NO KILL NO THRILL

Darcy Henton and Greg Owens

Red Deer Press

The Publisher
Red Deer Press
813 MacKimmie Library Tower
2500 University Drive N.W.
Calgary Alberta Canada T2N 1N4

Credits
Edited for the Press by Bob Weber
Cover design by Boldface Technologies Inc.
Text design by Dennis Johnson
Printed and bound in Canada by Friesens

Acknowledgments
Financial support provided by the Canada Council, the Department of Canadian Heritage, the Alberta Foundation for the Arts, a beneficiary of the Lottery Fund of the Government of Alberta, and the University of Calgary.

THE CANADA COUNCIL | LE CONSEIL DES ARTS
FOR THE ARTS | DU CANADA
SINCE 1957 | DEPUIS 1957

Canadian Cataloguing in Publication Data
Henton, Darcy, 1957–
No kill no thrill
ISBN 0-88995-209-4
1. Ng, Charles Chitat. 2. Serial murderers—California—Biography.
3. Serial murders—California—Case studies. 1. Owens, Greg, 1962– 11. Title.
HV6533.C2H46 2000   364.15'23'092   C00-911075-5

5 4 3 2 1

Dedicated to the Wilseyville victims and their families

Contents

AUTHOR ACKNOWLEDGMENTS

This book has been very much a team project. We extend our thanks for the extensive research provided by our good friends Rick Mofina and David Staples, two fine journalists and authors in their own right. We are also deeply indebted to our very capable editor, Bob Weber, our publisher, Dennis Johnson, and our partners Gordon and Warren Yake, who were the impetus behind this effort. Special thanks also to Debbie Weismiller and Jack Owens for their hours of work on the project. We would be remiss if we didn't thank a host of others who provided considerable help and guidance along the way, including Ray Ambler, Jim Farrell, Russel Fleming, Richard Helm, Mitch Hrdlicka, Judy Krauskopf, David McCann, Nancy Moss, Ray Munro, Joyce Owens, Joanne Owens, Scott and Sandy Owens, Sharon Sellitto, Dwight and Lola Stapely, Karen Tuck, and Don and Dorothy Weismiller.

In this sad world of ours, sorrow comes to all, and it often comes with bitter agony. Perfect relief is not possible, except with time. You cannot now believe that you will ever feel better. But this is not true. You are sure to be happy again. Knowing this, truly believing it, will make you less miserable now.

—ABRAHAM LINCOLN

Prologue

IT WAS ANOTHER SCORCHER in California's mother-lode country. Reg Heijne leaned on his shovel, wiping away the perspiration from his deeply tanned brow. Damn, it was hot. The sun pounded down with such ferocity that it felt like God was using the two-acre backwoods lot as his personal anvil.

Heijne was a big barrel-chested man pushing 60, a former biker whose thick mop of graying hair and large drooping mustache reminded people of Grateful Dead rocker Jerry Garcia. Locals claimed he was "afeared of nuthin'."

The retired building contractor certainly wasn't superstitious. He had snapped up the parcel of land in the Sierra foothills in November 1989 at a ridiculously low price, fully mindful of its reviled history. Hell, everyone in California had heard of the grisly murders committed here by Leonard Lake and Charles Ng (pronounced *Ing*). Who hadn't read about the cinder-block bunker torture chamber and the buckets of human remains found scattered around the place? Just in case he had been on Mars when the pair of serial killers turned the property near Wilseyville into a killing field seven years earlier, locals had tacked to his fence newspaper accounts of the murderous exploits on his property. But that had gradually stopped.

9

Heijne wasn't about to be chased off by ghosts. He liked his privacy, and the property had plenty of that. Secluded by dense thickets of oak and sugar pine, his place wasn't often bothered by strangers. The locked steel gate and signs warning folks to keep off discouraged all but the most brazen. The weirdos, too, were undeterred. The thrill seekers, satanic cults and sick-os wanted to practice their voodoo on deadly ground. He had run off more than a few. Visitors were well advised to call ahead.

Thankfully, interest in the case was dwindling now. Occasionally, families of the victims would come in search of bodies that had never been recovered. But most local folks just wanted to forget the whole affair and get on with their lives.

Heijne had already made improvements to the property, and he was planning more. The house was small with few outbuildings, so he had decided to erect a tool shed. He had really just started excavating the hard red earth when the blade of his shovel struck what he initially thought was a rock. When he pried it to the surface, a dirt-caked skull grinned sinisterly back at him. Heijne dropped his shovel and trudged to the cabin to get the sheriff's office on the phone.

"Better get the boys back out here," he advised. "I found another one."

The Sierra foothills of Calaveras County, California. Only a few hours from San Francisco, it is a place where locals respect one another's privacy.

For Leonard Lake and Charles Ng, the lonely Sierra foothills became a survivalist stronghold where the two could live out gruesome fantasies of sex and murder.

The gated entrance to the Calaveras County property once occupied by Charles Ng and Leonard Lake.

1

The Killer, the Con, the Cop

CALGARY ALBERTA / JULY 1985

CHARLES NG WAS SO INTENT on nonchalantly slipping a two-liter Pepsi bottle into his bag that he didn't notice two middle-aged cowboys watching him closely from the children's clothing department. A fugitive on the run in Calgary, Alberta, he had fallen back to his old habit—shoplifting—to stretch out his last few dollars. He was hoping to convince his eldest sister, Alice, to lend him enough money to get to Vancouver, board a freighter and head back home to Hong Kong. There he could disappear.

He had been camped out in a lean-to in a grasslands park in south Calgary for several days while he waited for an opportune time to rendezvous with his sister. Alice had made it clear she didn't want to have anything to do with him, but he had nowhere else to turn. Tired and hungry, Charlie had slipped up to the house once, but no one had been home. He had been reluctant to call ahead for fear of tipping off police that he was coming. It was a good bet they had her phone tapped.

He was almost broke—down to his last $5—and was getting weary of hiding out. Two young boys had already stumbled onto his hideout in Fish Creek Provincial Park, disturbing his sleep and raising his fears that someone might eventually recognize him and call the police. Since he had fled California a month earlier, his photograph had been plastered across newspapers all over North America, and it was a cinch the FBI would guess he was headed to his sister's.

But in downtown Calgary he felt reasonably safe. In early July the cowboy city was awash with strangers, many of them Asians, taking in the famous Calgary Stampede with its rodeo, chuck wagon races and beer halls. Everyone, it seemed, was outfitted in boots, jeans and cowboy hats. At noon the basement grocery department of the downtown Hudson's Bay department store was bustling.

Charlie wandered over to the specialty foods section, taking no notice of the lone cowboy, George Forster, dogging his heels. Forster's partner had slipped away. Sean Doyle, a 46-year-old school teacher moonlighting as a department store security guard, had ducked into a secret corridor behind the meat counter and was watching Charlie through one-way glass.

Doyle, who usually worked internal store security, had that morning been goaded into betting that he would nab a shoplifter before the regular floor staff. He had glanced over to the grocery department just in time to catch Charlie slipping a can of smoked salmon into a white plastic Bay shopping bag.

"Bingo!" he exclaimed to his beefy 48-year-old partner. "We've got one." Doyle was absolutely delighted. He had won the bet.

Neither of the part-time loss prevention officers, as they liked to be called, was armed with anything more than a two-way radio and a set of handcuffs. They had no inkling the diminutive young man they were about to approach in the early afternoon of July 6, 1985, was wanted for a raft of sadistic random murders. Charlie was not an imposing figure. He stood only 5' 7" and weighed barely 150 pounds. In fact he looked rather nondescript in jeans, faded blue T-shirt and running shoes. He had a mop of black hair and sad-looking brown eyes.

The kid is probably just hungry, Forster thought. He and Doyle had seen many like that. Often they were young native men down on their luck. Sometimes the pair let the hungry shoplifters go with a stern lecture. If they heard a particularly heart-wrenching tale, they would slip the would-be thieves enough money for a meal. Times were tough in Alberta. The boom and bust oil-fueled economy had busted flat, and the unemployment numbers were skyrocketing.

Dressed in their Stampede best, Doyle and Forster followed Charlie past the cashiers and out of the store. He took only a few steps down busy Seventh Avenue before they sidled up to him, one on each side, and flashed him their store security badges.

"You're under arrest, son," Doyle explained. "Please come with us to the office." Doyle took the shopping bag from Charlie and reached for Charlie's powder blue fanny pack.

"I'll take that, too."

"No, it's mine," the lad hissed.

Not wanting to argue the point on the street, Doyle, a former boxer who was about Charlie's height and weight, clamped hold of one arm while Forster, a stocky 5' 10", 210-pound fire department captain, grabbed the other. With their captive between them, they marched back into the store.

Forster was surprised by the young man's biceps. Seldom did he encounter shoplifters with such muscular arms.

Charlie went along in stunned silence, but once inside the store, he began fumbling in his fanny pack.

"I need my wallet," he explained. Doyle told him to forget about it.

"You can get it out when we get to the office."

Doyle could feel the lad's biceps tensing. Sensing Charlie was set to flee, he tightened his grip on both Charlie's arm and the shopping bag. His instincts were screaming, Watch him! Watch him!

But Charlie wasn't running. He plunged his hand into his fanny pack and pulled out a small black pistol. Forster caught a glimpse of the dull gleam of metal emerging from the pack and shouted to his partner, "He's got a gun! He's got a gun!"

Doyle reacted instinctively. He kicked Charlie's legs out from under him and rammed him with his shoulder. They landed on the floor in a heap with Doyle grabbing for the 10-shot Ruger .22-caliber pistol.

Forster tried a choke hold, but Charlie wriggled free and began slamming his knee into the back of Doyle's head, desperate to loosen the security guard's grip on the pistol. Grunting and groaning, the threesome thrashed about in the aisle of the men's suits department as spectators, drawn by the sound of the scuffle, gathered around to watch.

"For God's sake, get away," Forster shouted at the crowd. "The man is armed." Straddling Charlie's legs, he managed to clap a handcuff around one of Charlie's wrists, but he couldn't get the other cuff around the base of a nearby clothing rack.

Charlie was a writhing ball of fury. He squeezed off a shot that barely missed Forster's leg, then rattled off the base of the clothing rack. His desperation grew as he realized the two larger men were gaining control. He knew he had to get the gun free. Charlie clamped his teeth on Doyle's wrist and swung the revolver at his head. Just as he pulled the trigger, Doyle got a hand up to push the barrel aside.

A shot rang out, and Doyle felt his left hand go numb. At the sight of his blood streaming from the wound, he exploded. Erupting into an adrenaline-fueled rage, he picked up Charlie and slammed him facedown on the floor. For a long moment the three men lay panting in a heap on the floor. Doyle had both hands locked on the Ruger, which was pinned under Charlie's belly.

Geez, I'm getting too old for this job, Doyle remembered thinking. But he hung on desperately, fearful Charlie would catch his second wind and resume the battle.

Out of the corner of his eye, Doyle saw a black boot and a red-striped pant leg approaching, and he knew it was over. A customer had summoned a pair of beat cops off the street.

The pair disarmed and cuffed Charlie and led him to a patrol car now waiting at the curb. As the vanquished gunman rose to his feet, shoppers, who had watched what they thought was a staged wild west show, burst into applause. But the blood drenching Doyle's shirt was real. Forster applied pressure to his partner's injured left hand to staunch the flow of blood as they waited for an ambulance. Both men were in a state of shock, grateful they had survived and barely believing what had just happened. It was only now dawning on them that they owed each other their lives.

The shoplifter was hauled down to police cells. The identification he was carrying indicated he was Charles Ng. An interview confirmed he was the man wanted by the FBI and several police agencies in California. Fingerprints corroborated the statement. A month-long North America–wide manhunt was over.

BEYOND THE GRAIN FIELDS northeast of Alberta's capital, Edmonton Institution has operated in relative obscurity for more than two decades. To passersby on the divided four-lane highway that connects Canada's northernmost major city to the bedroom community of Fort Saskatchewan, the $15 million maximum-security federal prison could easily be mistaken for a community college or an office complex. The modern red-bricked structure is built low to the flat prairie landscape with narrow windows overlooking an expanse of farmland. But windowed towers at the corners of a 14-foot high razor-wire perimeter fence give away its true purpose. A local newspaper once called Edmonton Institution a jail in resort clothing.

Built in 1978 to house about 200 inmates, the Max, as it is known locally, has a relatively crisis-free history. Only a handful of prisoners have defeated the electronic gadgetry that replaces the stone walls of older fortress-style prisons. Should an escapee befuddle the sophisticated motion detectors between the double row of fences or the sensors built into the fence wire, he still had to evade the security cameras, the razor-sharp coils of wire, the armed roving vehicle patrols, the search lights, the dogs and the rifle-toting tower sentries.

The one inmate who did it twice is something of a legend. Harvey Andre, a brutish biker who murdered a British Columbia woman and shoved a shoe into her vagina, slipped beyond the gates inside the compactor of a prison garbage truck just three years after the prison opened. Recaptured several weeks later, he was wounded in a gunfight with Calgary police. Yet he staged another successful breakout exactly a year later. Under the cover of a blinding snowstorm, he clad himself in white and cut through the fences to short-lived freedom and another near-fatal gun battle with police.

Today such troublesome prisoners are contained in a separate wing of the prison just inside the main entrance. Prisoners held in the 72-man unit are locked in solitary confinement cells 23 hours a day. The heavy steel doors clank open and shut only to let them out for an hour of exercise, weekly showers or appointments with visiting medical staff and psychologists. The cells are lit by recessed florescent lights and whatever daylight squeezes through the slit windows. The walls, painted institutional green, are spattered with blood and feces, and marked with the barely decipherable scrawls of previous captives. The jingle of keys and handcuffs and the nerve-jarring clang of steel gates echo through the dank air of the concrete cavern throughout the day. Nights, often punctuated with screams and sobs, are much worse. Corrections Canada refers to the area as the Disassociation and Segregation Unit, or, in the acronym-laden vocabulary of institutions, D&S. The public knows it as solitary confinement. Inmates just call it the hole.

It was to the clang and clamor of the hole that Maurice Laberge arrived in February 1986, transferred in from Prince Albert Penitentiary, where he had spent the previous two months. Mo, as he was known to guards and inmates alike, was familiar with the Max, having begun serving his sentence there three years earlier. He still had 22 years to go on a 25-year hitch for robbery and kidnapping, but the 34-year-old small-time hood was making the best of it. He spent his time immersed in study. In the long hours of the long days, he sat at the tiny steel desk in his cell and persevered through university correspondence courses. The work connected him to the outside and gave him an opportunity to think—a little used skill in a world where guards managed every detail of inmates' lives.

When Mo returned from the PA Pen, he was locked in the solitary confinement unit's D-range in cell 206. He overheard the guards talking about the prisoner in the next cell, Charles Ng, the accused California serial killer who had been arrested in Calgary with a great deal of publicity the

previous year. Mo was anxious to see this suspected murderer who had out-
smarted the FBI, Interpol and the RCMP for 35 days, only to be picked up
for shoplifting. The next day, as Mo was escorted out to one of the unit's
two exercise yards, he saw Charlie working out in the other, his warm
breath visible in the frigid February air. Mo gave the slender young man a
cordial nod and began his exercise routine of push-ups, sit-ups and jogging
on the spot. Hell, he's just a frightened little kid, Mo thought as he worked
up a sweat under his green prison-issue parka. He had read that Charlie's
partner had killed himself and that Charlie was something of an enigma.
No one really knew who had done what to whom in the Sierra Foothills.
But many people were anxious to know. Mo glanced through the glass wall
into the other exercise yard, where Charlie was performing some sort of
martial arts routine. Mo wondered what the police would give to find out.

SEVEN MONTHS LATER, Chief Superintendent Gordie Grieg, commanding
officer of operations for Alberta's contingent of the Royal Canadian Mounted Police, was seated at his desk, looking all business. Dressed in the standard RCMP tan shirt and yellow-striped blue slacks, the K–Division commander had just summoned his head of homicide, a 15-year veteran Mountie named Raymond Munro, to his office at K–Division in Edmonton.
K–Division handled the province's specialty policing, assisting city forces
when requested, working on drug enforcement and overseeing the policing
of rural and highway detachments. Ray—short, balding and developing a
paunch already at 39—was dressed in plainclothes. It had been many years
since he had worn his scarlet tunic. Having put on a few pounds since joining the force in 1970, he doubted he could even fit into it. If he could even
find it.

"You wanted to see me?" he asked his boss.

Grieg was always gruff and to the point.

"Justice needs assistance with the Ng case," he explained. "Something
has come up. I want you to make immediate contact with the federal justice department lawyer involved in his extradition. She'll tell you what she

needs." He paused, looking up from his paperwork and into Ray's blue eyes. "Handle it."

Ray recalled the Ng case from clips he had seen on television. Watching reports from the scene of the grisly California mass murder, he had felt an immediate kinship with the American cops on their hands and knees, sifting through the red earth of the Sierra Nevada foothills, searching for clues. Poor bastards, Ray had thought. His crude vote of sympathy was directed not to the unknown victims but to the cops sweating their guts out in that sunbaked compound. Ray bled for them. After 11 years in homicide, he knew what they were up against. A pile of bodies and a cold trail. Random killings were the most difficult to solve, and it looked like the killers didn't discriminate. Men. Women. Babies. It was diabolical.

Before Grieg's call, Ray had been attending the postmortem of a native woman who had been found in a culvert with apparent stab wounds to the chest. When his pager had gone off in the morgue, he had assumed it was a development in the case. Now he had to leave that investigation with his subordinates and take up an assistance case. Ray could barely contain his annoyance. As if he didn't have enough on his plate. Now he had to hold some American cop by the hand for some case thousands of miles away. Great. But he got on the phone immediately to try to figure out what it was all about. It took him only a few moments to reach Shelagh Creigh, who advised him that a San Francisco police investigator was in Edmonton looking for evidence. The inspector was over at city police homicide. Ray was instructed to assess the situation and report back.

Ray rang up City Homicide and asked the staff sergeant, whom he knew well from many previous cases, what was going on. Apparently, a jailhouse informant at Edmonton Max was offering San Francisco authorities information on the Wilseyville killings, the sergeant explained. Ray rolled his eyes. This was going to be a real pain in the ass. It was bad enough when he was dealing with a multi-jurisdictional case with legal complexities. Now he was going to have to contend with a prison informant. And that, he knew from experience, was like climbing into a sleeping bag with a rattlesnake.

Great, he thought. Another jailhouse rat looking for some cheese.

Charles Ng with Detective Barry Whistlecraft following Ng's arrest in Calgary, Alberta.

Sean Doyle, former Bay security guard, was shot in the hand while arresting Charles Ng for shoplifting.

George Forster, former Bay security guard, helped capture Charles Ng.

Jailhouse informant Maurice Laberge in the gymnasium of Edmonton Institution, known locally as the Max.

Royal Canadian Mounted Police Staff Sergeant Raymond Munro.

2

Little Brother Dragon

CHARLIE'S ARREST LEFT HIS FAMILY to explain the inexplicable. For the most part they didn't try. "We don't understand why he was the way he was," his sister Alice admitted. Charlie's parents, still in Hong Kong, shut out the world. Charlie had always been different. While some kids dreamed of wealth and fame, Charlie dreamed of war and killing. Death had been his obsession since his youth.

In Calgary, Alice emerged from hiding to tell the *San Francisco Chronicle* how ashamed she was of her little brother. She said she wouldn't go to the Calgary jail to see him. She wouldn't talk to him. She wouldn't write. She wouldn't be going to his trial. She wouldn't even admit to anyone he was her brother.

"I still care for him," she explained, "but we can't just let him ruin all of our lives. I hope and pray that he can finally get some help from a psychiatrist. He's still my brother."

While on the run Charlie had twice phoned her collect to beg for money and help, but she had refused him. She told him the Chinese community would not hide him. She pleaded with him to turn himself in to police, but he was terrified of going to jail again. He had vowed he would not be taken alive. "I won't be hurting people anymore," he assured her. "I'll be hiding."

Charlie's arrest was terribly hard on his parents, who blamed themselves. "They think they may have done something bad in their previous lives," Alice told the *Chronicle*.

But the Ngs were decent people who had made tremendous sacrifices to give their three children the education they never had themselves. Charles was the youngest of three children in the Christian Methodist family. Kenneth Ng, a successful electronics shop owner, had to beg his wife, Oi Ping, to have one more child after their two girls, Alice and Betty, were born. He desperately wanted a son to carry on the family name.

Charles Chi-tat (pronounced *Cheetah*) Ng was born on Christmas Eve 1960. "I thought God gave me a present," his father would say later.

Kenneth Ng surely deserved a present for the sacrifices he had made. As the oldest boy in a family of seven, he had struggled to survive in war-torn Asia. Born in Rangoon, Burma, in 1930, he was still a toddler when he moved to Hong Kong with his family. His mother died when he was only seven, and he was left to help his widowed father raise his younger brothers and sisters. Then the war came, and the family nearly starved to death when the Japanese invaded Hong Kong. Kenneth's father dragged the children back to China, running just ahead of the invading Imperial Army. But conditions weren't much better in China, and the family struggled to survive until the Japanese surrendered four years later.

After the war the Ng family returned to Hong Kong, and 17-year-old Kenneth began doing odd jobs for the occupying British armed forces. A friendly soldier, taking an interest in Kenneth, gave him the book *Treasure Island* and taught him English. Kenneth married Oi Ping in 1957 and opened a small shop a decade later.

By working long hours and forfeiting holidays for themselves, Kenneth and Oi Ping placed all three of their children—Alice, Betty and Charlie— in some of the best schools in Hong Kong. Lacking a formal education themselves, they wanted to give their kids more opportunities than they had been given. Sometimes they had to beg officials at the exclusive schools to enroll their children, and they would not take no for an answer. If they were refused, they would return every day to plead until officials were worn down and relented.

When their girls finished secondary school, the Ngs sent them abroad for further education. Alice, the eldest, was accepted into the University of Alberta at Edmonton while Betty attended schools in England and the United States, where she worked on a laboratory science degree. Although his sisters excelled at school, Charlie didn't respond to the opportunity his parents struggled to give him. He was at best an average student. He had some artistic talent, but he never really pursued it. He had above average intelligence, but he didn't apply himself, and that kept him at odds with his workaholic father. When they were together, Kenneth was constantly harping at him for being so timid. It angered him that Charlie was so quiet. He would bind the boy's hands and feet and beat him with a cane, often so severely that Charlie's mother and sisters would beg him to stop, but Charlie would just quietly take it. Punishment never seemed to change his behavior in any constructive fashion. If anything he became even more moody and began to develop a rebellious streak. He started getting into trouble. Vandalism. Arson. Stealing. Anything to get attention.

Charlie craved affection, but he didn't feel he was getting it from his parents. He wondered if they loved him. If they did they didn't seem to show it in the usual manner. There were no hugs and kisses for little Charlie. When he did meet someone for whom he felt great affection, he became almost smothering. Few pubescent boys would put up with his cloying behavior for long.

Charlie's difficulty finding friends transformed him into a loner at a very early age. He spent his time reading or practicing martial arts by himself. He had a few pets, but was never allowed to keep them. His mother made him release a pet turtle he doted upon, and she refused to let him keep a stray dog that had followed him home. Worse still was the loss of his pet chicken, which ended up in the dinner pot one night. With nowhere to express his affection, Charlie withdrew even more and began to exhibit strange behavior.

Signs of abnormal behavior surfaced when he was visiting a classmate's house and stole a photograph of the boy's sister. When his parents caught the 10-year-old wearing his mother's pantyhose and engaging in other bizarre behavior, they took him to a psychiatrist. Therapy seemed to have little effect.

Charlie's parents, however, refused to give up. Although they had taken both of Charlie's grandmothers and an aunt into their crowded and aging twelfth-floor apartment in North Point, they still managed to send Charlie to St. Joseph's College, a reputable, century-old Catholic school attended by the children of Hong Kong's elite. But Charlie didn't fit in. He barely spoke in class and had few friends outside of other shy loners like himself. He expressed little interest in learning, although he was a bright kid.

Charlie's life revolved around the martial arts. Like many Asian children at the time, his hero was martial arts film star Bruce Lee. But for Charlie, Bruce Lee was an obsession. He called him Big Brother Dragon and had a poster of his idol in his bedroom. He studied martial arts in school, and he practiced constantly after classes until he could easily dominate other martial arts students his own size. He took his training seriously, having discovered something that gave him a sense of power and personal dominance. He believed abstinence from sex built strength and stamina, and whenever a martial arts partner couldn't keep pace with him, he would chide him for succumbing to weakness.

"You must have been masturbating," he would say accusingly to his less skilled adversary.

The martial arts fueled a hunger for danger and excitement in Charlie. Buoyed by newfound power and self-confidence, he turned his timidity into temerity. Armed with a slingshot, he would slink around the dilapidated high-density apartment block, seeking targets for his pent-up wrath. He would climb onto an outside staircase at the back of the building to unleash a barrage of glass marbles upon the windows of adjacent buildings and then take off laughing through the labyrinth of stairs and corridors, the curses of neighbors raining down on his ears. It was an adrenaline rush.

"I was thrilled just by watching," admitted classmate John Chan, who tagged along on some of Charlie's destructive missions. "He told me they would never repair their windowpanes because as soon as they put new glass in, he would make holes in it."

Charlie soon took to ambushing vehicles as they drove past his school. Hiding with Chan in the foliage on the edge of the schoolyard one day, Charlie scored a direct hit on the windshield of a passing car. The glass exploded into a spider web of cracks, splintering outward from the point of impact to engulf the entire screen. The car veered to the side of the road and screeched to a stop. As the bewildered driver stepped out to survey the damage, Charlie and his companion fled laughing.

From the mercenary magazines Charlie bought and devoured, he learned to make Molotov cocktails. With Chan in tow, he climbed to the roof of an apartment building with two gasoline-filled bottles, lit the gas-soaked rags stuffed into their necks and hurled them down onto a playground. Chan watched in horror as the bottles exploded upon impact, sending flames dangerously close to children playing nearby. Chan was incensed.

"You could have gotten people killed," he shouted at his friend. Charlie laughed. Chan began to have second thoughts about their friendship.

"Charlie enjoyed destroying things at random, just for the sake of destruction," he recalled. "It was fun and exciting, but after a while I got scared by his recklessness."

Spurred on by his new sense of physical power, Charlie launched a series of unprovoked attacks on unsuspecting strangers. Wandering through parks in the affluent neighborhood surrounding his school, he sought out the children of wealthy whites and launched frenzied attacks on them without a word of warning. Then he would walk away, leaving his victims stunned and bleeding on the ground.

When Chan tried to break off his friendship with Charlie, he found out what it was like to be on the receiving end of those vicious attacks. Charlie harassed Chan so much that it was a relief when Charlie was finally hauled off by police for setting fires in and around the school. Students later learned that Charlie had also been sending threatening, mocking and obscene letters to a female school teacher who had disciplined him. Charlie avoided jail, but not expulsion from St. Joseph's.

His frustrated parents decided to go farther afield for help. After consulting Charlie's Uncle Rufus Good, a teacher at Bentham Grammar School in northwest England, they decided to send the recalcitrant teenager to the centuries-old private boarding school on the River Wenning. Charlie, still obsessed with guns, knives and martial arts, tried to assert himself and resist. He desperately wanted to join the army. He talked to a recruiter about his dream of joining the elite British Special Forces, but his father, a former reserve officer, insisted he finish school and get a university education. If his son wanted the military life, it could wait until later.

Charlie got decent marks, particularly in biology, physics and math, but failed dismally in the social curriculum. He was still painfully shy. His parents may have hoped their son would bond more closely in a boarding school environment, but Charlie remained aloof. He didn't fit in with the bright socially active children of Britain's establishment. He often seemed acutely tense. When students approached him, he was unable to make eye contact and his legs often twitched nervously. It didn't help that they nicknamed him Charlie-boy. He hated the name.

"All of us boarders tended to clan together, but Charles never really seemed to fit in and was very much a loner," recalled a classmate. "He spent all his time practicing the martial arts, and I believe he thought of himself as something of a Bruce Lee." He didn't smoke or drink or socialize with the other students, preferring to spend his time shadow-boxing.

Charlie didn't make many friends, but he didn't like to give up the ones he had. He thought Angelos Solomon, a fellow Bentham student, was a true friend. But when Angelos rejected him, Charlie tried to punish him just as he had tormented Chan in Hong Kong. He crept into Angelos' room and stole a small chest of money and valuables.

Word of the theft swept through the school even before police arrived to begin searching the dormitory and questioning students. The following day Gary Cook, a good-hearted dormitory prefect who had often spent time with Charlie, found the stolen box on the school grounds near the river and turned it in to the house master. The stolen cash, a little more than $50 in English notes and coins, was not recovered.

As the student supervisor of the boys dorm, Cook had offered a general invitation to his charges to come to him for advice or help when they ran into problems at school. Usually, they approached him when they were homesick, and he consoled them and encouraged their peers to help them through the rough spots. Charlie would wander up to Cook's room to chat whenever he was lonely. Once, when Charlie had nowhere to go during a short school break, Cook had invited him to spend a few days with him at his grandmother's house.

In the days following the theft, Cook sensed that Charlie was avoiding him. He found Charlie in his room, and the two chatted about Angelos' plight. It didn't take Cook long to figure out that Charlie was the culprit. Crying, Charlie confessed that he had stolen the money because Angelos had rejected his friendship.

"You've got to tell the head master or at least give back the money," Cook urged. But Charlie was too scared. He finally agreed to give the stolen loot to the student supervisor when Cook promised not to tell police where he had found it. The plan soured when police threatened to charge Cook. When it became clear that Cook would go to jail rather than squeal, his girl friend begged the real thief to come forward. Reluctantly, Charlie admitted he was the thief.

Two police officers from the North Yorkshire police department questioned Charlie the following evening.

"We spoke to you last night about the theft of cash from one of the dormitories," one of the officers began. "You denied knowledge of it at that time. We now understand you want to say something about the matter."

"Yes," Charlie replied in a voice just above a whisper. He was frightened. His voice trembled and his hands shook. "I took it for revenge because Angelos had found another friend instead of me. I am very sorry I didn't tell you last night. I was scared."

"We have recovered some money. Is there more?" the officer inquired gently.

Charlie murmured yes and then began fishing in his pocket for a handful of coins. He handed them to the second officer.

"How did Gary Cook get the money?" the officer continued.

"I told him I had taken it. I was scared last night, and I asked Gary to help me. He is better at English than me. I gave him the money. As I said, I did it for revenge. I wanted to stop Angelos from having a good weekend in Lancaster with his new friend."

Police charged and fingerprinted Charlie, and he was required to appear in magistrates court. A short time later he was arrested for shoplifting at a Lancaster department store. His Uncle Rufus suggested to Charlie's mother that perhaps the boy would be better off in Hong Kong. She came to collect her son, and Charlie cursed his uncle as he left.

Even in early childhood, and almost certainly by his teen years, Charlie was exhibiting signs of an antisocial personality disorder, according to forensic psychiatrist Dr. Russel Fleming, who has treated scores of psychopathic killers at the maximum-security Penetanguishene Mental Health Centre on Georgian Bay. "He seemed to have no reservations about hurting people," Fleming notes. "There was a level of aggressive conduct in his childhood that goes just another level above normal." Fleming believes that long before Charlie reached Bentham, a pattern of deviant and violent behavior was firmly established. The boy without friends had developed into a young man devoid of empathy for others. People in his life became pawns to manipulate for his self-gratification. Expressions of love and affection were faked in order to achieve his desires. He used others for his own purposes and took pride in his ability to leave them ignorant of what he had done.

Psychiatrists still do not know for certain what causes psychopathy or what triggers some psychopaths to become violent (not all are), but a child's environment during his formative years is believed to be a major factor. However, Fleming says that the beatings inflicted upon Charlie, his stern upbringing and his feelings of being unloved may have had little bearing on his behavior. He cites growing evidence that psychopathy may be a product of genetics. "We're only just beginning to understand how complex the genetics of such things may be," he explains. "Some of these folks, for reasons that aren't clear, may be hard-wired for violence, antisocial lifestyles and sexual misbehavior, and it really doesn't have a lot to do with their families or whether they were abused by their fathers or mothers."

Dr. Fleming says that efforts by Charlie's parents to get their son treatment were commendable, but chances were few that psychiatric intervention would have been be successful. "At the age of 10 there may not have been anything that could be done therapeutically that could have altered the pattern," he says. "The parents go through life feeling guilty, but the hard reality is that there may have been nothing they could do."

Psychiatrists do know that there has been no successful treatment or cure found for violent psychopaths. Studies out of Penetanguishene, where one out of two patients has either killed or attempted to kill, have shown that almost 100 percent of violent psychopaths reoffend violently if released. Although it was once believed that violent tendencies in psychopaths wane as they grow older, research has shown that older psychopaths tend to simply choose weaker, more vulnerable victims.

After Bentham, Charlie was shipped to another Catholic boarding school near San Francisco, where his Aunt Alice could keep an eye on him and report any further problems. He obtained a one-year student visa and enrolled in the exclusive 1,700-student College of Notre Dame, just outside the Bay city in San Mateo County. His parents paid the $21,000 tuition without complaint. But Charlie had little interest in school, and his marks showed it.

He was still obsessed with the idea of joining an elite military force and proving himself on the field of combat. He now saw himself as an Asian Chuck Norris. Like the soft-spoken, cool-headed movie GI, Charlie fantasized about performing heroically on the battlefield with an array of weapons and martial arts skills. Rather than studying he read combat books and weapons manuals and hungrily devoured *Soldier of Fortune*–type magazines glorifying war and killing. He was convinced that he was a born fighter and a brilliant tactician. All he needed was an opportunity to prove it.

Far from the battlefields of his dreams, Charlie struggled just to become mobile. He was a notoriously poor driver, a failing that would come back to haunt him. After first getting his driver's license at age 18, he had four accidents in just three days. Then, driving his aunt's car in San Leandro, he slammed into a telephone pole and fled without reporting the accident. When police eventually caught up to him in the autumn of 1979, he ducked into a recruitment center and signed up for a six-year hitch in the Marine Corps. Charlie told the recruiter he was an American, born in Bloomington, Indiana. He went off to boot camp still owing Alameda County $1,900 for the damage he had caused.

After basic training in San Diego, Charlie was transferred up the California coast to Camp Pendleton for infantry training. He was a good soldier. He followed orders, listened to his instructors and cooperated with his peers, but he quickly became disenchanted with the quality of his fellow recruits, his officers, the training programs and the chain of command. They were slackers and unprofessional, Charlie thought. Hoping military life would get better as he advanced, he kept his mouth shut, collected his $677 a month and did as he was told. He made private, first class, in May 1980, and after training as an antitank gunner, he embarked on his first tour of duty at Kaneohe Bay, Hawaii. The base for 5,000 marines on the island of Oahu was known locally as K–Bay.

He found a friend in Corporal Jeffery Cox, his fire team leader in Weapons Company, First Battalion, Third Marines, First Marine Brigade. Cox shared Charlie's interests in books and martial arts. Rather than drink and carouse with the other marines, the pair would visit bookshops, libraries and movie theaters when they were off duty. Charlie had no contact with his family. It was only through a letter from Charlie's aunt that his parents learned that he had left Notre Dame and joined the marines. His mother cried upon hearing the news, but his father consoled her by telling her the marines were regarded as the best fighting force in the world. Through their grueling training, perhaps, Charlie might learn the discipline that seemed to be lacking in his life.

Charlie earned his marksmanship badge with the M-16 rifle. He also scored high marks in rifle squad tactics and map and aerial photo reading. He was proud to be a marine, a death technician, an expert in the art of killing.

But his fondness for weaponry soon landed him in trouble with the military police. They charged him with possession of hand grenades, but the case was thrown out on a technicality. The Corps judged the incident as an unfortunate mistake made by a misguided greenhorn with an overzealous love for armaments. Charlie would soon prove them wrong.

Class photo of Charles Ng (center, second row) in a private Catholic school in Hong Kong. Charlie's parents worked hard to give him opportunities they never had.

3

Gunning for Trouble

THE WEAPONS COMPANY ARMORY at K–Bay Marine Air Station was a nondescript one-story building attached to the Bravo Company barracks and supply office. The entire armament of the company, everything from machine guns and grenade launchers to rifles and pistols, was secured in locked racks, cages and strong boxes within the cinder-block walls of Building 1029. It was kept under 24-hour guard, its doors locked and its windows covered with heavy-gauge steel screens.

Charlie was standing guard duty outside the armory in September 1981 when three large metal Conex storage boxes, each about the size of a garbage dumpster, were unloaded from a flatbed truck near the building's front wall. The bins had been brought in to provide extra storage space for Bravo Company. This was the wrong place to put them, Charlie thought. As they were jockeyed into place in front of the windows, he shook his head in disgust. Another military screw-up. Any fool could see that the bins would provide cover for a burglar raiding the armory. The idiots deserved to be ripped off.

Once Charlie got the notion into his head, he couldn't shake it. The more he thought about it, the more he realized the place was ripe for picking. Shrubs along the back of the building would hide anyone climbing in through the windows. A heavy-duty bolt cutter would easily cut through the steel mesh and the locks securing the weapons to racks along the walls inside the armory.

Charlie figured the robbery would be at least a two-man job. He would need someone to keep a lookout and to pass the weapons to from inside. He casually broached the idea to 21-year-old Corporal Christopher Carlisle Thomas, the chief armorer for Weapons Company. The two knew each other well because they exchanged survivalist magazines and shared a fascination for weapons. Thomas, or C.C. as he was known in the unit, told Charlie that Bravo Company had been told to remove the bushes because they were a security risk, but no one had ever done it. The goofs. What kind of security was that? Thomas liked the idea of ripping off the armory. It would be great to have a selection of military weapons for personal use once he left the Marine Corps. Perhaps they could even sell a couple to make a few bucks. Many soldiers yearned to have an M-16 rifle or M-60 machine gun for their personal collections.

Several weeks later, in mid-October, Charlie approached the soldier who had been assigned to sentry duty that night to seek help with his plan. He didn't think Ken Armeni was particularly bright, and he was confident he could coerce the man into going along with the break-in.

"If something happened to the armory tonight, would you ignore it?" he asked.

Armeni was noncommittal. "I don't care," he responded. "What are you going to do?"

Charlie laid out his plan. When Armeni appeared to be wavering, Charlie assured him that all he had to do was his normal duty. "Just walk your post and hear nothing," he advised.

"Okay, but I don't want anything to do with it."

Charlie caught up with Thomas about noon in the parking lot near the Weapons Company barracks to tell him the plan was going ahead that night. His timing appeared perfect. Thomas, who had worked late the previous night, had forgotten to lock the weapons into their racks. Monday was a base holiday. The theft wouldn't be discovered until Tuesday.

"Can we use your car?" Charlie asked Thomas.

"Nah, it isn't working."

Charlie had seen Armeni driving around in a beat-up Chevy. He asked to borrow it, and Armeni reluctantly handed over the key. "If you get caught, just say the key was in the car," he told Charlie. He agreed to signal a warning by rattling the armory door if anyone approached while Charlie was inside. But that was all he would do. He didn't want any part of the haul. He didn't need the grief.

That evening Charlie caught up with Thomas in the TV room to tell him the car was a go. They briefly discussed which and how many weapons to take. Charlie wanted to get in and out quickly and was planning to grab whatever was close by. He set the operation for midnight when Armeni came on duty.

Thomas was sleeping when Charlie arrived at 11:15 P.M. with Armeni's keys and told him to drive the vehicle to the parking lot behind the armory. Thomas moved the car and then settled down in the TV room to wait.

About a half hour later, Charlie appeared, wearing green camouflage-colored shorts, a dark T-shirt and carrying a pair of gloves.

"Let's go," he said.

He posted Thomas on the south side of the armory, slipped behind the hedge and began to snip through the mesh window screen. From his vantage point, about 50' away, Thomas could hear the faint clipping of the bolt cutters on the metal, and he could see Charlie's shadow. Charlie cut a hole in the wire and slipped silently through. As he plunged headfirst into the dark armory, a sharp pain stabbed his right thigh. When he touched the spot, his hand came away wet with blood. Damn! He had cut himself on the metal screen.

No time to think about that, he thought. He rose to a crouch and darted over to a nearby pistol box that he could make out in the gloom. He scooped out a bag containing seven .45-caliber pistols and set it down beside the window. From an adjacent rack he grabbed three M-16s with attached grenade launchers. Spotting three M-60s lying on a workbench, he took them, too. Charlie stayed mostly in the back of the armory, but ventured near the front to grab a starlight night scope from a box near the entrance. When he had all the loot piled just inside the window, he waved to Thomas to come and get it. There was no response. Charlie cursed. Where was that asshole?

Suddenly, the main entrance door rattled. Charlie jumped feet first from the window and scrambled through the hedge into the parking lot. Then he walked as nonchalantly as he could toward the Bravo Company office. He spotted Thomas coming toward him.

"Why didn't you come over when I called for you?" Charlie hissed.

"It was too dark," Thomas explained. "I didn't see you."

The door rattling had been a false alarm, so Thomas and Charlie headed back to the window. Charlie slipped back inside and passed the weapons out to Thomas, who stacked them quietly on the ground. First came a machine gun and the bag of .45s. Then the rifles. Then the scope. By the time Charlie slipped out the window, Thomas had brought the car around and was struggling to open the trunk. He finally gave up and began throwing the weapons in the backseat.

Almost immediately, they heard the rumble of an approaching vehicle. As headlights rounded the corner, they leapt for the hedge. Their hearts pounded as they watched a bus pull up next door and unload a crowd of boisterous soldiers who had been out on the town. Whew! That was close. The two thieves giggled nervously as the bus pulled away. They quickly loaded the last of their haul and jumped in the car. Thomas nosed the Chevy toward a clump of bushes near the Amtrak station, where they planned to hide their haul. They field-stripped the weapons, slipped the pieces into two waterproof duffel bags and hid them in the bushes.

The two returned to their barracks and hit their bunks, but Charlie couldn't sleep. He had to get the weapons off base, and he wasn't sure how. Early Sunday morning he woke up 26-year-old Ricardo Dailey, a noncommissioned officer who had befriended Charlie on his first stint at sea. Dailey had just come off a leadership course, and after eight weeks of training in the Kahuku Mountains, he wasn't thrilled to be disturbed at 8:00 A.M. on his day off.

"Whadda ya want?" he demanded.

"I need to talk to you," Charlie said. "It's important."

Charlie told Dailey that he desperately needed him to rent him a car. Dailey refused. Charlie was practically pleading.

"I'm in trouble," he cried. "I need help." He told Dailey he had ripped off some weapons from the armory and needed a vehicle to get them off the base. Dailey, still groggy and only barely comprehending, told Charlie a friend was planning to drop by later, and he would call him to come earlier.

"Something has come up," Dailey told his buddy, Mark Campbell. "Can you come earlier? Meet me at the front gate in an hour." It was a call he later wished he had never made. He could never explain why he helped Charlie. It seemed he had taken the Marine Corps slogan *semper fi* too literally. Ever faithful, perhaps, but to whom?

Dailey was waiting at the gate when Campbell arrived in his girl friend's green Plymouth Duster. He got a visitor's pass for the car, and they went to get Charlie. The plan was simple. Charlie and Dailey checked out the cache, and when no one was around, they called Campbell on a two-way radio to come for the weapons. The plan went off without a hitch. With the weapons stowed in the trunk of the Duster, they headed to a storage facility in town where Charlie had a locker. But when they found it closed, they had to come up with a new plan. Finally, Dailey offered to hide the weapons for Charlie for $500. After dropping Charlie off at a mall near the base, Dailey and Campbell considered the situation. They both realized that they were nuts to be involved with Charlie and they'd better ditch the weapons fast. They headed up to a popular lookout point in the mountains and stashed the two bags in some bushes, covering them with leaves and branches. Then they waited for all hell to break loose. They didn't have to wait long.

Minutes after Thomas reported the break-in Tuesday, Naval Investigative Service agents were at the scene, and the base was placed on full alert. Sentries were advised to be on the lookout for terrorists. All vehicles leaving the Marine Corps Air Station were stopped and searched. The military brass was having fits. As Dailey would later remark, "The shit hit the fan."

NIS agents found few clues. Two footprints along the east wall of the armory, fingerprints of questionable value and cloth fibers on the severed edges of the window screen were about all. The haul was estimated at $11,000, but it wasn't the dollar value that had the Marine Corps in an uproar. It was the use that might be made of the weapons. Good God. That was a lot of firepower.

A nervous Dailey and Campbell holed up in a hotel in Waikiki the following weekend to figure out what to do next. They considered just dumping the weapons into a reservoir and phoning in a tip to Naval Investigative Service, but they figured it would only intensify the hunt for the culprits. They were determined to keep the weapons out of Charlie's hands, fearing that he would give his accomplices up in a heartbeat if he was caught. They finally decided to bury the weapons in the mountains, and in a few months, when the entire U.S. Marine fleet was out on a lengthy training exercise, Campbell would tip the NIS to their location. That way everyone on the base would have an alibi, and if they all kept their mouths shut, it just might blow over.

The NIS already suspected the robbery was an inside job. They interviewed Charlie after someone in his barracks claimed to have seen him oiling a bolt cutter before the heist. But Charlie denied even owning a bolt cutter. So the investigators turned their attention to the three weapons company armorers, calling them in one by one to take a polygraph test. Thomas failed the test miserably, but refused to talk. Investigators grilled him for several hours.

"We know you are guilty," they charged. "If you don't tell us the truth, no one will ever believe you again. The machine doesn't lie. No one will ever again have anything to do with you. You won't have any friends. You're going to prison for a long time—probably at least 15 to 20 years."

They would grill him intensely, then leave him by himself in an office. Then they would grill him some more. They told him that if he talked, he would get a lighter sentence. They told him that if he cooperated, he might only get five years in prison.

Finally, after six hours, Thomas broke. He told them everything he knew. Since he didn't know where the weapons were stashed, the agents didn't want to make any sudden moves that might panic the others. But they might as well have announced the confession on the local radio station. When Dailey heard that Thomas had been arrested, he called Campbell and told him to clean house. It was only a matter of time before the police came for them. Everything that could be remotely connected to the crime was ditched, including the tools used to bury the weapons, the case for the starlight scope and the bag that had contained the .45s. Then they called a lawyer.

While his accomplices were disposing of the evidence, Charlie was sitting in the Naval Investigative Service offices laying out every detail of the escapade, right from its inception. He had already cut a deal to reduce his prison time. Once he scrawled his name on his four-page statement, he was sent to Pearl Harbor to spend a long anxious night on a military prison ship there. The following day he was returned to K–Bay, where a military magistrate ordered him to be held in custody. Although his fate was looking pretty bleak, what really galled Charlie was the endless delay. That was the military way: hurry up and wait. Charlie got angrier and angrier as the day dragged into night. Still no escort back to Pearl Harbor. By 2:00 A.M. he was livid. Stupid assholes! The two marines assigned to guard him were a couple of goofs, he thought. One was sitting with his feet up on a desk smoking a cigarette while the other was on the phone to the officer of the day still trying to get a vehicle to take Charlie back to the brig. Neither was paying any attention to him whatsoever. It wouldn't take much to slip away from these bozos.

Screw them, Charlie thought, as he sidled over to a window. Stealthily, he slid over the sill and pulled the window closed behind him. Through the glass he could see his escorts still blithely unaware that he was gone. He turned, dashed across the field behind the office and made his way quickly over to a friend's quarters on base. Telling his friend that he had been framed for the armory theft, he convinced his friend to hide him for the night. The next day he borrowed some civilian clothing and slipped off the base in the trunk of his friend's car to hide out in a remote area on the island. He had asked his friend to try to raise some cash from his friends, but no one would help him. Finally, his friend gave him $20 and provided him with food and clothing, but Charlie had to rough it in the wet weather without even a tent. He was cold, wet, mosquito-bitten and had severe diarrhea.

After two days he could take it no more. He contacted a survivalist friend, Mark Novak, who lived on an army barracks on the island. Schofield Barracks was an ideal place to hide out. With his military haircut, he would blend in with the soldiers. No one would look for a fugitive marine on an army barracks.

Wanted posters bearing a photograph of Charlie in a T-shirt and tinted glasses appeared in the island's two newspapers and in the communities around the islands. One radio disk jockey fueled the indignation of the marines by ripping them on the airwaves. First they let a thief steal weapons right under their noses, and then they let the suspect escape. Talk about incompetence.

Charlie stayed in the barracks for three weeks, waiting for the heat generated by his escape to cool. Novak told him about another survivalist and ex-marine he knew in northern California who might be willing to hide him out. He said he would put in a good word for Charlie. When Charlie's parents sent $300 for a plane ticket back to the mainland, Charlie flew to San Francisco and stayed with his aunt. After a few days he contacted the ex-marine Novak had told him about in Mendocino County, north of San Francisco. Leonard Thomas Lake was expecting the call.

4

The Horn of the Goat

MARK NOVAK had introduced Leonard Lake to Charlie as a Marine Corps sergeant who had done a few stints in Vietnam. All he said was that Leonard was a weapons freak who might be able to hide him out for a while at a motel he was managing in a little California town called Philo. Lennie, as his family called him, was a husky overbearing man with a balding scalp and a thick black beard. He was the son of a navy seaman.

At 39 Leonard was nearly twice Charlie's age. Although Leonard stood only 5' 9", he had an arrogant way about him that exuded power. Charlie just assumed Leonard had seen combat overseas, and the older man did nothing to correct the impression. Leonard often embellished his warrior image with combat stories, talking about mortar rounds pounding down on his platoon and seeing his friends dying all around him. It could as easily have been him who was dead, he would say. But it was all a façade. Leonard had never seen action.

But Leonard had more in common with Charlie than military service and a weapons fetish. He, too, came from a troubled background. His mother, Gloria May Williams, had abandoned him when he was nine after she and her alcoholic husband, Elgin Lake, separated. Gloria packed up her other three kids and set off for Seattle to try to reconcile. She shuffled Leonard, the second youngest of four, off to her elderly parents in San Francisco. Leonard pretended he didn't mind, but when they said their final good-byes at the train station, he tearfully begged to come along. "Take me with you," he cried. That heart-wrenching scene still haunted Gloria decades later and fueled in the boy a deep loathing for, and mistrust of, all women.

In San Francisco Leonard's grandparents were loving but strict. They provided for him in their two-story house in the city's Glen Park district, but Leonard, like Charlie, grew up without the warmth of parental love. In school he was an average student who did well when motivated, but he was usually content just to get by. Leonard focused his attention on animals rather than people, sometimes using them in bizarre experiments. He dutifully tracked and recorded the litters and genetic traits of hundreds of mice. When they mastered the tricks he taught them, he would reward them with candy. When he was finished with them, he had no qualms about killing them. Watching them die was just another experiment. He used various chemicals—acid and lye—to dissolve them into a lumpy green fluid.

Leonard loved to mix chemicals, and, like Charlie, he enjoyed scaring his friends with his concoctions. Once, when he was 16, he terrified his eight-year-old cousin by smashing a glass of chemicals against his bedroom wall and setting it ablaze.

"I panicked, but he stopped me, and the fire just burned and went out by itself and didn't do any damage to the wall," his cousin recalled later. Leonard was fascinated by medieval history and its characters: kings, queens, knights, jesters, dragons and unicorns. He read everything he could get his hands on about the topic, even venturing into the dark side of witches and the occult.

As a young adult, Leonard rekindled a relationship with his mother and sisters, but he came to despise his brother, Donald, whom his mother spoiled even before a train accident left him brain injured and slow. Privately, he called Donald a leech.

After high school Leonard wanted to go to college or university, but without money he had to settle for a stint in the marines. He wanted to see if he was tough enough. Seeing Leonard in the marines wasn't a great surprise to friends and family since his military-style brush cut had already earned him the nickname Butch.

He signed up in April 1964, a slim young man in excellent health, and received his basic training at the Marine Corps Recruit Depot in San Diego, the same training center where Charlie would go 15 years later. From San Diego, Leonard was sent to Fort Bliss to learn to maintain and repair radar equipment and the Hawk missile battery. After stops in Camp Pendleton, California, and Okinawa, Japan, in late 1966 he finally arrived in Vietnam.

Leonard made it through only eight months of his ten-month stint before being sent home. He had smashed the baby finger of his left hand with a hammer, crushing the tip. Although he denied doing it deliberately, his superiors weren't so sure. He spent seven days in hospital while doctors monitored the compound fracture. Once he recovered he was sent to the naval missile center at Point Mugu in California's Ventura County. It was here that he met and married Illinois-born Karen Lee Meinersmann, a 20-year-old math major living in nearby Oxnard.

The couple had a quirky relationship. Leonard encouraged his new bride to work in a topless bar and to sleep around with strangers. The idea of her promiscuity excited the newly promoted staff sergeant, but his timing was bad. He was on his way back to Japan for a three-month posting when Karen landed a job as a topless go-go dancer. Somehow the idea didn't seem so great when viewed from the other side of the world, particularly after Karen revealed in her last letter that she was enjoying 4:00 A.M. breakfasts with customers after her shifts. Leonard had been assigned to special duty in Vietnam. When the letters from home stopped coming, he began to get jealous and angry.

After 22 days Leonard snapped. In a raging wind he climbed an 80-foot communications tower and howled into the storm. In his convoluted logic he had to feel the icy fingers of death before he could feel alive again.

When his anger was spent, he realized he desperately needed professional help. He checked into the First Medical Battalion Neuropsychiatry Unit on November 2, 1970. Staff there found him a psychological mess—manipulative, evasive, tense and, most of all, psychotic. Using his finger as an imaginary machine gun, he occupied himself by mowing down imaginary Viet Cong. He was belligerent to staff, and when he did consent to talk to them, his speech was almost robotic, devoid of all emotion, sounding at times like a Marine Corps manual come to life. He disrupted group therapy sessions and pushed ward rules to the limit. When his doctors ordered Leonard held in a locked psychiatric ward for further observation, his anger only intensified.

"I regret ever coming to First Medical Battalion," he seethed. "I resent being removed from my unit, being confined and being treated like a prisoner."

Leonard's symptoms of depression eventually subsided with little help from Leonard or the unit. Since he was refusing treatment, doctors decided it made little sense to keep him locked in the hospital. He was discharged with a diagnosis of hysterical neurosis and schizophrenia brought on by specialized duty in a combat zone. On January 28, 1971, a hospital medical board found him unfit for further military service and sent him home.

His wife, however, no longer wanted him. He was just too weird. He tied her up during sex and beat her, and she'd had enough. A year after he returned home, they were divorced. But Leonard continued to stalk his former wife, breaking into her home three times. The marriage had lasted only two years and seven months. The anguish lasted much longer. Leonard wept when Karen walked out—the first time anyone could remember seeing him cry since his childhood. There was no getting used to rejection. Leonard was now convinced women were evil. First his mother, now his wife. God, it hurt.

Cut loose from marriage and the marines, Leonard drifted aimlessly across California during the 1970s, doing odd jobs and stealing to get by. He was arrested for petty theft in Santa Clara County in June 1972 and fined, but it didn't stop him from helping himself to others' property whenever the opportunity presented itself. He tried university courses in San Jose, but decided he was wasting his time. What good was an education? Mankind seemed determined to blow itself into oblivion.

Leonard decided he would be ready. He would be prepared for it, and he would survive. He planned to build a bomb shelter and stock it with all the supplies he would need, including women. Especially women. Surviving in the aftermath of the cataclysm would mean being the fittest and, in his case, the best armed. It would be up to him and whoever joined him to repopulate the world. He was prepared. He would be ready. The Day After would be his day.

By 1976 Leonard was tired of drifting, and he settled in with a back-to-nature crowd in a commune nestled in the wooded hills near Ukiah, about two hours north of San Francisco. Leonard spent five years on the 5,000-acre Greenfield Ranch raising chickens, pigs, goats and turkeys, and tending a small orchard. He moved in with a woman and pursued his medieval fantasies, from Nordic mythology and paganism to the occult and witchcraft. When neighbor Oberon "Otter" Zell grafted a horn onto the head of a living goat to create a phony unicorn named Sir Lancelot, Leonard offered to take it around to county fairs, charging people money to see it. He had stationery and business cards printed with the image of a unicorn and the legend, "The Living Unicorn." Leonard solicited young women to dress as medieval maidens and pose for photographs with the goat for a unicorn calendar he claimed to be producing. But it wasn't business Leonard was after—it was girls.

Leonard loved to photograph women in various revealing poses, but he seldom shot full nudes. He felt photographs that teased the eye were far more seductive than ones that served up the goodies like a banquet table. He was fascinated by the metamorphosis of young girls blossoming into womanhood, and he was eager to record the various stages with his camera. He had few hang-ups about the age of his subjects. If a girl had breasts, she was plenty old enough for Leonard. But he was always mindful of potential repercussions. Occasionally, he managed to seduce a 16-year-old, but he forced himself to steer clear of attempting to have sex with girls in their preteens.

Ripping off people was an entirely different matter. To his mind, Leonard was merely punishing them for their stupidity. If people left valuables lying around, they were inviting thefts. Stealing building materials from a construction site in 1980 earned Leonard a year on probation, but that didn't seem so bad when Leonard considered all the other times he hadn't been caught. An arrest here and there was merely an inconvenience. Leonard's criminal activity didn't, however, go over very well with the other members of the commune who never really liked or trusted him. They thought he was just too creepy. "He was kind of a misfit," recalled former neighbor Zell. "The rest of us were hippies, and he was a pretty straight guy."

The other commune members asked Leonard to leave. It wasn't only the theft that bothered them. He was starting to act like he was the sole owner of the place. He sold out his share, bought a mobile home and found a job managing a small eight-unit motel in Philo, a town of about 150 in the Anderson Valley just a half hour southwest of Ukiah. It was time to get out on his own again. He had found a lover and was thinking about marriage.

The woman was Claralyn Balazs. Blame it on the unicorn. The horned goat shtick had captivated the perky Bay area teacher's aide when she had encountered Leonard and the mythical beast at a county fair. The gangly blue-eyed young woman was swept up by the unusual man who introduced her to a strange and exciting world of witches balls and ritualistic ceremonies. They were married in 1981.

A plain-looking woman with thick glasses and dark hair, Balazs had a beautiful smile and a healthy appetite for sex—especially kinky sex—that surprised and fascinated Leonard. He soon came to call her Cricket, a pet name apparently inspired by her noisy vocalizations during wild sex. Cricket quickly became the focus of Leonard's life. She didn't mind posing for his cameras or his recordings. Life with Cricket was intense and extremely exciting.

It was into this happy union that Charlie arrived in November 1981. He was astonished that these strangers would welcome him into their home. The young fugitive marine didn't quite know what to make of their generosity. He was quiet, respectful, polite and desperately afraid of offending his hosts. If he wore out his welcome here, he had nowhere else to go. They made an unusual threesome.

Charlie felt like he belonged for the first time in his life. It was as if he had finally found the family he had yearned for all his life, a loving and affectionate family that accepted him as he was. No one harassed him for his stoic silence or sullen moods. They gave him space.

Publicly, Leonard treated Charlie as his personal houseboy. But privately, the older man embraced and mentored the younger. Charlie bowed to Leonard's dominance, looking up to Leonard as a son looks up to a respected father. Under the older man's tutelage, Charlie learned how to grow his own food, how to chop wood, how to be self-sufficient. He was even allowed to have a dog. After spending most of his adolescence in schools and the Marine Corps, living with Leonard and Claralyn was a refreshing taste of the good life outside an institution. Charlie soon became very happy in his new home.

Leonard was just as happy. He now had a protégé who shared many of his interests and was eager to learn and oblige. Charlie also was a highly skilled marksman who could plan and carry out precise military operations. The two would spend hours in the countryside outside of Philo shooting at human silhouette targets. They had to lie low for a while after a local resident stumbled onto their target range and made a fuss, but otherwise they were pretty much free to hone their skills.

Charlie loved handling and firing the weapons. In his mind he was a killing machine. Give him a small-caliber handgun, and he could empty the clip in a tight-shot group in the center of a man's forehead. He often talked about killing another human being.

"Wouldn't it be nice to blow somebody's brain apart?" he would routinely and casually remark. He and Leonard began using their army training to plan military-style criminal operations to supplement their income.

The two worked well together, studiously casing gun shops and pawnshops and then returning later to burglarize them. The robberies brought in good cash. Charlie and Leonard also made a few forays to the Greenfield Ranch to steal marijuana, which they sold on the streets. All the while Leonard enlarged on his his fantasy to kidnap women and enslave them for sex, and Charlie proved an eager accomplice.

Working together the two psychopaths fueled each other's lust for sex and crime. They hatched plans to scoop prostitutes off the streets of San Francisco for free sex. One of their first victims was a woman who worked for an escort agency. Leonard took her to a motel near the international airport, where Charlie was hiding in the bathroom. When the woman entered, Charlie, naked and wielding a knife, leapt out and violently raped her, stabbing the bed with his knife to further terrorize the woman during the attack. This was sex the way Charlie liked it.

When he wasn't out on operations with Leonard, Charlie helped around the motel. Later, when Leonard got a job as a waiter at the New Boonville Hotel, Charlie went along as dishwasher. Leonard and Cricket moved out to the nearby Indian Creek Ranch in March 1982, when Leonard was hired as the youth camp's caretaker. Charlie, using the alias Charles Lee, tagged along again. But before leaving Philo, Charlie had written a letter to Mark Novak to fill him in on his exploits and to urge him to join their brotherhood of survivalists. The letter fell into the hands of Naval Investigative Service personnel, who was still anxious to bring Charlie to justice for the armory burglary back at K–Bay. They weren't going let Charlie slip away again.

The NIS contacted the Mendocino County sheriff's office, staked out the motel and eventually traced Charlie to the Indian Creek Ranch. A few days later, on April 29, 1982, a team of heavily armed agents in trucks and helicopters stormed the ranch. Before Charlie and Leonard could flee, gun-toting agents burst into the ranch house and hauled them away in handcuffs.

Agents found a cache of automatic rifles, machine guns, pistols, dynamite, exploding bullets, throwing stars and brass knuckles. They also uncovered $50,000 in stolen gold and silver coins and camera equipment. Police believed the items had been taken in three area burglaries. Leonard was charged with 17 felony counts of burglary, grand theft and various weapons offenses. He was freed on $3,000 bail.

Charlie was to be flown back to Hawaii to face a raft of charges stemming from the break-in at the Weapons Company armory at K–Bay, Hawaii, seven months earlier. He was facing an 18-year prison term for conspiracy, larceny, burglary and escaping custody. The young marine had become a major embarrassment to the American military. His boyish face had been plastered across the island, seemingly taunting the might of the military establishment for its inability to apprehend him. One doctored copy had even been hung on a wall in the Staff Judge Advocate's office. Someone had scrawled, "Having a good time in Hong Kong. Wish you were here. Charlie."

After Charlie was taken away, Leonard fretted about having to serve a prison term for possession of the illegal weapons. He just couldn't face the prospect of going to jail. Being locked in the mental hospital after his episode in Vietnam had been horrible enough. He told Cricket he wouldn't be locked up like some animal. He jumped bail and headed back to San Francisco with a $50,000 warrant hanging over his head. It became apparent to both Leonard and his wife that their marriage couldn't be sustained under the circumstances. A divorce was arranged, but the couple planned to maintain a close relationship and to get together whenever circumstances permitted. Leonard gave Cricket power of attorney over his affairs. Then he dropped out of sight.

Life as a fugitive fueled the paranoia smoldering inside Leonard Lake. In his delusions he was a hunted outlaw. In reality no one was looking terribly hard for him. But in his status as a wanted man, Leonard saw a golden opportunity to use the military training he had received from his country—the courses in counterinsurgency operations, chemical warfare, map reading, combat intelligence, explosives and demolition, guerrilla warfare. He would live by ruthlessness and cunning. He had crossed the line and there was no going back.

The street where Charles Ng lived in San Francisco.

5

From Willow Bunch to the Wild Bunch

I N 1958 MAURICE LABERGE was a six-year-old prairie boy with big dreams. From his upstairs bedroom in the tiny southern Saskatchewan community of Willow Bunch, he watched cars coming and going from the dentist's office and the tire shop across the street. He fantasized about cruising across the grasslands, windows open, Buddy Holly blasting on the radio and a mile-long dust plume in his wake. His attraction to chrome and steel was almost magnetic. He loved to hang around the tire shop, running his grubby hands over the big gleaming two-tone Buicks and Chevrolets the local ranchers drove. It was automobile heaven.

There wasn't much else for a youngster to do in the sleepy town of 500. It was one of Saskatchewan's oldest settlements, founded by Métis who followed the buffalo herds into the valley around 1870. The Willow Bunch that Mo knew was a francophone community that thrived on farming and ranching. The Métis lived on one side of town, the whites on the other. Life revolved around the Catholic Church. Given that his mother was a former nun, Mo, the fourth of 11 children, was expected to be a good Catholic boy. His education took him to one Catholic boarding school after another, but as he got older, Mo's religion became fast cars and fast women. He started leafing through his father's *Playboy* magazines and skipping school. He graduated to petty crimes like vandalism, theft and calling in false fire alarms.

Mo wasn't dumb. School simply bored him because he was usually far ahead of his classmates. His father, Armand, a farm implement dealer, insurance salesman and small-town entrepreneur, had fiddle feet. He had taken his family to Detroit in 1956, when Mo was four. Armand had tried to make a go of it selling cooking pots and even goldfish door to door. But after just two years, the family returned to Willow Bunch. In Michigan, Mo had vaulted from kindergarten to Grade 3, but back in his hometown, over his mother's objections, he was plunked into Grade 2. He hated it. When he did attend school, Mo spent his time daydreaming, reading and doodling in his scribblers.

Although advanced beyond his years intellectually, Mo was a very immature kid. He wet the bed, sucked his thumb and dragged around his favorite blanket through his early school years, and that made him the target of scorn and ridicule. He liked to go over to his grandmother's to watch *Roy Rogers* on her TV even though he knew the Métis kids on that side of town would beat him up if they caught him. He knew there were safe houses along the way, and he planned his route meticulously. He knew it was dangerous, but the challenge thrilled him. He liked to run the gauntlet, establishing patterns of behavior that would continue throughout his life.

The early years at home were turbulent. His parents didn't get along. Feeding and caring for so many children, aged 16 months to 12 years, under one roof put an incredible strain on their marriage. To relieve some of the burden, Mo and his two elder sisters were sent off to boarding school. They joined their aunts, also nuns, at a convent in the nearby francophone community of Forget (pronounced *For-jay*).

Mo grew close to his sisters during those early years. "We held each other and cried when my mom was fighting with my dad," he would recall later. "Though we were quick to get on each other's case, there was a healthy bond and lots of love between us."

In September 1959 the family moved to Moose Jaw, a small city of under 40,000, just 44 miles west of the provincial capital of Regina. Mo was stunned by what he thought was the fast pace of city life. He would stand on a curb, mesmerized by the speed and variety of traffic. Everyone was in a hurry. The city gave Mo the freedom he craved. It was big enough that he could do what he wanted without fear of word immediately getting back to his parents.

In the city Mo kissed his first girl, smoked his first cigarette, played hooky from school and began to test the limits of his parent's authority. Before long the slender dark-haired lad became familiar to detectives in Moose Jaw's juvenile crimes division. In an effort to stave off full-scale juvenile delinquency, Mo's father shipped him off to another boarding school in the francophone community of Gravelbourg. Later, after Mo recovered from a bout of pneumonia, he was sent to Saskatchewan's famed Notre Dame College at Wilcox. The school was well known in Canada for its academic standards, its willingness to take tough kids and its gritty hockey team, the Notre Dame Hounds. Many NHLers ascended to the pro ranks under the guiding hand of Father Athol Murray, who ran the school. Mo played hockey and served as an altar boy for the daily mass services.

"My fondest memories of school are at Notre Dame," Mo would say later. "I was well liked by the older Hounds and always had numerous places to go and things to do. I didn't want to leave when the school year was finished."

Mo couldn't accept his father's refusal to send him back the following autumn. He was furious. He called Father Murray and begged to be taken back. When that didn't work, desperation set in and he hitchhiked the 40 miles from Moose Jaw to Wilcox to plead with the legendary Catholic priest. But Père, as the boys called him, was away on business, and Mo hitchhiked home in tears.

Resigned to attending school in Moose Jaw, Mo made extra cash by getting a newspaper route, baby-sitting and helping his aunt with her laundry. It seemed like he might make a go of it. But when he was 12, he had another crisis to confront. His father's tax accountant, a friend of the family, sexually abused Mo during a boy scout camping trip. Mo kept the rage inside for about a month before letting loose in his school with a crowbar. He smashed a toilet and splashed ink on the desks of teachers he didn't particularly like. The investigating detective was his little league baseball coach, and the cop read him like a lineup card. Mo admitted to the vandalism and tearfully revealed that he had been molested by the man he called the Taxman. Mo's parents recognized that he needed help, and rather than sending him to a boarding school in Regina, as a social worker had suggested, they chose to send him to Winnipeg, where it was less likely he could immediately thumb his way home. Instead of having the abuser charged for molesting their son, they instructed Mo to stay away from him. His parents didn't want to pursue charges. Mo never forgave them for that.

He settled into the new boys school in Winnipeg without any problems. Many of the counselors who worked there were old pals from Notre Dame. Before long Mo had cornered the black market on cigarettes, which he sold three for a quarter from a stash he had under the floor of one of the school's garages. The cigarette trade provided him with steady income, and let him to pick and choose his friends and exert some influence over the older bullies. It was a lesson that would help Mo immensely in his later life when the bullies in the joint were murderous thugs.

By the time Mo was 14, he was already sexually active. He was an attractive kid with a charming smile and a mop of raven black hair. He ran away twice with his first love, earning him a weekend stay in a detention home. He had a romance with an older girl at summer camp at Manitoba's Whiteshell Provincial Park, spending many nights with her in her old Studebaker. He loved women. He enjoyed their scent, their conversations and the way they looked at life, which was so different from the boys he knew.

In 1967 Mo was sent to an elite private boarding school, St. John's Ravenscourt, also in Winnipeg, and like Charles Ng a half a world away, Mo had to get used to wearing a sports jacket and tie to his classes. He didn't fit in at all. "There was no room for my behavior, and I was constantly being punished," he would say later. "The headmaster was a good man. I just refused to follow the rules." One day he skipped study period to meet a girl in the skating shack for a little daytime romance. When he was caught he was given the option of a strap or expulsion. He went home.

His father was furious. Mo only avoided being grounded for life by agreeing to join the militia, Canada's reserve army. Armand thought a little military discipline might accomplish what expensive boarding schools could not. Mo made the best of it. Against his father's wishes and by forging his signature, he had acquired his driver's license. Now Mo could sign out jeeps from the armory twice a week. Oh, how he loved automobiles.

Walking home from the armory one wintry Friday night, he came upon a white Corvair parked and running outside a house. The car was warm, the radio was playing, a light snow was falling and the interior was rich with the scent of the new leather seats. The lights on the dashboard emitted a soft green glow. It was as if the car were saying to him, "Take me, Mo. Take me." Without really thinking, Mo hopped in and drove the sporty vehicle home, parking it at the house behind his parents'. Stealing the car was a rush. Mo was both terrified and excited.

The next day Mo was in the yard helping his father build a new fence. Worrying that he shouldn't have left the stolen vehicle so close to home, he slipped away to move it. No sooner had he pulled onto the street than the police appeared out of nowhere. They had staked out the vehicle, waiting for the thief to return, and they had Mo red-handed. Mo's father was oblivious to his son's arrest until he received a tearful call from the boy pleading to be bailed out of jail. Armand, well beyond the breaking point, left Mo in police cells over night, hoping the experience would put some sense into him.

It was a long night for the first-time car thief. The cell block was cold and the fans blew loudly. Mo, stretched out on a steel bed with a rubber sheet, couldn't sleep. He kept thinking that a fire might break out at the police station and he wouldn't be able to get out of his cell. He was terrified of his cell mates—hard-looking men who gave him menacing looks.

When his father eventually arrived after Sunday mass, he ripped into Mo for putting the family name in the court docket column of the *Moose Jaw Herald*. But he told Mo that if he smartened up and helped out around home, he would be allowed to drive his mother's car. Mo jumped at the chance. He promised to stay out of trouble.

The promise was one he couldn't keep. If it wasn't cars, it was women. Unlike Leonard Lake, Mo had no need of a fake unicorn or a camera to meet and seduce girls. They loved him. At a militia camp barbecue one weekend, Mo wound up in bed with a young girl. Mo thought she was 15 or 16, but it turned out she was only 13. The following morning two police officers came looking for Mo on a rape charge. Mo pleaded guilty and received a suspended sentence, but as they walked out of court, his date's father had a few choice words for Mo's father. "Can't you control that kid?" Armand looked grim.

"Keep your pecker in your pants from now on," Armand warned his boy.

Mo spent the summer working on a ranch in southern Saskatchewan, saving enough to buy a 1957 Chevy two door. Excited, he drove the car home to show his father and was heartbroken when his father ordered him to take it back. The order was too much for Mo. He packed up and headed back to the ranch. Cars were his life, he knew, and he wouldn't be treated like a kid anymore.

He tried going back to school in Moose Jaw, living with his sister and her husband, but that didn't work out either. Mo didn't like anyone telling him what to do. After moving back briefly to his parent's new home in Regina, he got a job in Saskatoon. Within a month he was caught breaking into a house and was sentenced to two months in the Provincial Corrections Centre in Regina.

Seeing his son in prison was the last straw for Mo's father. Armand disowned him. Mo's mother and sisters visited him, but his father refused to come and would not even discuss his son at home. Mo, now 18, was released from jail in November 1970 and registered for school. But he continued with his pattern of petty thefts, burglaries and frauds and was quickly sent back to jail. Like Charlie and Leonard, the die had been cast. He was spiraling downward.

The free fall continued after his release. He was sharing an apartment and a bed with two Grade 10 girls when a noise outside his door jolted him awake. Seconds later the door burst open and several armed men rushed into his room, members of a north-side gang, one wielding the ax he had used to smash open the door, another waving a .22 caliber rifle. The girl at Mo's side awoke screaming.

"What the hell do you want?" Mo roared as he climbed out of bed and hastily slid into a pair of jeans.

The gang claimed to be looking for a friend of Mo's who had stolen their car. Mo's buddy had been hawking stolen leather jackets to gang members, and apparently, when they stiffed him for payment, he took off with their car. They wanted it back. Now.

Mo didn't know what they were talking about. "Get the hell out of here," he shouted.

"Hey, buddy, I'm in charge here," the gunman retorted.

Mo laughed in the gunman's face. When the man became distracted by Mo's still-screaming bedmate, he leaped for the gun. As they wrestled for control of the gun, bullets sprayed around the room, knocking out a window, striking a photo on the wall and exploding a wine bottle Mo had been using for a candleholder. Mo took the last two shots in the abdomen. Pumped with adrenaline, he wrenched the weapon free and tossed the man down a flight of stairs. As the gang members fled, he collapsed to the floor, his guts on fire. Sure that he was dying, he took a last look around. He told the sobbing roommate to give his love to his mother. Then he blacked out.

Mo awoke looking into his father's eyes. The old man had been crying, but he smiled when he saw his boy was awake. Like the story of the prodigal son, Armand reached out to his wayward child. He still loved his boy.

Mo, however, was anything but repentant. The moment he got out of hospital, he began searching for the shooter, determined to exact his revenge. He staked out the man's house for several nights without success. Fortunately, police caught up to the man and charged him with attempted murder.

Soon after, a woman Mo had seduced at a party had him charged with rape when her boyfriend found out about the liaison. When she testified at his trial, the judge instructed the jury to return a verdict of not guilty.

At about this time Mo's long-standing girl friend, Brenda, gave birth to a little girl. They named the baby Theresa after Mo's mother and decided to settle down. Amazingly, they actually did. Mo took a job working on his brother-in-law's hog farm. He later rented a farm just north of Moose Jaw and went to work for one of the area's most successful farmers. Mo also helped his brother, Rene, manage a large herd of cattle. He liked the cowboy life—herding cattle, breaking horses and hauling livestock feed. When he applied himself, Mo was a hard worker and skilled in a number of trades. He had taken a couple of welding courses and had plans to take others in livestock breeding.

Mo and Rene soon got into curbing cars. They picked them up cheaply in Quebec and resold them on the prairies. With money flowing in, Mo could drive the newest and most expensive automobiles without having to steal them. Mo and his girl friend began talking about getting married and having another child. It seemed nothing could go wrong. "I was happy with myself and pleased with life at home," Mo would later recall. "I was confident that everything I touched would turn to gold." Then, just as quickly, Mo lost the Midas touch.

Brenda suddenly became ill. Mo rushed her to the hospital when she began screaming and clutching her stomach one night. Tests revealed she had a venereal disease. Brenda later admitted to having an affair with a musician. Mo was devastated. All his dreams, his hopes, his plans were a crumbling ruin. The couple made a halfhearted effort to keep the relationship going, but it couldn't work. The trust was gone.

Amid the marital crisis, Mo's brother, Rene, accidentally shot himself in the foot while fox hunting. On the way home from visiting his brother in the hospital, Mo wound up in trouble again after a bout of road rage. He met a truck that had cut him off earlier in the day, and he went after it, seeking revenge. He cut it off, flashed a one-finger salute and roared off. When the truck came after him, he slammed on the brakes to have it out with the occupants. But Mo was no match for the two men in the cab. They laid a licking on him, and as they drove away Mo grabbed his .22 rifle from behind the seat of his truck and shot at the truck's back bumper. The next day he was arrested for illegally discharging a firearm.

Mo became convinced that a black cloud was hanging over his head. Within weeks he and his brother, Rene, were charged with possession of stolen goods over some gold coins they received as payment for a gambling debt. Although they eventually beat the charge on appeal, it was a long expensive court battle. While that was dragging on, the farm went down the drain. First the vehicles, then the livestock. The motor in Mo's pickup truck seized and his car quit running. He rolled his one-ton farm truck while hauling hay. He bought a new pickup but had to take it back because it was a lemon. He wrecked its replacement the very next day. Then his hogs got sick and his horse got mange. To top it off, a neighbor shot his dog. When Mo's basement flooded, destroying his furnace, he hoped his unlucky streak had run its course. He was wrong. He was convicted of possession of stolen property and sent to jail for six months. It was a run of bad luck, Mo decided, that could have made a great country song.

Even in jail Mo seemed cursed. He got drunk on smuggled booze, got angry and stormed away from a minimum-security prison bush camp, where he had been sent to serve his sentence. The next day, back in police cells, he told Brenda he never wanted to see her again. He figured he had finally hit rock bottom. There was no point in pulling her down with him.

"I had completely screwed up my life," he said later. "I felt that I was destined to be a loser, and no matter what I did, it would turn out bad."

For a long time it looked like he was right. When he was released from the Regina Correctional Centre in February 1976, he went on a rampage that lasted six months. He got into fights. He stole. He fenced stolen goods. He was out of control. After he blinded a man with a broken beer glass during an argument over a game of pool one night, he was shipped off to Prince Albert Penitentiary to serve a three-year sentence. He had finally made it to the big time: a maximum-security federal prison. To welcome him his fellow inmates beat him the day he arrived.

Mo decided he needed to give his head a shake. If he was going to survive in the joint, he was going to have to learn some new skills. He learned to stay out of people's faces and to encircle himself with friendlies. He survived the rest of his prison term without incident.

But he still couldn't get it through his head to stay off the liquor. Just after his release from an Edmonton halfway house, he got into a fight with the best man at a wedding he had been invited to attend. He pleaded guilty and escaped with a $1,000 fine.

After that embarrassing incident, Mo took another stab at normal life. He settled in the Saskatoon area, in central Saskatchewan, and took up carpentry. He joined Rene in the stucco business and eventually purchased an acreage north of the city. For the most part he kept out of trouble. He stayed home, working on the acreage, equipping a workshop and breeding purebred dogs. He also found a new love, an attractive 21-year-old named Debby, who was a good friend of Rene. It was another bizarre relationship.

The couple met at Saskatoon's seedy Baldwin Hotel on St. Patrick's Day. An hour after they met, Mo invited the young lady to his acreage. "I put some music on the stereo and went into the kitchen to get some wine," he remembered. "When I came out, Debby was naked on the couch."

They got married a few months later. With Debby, Mo was a Material Boy. Anxious to please her and keep her happy, he showered her with every excess. He didn't care that he couldn't afford it.

"I had toys I didn't even use," he admitted later. He bought a boat, a snowmobile, a three-wheel all-terrain vehicle, a motorcycle and a pair of tractors. Of course, Mo indulged his passion for automobiles. He bought three new trucks between June and September 1980. In the first months of his marriage, he owned in rapid succession, a Corvette, a Toronado and a Cadillac.

But it wasn't long before the fantasy world Mo had created collapsed. The creditors were already starting to move in when Mo's truck was spotted at the scene of a bank robbery in the tiny Saskatchewan hamlet of Marquis in early February 1981. Although Mo later claimed a friend had borrowed his truck for the job, police were hunting for him and the vehicle within hours of the robbery. Mo's sisters begged him to turn himself in to clear up the mess, but Mo was determined to be on hand for his second youngest sister's Valentine's Day wedding in British Columbia. He picked up a few personal items at his Saskatoon acreage and flew to meet Debby in the southern Alberta town of Lethbridge. They holed up in a motel under an assumed name. Mo said he had some work to do there before heading to British Columbia.

He knew it was just a matter of time before the police and his creditors closed in, but he was determined to hold out as long as he could. His mother had arranged for family photos to be taken at Denise's wedding. It might be the last time the family got together. It had been 14 years since the whole clan, now scattered between British Columbia and Ontario, had gathered in one spot. The photo session was in the morning, the wedding in the afternoon. That turned out to be lucky for Mo.

It was a dull rainy day in the west coast town of Chilliwack, a day Denise and her new husband, Don Johnston, will never forget. As they strode happily out of the church to begin their lives together, they were met by a SWAT team in the parking lot. Invited guests gaped as gun-toting police officers in bulletproof vests closed in on the astounded wedding party. With guns pointed menacingly, police ordered the men to strip to the waist. They weren't certain just which of the guests was the suspected bank robber, and they weren't taking any chances in their search for a man who might be armed. Meanwhile, Mo had spotted the converging police through a church window and had slipped quietly out of town before they had closed the net around the church. In the three-piece suit and a new pair of shoes he had bought for the occasion, he stepped onto the rain-slicked highway and hopped into the first car headed toward Vancouver. A well-dressed man standing in the rain didn't have to wait long for a ride. Rene brought Debby to meet Mo at a Vancouver motel the next day. His brother also brought bad news. Mo's bank had called in his loans and police had seized his vehicles.

"I knew I was going back to jail," Mo explained later. "I knew this stage of my life was finished."

But Mo wasn't finished yet. He wanted to leave Debby with enough money to tide her over for at least a few months. The dreamer needed one more big score, and he knew only one way to get it.

Cowboy Maurice Laberge.

Maurice Laberge relaxes by a campfire. He loved working out of doors and was fond of camping and horseback riding.

6

The Red Serge

IN THE SPLENDOR of the Canadian Rocky Mountain foothills, Ray Munro trudged cautiously along the national rail line that linked Canada's east coast to the west. On a stretch of track just out of the view of motorists on the parallel Yellowhead Highway, not far from the east gates of the world-famed Jasper National Park, the unthinkable had happened on February 8, 1986. A freight train and VIA Rail passenger train had collided head on.

Ray surveyed the scene. A wrecked train engine stood on end, towering over piles of smoldering grain. The acrid black smoke of a diesel fuel fire drifted over the rubble. Much of the wreckage was unrecognizable, a jumble of twisted steel. Somewhere below the tons of metal and grain, passengers and crew members were entombed in the few rail cars that remained relatively intact.

God, what a mess, Ray thought as he approached the still-smoking engine. Debris was scattered down the track as far as the eye could see. It would be years before they can clean up this site, he thought. If ever.

Called in the day after the crash to determine if criminal activity had caused the death of the 22 victims, Ray had been given absolute authority over the scene. Nothing would be moved, no bodies would be recovered, no evidence would be disturbed unless he gave approval. It was not an enviable position. He was under intense pressure from his bosses at the Royal Canadian Mounted Police provincial headquarters in Edmonton to move quickly. The spotlight was on him. The event had attracted world media coverage. VIA Rail and Canadian National Railways were anxious to get the scene out of the public spotlight. They needed the line open again quickly. Every day of delay cost millions.

Ray was used to such pressure. He would not be hurried. No quick half-baked conclusions would be drawn. A veteran homicide investigator, he was well aware of that trap. The investigation would proceed slowly and steadily. No debris would be left unturned. Every seeming dead-end clue would be painstakingly checked out.

Ray often thought of his job as that of a biographer. Often it was his task to write the last chapter in a victim's life, to record in minute detail the motives and events that had led to the end. This was the biggest investigation of his career, but he wouldn't change his standard operating procedure. His team would spend hundreds of hours putting together the last chapter of this tragedy, and no one was going to tell them how to write it.

Ray Munro's stubbornness was the product of an impoverished childhood. He never knew his father, never asked about him and didn't want to know who he was. All he knew was the man had died, leaving his mother destitute. His two older sisters and brother had already been sent to live with family and friends before he arrived on November 23, 1948. His mother, Jessie, was 36 years old and barely making ends meet as a waitress and a maid. Ray's arrival was just another in a long line of setbacks for her. Since she had no income and nowhere to go after his birth, staff at Calgary's Holy Cross Hospital conspired to keep her there for three months while she looked for a way out. She finally found work as a nanny in Vancouver, where she worked for a year before being summoned to Orange County, California, to care for an ailing sister. Mother and son returned to Vancouver when Ray was three.

It was 1951. Times were hard on Vancouver's impoverished east side, a waterfront slum populated largely by immigrants with dreams. Ray's mother worked as a waitress at the Milky Way restaurant, earning about $30 a week. It barely covered the rent, utilities and food. By the time Ray was seven, he was selling *Liberty* and *Chatelaine* magazines to help pay the bills.

With his mother at work and no one to watch over him, he looked after himself. He was a latchkey kid in a tough neighborhood. The police were frequent visitors. The Rebels motorcycle gang had a clubhouse on the corner, and neighborhood boys were feeder stock for the local street gangs. It was hard to be good, but fate stepped in to keep Ray out of gang colors. When a downturn in the economy threw Jessie on to the unemployment line, she packed up and moved her 12-year-old son back to her hometown of Trail, British Columbia.

Mother and son moved into a tiny one-bedroom house she had purchased with her first husband in the late 1920s. It wasn't much of a place. Shortly after they arrived, the home was condemned by the local fire marshal. An uncle helped bring the house's wiring up to standard, and the condemned conditions were removed. The house was livable, but just. Once the dining room had been converted into a second bedroom for Ray, there was only a kitchen and bathroom. The place was heated by a tiny coal and wood stove.

In Trail, a mining town of 12,000 in the British Columbia interior, Jessie found work as a waitress, then as a saleswoman at a local meat market before finally landing a decent-paying job at the hospital laundry. With steady money now coming in, Jessie bought a 1950 Plymouth. Ray attended school, maintained a newspaper route and also worked part time for his best friend's father in the roofing business. Eventually, he got a pump jockey job at a local service station. Ray gave his mother half of everything he earned to help with household expenses.

Ray joined the Air Cadets when he was 14 and moved quickly up the ranks to sergeant. He enjoyed the military and stayed with it for five years. He spent his summers traveling across the country to attend camps and take courses at military bases. He planned to join the military when he graduated school, but that all changed the day an RCMP officer came to cadets to encourage the boys to consider a police career. What got to Ray was that the Mounties, despite being a top-down paramilitary operation, seemed to encourage individual skills and abilities more than the military. He was told he would be a good candidate. He was single, 5' 11" and had a quick mind and a drive to succeed.

Ray joined the RCMP on his nineteenth birthday. He was engaged to his high school sweetheart, Margaret Forrest, but their marriage plans would have to wait because, at the time, only unmarried men were accepted into the force. The ball-busting backbreaking regimen of the RCMP training program in Regina, Saskatchewan, was legendary. The three-month course literally spat out candidates who couldn't handle the physical demands or lacked the mental toughness. The training regime was go, go, go, and then go some more. Recruits were required to run everywhere on the grounds: from class to class, from crime scene investigation to swimming, from swimming to hand-to-hand combat, from combat training to typing, to law, to gym, to firearms training, to driving courses. And when they had mastered all those skills, they had to climb on horseback and ride until they were one with their beasts. The force was, after all, the Royal Canadian *Mounted* Police, and every recruit would be steeped in the tradition. The recruits were often reminded that while a horse cost $300, they cost the force nothing. They were expendable. Ray bedded down exhausted every night in a dorm with 32 other recruits in Troop 24.

Ray's years as a cadet were a tremendous advantage during the difficult training. He was used to getting up at dawn and running several miles. Push-ups. Sit-ups. Full equipment marches. Parading in the drill hall. Although he never had what one would call an athletic build, he was in good physical condition. And academically he was more than capable of handling the avalanche of information that poured down on the troopers. The only class he truly dreaded was swimming, but he persevered and graduated at the top of his class.

The RCMP ranks were experiencing tremendous expansion, and every recruit was pushed into the field as quickly as possible. The day after Ray's graduation in traditional red serge with riding breeches and knee-high boots, he was shipped off to a small northern Alberta community. He had two days to drive from central Saskatchewan to his new posting, a distance of more than 600 miles. He tucked away his red serge and pulled on his working clothes: the dull brown tunic of an RCMP patrolman.

Ray arrived in Faust, Alberta, in mid-September 1969 like a man from Mars. He thought he was used to small towns, but this was ridiculous. Faust was a northern community of about 1,000 people, mostly aboriginals and Métis, located on the south shore of one of the largest lakes in the province, Lesser Slave Lake. There were no stores. Area roads were surfaced with gravel. The dying industries of mink farming and commercial fishing fueled what was left of a local economy. The American Indian Movement had spread to Canada, and the self-proclaimed leader of the Canadian contingent was based in Faust. The sudden emergence of warriors in red berets kept the small police detachment on alert, but despite concerns of a pending rebellion, the RCMP and the native community remained on relatively good terms.

The detachment's four officers lived in the headquarters building, sharing the same putrid sulfur-reeking water that was pumped into the three prisoners' cells. It was undrinkable. Newcomers amused themselves by setting it afire. The officers were on call 24 hours a day. Besides doing their police work, they were called upon to be janitors, secretaries and grounds keepers. Since there were no prosecutors in the area, the officers both investigated and prosecuted the crimes.

The money wasn't very good considering the hours the officers worked. Ray was making $460 a month, but more than half his pay went to rent and utilities. Not that he had any time to spend money. He had no days off during his first three months on the job.

Ray's training officer, Constable Dale Crewson, was a bit taken aback with his new protégé. Portly, balding and often sporting the worst case of five o'clock shadow Crewson had ever seen, Ray looked more like the Coca-Cola trucker he'd been before joining the force than the stereotypical Mountie. Still, the recruit seemed brighter than most. He was asking in-depth questions well beyond his experience and seemed to have a feel for the street.

Ray's first night patrol with Dale earned him the nickname that would stick with him for the rest of his career. They were spending the shift performing random checks for impaired drivers. Rain had turned the gravel roads into mud slicks, and driving was treacherous. Ray hopped out to check their first stopped vehicle, brushing along its side as he approached the driver. He cleared the driver, sending him on his way and returned to the cruiser. When he stepped in front of the headlights of the police car, Crewson gawked at the sight of the rookie. Ray was covered with mud from his knees to his neck. When he slid back into the front seat of the cruiser, Crewson asked him what the hell had happened.

"You look like you've been in a pigpen," he said, chuckling at Ray's discomfort. Ray returned to the detachment to remove the muddy clothes, but the name stuck. He was Pigpen forevermore.

What he lacked in Mountie spit and polish, Ray more than made up for with his investigative skills. Crewson saw that Ray was a natural interviewer. His affable easygoing personality took him places other investigators could never go. Officers would be hammering away at a suspect who wouldn't give them so much as his name, when Ray would wander in. Within a few minutes he'd waltz out with a signed confession. In addition to using his nickname, fellow officers began calling him Father Ray.

Ray's interrogation skills weren't tricks. He genuinely liked people and treated them all the same, whether they were heinous criminals or his next-door neighbors. He didn't pound on tables and bark at suspects, and he never seemed to get angry. He gave them a cigarette and engaged in harmless chatter until they were comfortable with him and realized he was a guy who would listen. His often disheveled appearance and offhand manner reminded Crewson in later years of Peter Falk's TV detective. The more Crewson thought about it, the more Ray became the Lieutenant Columbo of the Mounties. He disarmed suspects with his charm and easygoing manner.

He also was a self-starter who needed little supervision. Within a week of arriving in Faust, Ray was working on his own, investigating complaints and responding to accidents and incidents. The learning curve was

steep. Over the next two years, he would investigate accidents, armed robberies, break and enters, thefts, deaths, attempted shootings and attempted murder.

In 1971 Ray received permission to marry. He hauled out his red serge
and, on June 5 in Trail, married his 20-year-old sweetheart, Margaret, before
reporting to his new posting in Slave Lake, a seven-member detachment in
a town of 5,000 and just down the road from Faust. With the surrounding
oil patch bursting with activity, the workload was enormous. Oil rigs and
big money had attracted some pretty unsavory characters. In Slave Lake the
oil boom meant each officer shouldered a caseload of 40 to 50 ongoing
investigations at any given time. But it was here that Ray developed his
forté. It seemed for a while that every death in the detachment area
occurred on his beat. He soon found himself probing murders, industrial
and motor vehicle deaths, and other sudden deaths.

Slave Lake provided a brutal orientation. Ray's first murder call in 1974
sent him to the small northern community of Loon Lake, population 300.
A man had blasted his wife with a shotgun. She had been eight months
pregnant at the time. It took Ray six hours to drive to the area to recover
the body, conduct a crime-scene investigation and make the arrest. Then he
had to transport the body of the victim to Edmonton, three hours distant,
for an autopsy. He asked Margaret, who was pregnant herself, if she wanted to accompany him on the trip. She declined.

Over the next two years, Ray investigated about 40 deaths. The cases
often brought him to RCMP provincial headquarters and put him in close
contact with the force's elite homicide and major crimes detectives. He
quickly emerged as a candidate for plainclothes detective work. Ray applied
for a promotion to detective ranks and got it, working under the wing of
veteran homicide investigator Floyd McAusland in Calgary, Alberta. The
pair was responsible for investigating all homicides in the southern half of
the province. They spent most of their weekends driving from one death
scene to another: vehicle accidents, suicides, murders. Then they spent the
next three days watching the coroner carve up the bodies.

Autopsies were not for the squeamish, but looking at death never really bothered Ray—at least not physically. He never felt nauseated by the hor-ror he saw routinely, but it bothered him to see what people were capable of doing to one another. It fueled his desire to get better at catching the peo-ple who committed such grisly acts.

He found forensic pathology fascinating. The minutia grabbed him. It constantly amazed him that so much could be gleaned from so little, and tiny bits of evidence were sometimes the difference between making an arrest or not. But he never lost sight of the fact that human lives had been snuffed out, and he never let himself forget the despair left in the wake of a violent act.

By the mid-1980s Ray was a veteran homicide investigator and had been promoted to corporal. He also had transferred to Edmonton, where he would eventually become a sergeant heading a major crimes unit. Oil prices had crashed, the economy was in a slump and murder rates were still climbing.

A killing one Sunday evening, January 13, 1985, shook Ray to the core. In the small farming community of Vegreville, about an hour and a half east of Edmonton, neighbors had called the local police detachment to report that Tom Ziaec, a single, middle-aged, unemployed and extremely paranoid local resident had been brandishing a rifle during an argument.

Constable Gary Griesbrecht, a recruit Ray had trained in Slave Lake, arrived at Ziaec's ramshackle home to back up the investigating officers. Like most other members of the detachment, the 32-year-old Mountie had experience dealing with Ziaec and was well aware of his distrust of the RCMP. Deciding against calling in a tactical team from Edmonton, the officers decided to rush the house and attempt to disarm Ziaec. When they broke down the door, they were surprised to find Ziaec's mother sitting by herself at the kitchen table as if nothing were wrong. But as Griesbrecht sidled past her to enter the living room, a rifle shot cracked, and a bullet from a .270 caliber magnum ripped into his stomach just below his bullet-proof vest. The blast sparked a cacophony of gunfire in the tiny house. In the ensuing battle, Ziaec sprayed the walls with bullets from his high-pow-ered weapon, wounding another officer in the next room. Police returned fire with a volley of shotgun blasts while two wounded officers and the bewildered mother were dragged to safety. The shaken officers set up a cordon around the perimeter and called for the RCMP tactical team and a police negotiator from Edmonton.

Ray, who had been trained as a hostage negotiator, got the call. He learned immediately upon his arrival that Griesbrecht, who had remained a close friends through the years, had died. But he had no time to mourn and no mandate to avenge the killing of the 12-year veteran. It now fell to him to convince Ziaec to surrender peacefully. The gunman, fearful he would be shot on sight, would not relinquish his weapon. After an eight-hour standoff, when it became clear there was no way out, he turned his gun on himself.

The homicide investigation fell to Ray, but this time the last chapter he would write of the victim's life was that of a friend. He never attended Griesbrecht's autopsy. He wanted to remember the man the way he was on the job and at his wedding.

Ray built a solid reputation as a tenacious investigator. He drove the people who worked for him hard, but they respected him. He took investigation work to the forefront, working with other senior investigators to transform the RCMP's top-down paramilitary investigation process into a much more efficient and productive team process. His idea was met with enormous resistance from his superiors, but it was eventually adopted. It was a small but costly victory for Ray, who then faced accusations of empire building. But give him straight police work without the politics and he was happy. Although he was on call 24 hours a day, seven days a week, Ray relished the life. He worked hard and then he played hard. But his lifestyle put considerable strain on his family, and his battles to keep upper management from interfering with his unit's style of operation were becoming tedious. It was time for a change.

He often thought it would be interesting to run an RCMP detachment in southern Alberta ranch country. East of the Rockies was open space. It would be a much different kind of policing than what consumed him now, but it was strangely appealing. The scattered towns were so small they relied on one central RCMP detachment to keep law and order. With long distances to travel, police response times were so slow that thieves sometimes broke into small-town stores, loaded up the safes and carted them away before police arrived. Ray knew of a guy who did stuff like that. His name was Mo Laberge.

7

The Big Score

NINETEEN-YEAR-OLD BOB MCLAUGHLIN peered into the darkness
shrouding the second-story verandah of his parents' home, hoping to
see what had startled his younger brother. He and David, four years
his junior, were alone at their parents' Lethbridge residence after returning
from evening church services. They had arrived home about 8:30 P.M., and
only a few minutes later David came racing breathlessly down the stairs,
yelling that someone was climbing the balcony. Bob went up to investigate.

"Who's there?" he called out hesitantly from the door to the deck.
David was at his back, trying to catch a glimpse of the shadow he had seen
a moment ago on the ladder. In the blackness of that late March night in
1981, the boys heard someone stumble over the patio furniture. Then the
outline of a figure emerged. At first the boys thought it was their neighbor,
who sometimes borrowed their father's ladder. But as the dark shape
stepped out of the shadows, the boys realized in a terror-filled heartbeat that
this was no one they knew. They both turned to run.

"Stop right there!" the intruder ordered as they bolted into the hallway.
"Stop or I'll shoot!"

Halting at the last command, the boys turned around slowly to see a large man, clad in a ski mask and green parka, entering the hall. Their eyes were fixed on his gloved hand, which held a very large silver handgun with a long barrel.

The man immediately began barking out questions. "Who else is in the house? Where are your mother and father? Are there any guns in the house?"

Stammering nervously, the boys explained that their parents had gone out for drinks at the Royal Canadian Legion and would be home in a couple of hours. Bob told the intruder of an old shotgun in the closet which had been dismantled. The gunman wanted to know if the boys' parents would be bringing anyone home with them. He wanted to know exactly where they would park.

He eyed Bob a moment and then asked if he worked in his father's store. Ed McLaughlin was manager of the Super-Valu Store, where Bob sometimes filled shelves or packed groceries. The intruder asked Bob if the store had an alarm system. "What kind is it, boy?" he demanded.

When he was satisfied there was no one else in the house, the gunman escorted the boys down the stairs to the main level and directed them to lie facedown on the floor. He continued to question them as he taped their hands and feet. He then tied their hands to their feet with a package of new rope.

Once the boys were securely bound, the gunman looked around the room. He quickly spotted a bar in one corner and asked the boys if the bar had a fridge. "Where is it, boy?" he asked Bob. He walked over and helped himself to a beer and took the bottle with him when he went upstairs to explore the remainder of the house. When he returned he tied Bob to the bar. He then pulled David across the room and tied him to the leg of the piano.

Once he was in control, the masked man was soft spoken and polite. In a gentle voice with a slight drawl, he inquired if the boys were comfortable. He then took another beer and searched the home's drawers and closets, stopping frequently to peer out the window. At one point the doorbell rang, but when no one answered, the callers, friends of the boys, departed in a van.

Underneath the knit ski mask, Mo Laberge was getting warm. But he couldn't complain. So far everything was proceeding according to plan. Mo, who had been staying at a local motel under an assumed name, had followed the store manager home from work to find out where he lived. He had arranged for the clothes, ski mask, rope and other paraphernalia to be sent up to Lethbridge by bus. He also had located a truck to use as a get-away vehicle.

This was going to be the big one he had dreamed about. It would keep Debby going and maybe he could stash enough away to set himself up when he got out of jail in a few years. He planned to turn himself in after this job and settle accounts for the string of outstanding charges against him.

It seemed like an eternity passed before the boys' parents arrived. Dorothy McLaughlin went immediately to the washroom while her husband went into the kitchen with a bag of takeout Chinese food he had stopped to pick up on the way home. He was flabbergasted when a gun-toting masked bandit suddenly appeared behind him. He thought it was a joke.

"You've got to be kidding," he said. "Come on, what's going on?"

Mo waved the gun barrel toward the master bedroom.

"Okay, McLaughlin," he said sternly. "Lie down with your face on the floor. And keep your head down."

Mo was putting the last strips of tape around Ed McLaughlin's legs when Dorothy walked into the bedroom. Unexpectedly confronted by a gunman in her bedroom, she let out an involuntary screech.

Mo didn't bat an eye. "Get down, lady," he said, gesturing to the floor, where her husband was already lying. The gunman moved quickly to tape her hands and legs together and then tied her to the leg of the bed. When he was finished, he began prodding Ed about the whereabouts of keys to the mall, where the store was located, and the location of the keys to the store itself. He also demanded to know the combination to the safe. He took about $80 from Ed's wallet and about another $100 from Dorothy's purse.

When she overcame her initial shock, Dorothy began asking Mo if her kids were all right. Mo assured her they were fine, but she didn't seem to believe him.

Mo turned to Ed. "What's the name of your youngest son?"

"David," Ed replied.

Mo called out David's name. "Your mother wants to know if you are all right." When David answered yes, Mo asked him how his brother was doing.

"Bob is okay," the boy responded.

Mo then asked Ed for the keys to his car, brought the vehicle around to the back door and hustled Ed outside. Seeing the panic in Dorothy's face, he assured her he wasn't going to harm her husband.

"Don't worry," he said softly. "We'll be right back."

Ed had tried to convince him there was no need to tie him up. He said he was willing to go retrieve the money from the store safe. Mo shut him up.

"You're damn right you will," he snapped. He opened the trunk of Ed's Pontiac LeMans and began pushing Ed inside.

"Hold on," Ed protested. "I have a dirty oil filter in the trunk. Can you at least move it or take it out?"

Mo tossed the oil filter aside and then helped Ed into the trunk. He eased the Pontiac into the street and headed for the store, which was just a short distance away. He parked beside the shipping and receiving entrance on the east side of the store and tried the keys he had taken from Ed's suit pocket on a fire exit door. It opened without sounding an alarm. Mo then returned to get Ed. As he walked toward the car, Mo felt conspicuous as hell in the new clothes he had obtained for the job, particularly the bright tan work boots that practically gleamed in the dark. Before opening the trunk, he cast a wide glance. The streets were deserted. It was past 11:00 P.M. He popped the lid. Ed seemed relieved to be getting out of the trunk. But just as he slid over the rear bumper and eased his weight onto his shaky pins, a car came down the street in the direction of the pair.

"Just pretend we're talking," Mo directed, turning his back to the

approaching vehicle but watching Ed intensely with steely eyes. When the
car had passed, Mo escorted Ed to the fire exit door and ordered him to wait
at the rear of the store. The safe was near the front window, and people were
walking past on the sidewalk. When they had disappeared from view, Mo
cut the tape off Ed's hands and handed him a green garbage bag he had
pulled from his pocket.

"Put the money in this," he directed.

When Ed had finished emptying the cash from the safe, Mo directed
him to close the safe and lie facedown at the back of the store. He taped
Ed's hands and feet and cut open the canvas sacks, dumping the contents
onto the floor. There must have been close to $7,000, including about
$1,000 in new hundred-dollar bills. Those might have to be stashed. They
were new and in sequence and too noticeable. Mo scooped the bills into the
garbage bag and slipped out the side door, locking it behind him. Ed began
working on his bonds when he was sure Mo had left. He freed his hands
within a few minutes and called police.

Outside, Mo ditched the ski mask, rope and some loose-fitting coveralls he had worn over another set of clothes. Mo cruised out of town in his
getaway vehicle. The bold robbery was front-page news in the *Lethbridge
Herald* the following day. A front-page headline trumpeted, "Extortionist
Forces Way into Store Safe."

Ed McLaughlin accommodated the local press by posing in front of
the store safe. "Nothing like this has ever happened to me after 35 years in
this business," he told the paper's reporter. "It shook me up."

He remarked that the masked gunman was one cool customer. "He
was cool about it," he said. "He didn't seem anxious, and he did know what
he was doing."

As he had planned Mo turned himself in to face several outstanding
charges against him. Police charged him with the February 2, 1981, credit
union robbery in Marquis, just outside of Moose Jaw, and with the robbery
of a hotel in Sutherland, a bedroom community on the outskirts of Saskatoon. He was transferred to Regina to face fraud-related charges there.
While awaiting bail in cells at the courthouse, Mo encountered his broth-

er, Armand, who was about to be sentenced for escaping from the city's provincial jail. They chatted a bit about their situations before Mo was called aside to sign some legal documents. When Mo returned, Armand was furious.

"What's bugging you?" Armand asked his older sibling when he returned to the cell at the Regina courthouse. At first Mo didn't respond. He lit a cigarette and paced angrily about the cell. Eventually, he explained that he had been hit with new charges and that his bail application had been revoked.

RCMP in Lethbridge had pieced together enough evidence to charge him with the Lethbridge Super-Valu robbery and a February 11 robbery of a Lethbridge Safeway store. All four robberies had been committed by a man wearing a green ski mask. Police also had determined that Mo, who was earning his living applying plaster to houses, had been in Lethbridge on both occasions to visit his sister-in-law. But the evidence in all the cases was largely circumstantial.

Two weeks later police in Calgary staged a unique event. Using actors and a speech sample obtained surreptitiously from Mo during a police interview in Moose Jaw, investigators set up a voice lineup. One by one, members of the McLaughlin family were brought in to listen to seven voices on the tape to determine whether they could pick out the masked man who had tied them up and robbed the store.

David McLaughlin was first. Although he fidgeted nervously when he heard Mo's voice, he didn't identify him as the robber. But when his mother heard the same clip, she became visibly agitated. Her head jerked back, and she asked to hear the tape again. As she listened to Mo's voice a second time, she tugged nervously at her lip with shaking fingers.

"It sounds like him—the guy that did our house," she told investigators.

Ed also picked out Mo's voice from the lineup that included a radio disc jockey, a couple of school teachers, a social worker and a few others. As he listened to Mo's voice, he removed his glasses and sat forward with his elbows on his knees, his hands clasped and his eyes closed.

"That's the voice I remember from that night," he said finally.

His son, Bob, picked up Mo's voice right away. "Whew!" he said. "I'll listen to the rest of the tapes, but I want to listen to this one later."

David asked police if he could listen to the tapes a second time. Although they mixed up the order of the voices, David picked Mo's voice out immediately. "Stop, that's him. I'm positive of that now," he interjected.

Mo was charged with ten counts related to the armed robbery, kidnapping and unlawful confinement of the McLaughlin family and the earlier Safeway store robbery. He pleaded not guilty at the trial in Lethbridge and elected to be tried by a judge without a jury. The charges relating to the other robberies were either withdrawn by the Crown or dismissed by the courts for lack of evidence. Nearly 100 witnesses were called to testify at a two-week trial in early November 1982. The Crown took eight days to outline a case based largely on the testimony of the McLaughlins and the audio-tape lineup. Mo's brother, Armand, testified against him, giving a version of events that didn't jive completely with the facts but that seemed to incriminate Mo.

Mo's lawyer, Charles Darwent, challenged Armand's testimony, arguing that the Lethbridge city police detective sergeant bought it with dinner, a free airline ticket to Toronto and $200 in cash. He also attempted to discredit the use of voice identification, which was an investigative tool not widely used in Alberta.

David McLaughlin took the stand to testify that the robber had "sad blue eyes." Mo's eyes were green. Darwent would later complain that the presiding judge, Alberta Court of Queen's Bench Justice L.D. MacLean, refused to let him cross-examine the teenager.

Mo took the stand when his defense wrapped up its four days of evidence, but the career criminal didn't impress Judge MacLean. He repeatedly denied committing the robberies. The judge dismissed his claims of innocence and accorded significant weight to the voice lineup. MacLean said the evidence painted a picture of guilt beyond any reasonable doubt. It was patently clear to him that Mo was arrogant, evasive and coldly aloof while on the stand. When he sentenced Mo a week later, MacLean suggested that if Mo really believed he was innocent, that police had fabricated evidence against him and that his brother had perjured himself, he was clearly suffer-ing from delusions.

"This is a very dangerous man," he said, noting Mo's 40-odd convic-tions in the past 14 years. "The most predictable thing about him and about his personality is the likelihood of him returning to a life of crime at the first opportunity. A man of this kind knows no restraints. His potential for committing a serious crime with serious consequences is unlimited. He is unstable and sufficiently dangerous to the community that he cannot be allowed to be at liberty until the passage of time and the natural aging process has burnt him out."

MacLean sentenced Mo to a total of 25 years for three charges of unlawful confinement, two of robbery and one each of kidnapping and using a firearm in the commission of an offense. An application to appeal, filed on his behalf by Calgary lawyer C.D. Evans, was dismissed, and the Supreme Court of Canada refused to hear the matter. Mo was going to prison for a long time.

He sighed heavily as he was led out of the courtroom, but he remained upbeat. He was battered, but he refused to be beaten. He continued to maintain his innocence even as he was hauled off to prison toward his even-tual meeting with Charles Ng.

8

The Brotherhood

A FTER FBI and Naval Investigative Service agents scooped him at Leonard's, Charlie spent two nights at the Sonoma County jail, just north of San Francisco, while arrangements were made to fly him back to Hawaii. He wasn't looking forward to going back to the Pearl Harbor Joint Armed Service Confinement Facility. He despised the brig and its stupid rules.

Charlie was infuriated at being awakened at 4:30 A.M. to do nothing all day. For the first week he wasn't even allowed to have a library book to read. In the evening he had about 30 minutes to write letters or read the Bible. There was no television, and he was not allowed outside for exercise. He had been placed in a maximum-security unit and confined on a cell block with eight other soldiers, each locked into an 8' x 8' concrete cell with a steel cage door. He had a steel bunk, but he was not allowed to sit or rest on it during the day. A mattress was brought into his cell only at night. He was entitled to have his uniform and nothing else.

On the few occasions he was taken to K–Bay for court appearances, Charlie was handcuffed, placed in leg-irons and accompanied by two escorts or chasers as well as an armed military police officer. Having been once burned, marine command was taking no chances.

After about two weeks Charlie was transferred to general population, where he had a bit more freedom. He could walk around the 80-inmate facility, eat meals in the chow hall, go out on work parties, exercise and watch television. He got a job in the prison laundry and played the part of a model inmate. But all the while he was plotting an escape.

He hatched a plan with two other prisoners to break out of the brig. The three persuaded a released prisoner to carry a letter about their escape plans to friends on the outside. But the man they enlisted to carry the letter tipped off the authorities, giving prison officials the opportunity to lay a trap for the would-be escapees. Prison staff planned to search the departing prisoner and intercept the letter before it got outside. But they screwed up. Communications got confused, and the prisoner was not searched before his release. They couldn't find him for four hours. They finally got him on the phone when he reported back to his military unit. He told them Charlie had somehow discovered the plans were going to be intercepted and had scrubbed the operation. Prison staff were skeptical. Had the plans been delivered? They had no way of knowing.

Guards tore apart the prisoners' cells looking for the letters but couldn't find a trace of any escape plan. All the while Charlie protested his innocence. "Why are you doing this?" he repeatedly asked his captors. They ignored him. They ordered him to pack up his stuff and marched him and his co-conspirators back to maximum-security cells.

Charlie was locked in maximum security for over a month, and throughout his time in the hole, he maintained he'd done nothing wrong. "I never did break any rule," he lamented.

He complained that 24-hour lockup was making him nervous, tense and angry. Eventually, a military board approved his return to general population provided he was not allowed outside.

Charlie had won a small but important victory. He was learning how to manipulate the system. Even in prison, he discovered, there are ways to get what you want. Still, time passed slowly in the brig. In all he spent 79 days in jail awaiting his fate. It was mostly dead time. Leonard had written to Charlie of his plans to come to Hawaii to visit, but he never showed up.

Charlie's only escape from the tedium of prison was in books. He was allowed to check out a library book three days a week. Reading kept his mind off things.

Charlie was more upset that he had been caught than he was remorseful for his crimes. He knew he was going to jail and expected to be deported back to Hong Kong when he was released. It was a depressing thought.

Several of his co-conspirators had already been sentenced. Ricardo Dailey, the 26-year-old sergeant who had helped Charlie move the stolen weapons off the base, had been demoted to private, sentenced to three years in the brig and dishonorably discharged from the marines. Corporal Christopher Thomas, the 22-year-old chief armorer for Ng's company, had been convicted of larceny, wrongful disposal of military property, and break and enter. He also had been sentenced to three years at hard labor. Both soldiers had cut deals with the military to dramatically reduce the time they would serve. Dailey served only six months, but a promising military career and plans to enter law enforcement had been snuffed out.

Charlie was recovering in hospital from a laundry room accident when he was contacted by the lawyer for Ken Armeni, the soldier on guard duty the night of the burglary. Armeni was facing a court martial. Charlie had stuck his leg into an industrial dryer to stop it from rotating and had badly wrenched his hip. It seemed like a stupid accident, and no one could be sure it hadn't been done deliberately to get out of the brig. But Charlie wasn't going to be able to run away on that leg for a while. He told Armeni's lawyer, Earle Partington, to visit him at the Tripler Medical Center in Honolulu to talk about his client's situation. Charlie, his leg in traction and wrapped in a large cast, told Partington that he had threatened Armeni to get his help in the armory break-in.

"I said I would kick his ass—and then he agreed to do it," Charlie said. "I was confident Armeni would go along with my plan because he seemed like a weak-willed individual, and I could exert control over him." He said Armeni was so weak-willed that he could easily have "wound up in Jonestown, drinking Kool-Aid."

Armeni denied he had been threatened by Charlie, but there was ample evidence to show that Charlie had manipulated him to do his bidding. The lance-corporal was acquitted of most of the serious charges, sentenced to two months at hard labor and demoted to private.

Partington walked away from the interview shaking his head. "He was a well-spoken figure, but very bizarre," he would tell others later. "He appeared very intelligent. I think he is one of those people with a lot of brains and zero common sense."

Charlie bragged to one of the military lawyers about his ability to manipulate others. "I consider myself a good liar," he told Major R.D. Gloger, when he was interviewed regarding the burglary. "If you want to kill someone, you make him think you like him. Then it will be easy. They never know who you are. Your best friend is your best enemy."

He bragged to the major about just what a bad dude he was. He took credit for a California murder, claimed to have blown up a house and killed livestock. He said he had put potassium cyanide in a salt shaker in the marine mess hall and had tried to blow up a staff sergeant he didn't like, but the grenade he had tossed at the man failed to detonate. He insisted he had blown up two vehicles. Gloger dismissed the claims as fantasy and suggested Charlie see a psychiatrist. Police found no record of any of the crimes.

On July 14, Charlie was escorted by the usual complement of guards to the Marine Corps Air Station at K–Bay for his court martial. He walked into the courtroom in his marine dress uniform displaying the ribbons and decorations he had earned during his four-year military career: the Marine Corps expeditionary medal, the sea service deployment ribbon and the M-16 rifle marksmanship badge. It would be the last time he would wear the Marine Corps seal depicting a globe, an eagle and an anchor. He pleaded guilty to the bulk of the charges against him: larceny, conspiracy, break and enter, being absent without leave and escaping custody. A charge of illegally disposing of the weapons was dropped.

The defense called several character witnesses, including Charlie's fellow marines and his father. Corporal Hugh Daugherty testified that Charlie was a loner who didn't really socialize with soldiers in his company, although he appeared to get along with them. Corporal Jeffery Cox, who had met Charlie shortly after he arrived in Hawaii in 1980, described him as a quiet above-average soldier. No one could explain why he would do such a thing. It was left to Charlie to try.

When Charlie took the stand, he admitted to committing the burglary just to see if he could do it. Speaking so softly that his voice could barely be heard above the drone of the air conditioner, he said he ran away because he believed his life was in danger. He said he had been tired, frustrated and annoyed over his betrayal at the hands of his friends.

"I thought that going away is the best solution," he mumbled. He now worried about what would happen to him. "So much things happen in so short a time. I know I disgraced my family, first of all, and the unit I was in. I just want the thing to be over with as soon as possible so I can get on with my life, but I don't do much planning yet. I just want to think—or go some peaceful place to think it over."

Charlie's distraught father, Kenneth, followed his son to the stand. Testifying in limited English, he struggled to express his shame over his son's actions. At times he broke into tears. "I realize my only son . . . what foolishness and stupidness that he doing."

In his closing arguments the trial counsel, Marine Corps Major T.R. Henry, noted that Charlie wasn't a minor player in the crimes. "He is *the* player," he insisted. "We ask you to take into consideration that Corporal Ng does come from a good family, a strong family, but that also cuts two ways," Henry told the court martial panel. "He did have a proper upbringing. He did have a disciplined upbringing. He would apparently know right from wrong. He came from a Christian household, which I assume followed the Ten Commandments and one of them was 'Thou shalt not steal.'

"He doesn't have a reason for committing this crime, other than that it was just something to do on a Saturday night. The accused has not shown any remorse. He has not shown that this has had any effect on him whatsoever."

Charlie's lawyer, Steven Pingree, argued that with the exception of the break-in, Charlie was a good marine. He blamed the situation on Charlie's inability to adequately express himself because of cultural differences and his difficulties with the English language.

"We've got a 21-year-old lance-corporal in the Marine Corps, a young male human being who still has a lot of life before him. There is a very good possibility that he can be punished in a way that will satisfy the need to set an example and still allow this young man to have a life, to perhaps begin anew."

He argued against giving Charlie a dishonorable discharge, calling it the "most heinous label that can be put on a person." He urged that any period of confinement chosen be sufficient to impress upon Charlie the seriousness of the offense without destroying his future.

"Now granted, it is a serious offense and he does deserve to be punished. But he's not a dope-smoking, boozing, trouble-making slack-off."

The court martial panel didn't buy the lawyer's pleas. Less than 90 minutes later they returned with grim faces and a grim sentence. The military judge ordered Charlie and his lawyers to stand to face the court while the president of the panel read the decision aloud: dishonorable discharge and 14 years of confinement at hard labor. He had disgraced the uniform of the 200-year-old fighting force spawned by the American Revolution.

The panel wasn't aware, however, that in exchange for his guilty pleas, Charlie had signed an agreement with the military limiting whatever sentence he received to just three years, less the three months he had already served in custody. Media reports noted the 14-year sentence, but there was no mention that 11 years would be suspended after Charlie served his first year in prison.

After the court martial panel was dismissed, the military judge called Charlie back to the courtroom for what is known as an Article 39(a) session to explain the agreement to him and ask him if he had any questions about it.

"No, sir," he responded.

Charlie complained that he should be given credit for extra time in jail because of the cruel and inhumane treatment he endured in solitary confinement. The motion was denied, but he was learning the system.

Now he was off to Leavenworth, Kansas, a Midwest city of 12,500 that included more than 5,000 prisoners in four state, federal, military and private jails. He would be joining about 1,000 other soldiers, airmen and sailors behind the red-brick confines of the U.S. Military Disciplinary Barracks on the oldest military base west of the Mississippi. Fort Leavenworth, founded in 1827, was home to the only maximum-security military prison in the country.

Charlie quickly established himself as a serious dude in his own right. "He was the best martial arts guy I've ever seen, and he would do a lot of show-boating—spin kicks and all that," explained fellow inmate John Carty, who served three years in Leavenworth for the theft of a jeep. The private, who had a history of unauthorized absences from his military duties, was immediately drawn to Charlie by a shared interest in weapons and martial arts. Both were sharpshooters with the M-16 rifle.

Charlie talked incessantly about forming a group of rogue marines who would hit banks and military installations for cash and weapons. He called it the Brotherhood. It was his obsession. The idea intrigued Carty. "I thought he sounded like he knew his stuff, and if we could put a band together, like a special forces group, we could make it work," Carty recalled. "But he went from just simple bank jobs to wanting to steal military missiles and shoot down 747s. The idea was the more people you could kill at one time, the better."

Carty played along with him, but the more he listened the more he was convinced that Charlie was a certified and very dangerous wacko. Charlie reveled in talking about torture. He fantasized about torturing women. He would come up with all kinds of bizarre ways to inflict pain. He told Carty that he used to staple mice onto planks and run them through a table saw just to watch their frenzied reactions as they approached the blade. It was all pretty sick, even for a hardened ex-marine like Carty.

"I'd try to get him to concentrate on ways of making money, and his response was, 'Hey, if you are not into torture, that's okay. We'll do the operations together, and I'll just do my thing on the side.'" Charlie was always talking about killing people. His favorite expression was "No kill, no thrill."

Charlie liked to brag about his prowess on military operations, how everything was planned down to the last detail. He bragged to his prison pals that he could make himself invisible, telling them how he slipped off Oahu in spite of a full-scale manhunt. He held himself out to be the mercenary–terrorist he dreamed about as a child.

Charlie was actively recruiting other jailed marines for his gang. He rounded up four prisoners with skills that would be useful—including a helicopter pilot—and told them about Leonard and the base of operations he was establishing in the foothills of the Sierra Nevada Mountains. He talked about a life of plunder and excess, which would be training for the day when nuclear war left the spoils of the world to the survivors. He and Leonard would be ready. It all sounded pretty wild to Carty, but when he was shown photographs Leonard had sent Charlie of a torture chamber under construction, he began to believe it.

"It was going to have video cameras, the whole nine yards, and it was out in the woods somewhere," Carty said. He decided he'd better do something to stop the pair of maniacs. He contacted the prison's criminal investigations unit and told them he needed to talk to the FBI. When a couple of agents from the Kansas City office came to see him in prison, Carty told them all about Charlie and Leonard. He also told them that Charlie bragged about killing a man in Hawaii, but the FBI couldn't find any record of a crime matching the events Carty described. They also could find no trace of Leonard.

The FBI told Carty to play along with Charlie and keep them posted. But Carty wanted nothing to do with Charlie or his friend and kept his distance when he was released in 1984. "In my view, someone was going to die before the FBI did anything, and I wasn't too hyped up about hanging around with Charles on the outside."

Charlie had more luck with an imprisoned soldier named Michael Carroll. Carroll, who was from San Francisco, was interested in hooking up with the pair for some operations when they got out of the joint. Charlie also asked Michael Diaz, John Hudson and Charles Dyer to join the Brotherhood. Diaz, a lance-corporal from Chicago, was serving a 27-month stint for possession of hash, possession of stolen property and larceny. Hudson, a decorated Oklahoma-born Marine Corps staff sergeant, was serving a 20-

year sentence for a 1981 sexual assault. He had served time in the brig with Charlie, but didn't really get to know him until they were transferred to Leavenworth. Dyer was recruited to become the Brotherhood's helicopter pilot.

Charlie and Leonard wrote each other frequently through Leonard's half-sister and his ex-wife. Leonard, who never signed the letters with his real name, kept Charlie up to date on his nefarious plans and encouraged Charlie to recruit candidates from the military prison. The bond between them stayed strong despite the distance and the brick walls that kept them apart. Although Charlie feared he would be deported at the end of his sentence, he need not have worried. Bureaucratic bungling resulted in no one acting on Charlie's admissions at his court martial that he had lied about his birthplace to get into the marines. He wasn't going to end up back in Hong Kong.

Charlie walked out of prison a free man on June 29, 1984. He was anxious to get on with his plans. He wanted guns. He wanted sex. And he wanted revenge. He called Hudson in Oklahoma and asked him to get him a gun and to track down Ken Staff, a prisoner from Oklahoma who had slighted Charlie in prison. Charlie had given Staff protection in prison, expecting him to join his Brotherhood upon his release. But once out of the prison, Staff had cut his ties with the lunatic Asian. Charlie was worried that Staff knew too much. He had to be killed.

Charlie headed immediately to Oklahoma to hook up with Hudson. He wanted to hit an armory and load up on some heavy firepower. But Hudson, who was a decade older than Charlie and had a wife and three children, wanted no part of Charlie's plans. After five years in Leavenworth, he was anxious to get on with his life. He had a good job as a casual laborer, and he was now convinced Charlie was a psycho. Hudson was very anxious to rid himself of his guest, but not wanting to upset him, he played along. Charlie was already upset that Hudson hadn't located Staff and tracked his movements for a hit. So when Charlie insisted they head out looking for him, Hudson dragged him around on an aimless search, steering well clear of any places where Staff generally hung out. And when Charlie wanted to snuff a hooker, he took him out to try to find one, but stayed well clear of any areas they frequented. He also managed to talk Charlie out of hitting an armory by getting him a .45-caliber military-issue pistol. That seemed to placate him. Charlie lovingly called the pistol "his baby" and mailed it to himself at Cricket's address in south San Francisco. After a week in Oklahoma City, which included a motel romp with a female prison pen pal, Charlie finally headed off to California.

Hudson had been a big disappointment. All talk and no action. But he did deliver on the gun. The Colt .45 arrived in the mail shortly after Charlie arrived on the west coast. It was a larger caliber than Charlie liked, but it was a weapon with which he was familiar. It would do.

9

Operation Miranda

L EONARD L AKE couldn't take his eyes off the young woman sitting across from him on the San Francisco city bus. She was only 16 or so, but her long flowing hair, petite figure and clear complexion lured him like a siren's song. Fresh, young, unspoiled. Only a hint of makeup.

If only I were young and handsome, he lamented. It was a dilemma. None of the women he wanted would ever want a guy like him: middle-aged, chubby, balding. He knew that. What was a man to do? Well, Leonard had a few ideas.

It was January 4, 1983, nine months since Charlie had been arrested at Indian Creek Ranch, and Leonard was still on the run after jumping bail on weapons charges. He was taking the bus back from his sister Fern's house to the basement suite he had just rented on Nineteenth Avenue. It was a busy north–south thoroughfare that carried commuter traffic over the Golden Gate bridge, but it was only about 10 minutes away from the Castro district whose well-heeled gay community was easy prey for a cruiser like Leonard.

Leonard had been staying with Fern and spending time with his mother. Although he had reconciled with his mother, he could never really forgive her for abandoning him as a child. Still, having a family was important to him. He could never tell her that her other son, Donald, his half-brother, was dead and that he was responsible. Leonard had lured him out to the country under the guise of finding him a house-sitting job and had finally rid the world of him. The blood sucker. But it was a real pain to take buses all over the state to mail forged letters to his mother from Donald. He would write on Donald's behalf that he was still working in the bush without access to a phone. He would thank her for the socks and shirts she had mailed to him at a post office box that Leonard had set up. He would apologize for not calling. "No phones up here, Mom," the letters would say. Meanwhile, Leonard was cashing his missing brother's social assistance checks. One day, when the checks ran out, Leonard planned to tell his mother that Donald had run off to Reno with a bike gang. And that would be the last she would hear of him.

Leonard had milked Donald for about all he was worth and already had another target in mind. The sap who had been his best man when he married Cricket was too much of an oaf to live. Charles Gunnar had split up with his wife, Victoria, and would be moving out of their San Jose home to Morgan Hill, a bedroom community just to the south, with the couple's two children. Gunnar seemed broken up about it. Leonard figured he was mostly upset about losing his meal ticket.

Leonard had come to despise the old army buddy who once had been one of his best friends. Leonard had been Gunnar's best man when he had married Vicky, but now he saw him as a fat lazy slob who lived off the government teat. The postal worker claimed he had a back injury that prevented him from working, but Leonard saw him as an illiterate goof-off. He sat around reading comic books and watching mindless television shows like *Laverne and Shirley* and *Fraggle Rock*. He never watched anything of historical significance or educational value. He slept most of the day, and he beat his children. Leonard didn't have any problems with whipping a woman into submission, but it disgusted him to see children abused.

"He sows not, nor does he labor," Leonard recorded in his target book. "Ah, but how he reaps—gold, in the form of government handouts. Well, that will only last until his next trip up into the hill country. Charles won't be long for this life." Leonard began planning for the day. He would lure Charles away with the promise of a weekend getaway at Cricket's cabin in the Sierra foothills. Once Charles visited Calaveras county, he was never coming back. Leonard outlined the plan in his target book. Since Charles was so unnaturally huge—at over 300 pounds, a walking talking Moby Dick—he dubbed the mission Operation Fish.

Leonard liked to think about what a dangerous man he was. He had killed. He would kill again. It wasn't that hard if you didn't mind the dreams. Sometimes at night Leonard's victims came back to haunt him. But it was a mere tinge of guilt. "Poor Donald," he wrote. "Why don't I feel any remorse? Is it my subconscious that creates these dreams?" In his worst nightmares, Leonard saw himself on trial for his crimes. But he was determined to never let that happen. He never ventured far from base without his cyanide pills, which he concocted himself. He referred to them as death in his pocket and recalled scenes from old mob movies: "You'll never take me alive, copper!" Well, they never would capture him. He had made the vow. A man who does not fear death is truly a dangerous man.

Fish was a walking dead man. Leonard had the means. He had the motivation. All he needed was the right moment. In the meantime Leonard the fugitive lived in the shadows, resorting to petty crime to augment the disability checks he was cashing in Donald's name. He peddled soft drugs, recruited hookers to help him roll drunks and was constantly on the make. He preoccupied himself with a never-ending pursuit of sex from hookers, escorts, companion ads, his ex-wife and any shapely woman who came into his line of sight. He liked petite women. He was still deeply in love with Cricket. He called her to give her his new address and phone number. "A very foolish lady," he recorded in his diary. "Why do I love her so? Wish I could turn it off."

They knew they were hopeless together, but neither could seem to break the relationship off. Love wasn't enough for Cricket. She wanted money and security. She realized that Leonard was dangerous, but he excited her. Sometimes he would ask her to buy guns for him or case prospective burglary targets. Occasionally, he took her on one of his operations. She would recruit models for him. She would pose for him. She would perform on the homemade porno tapes that he sold. Even though he was supposedly on the run and any police officer could easily follow her to him, they got together almost weekly for dinner and sex. If Leonard was using her, he didn't realize it himself.

"Once I had a wife," he mused in his diary. "She was my connection to the rest of the world. Through her, I could love, trust and believe in things others are allowed to believe in. I would have died for her, killed for her, even gone to jail for her. I would be willing to give up my freedom in exchange for the security of her love."

There was no jealousy between them. They spoke candidly about each other's sexual partners. Sometimes they hired female prostitutes for threesomes. Leonard hoped Cricket would find a true mate some day and not someone who was just looking to take advantage of her. As for himself, he still fancied himself a romantic in search of true love, but he was perfectly willing to settle for sex or paid sex or forced sex.

Leonard was very conscious of his appearance. He didn't like being short. He didn't like being bald. He didn't like being overweight. He didn't even like the way his voice sounded on tape. It was a weaselly, wimpish, conniving voice—not the bold, brash, authoritative voice that commanded attention. But he had to work with what he had. He wore a hairpiece, but it just made his face appear plump. He tried to keep his weight down and his mind occupied.

He focused his attention on small projects, spent a lot of time cleaning his apartment and did roofing work for friends and odd jobs for family. He liked to play the board game Risk and video games. Above all else he was a voracious reader of books and magazines, particularly survival magazines, and gun catalogues and manuals. He loved science fiction and read a lot of Stephen King horror and Agatha Christie murder mysteries. To keep informed about the pending global conflict and the approaching Armageddon, he read *Newsweek, Time* and *U.S. News & World Report.* He regularly scanned the local papers, including the editorials, and was a history and electronics buff. He even had a copy of *Guide to the Bible.*

Leonard was checking the television listings early in 1983 when a familiar movie caught his eye. It was the tale of a timid butterfly collector in England who became so obsessed with a young woman he saw in London that he engineered a plan to keep her in captivity. The movie was based on *The Collector,* a startling book that sold a million copies for renowned author John Fowles in 1962. The victim, who eventually died of pneumonia in a basement prison, was a bright well-to-do woman named Miranda Grey. Leonard had read the book years ago.

He identified strongly with the book's main character, a sniveling wimp of a clerk named Frederick Clegg. Like Leonard, Clegg had no father and had been raised by relatives after his mother abandoned him. He was a loner with no one who really cared about him other than a couple of aging aunts. Leonard believed that being a nobody had advantages. "I suppose in my way, I am the same wimp as the hero and in my way just as crazy," he confided in his diary. "I have no doubt that we wimps have been compensating for our inability since the dawn of history. Sad, really. Still, how can we die if we never live?

"Society would worry if they knew I existed and what I was up to," he continued. "I don't exist in the official world. No job, no taxes. No one to keep track of me day to day. If I were to disappear it might be months before any one would even wonder—and then what could they do?"

Operation Miranda began to take shape in Leonard's mind. He fantasized about building a base of operations in a remote location—a soundproof hidden prison where he could confine women he selected randomly from the streets to do his bidding. In *The Collector,* Clegg purchased a rural home in Sussex, about an hour out of London, with money he'd won in a lottery. Leonard toyed with the idea of an urban location, but it didn't seem possible to find a suitable and affordable property that would conceal his activities from the prying eyes of neighbors.

As he plotted the murder of Charles Gunnar, Leonard became even more convinced he needed a rural property to carry out his fantasy. But unlike Clegg, he had no lottery windfall to finance it. Leonard thought Operation Fish might provide some of the needed cash, and that made its successful completion even more vital. But he was having difficulty luring Gunnar to Cricket's place in Calaveras County, about 150 miles east of the Bay area, where he planned to do the murder. Finally, he coaxed Gunnar out in the spring on the pretext of helping him install a gas line. But his plan failed. Once there, it occurred to Leonard that he would be unable to single-handedly move the dead Gunnar to the hole he had dug. The man was just too big.

Leonard was frustrated but undeterred. He dug a new hole closer to the cabin and got hold of a winch to help him move the body. He purchased a tub of hydrochloric acid to dissolve the gigantic body and prevent odors from rising to the surface. When Gunnar returned a week later to help with some more chores, Leonard's plans were foiled again. The poison Leonard slipped into Gunnar's food failed to kill him. All it did was give him a headache and an upset stomach. Leonard couldn't believe his bad luck. Well, the guy wasn't bulletproof. Leonard would get another chance.

In anticipation of his former friend's disappearance, Leonard moved into the Morgan Hill home with Gunnar and his children. Like a kindly uncle he played Monopoly with the kids, cooked meals, cleaned the house and weeded the yard. He took the oldest girl shopping, bought groceries, built bunk beds for the children and repaired their bicycles. The children's father, a one-time drama coach, often slept until 5:00 P.M. Leonard was tempted to begin sorting through his friend's property and liquidating it, but he decided it was too big a risk. He would bide his time. But by mid-May Leonard had reached the end of his patience. He watched furiously as Charles whipped his eldest daughter with his belt, swinging blows with all of his might. Twice that week, Leonard built himself up to kill Gunnar, but again he backed off. He was furious at his lack of resolve.

He began to wonder if he was a coward. He had the opportunity, but backed off because he was afraid of being seen or interrupted. The frustration over his inability to complete the mission was overwhelming. Finally, in late May, after a day at the beach with Gunnar and his children, he convinced Gunnar to accompany him to Lake Tahoe. This time Gunnar did not return. Leonard opened up on him with a pair of handguns, riddling his body with .22 and .38 caliber bullets. He used his block and tackle to move the body to the hole he had dug, buried it and poured a concrete slab over the site. The work was hard, but Leonard didn't mind a little sweat. He told the kids their dad had gone off into the mountains for a while, and he didn't know when he would be back—if ever. He told Gunnar's wife that he had run off with a woman and would not be coming back.

Phase one of Operation Fish was complete. In phase two Leonard planned to liquidate all of Gunnar's possessions and divert his social assistance checks to a new postal address. He changed Gunnar's mailing address and gave notice to the landlord that Gunnar was vacating the house. He had to pay $232 in back bills.

Leonard spent the next several weeks sorting through Gunnar's belongings. Cricket came by to help. A lot of the stuff was junk that they hauled to the dump or dropped off in a bin set out by the Goodwill organization. It was amazing how easily everyone bought the story that Charles had run off. Leonard had made discreet inquiries of friends to find someone willing to take the children. Gunnar's ex-wife was content as long as the alimony checks kept coming. The money was rolling in from the sale of Charles' possessions: $40 for his double bed, $300 for a pistol, $120 for the desk and $285 for his rat-eating pet snakes.

Leonard hadn't even started to move the big stuff and already he was flush with cash. His accounts were bulked up to the $4,000 mark. Money for sex. Money for drugs. Money for guns. He gave Cricket $520 with instructions to buy him a truly lethal weapon, a MAC-10 machine gun. The Military Armament Corporation semiautomatic pistol, which had been designed in 1963 for police and military use, could be easily converted to automatic fire. With a couple of 32-round clips, Leonard could hold off an army.

Leonard was generous with his newfound wealth. He used some of it to take Gunnar's children to a water park in nearby Milpitas and gave Cricket $250 to take them shopping. Operation Fish was proceeding beyond all expectations.

Most of Gunnar's stuff was gone by the time Flag Day rolled around.

June 14 always had special meaning for Leonard. He had been a foot soldier and a patriot. He believed that in his own way he was helping Uncle Sam. He was destroying the wasteful consumers, ridding the country of the stupids. "By the gods, I am right," he recorded in his journal.

He cleaned up the house, settled with the landlord and packed the kids off to a family in Watsonville, friends of Gunnar who had once offered to be guardians for his children if anything were ever to happen to him. Once Leonard tied up all the loose ends, he headed north. He wanted to look at a house and 30-acre treed property in Humboldt County, near Garberville. It had the privacy he was looking for, but he saw immediately it would only be a temporary base for him. The property didn't have a good spot to build his doomsday bunker. It would do for now until he could find something better. Cricket helped him move in. He told her about a woman he had met through a companion advertisement and how well they had hit it off. He doubted the long-range love affair would amount to much with the distance involved.

On a return trip to Morgan Hill to clear up some paperwork and do a few last errands, he stopped by Cricket's cabin in Calaveras to see if anything had disturbed Gunnar's body. He stayed overnight without incident. No ghosts came into his dreams to haunt him. No guilt. No remorse. Operation Fish was clean.

On the road to Morgan Hill, he couldn't resist the temptation of another rendezvous with the woman he had met. "A woman is only a woman, but every now and then a lady comes into my life that I know," he reflected on the relationship. "I can feel for her, look into her mind and heart. If she gives me the slightest chance I'll fall in love with her." He spent the night at her house and left his personal effects with her when he went into San Francisco for the day. That was a mistake. In his absence she went through his gear and found his guns and false identification. Now she was frightened and confused. Nothing he could say upon his return eased her fears. He had hoped to take her north with him, but now she wouldn't go.

"Now she suspects I am Jack the Ripper," he divulged in his journal. "I am compromised. What risks and foolishness I endure for women."

Up north and alone, Leonard began initial planning for Operation Miranda. He purchased several drums, filled them with his identification, silver coins and jewelry, and buried them on the property. From now on he was Charles Gunnar. Leonard Lake, the fugitive, was dead. He had taken another man's life, his possessions, his kids, his Volkswagen van, and now he was taking his name.

He wrote a letter to Charlie in Leavenworth to bring him up to speed on recent developments. They used a lot of computer game jargon in their letters to avoid problems should the letters be read by prison officials.

Leonard's new flame showed up unexpectedly in mid-July. He found himself telling her everything. He told her about Operation Fish. He had no idea why he blurted it all out. He put his trust in her not to betray him, but he doubted he would ever see her again. He spent the next few days digging holes to bury more barrels. He planned to fill one with medical supplies, one with survival gear and food and another with tools and potentially incriminating material. He burned a photo album containing sex photos involving himself and another one containing similar photos of Cricket. He mailed a third to his first wife, Karen.

Leonard spent the summer preparing for Operation Miranda and running down into the Bay area for a few ops to bolster his dwindling bank accounts. He made frequent forays to the Greenfield Ranch, the commune near Ukiah that he had been asked to leave. He would walk through the woods and pilfer marijuana plants and whatever the occupants had left lying around of value. Sometimes he was spotted slinking about the property, but seldom did anyone approach him. Nonetheless he was always prepared for capture or arrest. Before he left his home base, he always mixed up a fresh batch of cyanide pills. Death before dishonor.

Near the end of August he headed down to San Bruno for his sister Patty's wedding. Later he met with Cricket, and over dinner he asked her if he could move into her cabin at Wilseyville. While she didn't object outright, he could tell she wasn't keen. He would stay there for a while, and if it didn't work out, he would move on. Before leaving Garberville, he purchased a German shepherd pup from a local breeder. He named it Wubon.

The drive from Garberville to Calaveras took seven hours, and Leonard had to make several trips to move his belongings. The Wilseyville cabin lacked a lot of amenities, but he enjoyed being in the foothills. Perhaps it was just that the smell of pine and granite dust reminded him of summer camp, but he savored the clean fresh air and the quiet. Something about the mountains made him feel peaceful and free.

He began writing more frequently to Charlie. His buddy would be getting out in the spring, and Leonard was anxious to continue their partnership. Charlie, for all his faults, was a good companion. Leonard had lots of news to tell him. He figured it would cost about $4,600 to build a bunker that would serve as both an emergency shelter and a cell for his sex slaves. He could cover half of it with the incoming checks from Donald and Charles, but he would be forced to borrow the other half from Cricket. He was anxious to get started. He wasn't happy with his own personal fitness. He had ballooned up to 192 pounds, and he didn't carry it very well on his 5' 9" frame. A regimen of construction work and a healthy diet would slim him down.

In late October Leonard finally broke ground on his Miranda project. He contacted a neighbor to help him cut down some trees and arranged for a backhoe to come in the following day to dig out the side of a hill, where he had decided to build. He was about to embark on his fantasy. That evening he set up his video camera on a tripod. He slouched in a recliner chair in his living room, and with the camera rolling, he described his plans.

"The purpose of that cell and the main purpose, hence, of the building will be the imprisonment of a young lady," he explained in an easy conversational tone. "I want to be able to use a woman whenever and how I want. And when I am tired or satiated or bored, whenever and however, I simply want to put her away."

People might think he was crazy, but look at him, he intoned. How could he get women with a body like his?

"I'm a realist," he continued. "I am 38 years old, a bit chubby, with not much hair, and I'm losing what I have. I am not particularly attractive to women—or should I say particularly attracting to women. And all the traditional magnets—money, power—I don't have. Yet I am still very attract-

ed to a particular type of woman who almost by definition is totally unin-
terested in me."

Sitting relaxed, his arms resting on the sides of the plush brown chair,
Leonard mapped out how he planned to use the cell in the bunker not just
to hold women but to condition them to do his bidding.

"I can create a facility that is so stark, so empty, so cold, so quiet, so
totally removed from the world that, by a combination of painful punish-
ments and minor rewards, such as music or magazines, I can quickly condition a young woman to cooperate with me fully. This is my belief."

He admitted he was attracted to girls as young as 12 years old. He
would have any female he desired. He would just take her. Unlike the
romantic and misguided protagonist in *The Collector*, who merely wanted
to befriend the woman he adored, Leonard planned to use women for sex
and slave labor. When he was finished with them, he would discard them
like garbage. He was anxious to get on with Operation Miranda and excited about its prospects.

"Tomorrow evening a backhoe will arrive, and I will start excavating
the earth," he added. "It will be interesting to see how far this tape and I
actually go."

The next day work began as predicted. The ground was hard, laced
with veins of rock, and work was slow, but he was at last making progress.
He had little time to waste. The evening newscast left him bitter and apprehensive. More than 240 U.S. Marines and 40 French paratroopers, part of
an international peacekeeping force in Lebanon, had been killed by a suicide bomber. Elsewhere, U.S.-led forces were invading Grenada. The world
was going to hell.

"I hope I can get this building finished before the world ends," he concluded.

Weeks passed and the New Year saw Leonard Lake older, fatter and
balder, and in his own opinion, not much wiser. He opened 1984 with an
entry in his journal: "My second year as a fugitive, mostly dull day-to-day
routine. Still with death in my pocket and fantasy my major goal.

"Life seems to be too often a beauty contest," he continued. "The prettiest girl gets the job, the most opportunities and the richest men. The best looking man gets the same. People help out the person with the best smile and nicest personality. It is completely understandable, even admirable, but us not so great-looking types frequently take second, even third place at everything. I live to correct this."

By the time the snow came in February, Leonard had the cinder-block walls of the bunker built up five feet high. The cost of materials was an ongoing problem. He contemplated an armed robbery to help pay the bills. There was no more money forthcoming from Operation Fish. He had bled Charles Gunnar's life completely dry. He got a part-time job and held a garage sale in Wilseyville to get some extra cash.

He headed back to the Bay area in March to collect the last of Gunnar's checks and pick up a little more work. Scanning the local papers, he noted a personal ad from a man offering free oral sex. Thinking it might be a chance to grab some items of value, Leonard responded with his gun and full ops kit. The man, who said his name was Phil, gave great blow jobs. Leonard didn't reciprocate, but he enjoyed the experience. All the while during the sexual encounter, he was plotting to kill the man. With a few alterations to his own physical appearance, he might be able to pass for Phil. It would bear thinking over.

A few days later he called Phil to invite him up to Calaveras. He dubbed the operation Samson because, according to legend, Samson fought the *Phil*-istines. For two weeks he worked on the details. If Operation Samson worked, he would have a new car, new identification, new credit cards and new furniture. He was furious when Phil backed out. Something must have made him suspicious.

Leonard grew even more anxious to make a hit. He was scrutinizing the papers daily. He needed wheels. He needed new video equipment. In the meantime his neighbor, Jim Southern, had invited him over to join his bible study group. It was crazy to be praying one day and scheming murder the next, but Leonard didn't care.

Charlie was writing more often now. His time was short. They would be together soon. Leonard had purchased some things Charlie wanted and filled him in on his progress with the bunker. He was building the cell now. He had framed most of it but planned to put the furnishings in before he completed the job. He planned to borrow another page from *The Collector* and build a hidden door behind some wooden shelving just as Clegg had done. The shelving would conceal the entrance to both the fallout shelter and the cell. It would give him a secure place to store his possessions, both human and material. If need be he could hide out there himself.

But working alone slowed construction. Leonard considered grabbing some drunks and dope addicts off the street in San Francisco to use as slave labor, but his first attempt didn't work out as planned. He had one guy almost sold on the offer of free dope in exchange for work on his pot farm, but at the last minute the guy had bailed out.

"People don't trust me," Leonard lamented to Cricket. "While they have good reason not to, it definitely works to my disadvantage not being able to project a warm, friendly, trusting image."

By the Memorial Day weekend, Leonard had finished the interior paneling and wiring and had connected the power in the bunker. Cricket came visiting and surprised Leonard by suggesting a mutual acquaintance as a possible candidate for his first slave. Although he didn't think the woman was anything special, Leonard said he would think about it. But the next time he broached the issue with Cricket, she vetoed the idea. Exasperated, Leonard decided that from now on it might be best if Cricket wasn't involved in the project.

July was a scorcher. Leonard moved back into San Francisco where it was cooler. After baking in Calaveras, he welcomed the cooling mist. He needed to be in the city to launch the big adventure.

When Charlie flew into San Francisco in the early afternoon of July 9, 1984, Cricket was waiting for him at the airport. She took him around to Leonard's Nineteenth Avenue basement suite, and the two men hugged each other like brothers. It was great to be back. Leonard seemed so pleased to see him. Cricket noticed Charlie had aged appreciably during his two years in prison. He still had the boyish looks, but he seemed more mature. More strident. She spent the day with the two ex-marines catching up on

Charlie's adventures and listening to her ex-husband talking excitedly about his beloved Miranda project.

Leonard arranged for Charlie to move into his sister's place on Seventeenth Street for a month until he got settled. After that he'd have to find a place of his own. They spent the next day driving around the city. Charlie talked Leonard into giving him a refresher course in driving. As Charlie drove with white knuckles along the steep and narrow San Francisco streets, Leonard outlined the operations he had planned. He was extremely anxious to get on with Miranda and had scoped out several targets to score some money to really launch the program.

There was one he wanted to do that night. Leonard told Charlie about a gay man who was advertising free blow jobs in the *San Francisco Spectator*. He showed Charlie the ad: "Blow Job and X-Video for straight young guys by another young guy in San Francisco. Vince. 626-1581." He told Charlie about his encounter with Phil. These guys were easy targets. They had money. They had great stuff. The operation would be a pushover. They drove by the place, an old-style, tall two-story building at 153 Henry Street, shaded by giant maples and shrubs. It smelled of money.

But Charlie was hesitant. For all his bold talk he had never killed anyone. He didn't know if he could do it alone. Leonard couldn't believe what he was hearing. He had waited all this time for Charlie's help, and now he was balking. "He seems to want me to carry him everywhere," Leonard griped.

Charlie owed him. Leonard had taken him in as a stranger. He had hid him, fed him and nurtured him for six months when every law enforcement agency in the country was after him. He had shown him the ropes. He had taught him how to survive by his wits. It was time to pay up.

Grudgingly, Charlie came around. He did owe Leonard for what he had done. But he was extremely nervous. They would come back around 7:00 P.M.

That evening, 31-year-old Richard Carrazza was eating dinner in the kitchen of the second-floor apartment he shared with Donald Giuletti when the doorbell rang. He could hear Giuletti, five years his elder, go down the stairs to let someone in the door. Since he was aware Giuletti had an appointment scheduled, Carrazza didn't move from the table. But a few minutes later, the sounds of a scuffle and a loud grunt brought him to his feet to investigate. He stepped into the hallway, startling a young Asian man who was going through a chest of drawers. The man raised a long-barreled gun at him and opened fire, so many shots so quickly that Carrazza couldn't count them. One caught him in the chest, and he crumpled to the floor. The gunman turned and fled, hurtling down the wooden stairs to the street. Once Carrazza was sure the man was gone, he staggered to a phone and called police. Then he went in search of his roommate. Giuletti was lying facedown in a large pool of blood. He would later die in hospital, but Carrazza would survive.

Charlie was shaken and upset as he told Leonard what had gone wrong. His first operation had been a failure. They had not scored anything of value, and even worse they had left behind a witness. But Leonard consoled Charlie and told him not to worry about being identified. "All you guys look alike," he chuckled. Leonard wasn't terribly disappointed. The Giuletti killing had been a test, and Charlie had passed it. He could be trusted to kill on command. They would try again soon. And the next time there would be no screw-ups.

The bunker's hidden door led to the room where Lake imprisoned his sex slaves.

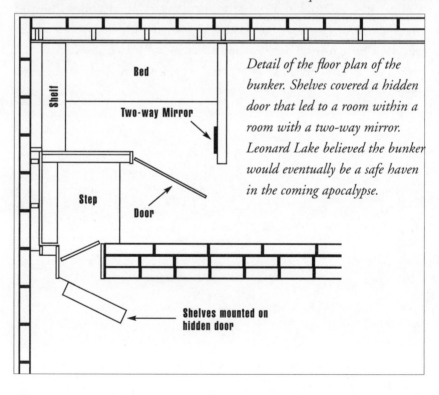

Bed

Shelf

Two-way Mirror

Step

Door

Shelves mounted on hidden door

Detail of the floor plan of the bunker. Shelves covered a hidden door that led to a room within a room with a two-way mirror. Leonard Lake believed the bunker would eventually be a safe haven in the coming apocalypse.

10

A Rat in a Cage

Edmonton Institution has seen a lot of bad men, but few gave the maximum-security prison more headaches than Mo Laberge. Sentenced to a 25-year term, Mo arrived at the northern Alberta facility in early January of 1983 with little fanfare. A strong southeast wind was blowing snow crystals across the four-lane blacktop highway. After a mandatory shower and skin search, Mo was handed his greens (the coveralls that all inmates were required to wear) and was escorted to his cell.

It took him about six months to settle into the routine with the other 240 prisoners. He latched on to a job as an institutional cleaner, which provided him with a prison salary to spend on confectionery items from the prison canteen. He began taking a raft of computer courses and landed a job as a tutor. Eventually, he was appointed coordinator of the prison's computer program. He then enrolled in correspondence courses and began working on his Bachelor of Administration, majoring in behavioral sciences and financial management.

Within a year Mo had the plum job of inmate committee grievance clerk, a position that put him in almost daily contact with the top prison administrators and gave him considerable clout among the inmate population. He also met regularly with the prison's director of security and worked with him to resolve prisoners' complaints. Often Mo provided useful tidbits of information to help officials keep order in the prison. It was a trick he had learned in Regina, Moose Jaw and Saskatoon, where he was on a first-name basis with many senior detectives, including one who was eventually elected mayor of Moose Jaw. In business it was called networking; in prison it was survival.

Mo would alert the prison security director when inmates were having trouble adjusting or getting along with fellow prisoners. Although he never saw himself as a snitch, he would tip him off when inmates were planning to lay a licking on someone and give the security director a chance to transfer either the offenders or the potential victim before trouble erupted. Mo never asked for anything for this service, but prison officials occasionally rewarded him with perks and privileges such as unsupervised 72-hour visits with family on the prison grounds or first dibs on the best jobs.

As part of his rehabilitation, Mo was required to see a prison psychologist to address the problems that lay behind his lengthy criminal record. He was asked to identify his strengths and weaknesses in order to build on the first and address the second. Mo saw himself as honest, candid, flexible and receptive to new ideas. He felt he was patient and noncritical, prompt and thorough, assertive and forthright. While he wouldn't admit to being a psychopath, he conceded he had a tendency to manipulate people.

"I have identified ways in which I attempt to control people, and I am aware of it and I am working on it," he assured the psychologist in a report he submitted. "I am developing depth of compassion for other people and their feelings. This is an area I must pay particular attention to so I'm not meeting my needs and short-changing someone in some way."

He thought he had made some progress since being jailed for the Lethbridge robberies. He told the psychologist he realized he had hurt people by his actions. He began doing thought-stopping exercises to curtail his criminal thinking. "I no longer use semantic gymnastics to rationalize dishonesty," he explained. He recognized he abused alcohol and wondered if it was related to the sexual abuse he had experienced as a child. He believed his sessions with sexual abuse counselors were making a difference. "I finally grew up and became a mature adult instead of a frightened 12-year-old in a man's body," he concluded.

Although he didn't recognize it at the time, Mo had developed many of the chronic psychological problems associated with men who have been sexually abused as children. He rejected authority in every form, had difficulty developing long-term relationships and couldn't stay on any course for very long.

When he wasn't working, taking classes or in therapy, Mo made good use of his time, following the stock market, reading self-help books and keeping fit with exercise programs. He was a health nut, exercised regularly and didn't smoke. He researched sexual abuse and family violence to learn more about its effect on him, and he studied Zen philosophy. He was close to his family and maintained regular correspondence with them. A sister in Edmonton came to visit him frequently.

While he claimed he accepted responsibility for his situation, he couldn't accept that he would have to spend more than 20 years behind bars. "I'm saturated with institutionalization, prisonization and the loser image I've carried for far too many years," he complained. "I've had enough of crime, jail, bail, courts, three hots and a cot."

In September 1983 Mo ruffled the feathers of prison management when he testified at a fatality inquiry into the hanging death of a fellow inmate. Mo, who had been working in the prison's isolation unit as an inmate cleaner, claimed that prison nurses routinely doled out codeine-based prescription drugs to keep inmates in 23-hour lockup under control. He said many inmates relied on the sleeping medication or a chemical cocktail they called bug juice to cope in the hole.

"They are very pleased to see the nurse come, I know that," he said of the inmates in the isolation unit. "I have seen her just *late* and there's been an awful commotion."

The headlines read, "Inmates Detail Bug Juice Therapy" and "Routine to Drug Inmates, Inquiry into Suicide Told." But Mo was just getting warmed up for what would become a full-scale assault on the prison hierarchy.

The following spring, his lawyer, Burke Barker, contacted the *Edmonton Journal* with an amazing story. Barker, an outspoken maverick University of Alberta law professor who often defended unpopular and impoverished clients, said he had uncovered a travesty of justice. Mo had been jailed for a crime he didn't commit, and the real culprit in the Lethbridge robbery had come forward. A fellow inmate had approached Mo in the prison gym and admitted to doing the job. Wilfred Anderson, a 33-year-old inmate, said he couldn't stand to see the wrong man jailed. Anderson, who was serving an eight-year sentence for manslaughter at the time, said he initially found it amusing when police charged Mo with his offense, but the joke ended when Mo was convicted.

Mo professed to be astounded by the development, saying he had given up hope of being freed when the Supreme Court of Canada had refused his appeal. He said Anderson offered to provide a statement admitting to his guilt.

"If it was me, I wouldn't have said nothing," Mo said in an interview at the prison. Federal justice officials began investigating, but before they got very far, Mo was charged with murder. Edmonton city police charged him along with four others in the prison-yard stabbing death of Tennessee racketeer Timothy Frank Collins. Collins was known as the Pinball King of Nashville and had a lengthy record of racketeering, income tax evasion, receiving stolen goods, torching pinball arcades and threatening to kill a witness who was to testify against him. He was convicted in February 1979 but escaped from a county jail just outside Nashville. The 41-year-old grifter wound up in the Edmonton Max after police nabbed him in a drug bust in Calgary. Collins was serving a six-year hitch for cocaine trafficking when he died.

A prisoner claimed Mo hired the other cons to kill Collins because he was sabotaging Mo's bid for a new trial in the Lethbridge robbery–kidnapping case. He claimed Collins also had circulated a magazine article that suggested Mo was a sex offender. But when the case went to trial, Mo was acquitted.

Other prisoners testified that Collins' murder was arranged by another inmate who had ripped Collins off in a drug deal and feared retribution. They testified that Collins had given the man money to buy drugs on the outside, but the man resold the drugs and kept the cash. The jury didn't know what to believe. In the end they convicted only the man who had wielded the knife.

Wilfred Anderson, the man who claimed to have committed the Lethbridge robbery, was brought to Edmonton from Quebec's Archambault prison to testify at the Collins trial. He refused even to tell the court his name. "I have nothing to do with this trial because I was thousands of miles away when it happened," he muttered. When asked to identify Mo, he gestured toward the prisoner's box where the four accused sat and said, "I think he's there somewhere."

Anderson refused to talk about the Lethbridge robbery even when he was threatened with a charge of contempt. "If God won't find me in contempt, I don't think this court can," he said.

The only light Anderson shed on the proceedings was that he and Mo were no longer buddies. "The only conversation I had with Laberge before I left Edmonton was that I was going to murder him," he offered. When asked why, he said the matter was between him and Mo and God and the attorney general.

Anderson wasn't cooperating with the justice department probe either. Barker argued that it wasn't necessary for the authorities to interview Anderson because he had already provided a signed statement. Barker said they also had a statement from Mo's brother, Armand, claiming he had lied at Mo's trial, and a statement from an unidentified man that corroborated Anderson's statement of guilt. Barker appealed to federal justice minister Mark McGuigan to pardon his client or at least order a new trial.

But the McLaughlin family never doubted that Mo was the man who forced his way into their home, tied them up and robbed them. "We know we have the right man," Dorothy McLaughlin said. "There is absolutely no doubt. There was no mistake."

"I think they got the right guy," added her son David.

Prison officials believed Mo coerced or bought the confession from his longtime friend, but somewhere along the way, the arrangement soured. Either Mo didn't pay or the deal didn't come off as it was initially sold to Anderson. But it looked like Mo was going to have to do his 25 years after all.

After the Collins murder, one of 13 stabbings at the prison that year, Edmonton Max was in an uproar. Guards threatened to lock out the warden if he wasn't replaced. They complained he was running the prison like a minimum-security farm camp. "It's getting far too dangerous out there," one guard complained to the press. "We want a new warden and we'll get one."

A new warden was brought in, but he fared even worse. In what has been called one of the most embarrassing chapters in Corrections Canada's history, a convicted killer released on an escorted pass to celebrate his birthday escaped from his escort and went on a violent rampage that left two people dead. Daniel Gingras, a muscular blond former mechanic with multiple tattoos, including one that reads "Murder Incorporated," overpowered his unarmed escort in the parking lot of West Edmonton Mall on June 29, 1987.

Once free, Gingras, who had killed a 28-year-old janitor the last time he escaped from a prison, armed himself with a pair of .357 magnums and began a 52-day crime wave. He executed a man he met on a train and dumped the body near the Edmonton Max to rub it in the faces of prison officials who had let him out. He then teamed up with another convict to pull off a supermarket robbery in the southern Alberta city of Medicine Hat, kidnapping and strangling a young woman whose truck he wanted to use as a getaway vehicle. The body of the 24-year-old woman was found in a thicket of rose bushes outside of the city. She had been strangled with a pair of shoelaces while her hands were bound behind her back.

When he was finally recaptured, Gingras was locked in the hole a few doors down from Mo. The two chatted in French several times a day when Mo stopped by his cell. Whenever Gingras revealed anything incriminating, Mo wrote it down in French when he returned to his cell.

Mo was working on a thesis for a psychology course he was taking. The unsuspecting Gingras, and his manipulation of the prison system, was going to be the subject of Mo's report. Mo also was well aware that a confession from Gingras could help him get out of prison.

At Gingras' trial, Mo's testimony was so shocking it set the court reporter to tears. "Mr. Gingras told me that the 'bitch was crying like a cow' and that he had to strangle her to keep her quiet," Mo testified. "He told me that after he strangled her, he just threw her out of the vehicle south of Medicine Hat. He told me he took her money."

He said Gingras was concerned police would accuse him of sexually assaulting the woman, and he vehemently denied he had molested her. Mo testified that Gingras had said, "Wanda, my dear, Wanda, my darling. I didn't touch her except to kill her." Mo then told the court that Gingras had "called her a swear word that doesn't translate into English."

Gingras' lawyer, Peter Royal, asked Mo if he considered himself a normal healthy heterosexual. Mo did.

"You're not a homosexual?"

"No, I'm not."

"Nor are you a pedophile?"

"No sir."

"You have no homosexual tendencies? Is that right?"

"That's correct."

Royal then asked Mo if he ever sexually abused a teenage boy during one of his offenses. Mo denied it.

Royal then produced a report from the Regional Psychiatric Centre in Saskatoon in which Mo admitted he wanted to experience sex with a male. The report said he stated he had assaulted the teen out of "a feeling of power and control," which was possibly linked to being sexually abused as a child.

Mo denied ever making such a statement.

Royal continued reading from the report.

"Maurice said that the boy was defenseless and he had fantasized about his wife's earlier and younger boyfriends and what happened between them sexually," Royal quoted from the report. "At the time of the offense, he thought nobody would know and that he would not be apprehended."

"Did you say that?" Royal asked.

"I don't believe I did. No."

"Well, did you or didn't you?"

"I can't recall saying that, and I don't believe I would have made that statement."

"That statement wouldn't, of course, be consistent with your position that you did not in fact assault this boy," retorted Royal.

"That's correct," Mo responded.

Royal was perplexed. He asked to have Mo excused while he argued for more latitude to cross-examine the prisoner. "There are many other references in these materials to him, in fact, having admitted that offense to various psychiatric personnel," Royal told the judge. "He will admit it when it suits his purpose. He will deny it when it suits his purpose. The whole purpose of this exercise is to show that this man is a liar."

When Mo was recalled to the witness stand, Royal asked Mo if he had lied when he claimed he was innocent of the Lethbridge robbery and if he had lied to his elderly parents about his involvement in the offense.

"My parents believe I have been wrongfully convicted," Mo admitted.

"As a result of what you told them, right?"

"Yes."

"Other people see you as being manipulative, Mr. Laberge," Royal continued. "You've been described as manipulative before?"

"That's correct."

"Would you agree with that assessment?"

"No," Mo replied.

Gingras was convicted and received two life sentences on top of the one he had been serving. Mo leaked his thesis to the media, sparking a Royal Commission charged with investigating Gingras' release and the subsequent removal of the warden.

Mo's paper, "The Gingras Affair: An Analysis in Leadership," was a comprehensive examination of what led the warden, Sepp Tschierschwitz, to approve a plan to send a convicted killer out on a pass to celebrate his birthday at the world's largest mall. The 44-page paper—which included an appendix of similar length with organizational charts, maps and a layout of the warden's office—showcased Mo's keen knowledge of decision-making inside the prison. It laid out the how, when and why. It established where the program went off the rails. Mo noted how Gingras, who had committed 15 armed robberies during his previous escape, put the warden in such a position that he felt obligated to approve the pass to a French Canadian in order to show that the prison system did not discriminate against minorities. While the analysis laid out the warden's good traits and his laudable goals, it also showed that he overruled his line staff and security officer when they refused to even contemplate the killer's temporary release. Mo claimed that when prisoners learned that Gingras was getting a pass from the warden, the move was mocked with cartoons that showed Gingras as a wolf among a flock of sheep and Sepp Tschierschwitz as the shepherd. He claimed that when Gingras left the institution on the pass, after having successfully lobbied to replace the burly guard assigned to escort him with a smaller prison escort, line staff immediately listed him—in an apparent show of black humor—as unlawfully at large. Mo claimed the warden just wanted to be liked.

"Men facing repression of their natural needs for extended periods of time are hardly contributors to harmony and goodwill and into this melee strode a 26-year veteran with plans for reform, avant-garde programming, and control without force," Mo wrote in his paper. "Sepp Tschierschwitz was too innovative a personality for a maximum-security penitentiary. The warden saw the inherent good in men he was charged with keeping and this is clear in his willingness to gamble with Daniel Gingras and take a chance that Gingras was sincere and had legitimate objectives. His estimation of the potential evil in the prisoners at Edmonton prison was naive."

Mo noted that Gingras may have been sincere but likely changed his mind as a result of a foolish move by his caseworker. Mo claimed that five hours before Gingras was about to leave the prison on his pass, his case management worker had told him he had no hope of being paroled at an upcoming hearing. Mo called it a "massive lack of judgment," saying that not only did the prison official shatter the prisoner's hopes, but he also failed to tell anyone about his conversation with Gingras.

Mo suggested that police officers and parole boards should be the ones who decide when prisoners leave maximum security. He had a dim view of wardens who allowed themselves to be manipulated. He claimed Gingras was permitted to have a 72-hour private visit with a female prison volunteer despite regulations stipulating that prisoners could only have conjugal visits with wives, family or common-law spouses whom they had known for at least six months before being jailed. The prison was now in a real mess, he said.

"The aftermath of Tschierschwitz's stay at Edmonton Institution is a prisoner population rife with distrust of management, staff wary of committing themselves completely to new management and careful public scrutiny of what is going on at Edmonton's penitentiary," Mo wrote.

Mo's essay triggered an almost volcanic reaction at the Max when it was leaked to a provincial crown prosecutor who used it to call for a public inquiry. "It is an understatement to say they are not pleased with its contents and opinions," the prosecutor stated in his request for an independent review.

The Gingras affair left Mo in a very precarious position. The prison officials wanted to rip him from limb to limb, and the inmates, who detested rats, wanted him dead.

11

The Vanishings

D EBORAH D UBS was chatting excitedly on the kitchen phone to her best friend, Karen Tuck. It was around dinnertime in late July 1984, and they were happily planning their annual joint-family vacation to Lake Tahoe. Sharing a cottage at the mountain resort had become a tradition for the two San Francisco families.

Debbie and Karen talked to each other every other day to catch up on their lives. Friends since childhood, they were now married with three children between them, but their relationship never changed. They had grown up as neighbors in Hillsborough, California, about 18 miles south of San Francisco, and although they attended different schools, they had spent almost every possible minute together. Deborah Ann, a vivacious and attractive brunette, was an only child, and she embraced Karen like a sister.

Debbie grew up in a posh two-story colonial-style house in an upscale suburb. Her father, book publisher Jim Nourse, built a putting green on the front lawn, but the girls spent most of the summer in the swimming pool in the back even though they often complained that it wasn't heated. When they weren't pretending to be water lilies in the pool, they could usually be found upstairs in Deb's pink bedroom. Deb's cream-haired poodle, Domino, often joined them. Those were happy times for the girls.

But tragedy struck when Debbie was 24 and away at school: her mother committed suicide. Jim called Karen to help with the funeral arrangements. To get through her mother's death, Debbie clung to Karen and grew even closer to her father. Jim had always wanted a boy, but loved his athletic and outgoing daughter deeply. Once, she had leapt into frigid Lake Tahoe on a blustery day just because he wanted to see her dive. He spent countless hours on the lake with her, spinning lazy circles in the boat with his water-skiing daughter in tow. When Deb had turned 16, he gave her the gear-shift knob from a Mercedes and promised her the rest of the car when she turned 21. She did get a car, but it wasn't a Mercedes.

Not long after her mother's suicide, Deb contracted hepatitis in a restaurant where she was working and lapsed into a coma. She was unconscious for three days, but Karen visited her daily and talked to her nonstop, convinced Deb could hear every word. Her aunt Maxine McFeeters took Deb into her home until she fully recovered. Soon she was back to normal, a lively young woman with an even greater appreciation for life.

When Debbie hooked up with Harvey Dubs, she caught everyone by surprise. They seemed so different. Deb met the typesetter at Petrographics–Typeworld, where she worked as a graphic artist. He was a quiet New York Jew whose work was his life. She was artsy and outgoing. Karen couldn't see the attraction, but the pair were obviously in love.

Harvey, an orphan with no ties to the Big Apple, had crossed the continent with his two cats and collection of Beatles albums to work at Petrographics. The office romance blossomed, and Harvey and Deb were married in a small ceremony at the quaint, nondenominational Swedenborgen Church in San Francisco in 1982. When son Sean was born March 30, 1983, Debbie asked Karen to be his godmother. She was the only one Debbie would trust with her boy, the only one allowed to baby-sit Sean. The boy was precious. Now Deb was 29 and Harvey was 33, and they were going into business.

On the telephone that day, July 25, Debbie was telling her friend all about the couple's business plans. Harvey had purchased a video camera and editing equipment and had advertised in the newspaper his availability to record and edit videos of weddings, christenings and bar mitzvahs. Videotape was a relatively new medium, but Harvey was hoping that professionally produced home videos of special family events would be popular with California yuppies. Already he had lined up a few customers. Deb told Karen that a man who wanted to rent the equipment for a wedding was stopping by that evening.

When the doorbell rang at 5:45 P.M., Deb wound up the telephone conversation with Karen. "I've got to go," she said. "That must be them."

The following day Petrographics owner Stan Pedrov was puzzled when Harvey didn't show up for work. No one had seen Harvey since he left at five-thirty the previous evening. It wasn't like Harvey not to call. He was very conscientious, punctual and seldom ill. After working together for 11 years, Harvey and Stan had become good friends. When his secretary, Lauren Bradbury, received a call from someone named James Bright, who claimed Harvey and his family had to make a sudden trip to Washington on a family matter, Stan couldn't make any sense of the events. Harvey had his home number. Why hadn't he called? And he had never heard of James Bright. Perplexed, he phoned Deb's father.

Jim Nourse was equally confused. He had eaten lunch at his daughter's home on July 25 and had taken his grandson on an outing to Golden Gate Park. No one had mentioned anything about a trip. Nourse didn't know of any relatives in Washington. There were certainly none on his side of the family, and he knew Harvey had few relatives. After Stan Pedrov's call the worried father phoned his daughter's home repeatedly throughout the afternoon and evening, but no one answered his calls. When he had no better luck Friday morning, he called Karen. Surely, she would know what was going on.

"Have you heard from Deborah?" Jim asked. "I couldn't get her all day yesterday."

But Karen hadn't heard from Deb since they had chatted on the phone two nights before. She called her husband, George, and asked him to slide by the Dubs' home. George, who operated a heating and air-conditioning business, was familiar with the address. He had helped move Harvey and Deb into their home at 158 Yukon. It was a unique street, more like a laneway, on the lip of the Eureka Valley. The top end of the street where the Dubs lived was almost screened from the rest of the thoroughfare by trees and shrubs. The Dubs rented the ground and second-floor levels of the brown shingle-sided building while another tenant lived downstairs.

As he made his way up Market Street toward Yukon, George figured there had to be some simple explanation. But when he arrived at the house and climbed the steep front steps, he froze. The front-door key was in the lock. George tried the door. It was open. He called out to Deb and Harvey. No one answered.

Cautiously, he entered and made a cursory check of all the rooms. There was no sign of anyone except for the family cats. George left, locking the door and taking the key with him. He phoned Jim Nourse to tell him what he had found. Nourse immediately called San Francisco police.

Nourse was waiting at the house when police arrived. George had left the door locked and Nourse didn't have a key, but a police officer entered through a second-floor window. The hungry cats, now meowing noisily, rubbed up against the legs of the investigators. No note was found to explain the family's absence and no clue hinted at their whereabouts. What Nourse did see was enough to churn his stomach—a kitchen sink filled with dirty water, a dirty diaper on top of a dresser in an upstairs bedroom. Something was very, very wrong. "Deb would never have left the house like this," the bewildered father informed the officers.

The family's disappearance was highly suspect; police were certain of that. People disappear for many reasons, usually of their own volition, but the disappearance of the Dubs didn't fit any typical scenario. It smacked of foul play, but that was a huge leap. Who would kidnap an entire family? And why? Police officers began taking an inventory of the house and canvassing the neighbors.

Sergeant Irene Brunn noticed immediately that items were missing from the home. Brunn, a 44-year-old investigator in the department's overworked missing persons unit, noticed dust marks on empty shelves in the bedroom and the living room, suggesting that someone had recently removed stereo equipment, cassette tapes and videos. Brunn had a feeling that this was not going to be a routine investigation. Working in a unit receiving about 500 reports of missing persons monthly, Brunn had developed a sixth sense for singling out the bona fide cases from the pack. "Everything indicated there was something out of character," Brunn recalled later. "I just got a sense, a gut instinct based on how the people who reported the disappearance reacted." Brunn poked around in the house for several days, locating receipts, serial numbers and photos of the missing property. Harvey had kept meticulous records, often even keeping the original boxes. He kept records of serial numbers and titles of music and film tapes, all dutifully recorded in his own handwriting.

The neighbors were also helpful. Yukon was a small street. People watched out for one another. Dorice Murphy, who lived at the end of the street at 175 Yukon, told police she saw an Oriental man remove a large box from the house and place it in the trunk of a white Honda parked under the kitchen window. She noticed a second man in the vehicle. She didn't think the Dubs were home because Debbie usually left a light on in Sean's room, and it hadn't been turned on the previous night. The next day the car was back with the same two men. Murphy also noticed the vehicle didn't have a license plate. The driver took off when he realized he was being watched. Murphy boldly got into her car and followed for more than a mile before she was spotted. The Honda lurched across three lanes of traffic and made a getaway down a side street.

Barbara Speaker, the basement tenant at the Dubs' residence, saw a Chinese man in sunglasses leave the home about 11:30 A.M. on Friday. He was straining under the weight of a white flight bag and a blue duffel bag. Speaker knew the Dubs weren't home because she hadn't heard Sean in the evening when she came home from school. The university student could usually hear the 16-month-old playing with his toys on the hardwood floor above, but on Friday the flat above had been strangely silent. Speaker had been on the sidewalk when the Chinese man walked past her toward a car parked on the street.

"Excuse me," she called after him. He turned and looked at her, then hurried to a tan-colored Volkswagen Rabbit that looked a lot like the Dubs' car. Another man inside the car opened the door for his partner. The man carrying the bags jumped in and they drove off. Barbara's boyfriend had earlier seen a man in a Greek fisherman's hat leave the flat. Bank security cameras later captured a photo of a similarly hatted man withdrawing money from the Dubs' account at a bank machine.

The family's disappearance soon made headlines in the San Francisco papers. Friends of Debbie and the Nourses, as well as fellow workers from Petrographics, printed and distributed posters seeking information about the family. They carried a heart-wrenching photo of the Dubs, Harvey wearing a San Francisco International Film Festival T-shirt, Debbie in long earrings and a knit sweater holding a wide-eyed Sean in her lap. Large black type above and below the photo read, "Help Find This Family."

––––––––––

SOMETHING STRANGE was going on at the Pink Palace, a popular three-story flophouse on Carl Street in San Francisco's Haight-Ashbury district. During the autumn of 1984, several tenants disappeared from the 30-unit building, which wasn't really pink but rather a pale green. Normally, the disappearance of tenants from the flophouse wasn't that unusual. After all, the place was hippie central. People came and went. But usually someone heard from them again.

The disappearances began after someone distributed flyers in the tenants' mailboxes advertising for casual laborers. Several people were also approached by a middle-aged bearded and balding man calling himself Steve and offering to work on a pot farm in the Tahoe area. Steve, one of several names Leonard Lake was using at the time, came by the flophouse fairly regularly to sell drugs.

One of the first tenants to disappear was 26-year-old Michigan-born Sheryl Okoro, a 5' 1" blue-eyed brunette. Okoro, who sometimes worked as a prostitute, told a relative of her plan to work on a farm. She had her heart set on getting off the street for a while. Okoro's roommate and sometime pimp, a young black man who went by the name of John Lacey, disappeared at the same time. The couple's landlord later received a letter saying they had moved, but Okoro's family never heard from her again.

Maurice Rock also told friends he was thinking about taking a pot-farm job. The reclusive 37-year-old African American guitar player wanted to get out of the city to get his head together.

A couple of months later, 35-year-old Vietnam vet Randy Vern Jacobson also disappeared. A few days after his disappearance, someone cleaned out his apartment. When his girl friend came home on October 15, Randy was gone and she never saw him again. She later received a letter from Randy saying he had left to help Steve with some marijuana deals.

LATER THAT AUTUMN Paul Cosner, a San Francisco car dealer, was making arrangements to meet the potential buyers of a 1980 Honda Prelude he had advertised for sale. Originally from Reynoldsburg, Ohio, a suburb of Columbus, Paul and his sister Sharon had moved out to San Francisco more than two decades earlier, shortly after she had graduated from Ohio University. Paul was 23; Sharon, 21.

They had arrived in San Francisco in 1970. They had missed the Summer of Love, but the lure of the west coast was still strong. It was the era of Janis Joplin, Jimi Hendrix and Jefferson Airplane. Days of free concerts in the park and $3 shows at the Fillmore. The two siblings were unusually close. Their mother and father had divorced when they were both toddlers, and their stepfather had died when they were in their teens. They were away at college when their mother, Virginia, married for a third time.

Paul loved cars and motorcycles. He earned a bachelor's degree in education at Ohio University, a master's in vocational rehabilitation from Kent State and was offered a job writing for the *Motorcycle News* out of Long Beach. The pair drove out with all their belongings in a Corvair.

Now 39, the 5' 10" Paul had thinning brown hair and hazel eyes. He had just sold his partnership in a small dealership called Marin Motors and was now selling cars through ads in the *San Francisco Chronicle*. He also dabbled in writing. His green-eyed sister liked to brag that he wrote in the style of American humorist James Thurber, also an Ohio University graduate.

On November 2, 1984, he told his girl friend of five years, Marilyn Namba, that he figured he had sold his copper-colored Honda to "that weird guy I told you about." He was meeting the guy at 6:00 P.M. He said he ought to return in an hour or so. Namba, an X-ray technician, lived upstairs in the same apartment building in the Marina District west of Fisherman's Wharf. They were saving for a trip to Europe the following spring. Paul had told his sister he planned to propose to Marilyn when they reached Paris. They were planning a quiet night in front of the TV eating chicken salad and watching *Raiders of the Lost Ark*.

Paul never showed up. When he was still missing the next morning, Marilyn called Sharon. She was really worried, but she didn't want to start calling all of Paul's friends like some meddling girl friend. Maybe something had come up. But Sharon had no such reservations. This wasn't like her brother. Something must be wrong. The two women went through his telephone directory and phoned everyone he knew. Then they phoned city hospitals and the police, getting the runaround that Paul wasn't considered missing until he had been gone for 24 hours. In the weeks that followed, Sharon distributed flyers throughout San Francisco seeking information about her brother's disappearance. She took out an advertisement in a magazine pleading for help in locating him. She hired a private investigator to follow up on any leads she received, but they were all dead ends. For seven months she kept Paul's apartment, paid his bills, monitored his bank account and kept his telephone answering machine on, hoping for a call that would lead her to her brother.

———

CLIFFORD RAYMOND PERANTEAU was happy to oblige when Alice Shum called to ask if he could find her nephew a job at the moving company where he worked. At age 24, Cliff was the senior man at Dennis Moving, a commercial office and computer moving company in San Francisco. His word carried weight with the boss, Dennis Goza, and his endorsement got

Charles Ng hired as a member of Goza's 18-person staff in September 1984. Charlie told Goza he had just gotten out of the marines. He never mentioned the time he spent in Leavenworth or the dishonorable discharge. A guy named Leonard Blake (Leonard was loathe to give his real name) came with Charlie on his first day of work to submit his own job application, but he wasn't hired.

Charlie was now living in the attached garage of a modest house on Lenox Way near San Francisco's West Portal transit station. The garage space had been converted to an apartment. It was easy to hop the Muni to the Dennis Moving office on California Street. Charlie was a hard worker, and he earned his $350 a week. But Cliff never really liked the guy much. Cliff's job was to delegate assignments, and Charlie didn't like being told what to do. They had a few arguments, which ended with Charlie telling Cliff just what he thought of him in front of other staff. Charlie would rail against other workers he considered slackers, too. And he was strange. He talked incessantly about guns and was always bragging about how many people he had killed or whom he would like to kill next. He claimed to have killed 12 people. No one ever took him seriously.

"What's going on, Charlie?" a fellow worker would greet him in the morning.

"No kill, no thrill," would come Charlie's standard reply. He was also fond of saying, "Daddy dies, momma cries, baby fries." He would say it out of the blue and repeat it frequently all day long. No one ever figured out what he was talking about, but it became a standing joke among the movers, and they would egg him on. "Daddy dies, momma cries, baby fries," Charlie would repeat.

About four months after Charlie started working for Dennis Moving, Cliff felt his new employee seemed to be warming up to him. Still, Cliff was quite surprised when Charlie invited him on an all-expense-paid weekend to Tahoe. The plans fell apart when Cliff had to work overtime that weekend. He learned Friday that he was needed to work Saturday at the Pacific Gas and Electric Company offices on Market Street. He went out for a few Friday night beers at the Rockin' Robin on Beale Street with a co-worker who had been assigned to work with him the next day. When Cliff dropped the man off at his apartment about midnight, he called out, "See you tomorrow." But he never did. When Cliff didn't come in for the 8:00 A.M. start, his friend assumed he'd slept in. He tried calling him throughout the morning, but no one answered the phone. Finally, about noon, the co-worker dropped by Cliff's home on Waller Avenue and pounded on the door. No one answered.

"That's funny," the co-worker thought as he walked away. Cliff's blue Suzuki motorcycle was there. He returned after work to see if Cliff was around. The house was still empty, but the motorcycle was gone. Cliff also had made plans to watch the Super Bowl game featuring the San Francisco 49ers against the Miami Dolphins at a friend's house the following day. His friend was surprised when Cliff didn't show up or call to say he couldn't make it. When Cliff won $400 in the office Super Bowl pool and still didn't call, his co-workers began to really worry. That wasn't like Cliff.

A few days later Dennis Goza received a note from Cliff requesting that he forward Cliff's last paycheck to a post office box in Calaveras County, about 150 miles northeast of San Francisco. "Dennis," the note read, "Sorry to leave on such short notice, but a new job, place to live, and a honey all came together at once." The letter was signed "Cliff." Goza sent the check. It was cashed a few weeks later. Goza's co-worker also received a typed letter asking him to forward the Super Bowl winnings to the same address.

It looked like Cliff was gone. Cliff's girl friend let herself into his apartment to collect a few personal items. Items belonging to Cliff and her were missing. Someone had cleaned out the apartment.

———

JEFF GERALD, another Dennis Moving employee, was still sleeping when the phone rang in his Geary Boulevard apartment early on February 24, 1985. Jeff's roommate answered. A soft-spoken man at the other end asked if Jeff was around, and she advised him to call back. When he called back later, still refusing to identify himself, Jeff, a sandy-haired, 25-year-old musician from Arvada, California, chatted to him for a few minutes. "I'll meet you at the bus station," he told the caller before hanging up. Jeff told his roommate he was going to catch a bus to Stockton, an agricultural community about an hour's drive east of San Francisco, to meet "Charlie from work" to help with a freelance move. Charlie had offered him $100 and bus fare to help him move his cousin.

The money was appealing. Jeff, who had come to San Francisco three years earlier with plans to take some business courses at nearby St. Mary's College, was trying to get his life going. Lately, things were starting to improve. His band, Crash and Burn, was hoping to record and had booked studio time. Jeff played drum and guitar and wrote music. He had seen an advertisement for work at Dennis Moving on a bulletin board at college and it had turned into fairly steady work. He didn't mind the guys, but Charlie gave him the creeps with all his talk about guns and killing. He claimed to have throwing stars and all kinds of weapons. Jeff wasn't impressed. During one heated exchange, Jeff had called Charlie a "gook," which didn't sit too well with the ex-marine. Charlie also was upset that Jeff had been reinstated with full seniority when he returned to work in February after quitting without notice the month before. The boss had been sympathetic when Jeff explained that he had been suffering from depression. But Charlie saw it as a personal slight. His chance to move another rung up the seniority ladder had been denied. Jeff thought Charlie was nuts. Who gave a rat's ass about seniority in a grunt job like this? He hoped to be back in class soon.

After taking the call from Charlie, Jeff headed down to the bus station to catch an afternoon bus to Stockton. He told his roommate that it was a small job, a couple hours of work. He expected to be back that night. He would bring home Chinese food for dinner.

Later that weekend a man identifying himself as a friend of Jeff's called the owner of Dennis Moving at home to advise him that Jeff wouldn't be back to work until Tuesday. The caller said Jeff had decided to visit friends in San Jose. Three days after Jeff's disappearance, his roommate came home from work to find the apartment empty of Jeff's belongings. He didn't even leave a note to say good-bye.

KATHLEEN ALLEN, an 18-year-old, was working at the Safeway in Milpitas on April 14, 1985, when she received a call that her boyfriend, Mike Carroll, was in trouble. She had been worried sick about him for the past two days. When he left the room they shared at the Best Inn in Milpitas, just north of San Jose, he said he was going into San Francisco to see a friend named Charlie. He was going in just for the day, but she hadn't heard from him since. The call confirmed her worst fears.

"Kathi," the soft-spoken man said gently. "Mike has been shot. He needs you."

"What?" she stammered. "What do you mean?"

"We don't know much yet, but something went wrong," the voice continued. "We don't know if he's going to make it. We'll send a car around for you. What time do you get off work?"

"Six," she said hesitantly. "Who is this?"

"We're old friends, Kathi. We've known Mike a long time, long before he met you. Watch the parking lot for a copper-colored Honda Prelude. And Kathi," the voiced paused, "don't say anything to anyone about this. Mike is in enough trouble."

The hours dragged by as Kathi mindlessly punched groceries through the store cash register. What had happened? She suspected that Mike, five years her senior, had been up to something illegal. He kept making trips into San Francisco to hook up with a guy he said was an old army buddy, and he always came back with cash in his pocket. Whatever he was doing, he wasn't saying. A friend of Mike's hinted that he had hooked up with a couple of guys who were rolling gays in the Castro area. But Mike wouldn't discuss it.

"Relax," he would say. "It's no big deal. Don't sweat your pretty little head over it."

The guys who called Mike weren't giving anything away either. Whenever one called for Mike, and she asked who was calling, he'd just say, "Tell him it's his friend from San Francisco."

And now it had come to this. Nervous and uncertain of what to do,

Kathi confided in her friends at work. They were horrified that she was even thinking about getting into a car with a stranger under such circumstances.

"Don't go," her friend Monique Mavraedis pleaded. "Don't get into that car with a stranger."

Kathi called a friend in San Jose at about 5:00 P.M. and explained her predicament. James Baio was just as concerned for her safety as her supermarket co-workers had been. But Kathi assured him that Mike had called and told her he had got into some trouble in San Francisco and was holed up in the Tahoe area. He said he was sending someone to pick her up.

When the friend called Kathi back at the Best Inn a little later, he caught her packing for the trip. She told him that she couldn't talk because a guy was waiting to take her to Mike.

"This guy is kind of weird," she whispered into the phone. "He claims to be some kind of photographer and wants to take pictures of me."

Baio grew even more worried. He didn't like the sound of this at all, but he couldn't talk Kathi out of going. "Call me as soon as you get to Tahoe," he said finally. "I want to be sure you are okay."

She never called.

The Dubs family—Harvey, Deborah and baby Sean—were among those murdered by Leonard Lake and Charlie Ng.

After the Dubs disappeared, friends created this missing persons poster, then circulated it all around San Francisco.

The Dubs' home on Yukon Street in San Francisco.

Murder victim Brenda O'Connor.

Murder victims Brenda O'Connor, Lonnie Bond and Lonnie Bond Junior.

Murder victim Scott Stapely.

Murder victim Paul Cosner, the brother of Sharon Sellitto.

Police excavate the trench where Leonard Lake and Charles Ng buried a number of their victims.

Sergeant Larry Copland of the Calaveras County sheriff's office investigated the deaths of victims who had lived at the Pink Palace.

12

Sex Slaves

WILSEYVILLE CALIFORNIA / APRIL 1985

KATHI ALLEN SAT FROZEN in the big brown easy chair scarcely believing what was happening. Since climbing into the car in the supermarket parking lot, she had grown more and more afraid. The guy with the beard was really creepy, and she became more nervous with each mile they drove. They traveled nearly three hours, turning off the freeway onto narrow, winding country roads until finally both the pavement and the flat landscape disappeared. She tried to keep track of where they were going, but she couldn't. They were in hill country. Dense groves of trees lined both sides of the road. It was dark when they pulled up to a gated lane. When the driver got out to unlock the gate, she was tempted to make a break for it, but to where? She prayed Mike would be waiting when they pulled up to the house.

She thought she recognized the Asian man who came out to greet them. It was Mike's Marine Corps buddy, Charlie. She had met him before. But there was no sign of Mike. When she asked them where he was, they told her he was dead. Charlie touched the butt of a handgun stuck into the waistband of his jeans. Kathi was stunned. Surely, they were joking. She looked at their faces. They were all business. No one was laughing. This

can't be happening, she told herself. She was still in a daze when they manacled her wrists behind her back and pushed her inside the house. The
room was very warm. She was escorted past a video camera mounted on a
tripod and seated in a chair set against the backdrop of a peaceful wall
mural of a forest in autumn colors. She winced as the weight of her body
caused the cuffs to bite into her wrists.

In a moment the room was flooded in the bright glare of a free-stand-
ing spotlight. The room got even warmer. The bearded man, whom she could
now see was wearing jeans and a green cardigan, was checking the camera.
Charlie, clad in a black T-shirt, stood nearby, the gun now tucked into the
back of his jeans. Kathi crossed her legs and waited, praying it was all a joke.

She was a doe-eyed, dusky girl with shiny raven black hair and high
cheekbones. Soft-spoken. Attractive even though she thought her hips and
thighs were too heavy. She had only been living in the Milpitas hotel about
a month, having just left her mother's Maraga Avenue home in San Jose to
move in with Mike. The second eldest of three, Kathi had been raised pri-
marily by her Japanese mother, Sumiko, after her father, a U.S. Navy seaman, had died in 1973 before she was six. Her parents had met and fallen in
love when her father was stationed in Japan. When they married, Sumiko's
family had disowned them. Kathi's older brother, Danny, had been born in
Japan, but the family moved to the United States in 1963. Kathi had been
born four years later. A younger sister, Dian, who looked strikingly like her,
was born in 1969. Thinking of them now had Kathi on the verge of tears.

The bearded man was talking to her now. Something about a debt
Mike owed them. "You can go along with us, you can cooperate, you can
do everything we tell you to willingly, and in approximately 30 days—if you
want a date to write on your calendar, the 15th of May—we'll either drug
you, blindfold you or in some way or other make sure you don't know
where you are and where you're going and take you back to the city and let
you go. And what you say at the time, I don't care.

"My name, you don't know," he continued. "His name's Charlie, but
screw it. You don't know where you are, and what you say, hopefully, can't
hurt us. By then, hopefully, Mike will have disappeared gracefully."

Leonard Lake paused for effect. This was the critical part of his pitch. He wanted to lay it out clearly and succinctly and leave no doubt in Kathi's mind. He had to make it clear he wasn't bluffing. His voice was flat, devoid of emotion. But his eyes were dancing. Operation Miranda was a success. He was in complete control.

"If you don't cooperate with us, if you don't agree this evening, we'll probably put a round in your head and take you out and bury you in the same area that we buried Mike," he finished, menacingly.

Kathi sat motionless, staring vacantly in his direction, fearing the worst. She kept thinking, they killed Mike. There was no other sound in the room except the even confident tones of the bearded man's voice. He was rationalizing now.

"We do this just because we're—we admit it—scared, nervous. We never planned on fucking up, much less getting caught. And we're not intending getting caught. It's the old 'no witnesses.' It's a little crude, but . . . uh . . . that's where it's at."

His voice dripping with arrogance, Leonard began outlining what he expected from Kathi, the web of subterfuge she would help them weave to keep people from becoming overly concerned about the disappearance of people they knew. With the exception of the Dubs and Paul Cosner, there had been no hue and cry raised over the other victims because Leonard and Charlie had offered explanations for their absences, just like Leonard had done after his first kill, when he had taken the life of his half-brother. He laid out the steps for Kathi. He wanted all the information she could provide regarding Mike's bank accounts and "who we need to write to make things correct." He wanted Kathi to write to Mike's foster brother.

"Tell him some bullshit story about how you and Mike have moved off to Timbuktu," he explained. "Basically, we want to phase Mike off, just sort of move him over the horizon. Let people know that, yeah, Mike moved off to God knows where, and we never heard from him again. If anyone wonders, they are not going to wonder too hard."

Then Lake moved to his ultimatum. It was his pat line for his new slaves. "While you are here, we'll keep you busy," he told Kathi. "You'll wash for us, you'll clean for us, cook for us, you'll fuck for us. That's your choice in a nutshell. It's not much of a choice unless you've got a death wish." He stopped again, letting his message sink in.

Kathi had been sitting motionless, frozen with fear since her arrival. The man seemed to want a response, but she didn't know what to say. She turned her head toward him, blinked and mumbled, "No, I don't . . ." Her voiced trailed off. Charlie, who had been listening quietly, grinned. It was amazing how reasonable a bitch could be given the right motivation.

Leonard sighed. He told Kathi he hadn't liked having to deceive her, having to trick her into accompanying him to the cabin. "Actually, Kathi, I like you," he said. "The fairness of what we're doing is . . . uh . . . not up for debate. We're not worried about whether we're fair or whether we're good. We're just worried about ourselves. Selfish bastards? Maybe," he chuckled softly. "You'll probably think of worse names for us in the next four weeks, but that's where it's at." He paused again for effect. Kathi stared back, expressionless, eyes locked. Leonard began again.

"In the last 24 hours, we've been tired, nervous, a little high-strung, perhaps. We expect you to do something about that. Believe me, we both need it. If you go along with us, cooperate with us, we'll be as nice as we can to you within the limits of keeping you prisoner. If you don't go along with us, we'll probably take you into the bed, tie you down, rape you, shoot you and bury you."

Kathi didn't say anything. She didn't move. She didn't blink. Fifteen seconds ticked by. Leonard rose and walked across the room, arms dangling at his sides, to take up a new position on her left. She didn't look at him.

"Sorry lady," he snapped. "Time's up. Make your choice."

Barely coherent, Kathi mumbled, "I guess I have to be available."

"Spell it out on tape," Leonard barked. "I want to hear it from your own lips."

"I can't spell it out," Kathi mumbled again, her voice barely audible. Then, resignation creeping into her voice, she added, "I'll go along with whatever you want."

"That's all we wanted to hear," Leonard replied, clearing his throat as he approached her and crouched down at her feet to manacle her legs with a set of stainless steel shackles. Kathi refused to acknowledge him in any fashion. He put his right hand on her knee.

"Mike was an ass," he said bluntly. He told her Mike was planning to ditch her. He had told them she was clinging to him too much and asking him to do things he didn't want to do. Kathi didn't buy it.

Leonard turned to Charlie and asked him if he had the keys to Kathi's handcuffs. He asked Kathy to stand up while Charlie fumbled to remove the manacles from her wrists. Totally resigned, she let her freed right hand dangle limply at her side while Charlie worked on the other cuff.

"If we're a little clumsy at this, forgive us," Leonard said softly.

Kathi dropped back into the chair but rose when Leonard commanded her to get back on her feet.

"Undress for us," he said crudely. "Let's see what we bought."

With a remaining flicker of indignation, Kathi folded her arms across her chest, cocked her hip and stared boldly back at Leonard.

"Undress for you?" she asked incredulously.

"Take your blouse off," Leonard ordered. Kathi stared at him for another long moment, then slowly pulled her arm out of the sleeve of her top, slipped the shirt over her head and let it drop to the floor. She slipped a hand into the pocket of her jeans and waited for the inevitable next command.

"Take your bra off."

Kathi slipped it off and let it drop to the floor. She was naked now from the waist up, except for her dangling earrings, a chain carrying Mike's dog tags and a small gold chain with a floating heart and her mother's wedding band. She stood facing Leonard with her arms hanging limply at her sides, her head cocked to one side, her face expressionless.

Leonard admired her breasts. "They are not all that bad," he mused.

His voice remained flat, uninflected, betraying little emotion other than a hint of amusement. He was about to fulfill his sexual fantasy, but there was no lust in his voice. It was as if he was unable to feel any real emotion and extreme measures were his attempt to feel something, anything.

Sex was but a momentary spasm for him. He had a great hole inside where his emotions were supposed to be, and Operation Miranda was his attempt to see if there was anything down there at all.

He bid Kathi to keep undressing: "Take your chains off."

Kathi slipped off the dog tags with one hand and then focused on the clasp of her gold chain. Charlie suggested he get the key to unlock the shackles in order to allow her to remove her jeans.

"Sure," agreed Leonard. "We'll run it through the shower." Kathi was now reduced to an object.

"Should I go, too?" asked Charlie. Charlie didn't say much, but he was excited. He was visibly frothing at the mouth.

Leonard picked up on Charlie's desire. "Oh, you want to take a shower with her?" He chuckled. "If you want to." He ordered Kathi to sit down so he could remove the manacles from her legs. She didn't look at him, but sat down, still engrossed with the clasp on her necklace.

"This is surprisingly cooperative," Charlie noted.

"Wisely cooperative, Charlie," Leonard observed. Then, turning to Kathi, he explained, "We were prepared to do practically anything to get you to agree with us. I'm glad you made that all unnecessary. But a few ground rules, Kathi. We're real serious about this. Do what you are told, cooperate with us, and there won't be any problems. If you create any problems whatsoever, you could very well die."

Leonard removed the manacles and stepped away.

"Keep undressing."

Charlie reminded her he had a gun. "The piece is on the table."

"I see it," Leonard acknowledged him.

Kathi removed her socks, then stopped and slumped forward, staring at the floor. She was leaning on her left elbow, her hand against her forehead.

"Keep going."

"Excuse me for being shy."

"I can understand, but don't be shy," Leonard said gently. "You're going to take a shower."

"This won't be the first time—it won't be the last time," Charlie added coldly. He loved playing the villain with these bitches. He called them holes. He enjoyed watching them suffer. For Charlie it was a chance at last to have power.

"Don't make it hard for her, Charlie," Leonard cautioned. "Kathi, undress please."

With a huge sigh, Kathi Allen slipped the jeans off, pulling up her panties modestly. She stood facing her kidnappers with her hands on her hips.

"Panties, too."

She stood with her hand on her temple, unmoving. Leonard prodded. "I don't want to have to make an example of what we need to do to make you cooperate."

"I realize that."

"Then please cooperate."

Another long sigh. Kathi slipped off her panties.

Charlie led her off into the shower. He enjoyed showering with his female captives. Soap, water and skin. It aroused him. Leonard insisted that his women be clean. He made sure they brushed their teeth and used mouthwash. He detested the smell of cigarette smoke that hung around them, in their clothes and hair, on their breath. And Kathi was a smoker. Later that night Leonard videotaped Kathi, naked except for her panties, astride Charlie's legs, rubbing massage cream onto his back. Charlie, face-down on the bed in the spare room, cocked his leg and rubbed it against Kathi's buttock. The first night was always the best.

The next day they had Kathi call her boss to explain her absence. She made the call just before noon. She told Fred Demarest that she was going up north with her boyfriend to the Lake Tahoe area, where her boyfriend had a job. She asked for the rest of the month off, using her annual leave and taking some time off without pay. They chatted for about six minutes. She was sitting at the kitchen table, naked except for a pair of pantyhose, with the barrel of Charlie's gun pressed into her crotch.

During the days that followed Kathi was their sex slave. They took her whenever and however they wanted. Charlie had ripped the crotch out of her pantyhose. That was his turn-on. He'd always had a thing about pantyhose. He liked the feel against his skin, making him feel rebellious. He often bragged about his favorite sex routine. He would tie a pair of pantyhose around a women's neck, and using a chopstick to tighten it like a tourniquet, he would sodomize the woman while she drifted in and out of consciousness.

With Leonard the forced sex was secondary. The photographs and videotapes turned him on. They were a constant irritant for Charlie, who thought recording their conquests was far too risky. It would be evidence against them at their trial. But Leonard would just laugh it off. "Do you know how much a snuff film is worth?" he would counter.

Leonard trotted Kathi out to the deck to photograph her standing in cutoff jeans and a white tank top against the backdrop of sunlit trees. Hands cuffed in front of her, she simply stood, her eyes mournful, as he snapped his photographs. Leonard took a second photograph of her topless.

He took most of the photographs in the bedroom, although he didn't like the way the lime green walls added a sickly green tint to his photos. But it was the room where they played out their sexual fantasies. The wooden bed frame, with bookcase headboard made of plywood, was equipped with eye-hooks that enabled Charlie and Leonard to strap down uncooperative captives spread-eagle on top of the homemade diamond-patterned bedspread. Leonard had picked up thick black leather wrist and ankle bands believing that they were more secure than simply tying his captives' hands and legs, but Kathi had already demonstrated that if left alone for a long period, she could free herself. They had caught her before she had removed all the restraints, but they were more cautious now, locking her in the cell when they were occupied for any prolonged period.

Although generally cooperative during the first days, Kathi had shown streaks of rebelliousness. Some things she refused to do despite threats that she would be killed or beaten if she continued to be obstinate. But she reluctantly wrote letters to Mike's foster brother explaining his sudden departure with the now familiar moving-to-Tahoe story. "Dear John," she wrote in neat large handwriting, "Mike and I have moved up to Tahoe where Mike got a job with some friend. Our place doesn't have a phone yet so Mike asked me to drop you a line and let you know. The car is not working and until we get the money to fix it, we'll have to have some friends get our stuff. We'll send you our phone number as soon as we get one. Take care, Kathi."

Leonard had already made arrangements for a friend to pick up Mike's car in Milpitas to see if it could be repaired and sold. He sent Charlie by bus to San Jose to deliver the keys and a map showing where his buddy could find the vehicle. But the yellow 1974 Mercury Capri was a wreck. The brakes were shot, and it probably needed a new front end. Leonard advised his buddy to sell it for whatever he could get and send any money that it might garner over and above the cost of his time. Mike, just out of Leavenworth, didn't have much in the way of possessions. All he had that was really worth taking was Kathi.

Throughout the days and nights of captivity, Kathi posed for Leonard's photographs but refused to give in to his demands for a smile. Although her captors repeatedly promised to release her, she no longer believed them. When she was asked to write a letter to her boss advising him she was quitting her job, her fears were reinforced. She was never going home. They were paving the way for her to disappear just as Mike had.

The nights locked in the bunker were the worst. It was cold and deathly silent. The air was dank and musty, tinged with the sharp scent of urine from the pail beneath the mattress of her bed. Alone and in the dark, away from their prying eyes, she cried.

On the third night, Kathi got angry. Using her shoulder, she launched herself against the heavy door again and again until she fell exhausted and crying in a heap on her bed. It would not yield.

Leonard was furious when he came to get her in the morning. He noticed immediately that the hinges were out of kilter. When he stepped back to examine them, he saw they had been badly bent. It was unlikely they would have broken, but the thought sent a shiver of fear up his back. If Kathi had managed to escape in the night, they might have been arrested in their beds before they had a chance to fight, flee or die. This was not good.

He dragged her into the house and left her in the bathroom. After a few minutes he heard chanting coming from the room. Fearing that she might be preparing to harm herself, he barged in. He found her in front of the mirror, saying her morning prayer. Satisfied that she was okay, he retreated.

When she came out, he tied her spread-eagle across the spare bed while he went back to the cell to survey the damage. He could probably hammer the hinges flat, but it would take some time. By the time he returned, he had calmed down considerably. He picked up his 35 mm camera, turned the flash unit on and snapped photos of Kathi while chatting with her in a friendly conversational tone.

He had shown her his suicide pills and warned her that no one would ever take him alive. He wanted her to know he meant it.

"Hopefully, no one's going to catch me at these weird things, but if someone ever did, I'd die," he reminded her, adding that if he died, she would also likely perish in that hidden cell before anyone found her. If she didn't want to die, she had better ensure he didn't get caught.

He crouched beside her head as she lay facedown on the bed, clad only in cutoff jeans and panties. He told her he had refrained from doing things to her that he knew she wouldn't like, as a courtesy to her, but she had let him down. He was upset that she had pounded on the cell door, and he wanted to know what he had to do to convince her he was serious about her obeying him fully.

"Are you asking if you can hit me?" Kathi asked.

"No, I'm not asking if I can hit you. I can very much hit you, very easily. I don't want to hit you, Kathi. Let me take this back. Erotically, it would turn me on. I would get a great thrill out of it, but let's say I'm still trying to keep a little bit of your sanity. Okay? I'm having a little war within myself between what I want to do and what I think I should do, and what we might call is the decent thing to do."

Leonard untied her hands and legs from the bed and tossed Kathi a powder blue nightie with black trim. Kathi, fumbling with the skimpy negligee, reminded him of a story about a three-year-old girl he had attempted to dress.

"I was 19 at the time and visiting her house," he began. "She got up at some ridiculous hour, and I took her out to play, but, of course, she was naked as a puppy when she came running into the room, so I put what I thought were her clothes on and let her go outside."

Only half listening, Kathi continued to struggle with the outfit. She slipped the panties on but discovered she had the top inside out. Leonard continued.

"When she got back, though, her mother gave me this big lecture. It seems I had done everything wrong. I put her panties on backwards. I didn't know they had a front and a back. And I put her shirt on backwards. I thought her shirts were like my shirts that buttoned in the front. Hers buttoned in the back. I put white trousers on her, which evidently is nothing to put on a three-year-old girl to let her go outside and play. In general, I blew it."

Kathi was finally ready. Leonard got her to hop back onto the bed and snapped a photo of her in the outfit. His German shepherd, Wubon, watched the photo session silently from the bedroom doorway. Leonard stood at the foot of the bed focusing his camera, trying to coax a smile out of Kathi.

"I know you are not trying to do anything foolish, like smile, but you have such a pretty face that even when you're not smiling, you have a sultry look about you that the guys would find very attractive."

He told her there were only two more photos to take and then he would let her go outside for a cigarette. He gave her a tan-colored bra and a black lace slip to wear for the next photo.

"Notice I haven't done any full nudes?" he asked.

"Uh-huh."

"Personally, I don't find full nudes very attractive. I think a woman should always—"

Kathi injected, "They don't leave nothing for the imagination."

"Right. Yes, I agree completely."

Leonard helped Kathi undo the stubborn clasp on the bra, took another photo and then escorted her outside for her first cigarette of the day. It would also be her last. He would have Charlie see to that.

Kathi Allen held prisoner at Leonard and Charlie's secluded Wilseyville property. Leonard Lake loved to photograph beautiful young women—especially when they were his slaves. He repeatedly implored them to smile for his photos.

13

Part of the Game

S THE BEAT-UP GRAY CHEVY PICKUP roared up Highway 99 in the early morning hours of April 20, 1985, 19-year-old Brenda O'Connor could see the lights of Stockton twinkling in the distance. She glanced at her year-old son buckled in the child seat between her and the driver, Scott Stapely. Lonnie Bond Junior was fast asleep. The drive from San Diego north to Wilseyville was lengthy, and they had left at night, hoping it would be cooler and that Lonnie would sleep most of the way. It was a long time for a one-year-old to be cooped up in the cab of a truck. Raising her voice to be heard above the rattling dashboard and the wind whipping through a partially open window, Brenda asked Scott if they would be stopping soon.

"Seems like a good idea," he drawled.

Scott, a tall 26-year-old with a reddish brown beard and a receding hairline, figured they might as well get out and stretch their legs when they pulled into Stockton. Maybe get a bite to eat. He was going to need to stop for gas anyway. The old Chevy he had just picked up for $1,250 sure burned gas. But Scott loved the old truck. Born Robin Scott Stapely on August 15, 1958, Scott, as he was known to friends and family, enjoyed the outdoors.

The truck, now crammed with his camping gear and Lonnie Junior's portable crib, playpen and high chair, was a perfect vehicle to make the runs into the foothills. He liked to take his guns up to target shoot; maybe do a little fishing and hiking. When he wasn't sailing on the ocean in his parent's 25-foot sailboat, *My Lady,* he liked to be in the woods. Anywhere but in San Diego, where he worked for National Home Medicare.

Scott thought the cities were a mess of crime and poverty, and he had done his part to clean up San Diego by founding a chapter of the Guardian Angels and helping establish branches in Las Vegas and Beverly Hills. It still seemed like a lost cause sometimes. Riding the subways and cruising the streets in the red beret of the volunteer crime prevention army was losing its appeal. He wondered if people really appreciated what the Guardian Angels were doing.

Scott had already made this trip several times since Brenda and her common-law spouse, Lonnie Bond, had moved up to a secluded cabin near the little town of Wilseyville two months before. He had come to know their neighbors, Leonard Lake and Charles Ng, although he didn't know them by those names. He had bought a handgun from Leonard. A 9 mm Walther PPK/S. Nice piece, too. But they were strange dudes.

They sure had scared the shit out of Brenda. Leonard, now living under the name of his murdered friend, Charles Gunnar, was always hitting on her and wasn't taking rejection well. Once, when Brenda had gone into town, she came home to find that someone had been in the house and locked her out. She had to break a window to get in. She had started referring to him as Fuckface behind his back. The man was getting freakier every day and Lonnie Senior wasn't around all that much. He had landed some roofing work in the hope of raising enough money to start a methamphetamine lab. He figured if he could get some working capital, he could be the crystal king of California. But Brenda hated being around Fuckface and his little Asian buddy. They gave her the creeps.

One night around Easter, when Brenda was alone at home with Lonnie Junior, she had glanced out the window of their cottage and saw movement around Leonard's cabin, about 70 yards away. From the darkness of her bedroom, she thought she saw them hauling a body off into the woods in a wheelbarrow. It sure looked like a body with one arm flopping down. What else could it be? Lonnie would kill her if she called the cops out near his speed lab, so she called friends in Stockton to come out and get her. She returned to the cabin briefly when Lonnie returned but insisted he take her back to San Diego, where they had been living before moving up north. After two weeks, however, she missed him. Lonnie Junior missed him, too. When he called, begging them to come back, she reluctantly agreed. She felt better going back with Scott, whom she had met through the Guardian Angels when he was chapter president. He was a big boy and he could take care of himself. She remembered the time a knife-wielding mugger had tried to rob Scott in an alley. Scott had crippled the man.

Brenda wasn't sure how long Scott was planning to stick around. She had planned to take the bus up to Stockton when he offered to take her. He did a lot of work with seniors, and three he had been visiting for some time had died within a short period. He needed to find some peace. He told Brenda he was looking forward to getting out in the mountains alone. It would be his last chance for a while because he had been accepted into graduate studies at San Diego State University, where he had earned his bachelor's degree. He was hoping to get his credentials in secondary education and counseling. The last thing he had done before leaving was call his folks to advise them that he was going to be out of touch for a while.

"You probably won't hear from me for a while because Smokey the Bear doesn't allow post office boxes in the forest," he joked with his 57-year-old mother, Lola. His father, Dwight, was nearing the end of his career as a high school principal in Lancaster, north of Los Angeles. Since his mother, who worked for IBM, had been transferred to Los Angeles his parents were living apart weekdays and spending weekends and holidays together in the Los Angeles suburb of Garden Grove.

Dawn was approaching when the gray pickup, with Scott's personalized license plates, AHOYMTY, pulled up to the gate across the driveway of the green A-frame Lonnie had rented. Locals called it the Carter house, after the family who had owned it for many years. Located several hundred yards up the road on the right and well into the stand of sugar pines, it was not visible from the road. Nor was the yellow two-bedroom cabin on the left where Leonard resided. Brenda and Lonnie shared a driveway with Leonard, and he was always complaining when they inadvertently left the gate open or unlocked.

The travelers were bushed when they arrived. They rousted Lonnie Junior and brought the suitcases in. Lonnie Senior carried the two containing Brenda and Lonnie Junior's clothes up into the second-floor loft. They could unpack later. Brenda and Scott hoped to get in a few hours sleep before it got too hot. It was going to be another cooker. So far April 1985 was turning out to be one of the hottest springs on record in California.

Later Brenda went into town to do some shopping, leaving Lonnie Junior to get reacquainted with his father. Scott decided to stay with the pair. He'd had enough of driving for now. Brenda was grateful for a couple hours respite from the baby, even if it was just shopping in nearby Jackson. She hated living in the sticks. The youngest of six children, she had left home in Coldwater, Michigan, to move to San Diego a couple of years earlier. She had gone out to visit her older sister, Sandy, who had moved there with her husband, Arthur Bond, in 1981.

In San Diego, Brenda had been smitten by Art's brother, Lonnie, an auto mechanic. Lonnie, eight years her elder, was a likeable guy. Although he had a deformed left hand and a small stature—about 5' 4" and 150 pounds with a stocky build and blue eyes—he had a big heart. If anyone needed help, Lonnie would drop whatever he was doing to assist in every way he could—even if it cost him his last dollar. They moved in together, and Brenda was soon pregnant. With the birth of Lonnie Junior in 1984, Brenda gave up her dream of being a model despite still having a petite figure, long legs and a narrow waist. She was 5' 3", barely over 100 pounds, with brilliant blue eyes, dimples and a dazzling smile. The couple planned to marry July 4. Brenda hoped she wouldn't be showing by then. She suspected she was pregnant again. It was time to settle down, be a homemaker and get back into the cooking and baking she loved to do. She just wished they didn't have to live up here in the woods with crazies for neighbors.

As scary as the neighbors were, Lonnie believed Calaveras County was safer than San Diego. And for good reason. Lonnie had been dealing drugs and had run afoul of some unsavory characters who now wanted him dead. He had initially sent Brenda back to stay with her parents in Coldwater while he went underground. He urged her to come back after finding this hideout in Wilseyville. Lonnie figured they would be safe there.

Before Brenda headed into town, Lonnie told her they had been invited for dinner that night with the neighbors next door. It was a peace offering. Leonard apparently felt bad about their strained relationship and had invited them over to mend fences. Brenda was less than thrilled, but at least she wouldn't have to cook. She wasn't feeling very well.

When Brenda returned from nearby Jackson in the late afternoon, there was no sign of Lonnie, Lonnie Junior or Scott. But Scott's truck was there. Where were they?

She didn't have time to dwell on it. Leonard and Charlie crashed through the door and flung her to the floor, spilling her packages around the kitchen. She screamed and struggled as they handcuffed her wrists behind her back and half-pulled, half-dragged her through the thin stand of sugar pines separating their yards and past the concrete bunker to their cabin. One on each side, they forced her through the carport, in the door, past the kitchen and into the living room, where a video camera was sitting on a tripod. They were all panting from the struggle when the two men pushed the nearly hysterical woman into the brown armchair against the mural-covered wall.

"What have you done to Lonnie?" she cried.

"If you must know, I didn't do anything with him," replied Leonard, still breathing heavily from the exertion.

"What did he do with them?" she asked, referring to Charlie, who was at her side, checking her manacles.

"I didn't do anything," Charlie replied. Brenda didn't believe them.

"Did you guys kill him?"

"No, we didn't kill him," retorted Leonard.

"Are you going to let us go soon?"

"Probably not."

"Never?" She sounded incredulous. "Are you going to kill us?"

"That's sort of up to you, Brenda," Leonard said menacingly. Hatred oozed from his voice. Brenda leaned forward in the chair, searching the faces of her captors, looking from one to the other. Her heart was pounding, chest heaving. She knew these guys. And they knew her.

"Why are you doing this?"

"'Cause we hate you," Leonard snapped.

"What did we do?"

"Shut up!" he barked. Then he said to no one in particular, "Oh, what a hairy day."

The operation against Lonnie, Scott and the baby hadn't gone as smoothly as planned. They had jumped the men while they were sleeping. Scott, with his size and experience, had been tough to bring down. He had leaped for his gun in the suitcase, but he didn't get to it. Charlie managed to hit Scott in the leg and shoulder with a volley of gunfire and bring him down. Charlie pounced on him, shoved the gun in his mouth and fired, smashing his teeth and jaw. He fired the fourth shot execution-style into his head.

Leonard had tried to get more information out of Lonnie before killing him. He was convinced his neighbor had stashed some cash in an old mine shaft somewhere nearby, but Lonnie swore it wasn't true. When they couldn't get anything more out of him, they killed him with a single shot. Leonard had handed Charlie a hammer and sent him to the bedroom to bludgeon the baby, now screaming in his crib. Charlie had argued that they should sell it, but that was too risky. Leonard told Charlie killing the baby would be good training for him. Yeah, it had been a hairy day.

Brenda was growing more hysterical, demanding to know where her baby was. Wouldn't she shut up?

"Your baby is asleep like a rock," he said brutally. He paused. Where to begin? Although he was angry, he kept his voice even. But venom dripped from every word.

"Brenda, the whole neighborhood doesn't like you. The neighborhood doesn't like Lonnie, and we haven't liked you since you moved in."

"So we'll leave," she countered.

"Oh, you have already left," he said sardonically. "We've closed you down. The Star Route Gang, if you want to call it that," Leonard said, referring to the neighbors along the postal route. "We got together and we took you away. We took Scott away. Lonnie's going to earn a decent living for the rest of his life, hopefully," he added, leaving her a glimmer of hope.

"I know he is," she said.

"Your baby is going to be taken away." He paused, trying to catch his breath. "Whew! Excuse the heavy breathing."

"Be taken away?" Brenda repeated incredulously.

"There is a family down in Fresno that doesn't have a baby."

"You aren't taking my baby away!" she screamed defiantly.

"They've got one now," Leonard retorted.

"It's better than the baby's dead, right?" added Charlie. His voice was quiet. Brenda wasn't paying any attention to him. She focused on Leonard.

"What do you mean they've got one now?" Brenda screamed. "That's my baby!"

"Brenda, you have a choice. We'll give it to you right now."

"What?"

"You can cooperate with us," Leonard said, launching into his now-familiar horrifying spiel. "By cooperating with us, that means you will stay here as our prisoner. You will work for us, you will wash for us, you will fuck for us. Or you can say, 'No, I don't want to do that.' In which case we will tie you to the bed, we'll rape you and then we'll take you outside and shoot you. Your choice."

"I'll cooperate," Brenda said quickly.

"That's nice," mumbled Charlie.

"That was fast," added Leonard.

"Are you really going to take my baby away from me?" Brenda was leaning forward now. She was working her wrists, trying to slip out of the cuffs, but they were tight. They bit into her wrists.

"Yes, we are," said Leonard, savoring the opportunity to drive in another psychological nail. "Personally, I don't think you are a fit mother."

"Where's Lonnie now?"

"They've been taken away," Leonard said lamely. "There's a place up in the hills where they will have to split wood for the rest of their happy lives."

Brenda wasn't buying it. "You haven't killed them or anything?"

"No, I haven't killed them," he answered, feigning disinterest. "If they die, that's their problem. To be honest I couldn't care less. They had better cooperate, too. They are getting the same choice you are getting. For all I know they could be dead now."

"Is that why you invited us for dinner?" asked Brenda, who, although still not wanting to believe it, was starting to put the shocking pieces together.

"Uh-huh," admitted Leonard.

"It's part of the game," chimed Charlie.

Leonard launched into Brenda, telling her what an asshole she had been. He said Lonnie wasn't as bad, except for his habit of shooting off weapons at all hours of the day and night and his drug factory.

"But you've been an asshole like I can't believe. You have been so damn rude, and for no reason that I can figure." He was sounding hurt now.

"'Cause I can't stand it up here," replied Brenda. "It's in the middle of nowhere."

Charlie urged her to explain why she wrote derogatory letters about Leonard to Lonnie when he was away. Leonard had broken into the house and read them. Brenda changed the subject.

"Are you going to keep me up here the rest of my life or something?"

"No," replied Leonard. "To be honest with you, I probably won't keep you here more than a few weeks, but after that I'll probably pass you around. There's other—"

"The light's hot," Brenda interjected. The light for the video camera was growing unbearable in the sticky hot evening. She felt faint. Leonard didn't care.

"Suffer!" he snapped. This was payback for every woman who had betrayed him—his mother, his first wife. He would take this angry terrified woman, and he would break her into submission. It would be glorious.

"Why do you guys do this?" Brenda asked, anguish in her voice.

"We don't like you," Leonard snarled. "Would you like me to put it in writing?"

"It's done," added Charlie, the fatalist. "Just take it—whatever we tell you."

"I can't take much of this," cried Brenda.

Leonard was chuckling now.

"We're going to, heh, heh, sit back and enjoy ourselves," he said matter of factly. "It's been a hectic day, and you are going to learn the true meaning of fuckface. That's me—if you haven't gotten that," he added.

Brenda asked Leonard to loosen her handcuffs, which were biting into her wrists. Leonard assured her that they would be taken off shortly, once Charlie slapped a set of leg-irons on her feet. But Charlie had something else on his mind. He walked up to Brenda, grabbed her by the back of her T-shirt and began slashing at the light cloth with a small pocket knife, pulling and ripping the material as he hacked at it.

"Since you say it's hot, I will take it off for you," he told the frightened woman.

"What?" cried Brenda.

Even Leonard was surprised. "Well, she could actually take it off herself, but . . ."

"Well, with the cuffs on it's hard," Charlie mumbled by way of an explanation. He continued to tug, hack and rip at the garment until all that remained was a portion of the upper left sleeve. He then went over to a nearby table to retrieve the leg-irons, dangling them in one hand as he returned.

The room was stifling hot under the floodlights. Charlie stripped off his black crew-neck T-shirt. He knelt at Brenda's feet, fishing in the pocket of his jeans for the key to open the leg-irons. All the while Brenda begged to be reunited with Lonnie Junior. On both knees in front of her, Charlie fumbled with the lock on the shackles. The chain linking them clattered against the floor. Seconds later Charlie snapped the bracelets around Brenda's ankles. They closed with a loud clank.

"Would you please go get my baby," Brenda cried. "You can't keep my baby from me for sex."

"We're taking your baby because your baby is innocent in this," began Leonard. "There's nothing—"

"Well, so am I," retorted Brenda.

Leonard and Charlie both laughed.

"You two are crazy," Brenda cried.

"Well, maybe the whole neighborhood is crazy," conceded Leonard. "The point is you haven't been particularly innocent while you've been here, Brenda. In fact, you've been something of a first-class asshole," he reminded her again. "However, we're going to give you an opportunity to make up for it."

He was still chuckling over Charlie's attack on Brenda's shirt. "You're so crude, Charlie. I actually like that T-shirt."

Charlie reached behind Brenda with both hands to undo her brassiere, and then in frustration he reached for the knife and cut it off, against Brenda's protests. "Let's see what we're buying," he said, stealing the line Leonard had used on Kathi a week earlier.

"Don't cut my bra off," Brenda cried. But Charlie was into it. Really into it.

"Nothing is yours now," Charlie seethed. "It'll be totally ours." He glared at her. "You can cry and stuff like the rest of them, but it won't do you no good," he said, chuckling. "We are pretty coldhearted, so to speak."

Leonard reminded Charlie to remove Brenda's handcuffs now that she was clamped in the leg-irons.

"I'll get my weapon handy, in case you want to try to play stupid," Charlie warned her.

"I ain't going to play stupid," Brenda assured him. "I don't want to get killed, you know." She was still feeling lightheaded and nauseous. She felt even sicker when she learned that she was going to have to have a shower with Charlie, who was now standing in his underwear, pointing a stun gun at her.

"You see, Charlie owes me one," Leonard explained to his captive as he caressed her breast with one hand. "So, uh, I get you first, but he's got his heart set on taking a shower with you. Who am I to turn him down?"

Brenda was having difficulty breathing. God, it was hot in the room. Her lips grew pale.

"I think she believes us," Leonard mused to Charlie. Then he turned back to Brenda. "You better believe us, Brenda, or you'll be dead."

"Right," added Charlie.

"I believe you," Brenda said quietly.

She was ordered to stand and remove her jeans. She warned them she was dizzy and might faint at any moment, but she didn't get much sympathy from either of the men leering at her lithe, tanned upper body.

"Well, you can pass out," Charlie sneered, "but we're going to wake you up."

Leonard threatened to whip her if she didn't comply, but Brenda was growing increasingly sickly in appearance. Noticing finally that her lips were pale and she might actually be ill, Charlie offered her a drink and an Aspirin. Brenda speculated aloud that she might be pregnant.

"Not the right time for that shit," muttered Charlie.

Brenda became nearly hysterical again. "Give my baby to me," she cried. "I'll do anything you want. He can't live without me."

"He's gonna learn," snarled Leonard. "Come on, stand up. Jeans off. Panties off and everything else." He stood over her as she undressed, then called after Charlie as he led her off, "Watch she doesn't fall over in the shower and split her head."

"I don't need a shower," protested Brenda.

"You do, too," countered Leonard.

"We have to make sure you're clean before we fuck you," explained Charlie. "That's the house rule. Traditional."

"Make sure she brushes her teeth and uses mouthwash," Leonard called.

———

WHEN MOTHER'S DAY came and went without a card from Scott, Lola Stapely was surprised. Scott had said he would be out of touch for four to five weeks, so she assumed he was still backpacking in the wilderness. But when she had heard nothing by May 26, her husband's birthday, she became alarmed. Birthdays were a big deal. Theirs was a close-knit family. But what to do? They knew he was supposed to be in Yosemite Park, but they knew they couldn't very well knock on the door and ask if their son was still in the park. And if they contacted authorities and nothing was wrong, Scott would be peeved. So they waited and prayed their instincts were wrong, prayed he would call to tell them he had met someone or gone somewhere and there would be a reasonable explanation.

Brenda's mother, Sharron O'Connor, also was concerned when she didn't hear from her youngest child on Mother's Day. Brenda always remembered special occasions. The O'Connors were simple people who lived a modest existence in Coldwater, where they had moved in 1972 after the State Mental Hospital in Battle Creek had closed down. Both of Brenda's parents had worked at the institution in various jobs until it closed. Sharron had raised seven children, including her baby sister after their mother had died. She had an instinct when one of her babies was in trouble. When her birthday came and went on July 25 and she still had not heard from Brenda, she knew something was wrong.

Scott's girl friend, Tori Doolin, who had met Leonard at the Bond's cottage on one of the earlier trips to Calaveras County with Scott, was surprised when the man showed up at the door of Scott's apartment about five days after Scott had left. It was 8:30 A.M. when the doorbell rang.

"Who is it?" she asked.

"Charles," said Leonard, who was still using Charles Gunnar's identity. Tori, who didn't recall anyone named Charles, asked, "Charles who?"

"Charles from up north," he responded. Then she remembered the Bonds' neighbor. She opened the door to find the man and a younger Asian whom she had never seen before. Leonard didn't introduce him.

Leonard advised Tori that he had found Lonnie, Brenda and Scott dead at the A-frame on April 22. He said he and his friend had burned the bodies because he didn't want the police snooping around. (In truth the bodies were still lying under his deck where he had left them the previous day.)

"There are clothes scattered around the cabin, but all their guns and identification are gone," he told her. "The baby is also missing."

He suggested the murders were drug related, and to keep police away, he wanted to make it appear that they had moved. For this, he said he needed Scott's bike, all his clothes, the receipt for the 9 mm Walther PPK/S pistol that Scott had purchased from him and the receipt for the truck. He handed Tori the key to the portable safe in which Scott kept his valuables. When Tori couldn't find the receipt for the gun or the truck, Leonard grew angry. He asked her to send them to him if she located them later.

Leonard and Charlie had driven Scott's truck down to San Diego to pick up Scott's belongings. Tori noticed the driver's door was smashed. Leonard explained they'd had an accident on the way down. Charlie followed Tori and Leonard to the truck to examine the damage but never said a word. They loaded up Scott's possessions and drove off. Tori never called police. She was going through a difficult child custody battle and being connected to something like this could prevent her from ever getting custody of her child.

When Brenda and Lonnie failed to pay their May rent, the realtor visited the A-frame to find it deserted. Leonard, who had alerted the realtor that the tenants had skipped, said the couple had left him their car. Summoned by the realtor, owner Bo Carter came out to investigate. He found the place in disarray, a window broken and two suitcases containing women's and children's clothing in a hidden room in the loft. But there was no sign of the tenants.

Leonard Lake's photo of Brenda O'Connor held captive. Leonard often photographed his victims on the deck, where the light was better.

14

A Simple Twist of Fate

IT WAS NOON at the South City Lumber Store, a large yellow cinder-block structure on the southern outskirts of south San Francisco near the corner of Spruce and Railroad. The place was not busy. Leonard had often stopped by the store when he was in the Bay area to pick up material for his bunker. It was not far from Peck's Lane, where Cricket lived, and it was on the way to nearby San Bruno, where Leonard's family resided. Leonard and Charlie routinely ripped the lumber store off. Leonard would distract the clerks with product-related questions while Charlie slipped out with the goods. The five-finger discount. Charlie was proud of his ability to slip in and out of stores unnoticed. But today would be a challenge. Leonard wanted a bench vise, a hefty piece of equipment weighing about 25 pounds. The vise they had was crap. Leonard had already spent $40 having it repaired once. It was a useful tool for working on weapons, especially when threading gun barrels for silencers. They could have purchased a new one, but at $75 it seemed a tad overpriced for what it was: a set of large adjustable iron clamps with a solid steel table mount.

Leonard wheeled the copper-colored Honda Prelude into the lumberyard parking lot, parking as close to the doors as he could. The pair walked in together but quickly split up after Leonard pointed out the vise he wanted: a gray Chinese-made Diamond brand multipurpose bench vise. Charlie waited nearby, pretending to look at other tools until Leonard engaged the clerks at the counter. When no one was watching him, Charlie nonchalantly scooped up the vise and headed for the exit. It was bad luck, really, that a customer was coming in at the same time.

John Kallas, a former United Airlines mechanic who had been dabbling in renovation work since his retirement, was a frequent customer at the store. He had just recently turned 61, but he liked to keep busy. It was convenient for him to shop at South City since he lived not far away. When he strode into the store on June 2, 1985, he was looking for hinges for a cabinet he was making. As he entered, Kallas noticed a small Asian man heading in the opposite direction with a large vise gripped in both hands. He saw the man come out of an aisle, bypass the cashier's counter and head straight out into the hot sun in the parking lot. After 28 years in the police reserve, he figured he could spot a shoplifter.

"Hey, did you guys just sell a vise?" he hollered to the clerks at the counter. They looked at each other and chorused, "No."

"Well, if you didn't sell it, you just got ripped off." He turned and dashed back out the door to see where the shoplifter had headed. A clerk, whom Kallas knew only as Glen, rushed to join him. As they stepped onto the pavement, they heard a car door slam off to their right.

"There he is," Kallas told Glen. "That's him." The shoplifter had paused beside a copper-colored Honda.

When Charlie saw the two men approaching, he turned and walked briskly toward the intersection of Spruce and Railroad.

"Hey, bud!" the clerk called out. "I want to talk to you."

Charlie kept walking. He didn't look back as he crossed the intersection and headed up the street. Since he was no longer carrying the vise, the men didn't pursue him. He had obviously dropped it near the Honda. Kallas and Glen went to check the car. Glen looked under the vehicle while Kallas walked around it, peering in the windows. There was no sign of the vise in either the front or backseats.

"I wonder what he did with the vise," Kallas mused aloud. By this time he had encircled the car and was standing beside Glen at the trunk. The lid appeared to be ajar. Glen lifted it.

"There it is!" Kallas exclaimed. In the left-hand side of the trunk compartment the vise was sitting in plain view, still bearing the South City price tag. Kallas made a quick inventory of the other items in the trunk. There was a box of pornographic photos, a bag of marijuana, a box of clothing, a couple six packs of diet Dr. Pepper bottles and miscellaneous other items. But what sent him scurrying back into the store to call the police was a bag containing a hand gun with an illegal silencer. Somebody has to be up to no good, Kallas thought. He asked a clerk if police had been called. When he learned they hadn't yet been summoned, he picked up the phone and dialed the familiar number. As he informed the dispatcher of the complaint, a bearded balding man approached him and began badgering him not to call police. Kallas ignored him. When he got off the phone, the man was still standing there.

"That was my friend," Leonard explained. "Can I pay for the vise?"

"You'll have to talk to the clerk about that," Kallas responded curtly. "I don't work here."

Kallas went to pick up his hinges, paid for them and strolled outside to await officers from the South San Francisco police department. One of the first officers on the scene was Daniel Wright. He checked the Honda's trunk for a receipt for the vise. Finding none, he searched two tote bags for additional stolen property. In one, in a light green and gray pistol case, he found the weapon that had set Kallas off, a Ruger .22 pistol with a silencer. Leonard approached him while he was examining the threads on the end of the barrel of the .22 and the corresponding threads on the silencer.

"I paid for the vise my friend took," he told Wright.

"Who owns the car?" asked Wright.

"Lonnie Bond," Leonard replied.

"And where is Mr. Bond?"

"Up north."

Wright asked Leonard if he had Bond's permission to use the car, and he said he did. But when he asked for Bond's phone number, Leonard said he didn't have a phone.

"Do you mind if I search the vehicle?" he asked.

"You might as well," Leonard replied.

"Does that mean yes?"

"Go ahead."

Wright asked Leonard for identification. He produced a California driver's license belonging to R. Scott Stapely. Wright then removed the gun and asked Leonard who owned it. Leonard said it belonged to Charlie Ng. But when Wright checked the serial numbers on the .22 pistol, he found the gun registered to Stapely. "It looks like you have more problems than anticipated," he told Leonard before placing him under arrest for possession of an illegal weapon.

While they were waiting for a tow truck to take the impounded Honda away, Leonard asked for permission to use the washroom. Kallas, who was still hanging around in case he was needed to provide a statement, escorted Leonard to the washroom and waited outside the door. He heard the toilet flush and the sound of Leonard washing his hands. When Leonard emerged, Kallas escorted him back to the officers. Meanwhile, Wright ran the Honda's vehicle identification number on the police computer. Something didn't add up. The car was registered to a man who had been reported missing eight months earlier, and the plates, which were registered in another person's name, didn't match the vehicle. A simple petty theft was starting to get complicated.

Charlie headed down the street several blocks before doubling back to see if Leonard was able to salvage the situation. When he saw the police cars arrive at South City, he feared the worst. From a pay phone not far from the store, he dialed up Cricket. "Come get me," he rasped. "The cops have got Leonard."

She scooped him up and circled the block while he explained the situation. She cruised by the store to see for herself. Charlie crouched on the floor as they drove past the parking lot. Police were still on the scene. It looked like they were going to arrest Leonard.

"Shit," Charlie exclaimed. "I've got to get out of here." Cricket drove him to his basement suite in West Portal, dropping him off a few blocks from the house as a precaution in case police already had his place under surveillance. Charlie did a quick reconnaissance, and when he was convinced no one was around he ducked in and began to make arrangements for a quick exit if it became necessary. He didn't know how much the cops would figure out. Cricket planned to bail Leonard out later in the afternoon. If she got a chance to talk to him, they could find out how much the cops knew.

Police took Leonard to the South San Francisco police station. Kallas watched the arrest with casual interest. He knew he would have to go down to the police station to give a formal statement, but he planned to go home first to change out of his work clothes. In the end he decided to go as he was.

At the South San Francisco police station, a female officer approached him as he was writing his statement. "John, you sure opened a can of worms," she said.

"What do you mean?"

"That Honda belonged to Paul Cosner."

"Oh, boy," Kallas exclaimed. He had been following the case closely in the newspapers. Cosner's sister, Sharon Sellitto, had raised hell over the handling of the case and had pressed the City of San Francisco to post a reward for information.

Kallas had just finished his statement and gone home when he was summoned back to the South San Francisco police station. This time, he was informed, his statement would have to include the fact that he had taken Leonard to the washroom.

"Why do you need that?" he asked.

"The guy tried to kill himself."

Back at the police station Leonard had requested a pen and paper to write a note to a girl. The police obliged. They believed he was lying to them about his age and possibly his name, and they thought the woman he listed as next of kin might be able to help them identify him. A police officer asked Leonard how he planned to deliver the note. Did he want police to deliver it?

"You may be calling her," Leonard said ominously. He added that when he finished the note he would tell police what they wanted to know. He admitted he had been lying to them earlier. "You always lie to police," he explained. As he began writing, Leonard asked for a glass of water. Again the police obliged, taking him across the hall to the washroom to get a drink.

When they returned to the interview room, Leonard took a deep breath and said his name was Leonard Thomas Lake. He began breathing hard and sweating profusely. "I'm wanted in Mendocino County on felony charges," he rasped, panting rapidly now. Suddenly, his whole body began to shake as he went into convulsions and then collapsed on the table.

The police officer taking his statement rushed from the room and called for help. He returned to find Leonard lying on his left side on the floor. His pupils were dilated. Paramedics, suspecting a heart attack, attempted CPR. Leonard was taken by ambulance to Kaiser Hospital and placed on life support. The prognosis wasn't good.

No one saw him slip the cyanide pill from under his shirt collar into his mouth. Police didn't even suspect cyanide poisoning until a search of the Cosner vehicle revealed a bottle of cyanide pills in the glove compartment. Leonard lingered in a coma for four days. After agreeing to remove him from life support, his family joined hands and stood around his bed to pray for his soul.

Leonard had fulfilled his promise—they never did take him alive. He would never face the state's punishment or the wrath of his victims' families. He would never have to acknowledge his crimes. The note he had written was of little use to police officers. It was to his beloved ex-wife, Cricket, an apology to her and his mother and sisters for the hell storm he was about to bring down on their heads. "Dear Lyn: I love you. I forgive you. Freedom is better than all else. Tell Fern I'm sorry, Mom, Patty and all. I'm sorry for all the trouble. Love, Leonard."

Police were stunned by Leonard's actions. Why would a guy kill himself just to avoid car theft and weapons offenses? They knew there had to be more to it. Were these guys involved in Cosner's disappearance? Who was Ng? And more importantly, where was Ng?

When Cricket got the call from police that Leonard was in critical condition in hospital and that they were looking for his accomplice, she immediately called Charlie to warn him. Charlie hastily packed a bag. He threw in his .22 Ruger, a set of handcuffs, a 35 mm camera, a towel and other supplies. He didn't know how much time he had before police would come knocking on his door. He had to get out of town fast.

Charlie felt betrayed. Damn Leonard. Damn his photos and his videotape. Damn him for keeping the property of the victims rather than selling it for cash. Damn him for popping that cyanide pill.

But Charlie had a plan. It had never been his intention to kill himself if apprehended. He had advised his friends John Hudson and Mike Diaz that he might be heading their way if he got into trouble. He had researched the possibilities in Leavenworth and had set up what he called a triangulation. Hudson and Diaz would be his alternative avenues of escape. Hudson, in Oklahoma, would be his jumping-off point into Mexico. Diaz, in Chicago, would launch him into Canada. Charlie figured Canada would be his best bet. He could lose himself in its large Asian population and seek help from his sister in Calgary or other military buddies now in British Columbia. And Canada's extradition treaty with the United States allowed it to seek assurances that an extradited fugitive would not have to face the death penalty. It was a no-brainer.

Charlie headed down to the West Portal station, hopped on the Bay Area Rapid Transit, and took the Trans-Bay Tube over to his Aunt Alice's Beatty Street residence in San Leandro. It was Alice Shum, his mother's little sister, who had secured him his job at Dennis Moving. She was duty bound to help him. He called his lawyer, Garrick Lew, to tell him he was in trouble and to ask him to represent his interests. His aunt loaned him $400 and drove him to the San Francisco International Airport. Using stolen identification in the name of Mike Kimoto, Charlie caught a flight to Chicago to hook up with Diaz.

The following morning, Monday, June 3, 1985, Charlie called his boss from a Chicago hotel to tell him that he needed time off work because a friend had committed suicide. It sounded to Dennis Goza like a long distance call, so he asked Charlie if he was calling from out of town.

"Yeah, I just got off the plane in Honolulu," Charlie lied. "I would like to stay a few days at least, maybe longer."

Goza agreed to let Charlie take off all the time he needed. Charlie said he expected to be back within a week. He was still hoping everything would blow over.

Within hours of Leonard's suicide attempt, Irene Brunn was called in to work on the case. She was the missing persons investigator working on the Cosner and Dubs disappearances. Although her office was closed when the call came in, Tom Eisenmann, who was on call, relayed a message to her. He briefed her by phone and suggested they meet at the office and head down to South San Francisco together.

Brunn was an interesting partner. She had already had four children before she got into policing in 1973. She had been working as a waitress at Mel's Drive-in, a car hop made famous by the movie *American Graffiti,* when a boyfriend, who was a cop, convinced her to write the police exam. She started out in the sheriff's department and later transferred over to the San Francisco police. Now she was a 45-year-old sergeant in the four-member missing persons bureau. Eisenmann, a child abuse investigator, had worked with her often enough to know that she often had hunches that paid off.

"She not only has women's intuition, but she picks out little things about people," he would rave. Eisenmann was a talker, Brunn a doer. While he yakked, Brunn would poke around. When she had sized up the situation, she asked direct and pointed questions. They were an odd couple, often in open disagreement, but respectful of each other's skills. Right now Eisenmann was going to have some talking to do. Brunn looked at her watch. He was late. It was 7:00 P.M. before he strolled in, flustered and apologetic. A chemical truck had overturned on the San Raphael Bridge, near San Quentin. He'd had to come in from his home in Novato, 25 miles north of the Golden Gate Bridge, the long way around over the San Francisco–Oakland Bay Bridge.

Twenty-five minutes later, they were down in South San Francisco being briefed by Wright and other detectives. Eisenmann drove the Honda back to San Francisco and parked it in a sealed room in the department's underground parking garage. Together he and Brunn did a quick inventory of the car. Three items caught their attention: a stun gun, photographs of seminude women and a Pacific Gas and Electric utilities bill for a residence near Wilseyville. Brunn was also interested in a black cap that was found in the car. She had seen a bank security camera photo of a man in a Greek fisherman's cap using the Dubs' bank card at an automatic teller.

It was late. The two officers prepared the car for an examination by the department's crime lab and contacted the on-call homicide inspector to ask if they should follow up on the utilities bill.

"Don't do anything more tonight," he said. "We'll see what develops tomorrow."

When Brunn and Eisenmann arrived at work on Monday, they arranged to meet Cricket and Leonard's sisters, Patty and Fern. Cricket assured the officers that Leonard could not have been involved in any illegal activity. She admitted she had property in Wilseyville but said no one was allowed to be there.

"We'd like to check to see if this Charles Ng is up there," Brunn explained.

"Well, it's very hard to find," Cricket replied. "I'll have to lead you there." Brunn and Eisenmann tried to press the issue, but Cricket insisted it was impossible. She couldn't make the trip today, but she would meet them in Wilseyville the following morning and guide them to the property. The two cops didn't like it, but they didn't have any evidence to suggest that Charlie was there or that it was the location of any illegal activity. Eisenmann called the Calaveras County sheriff's department and asked them to keep an eye on the place.

Charles Ng's attempt to steal this $75 vise led to his undoing.

Evidence found in murder victim Paul Cosner's car, which Leonard and Charlie were driving at the time of the petty theft, led to Leonard's suicide and Charlie's flight to Canada.

15

The Missing Pieces

I N 1806 a Spanish exploratory expedition venturing inland from the west coast came upon an ancient boneyard alongside a river in the Sierra Nevada foothills. They called the river *Rio de Las Calaveras,* or "River of Skulls." The name *Calaveras* was later applied to the entire county that stretched from the western foothills along the Stanislaus River from Poker Flats almost to the entrance of Ebbets Pass. To protect themselves from Indian attacks, the Spanish soldiers on that first expedition carried guns and lances and wore a five-inch thickness of sheepskin as primitive body armor.

Fear of the Indians residing in the foothills kept settlers away for some time. But eventually they came—Mexicans, Californians, Hawaiians and a mixture of Europeans—drifting in from the ocean or blown down from the mountains. They set up homesteads, scraping out a meager existence until gold fever swept through the county in the mid-1800s. The gold rush rocketed the population from a few hundred to more than 80,000 by the end of 1849.

The gold rush attracted adventurers and ragtag wanderers, but no one more famous than a shotgun-toting, poetry-writing stagecoach robber by the name of Black Bart. He robbed 29 Wells Fargo stagecoaches before he was captured and sentenced to six years in San Quentin. He was the stuff of legends, but he was only one of many. Books and articles about the mining camps by the likes of Mark Twain and Brett Harte shaped the world's perception of the Old West. Harte, who worked as a stagecoach messenger, wrote "Luck of the Roaring Camp" for the *Overland Monthly* while Twain penned "The Celebrated Jumping Frog of Calaveras County" about Angels Camp when he was 30 years old. The gold eventually ran out, as did the veins of quartz, silver and copper. But the county retained its affection for jumping frogs. Every spring crowds gather to watch 1,000 frogs hop at the Calaveras County fairgrounds.

It was in the wake of that annual event that Irene Brunn and Tom Eisenmann made the trek out from San Francisco. They had started out early in order to meet investigators from the Calaveras County sheriff's department in San Andreas before their 10:00 A.M. appointment with Cricket in Wilseyville. The 150-mile trip took close to three hours. They fought through heavy traffic east of the Bay area and then dodged in and out of the slow-moving farm vehicles on the narrow two-lane highways east of Stockton. As they passed through miles of blossoming orchards and vineyards, Brunn was thinking about a remark made by a veteran homicide inspector she had met in the Hall of Justice parking garage just before heading out. "Remember the Dubs," he had said. It seemed like a strange thing to say, but it made more sense the more she thought about it. Maybe he had something. Both Paul Cosner and the Dubs family disappeared after placing advertisements in the *Chronicle.* There was the hat found in Cosner's car that was similar to the hat worn by someone using the Dubs' bank card. An Asian man had been involved in the Dubs' case, and now they were looking for an Asian man in connection with the Cosner vehicle.

"Do you think the Chinese man in the Dubs' case could be the same Chinese man we're looking for in the Cosner case?" she asked Eisenmann.

"There's got to be billions of Chinese people in the world, including thousands in the Bay area," he responded. "What are the mathematical odds it could be the same guy? I don't think so."

Northeast of Stockton they could see the mountains low on the horizon, the snowcapped peaks glistening white in the California sunshine. The tabletop terrain gradually grew hilly, and the roadway began to bob and twist along sunburned ridges and through grassy brown valleys spotted with small clusters of scrub oak. They were climbing continuously now. The little engine of the department's high-mileage pool car was forced to work harder as the incline steepened. The vegetation was thicker at the higher altitude. Toyon and Manzanita shrubs greened up the brown hillsides. Oak and ponderosa pines crowded up against the edge of the pavement, occasionally forming a dense canopy over the road, blocking out the sun and plunging the interior of the little car into shadow. Calaveras County often reminded people of the Tennyson line about the place where it always seemed like midafternoon.

The two cops rolled into San Andreas in plenty of time to brief the sheriff's department, which had its offices in a new court and justice building on the outskirts of town. They met Calaveras Deputy Sheriff Norm Varain and Detective Steve Mathews, who would accompany them to Wilseyville. All they had was the Pacific Gas and Electric bill suggesting someone was living up there, but as far as leads went, it wasn't much. Still, it had to be checked out.

It took the better part of an hour to make the kidney-pounding 30-mile trip to Wilseyville on a narrow road that twisted through dense stands of pine. Here and there, a deer stood frozen on the edge of the pavement. Most of the homes and farms were set well back from the road, screened from view by trees and shrubs, and protected by locked iron gates across the dirt driveways. People in Calaveras County appeared to value their privacy, Eisenmann mused. It seemed odd to see so much security in such a sparsely populated area. The entire 1,200-square mile county boasted only 20,000 people, and most of them lived in the bigger towns to the south and west.

The locals couldn't have been worried about the tourists, Eisenmann concluded. There was little to bring people to Wilseyville. The county was home to Big Trees Park, with 2,000-year-old giant sequoias stretching more than 300' into the sky and numerous caves that had been commercially developed, but Wilseyville was on a road to nowhere. Unless they planned on camping at Schaad's Resort, a tiny campsite on the middle fork of the Mokelumne River, there wasn't anything to bring tourists this way. The pavement petered out in the Stanislaus National Forest only a few miles beyond the town—if you could call it that. It certainly wasn't a town in the normal sense of the word. There wasn't a road that could be called main street—just a scattering of barely visible cabins along a couple of intersecting roads. You could easily miss it.

The community had been built in 1944 by the Blagen Lumber Company, back when commercial logging fueled the economy. When the mill closed in 1967, many of the mill workers purchased the company homes they had been renting and stayed. Some retired and others picked up what work they could, often commuting a considerable distance to keep themselves employed. About 600 people remained in the area, but most resided in and around West Point, a neighboring derelict community on Highway 26, about two miles up the road.

The majority of Wilseyville's homes were tiny ramshackle cottages, heated solely with firewood dragged indoors from towering piles in the yards. At 3,000' above sea level, the winter often brought snow to this end of the county, and it took a heap of wood to ward off the chill. Locals joked that you could take another man's woman, but you wouldn't dare touch his woodpile. The community—made up of hound dogs, Vietnam vets, old bikers, burned out hippies, unemployed mill workers and prospectors—had a hillbilly flavor. Gun racks in the back of beat-up pickups. Cars up on blocks in front of houses. The deputies who patrolled the community jokingly referred to the partially dismantled vehicles as condos. But the people here were a likeable lot for the most part. If the deputies hauled them off to jail for being drunk, they drove them home the next day in their own vehicles rather than a patrol car to save their dignity. This mutual respect allowed deputies to work alone, knowing if someone took a run at them, they would be taking on half the town. Loyalties ran deep.

Brunn and Eisenmann were to meet Cricket at the Wilseyville General Store, which was located with the post office in a flag-draped white house off by itself near the intersection of Rail Road Flat and Blizzard Mine roads.

At one time it had been the company store, what the locals called the commissary. Leonard had often set up shop in the shade of a couple of old oak trees on the corner to sell the goods he had pilfered from his victims. Cricket was not at the store when the investigators arrived, but she breezed in with Leonard Lake's mother, Gloria Ebeling, shortly after 10:00 A.M. The cabin, as it turned out, was only four miles from the store, just off Blue Mountain Road, where it intersected with the road into Schaad's Resort.

"It wouldn't have been that hard to find at all with the proper directions," muttered Brunn, wondering why Cricket had been so insistent on accompanying them to the house. They pulled up to a locked metal gate and walked about 300 yards up the shaded lane until they reached a fork. Up the lane on the left they could see a yellow two-bedroom cabin built on a hillside.

"It's this way," Cricket said as she led the officers toward it. "The other road leads to the old Carter house."

They had to skirt around a couple of wrecked vehicles in the driveway. Eisenmann noted a bumper sticker on the old blue Plymouth: "If you love something, set it free. If it doesn't come back, hunt it down and kill it." Parked nearby was a disabled silver 1980 Honda Civic, which appeared to have been cannibalized for parts. A damaged gray Chevy pickup truck with the license plate AHOYMTY was parked alone off to the side. In the carport was a stack of dollies with the name Dennis Moving stenciled on them.

The cabin was empty, but it appeared to have been left in immaculate condition. It's almost too clean, thought Brunn.

While Eisenmann chatted up Cricket and Gloria in the kitchen, Brunn wandered around the house. She was in the living room, taking in the colorful wall mural and the potbellied wood stove, when she found herself staring at the video equipment in an adjacent wall unit. There was something astonishingly familiar about it. Then she remembered where she had seen it before. The Hybrid 8 special effects generator and the Sony cassette deck matched the list and the photographs that Harvey Dubs had so meticulously kept.

"Holy shit!" Brunn exclaimed aloud. Immediately, she realized she had blown it. Cricket, looking up in alarm, suggested that perhaps the police officers had better leave.

"I think this has gone far enough," Cricket insisted.

"Just a minute," said Brunn. She whispered into Varain's ear, explaining what she had seen. "I want to check this out." She phoned her office in San Francisco and asked a detective to pull the Dubs' file. The serial number on the generator had been removed, but the serial number on the cassette deck was a match. Varain suggested the investigators return to San Andreas to obtain a search warrant. They now had evidence to warrant a full-scale search of the property. He advised Cricket what they were planning.

Police would secure the property to make sure nothing was removed, he explained. Eisenmann and Mathews stayed behind with Cricket and Gloria while Brunn and Varain went into town to brief District Attorney John Martin. It was about noon when Brunn presented sworn oral evidence to County Court Judge Douglas Mewhinney to obtain a search warrant for the cabin and property. He questioned her about her evidence, then, satisfied, signed the warrant.

Out at the cabin Eisenmann tried to convince Cricket to ask the phone company to turn over the phone records from the cabin to the police. Investigators could get them through a search warrant, but it would be helpful if she asked for them herself, he explained. Cricket showed no interest in being helpful. Rebuffed, Eisenmann made small talk with Gloria. Inadvertently, he referred to Leonard as deceased. Gloria burst into tears. Sobbing, she explained that doctors had asked for permission to take Leonard off life support, but she hadn't made her decision yet. It was painful because Leonard was likely the only son she had left. She feared her other boy, Donald, might also be dead. Eisenmann's ears pricked up as Gloria told him about Donald's disappearance. The cop immediately wondered if perhaps Cain slew Abel. They talked awhile longer. Gloria explained to the amiable investigator that she had come up to the cabin the night before to do some housekeeping before the police arrived. "We wanted to clean the place up and make it presentable," she said.

Eisenmann was flabbergasted. What the hell is going on here? he wondered. This sounds a lot like disposing of evidence.

By midafternoon the two women got tired of waiting for the others to return and left. Eisenmann and Mathews seized the opportunity to look around. They spotted a number of things they hadn't noticed previously. The holes in the bedroom doorframe appeared to be bullet holes, as did other holes in the ceiling. A maroon stain that looked like blood was on the ceiling above the bed in the master bedroom. On a corner shelf near the ceiling in the bedroom, Eisenmann found clear plastic capsules containing what he suspected was cyanide.

Behind the house, there appeared to be fresh dirt covering a narrow 50' trench that ran uphill toward the road. A piece of plywood covered a portion of the trench. When the officers lifted the plywood, they saw a stream of ants coming to the surface, carrying tiny white larvae in their mouths.

"Those are maggot eggs," Mathews explained to Eisenmann. "It means there's something dead under there."

Later, when the search team arrived with the warrant, they began a methodical examination of the home, yard and bunker. They had barely begun when a police dog, which had been allowed out of the dog handler's vehicle to relieve itself, recovered what looked to be a human bone. No one had seen where the dog had found it, but a closer examination of a half dozen 10' diameter burn sites turned up small bits of bones and teeth, a shell casing, and handcuffs. It appeared the burn areas had been raked clean of larger debris and the ashes had been scattered in the woods. Before long investigators found what appeared to be a baby's charred liver and part of a human vertebrae. Everywhere they looked they found human remains.

"There hasn't been anything like this since the Nazi death camps," observed County Sheriff Claud Ballard. The 60-year-old sheriff was beside himself. It appalled him that something like this had gone on during his watch.

He was anxious to check out the 16' x 20' bunker. There was only one entrance, which opened into a workshop, complete with a workbench, shelving and tools. Saws, levels, pliers, wrenches, hammers—all stacked on the workbench or hanging from pegs on the wall. One officer spotted a leather handcuff case and two blood-stained rolls of duct tape.

When it became apparent that the outside dimensions of the bunker were significantly larger than the interior, the officers began to look for a secret compartment. A few workshop items rested on shelves mounted on the wall, but there was no doorway or entrance visible. The investigators probed deeper. They stripped away the insulation on the left-hand side of the wall to discover that the entire 4' x 2' piece of plywood sheeting holding up the shelves was mounted on hinges. They cleaned off the shelves and removed a couple of screws and the plywood sheet swung open to reveal an entrance to another large room. It was very dark inside.

Flicking on a flashlight, they entered. It was dank and musty and cool. The flashlight beam splashed across the room, revealing a bed, a closet, a desk and a filing cabinet. It was a makeshift living quarters. One officer found a light switch and snapped it on. Investigators saw a closet filled with camouflage clothing. Among the military apparel was a shirt and a baseball cap bearing the label "Dennis Moving Services"—the company where they now knew Charles Ng had worked. On the wall was a wooden plaque with an inscription entitled "The Warrior Creed." It read, "For those who thrive on the challenge of competition, whose being is intensified by impossible tasks and insurmountable odds, who even at the risk of defeat, will enter the arena in the quest for victory."

In the corner near the entrance was a heavy door that opened into a smaller room. It was more like a cell, roughly 3 ½' x 6 ½'. The hinges on the door had been bent outward, seemingly by someone on the inside straining to get out. The cell was Spartan—a platform bed, a five-gallon pail for a toilet, a roll of toilet paper. A limited selection of women's toiletry items—makeup and perfume—rested on a shelf. The officers discovered that the mirror in the cell was actually a one-way glass window that enabled the captors to spy on their captives. *What the hell is this?* wondered Eisenmann. *Some sort of torture chamber? Keeping someone locked up in the dark is sensory deprivation.*

In the cabin investigators noticed holes drilled in the corner posts of the bed in the master bedroom. In a dresser they found eye-bolts that screwed into the holes, obviously for tying captives on the bed. In the spare bedroom officers found a stack of padded blankets like those used by moving companies and a white shirt with the name "Dennis Moving Services" stamped on the pocket. It was sure looking like Charles Ng had been around.

When police began excavating the trench, they found the river of skulls all over again. Under the plywood where Eisenmann had seen the ants, they uncovered the skeletal remains of a black man in a tan three-piece corduroy suit. Most of the flesh had rotted, but the man's Afro hairstyle had remained intact. Police later identified the body as Maurice Rock, the musician who had disappeared from the Pink Palace the previous autumn. One foot had been partially exposed above ground, and some of the bones had been removed by animals. At the foot of the first grave, officers located a second black male whose body also was severely decomposed. Police suspected it was the man known as John Lacey, but they couldn't make a positive identification. Lacey had been the Pink Palace roommate of Sheryl Okoro, who also was missing. Both men had been struck with a pickax, and the man police believed was Lacey had been shot in the head with a small caliber gun. A pathologist later found the .22 caliber slug inside the skull.

Several days later investigators discovered the body of a third Pink Palace resident, Randy Vern Jacobson, buried beneath a chicken coop and doghouse. He had been poisoned with cyanide.

Eisenmann stayed in Calaveras to help with the investigation. He was assigned to sift through the soil and ashes in the trench. The shallow ditch had been originally excavated to bury the telephone line. Leonard and Charlie had used it to bury their victims and practically everything else that would be damning. Starting at the summit of a hill at the far end of the trench and working back toward the house, the investigators sifted through layers of dust, ash, bones, personal property, charred men and women's clothing, jewelry, perfume, tools and empty shell casings. Eisenmann used a small trowel and a bug screen to strain the earth, sifting out adult and baby teeth, fillings and buttons. The sheer magnitude of the killings was becoming more evident by the hour.

The meticulous work was tedious and backbreaking under the scorching sun. The officers drank gallons of water to replace the fluids they were sweating out in buckets and took salt tablets to prevent cramps caused by dehydration. They soon tired of the county jail's baloney sandwiches and of the long exhausting hours, practically from sunrise to sunset. Their golf tournament was cancelled. All vacations were off. Any officers on the 35-member force who were not digging at the site had to work longer hours to cover for those who were.

When the day crew went home, the night shift came on. Deputy Sheriff Mitch Hrdlicka babysat the property at night. It was an unsettling job for there was still a chance Charlie might return. Hrdlicka didn't like to think about the possibility. He made patrols around the perimeter, periodically checking the bunker and the grounds. But mostly he just sat out the long nights in the silent, darkened house, thinking about the evil that had erupted there. He started at every unusual sound, bristling when the oscillating fan would set the curtains rustling or a piece of paper fluttering to the floor. He hated every minute of it. The dawn never came fast enough.

Eisenmann was still on the scene two days later. It was another scorcher, close to 100 degrees. He took a break from his digging and sifting duties and ambled over to the ice cooler to fetch a Coke. The department had brought in a road crew and grader to remove a few inches of topsoil in the yard. Eisenmann wandered by to chat with the crew's foreman. As they stood beside the driveway making small talk, the foreman suddenly glanced at the ground below his foot with a look of surprise.

"There's a soft spot here," he told Eisenmann. He pushed down hard with his heel and made a deep indentation in the earth, but when he removed his foot, the ground popped back up. He'd been digging in the earth for many years, and he'd never seen it do that before. "There's something buried in here," he insisted.

The two men scraped away a couple of inches of topsoil and found themselves staring at the top of a five-gallon plastic pail. They summoned the others. One ran over with a video camera. Another popped off the lid.

"So that's where the videotapes are," Eisenmann muttered. They had seen the video equipment and the photographs Leonard had taken, photos of 20 young women in various poses mounted on the wall in the bunker. They had no idea if the women pictured were alive or dead. Now they wondered if they had unearthed snuff films. The pail also contained two hand-written and typed journals, dated 1983 and 1984. The typewritten forward was dated October 12, 1983. It began:

> Without question, this journal is dull. There are two main reasons for this: 1) My life is pretty dull. One day in 30 I am lucky something interesting, exciting and/or profitable happens. The rest of the days are just the basics of staying alive. 2) This book is really more of a log. It records what I do. . . . If anyone wonders why the term "abridged" is used, it is simply a bit of self-preservation. The depth of my sins are not recorded.

Also in the pail were several photo albums, including one of nude and seminude women.

The discovery prompted police to direct the grader to peel back the earth alongside the driveway to unearth more buried evidence. About 20' from the first find, they located another buried bucket containing another videotape and a number of envelopes taken from the Philo Motel. In an envelope labeled "Me," police found the driver's license, social security card and birth certificate for Leonard Lake. In an envelope marked "Randy," they found Randy Jacobson's driver's license. In an envelope marked "Kathi," they found an assortment of identification for Kathleen Elizabeth Allen and Michael Sean Carroll, including their driver's licenses, social security cards and some bankcards. Also in the pail were blank checks in the name of R. Scott Stapely and identification for Maurice Rock.

The investigators watched the three tapes that night in San Andreas, scarcely able to believe what they had found. One tape showed Leonard having dinner with his family the previous Easter at his mother's home in San Bruno. The second, labeled "M," was much more interesting. It featured Leonard sitting comfortably in a big easy chair, telling them all about Operation Miranda and his plan to enslave women.

They listened to him with jaws gaping. "The purpose of that cell and the main purpose, hence, of the building will be the imprisonment of a young lady," Leonard nonchalantly informed them through the miracle of video. "So having secret rooms—underground rooms protected by concrete and steel and buried by four feet of earth—these are fairly safe investments. The building and the whole of the ultimate series of buildings will not be designed around the cell, but ultimately around the concept of a secret, secure living place for myself and perhaps for friends. But this first phase," Leonard continued, "well, it would be a lie to say it was anything other than a cell."

The third tape, labeled "M Ladies—Kathi and Brenda," was shocking. While it didn't depict physical torture, and it wasn't the snuff tape they were dreading, it showed the gut-wrenching horror of two women as they were confronted with their fate: either submit to rape and slavery or die. The officers watched the videos in silence, dumbfounded. They were shocked but at the same time thrilled to discover the hard evidence, evidence like nothing they had ever seen before. Charlie was shown slashing the T-shirt and bra off one of the captive women and marching her off to the shower under the threat of death. The tapes would be powerful evidence for a jury. But it was a somber crew of investigators who retired to the lounge at the Black Bart Inn that night. They were haunted by the video images. Some of the victims now had faces and voices. They were no longer bits of bone.

On the third day media swarmed the cabin site, thundering overhead in a flock of helicopters and unleashing a deafening windstorm upon the investigators on their knees in the red earth below. Sheriff Ballard told the media about the videotapes and what he thought they had found. In his usual perfunctory style, he didn't mince words. He was visibly shaken as he described the scene in which a young woman is heard begging for her baby. "It's like a horror film—vicious, vicious, vicious," said Ballard, a career law officer who was serving his sixth year as county sheriff. "I've been in law enforcement for 27 years, and I have seen a lot of terrible things, but nothing like this."

Police in San Francisco executed a search warrant on the basement apartment Charlie had rented at 136 Lenox Way. Inside the cramped quarters they discovered a stash of .22 caliber and 9 mm ammunition, pistol grips and other firearms parts. A closet was stuffed with camouflage uniforms and survival gear, rolls of duct tape and mercenary magazines. In the center drawer of a black desk along the south wall, they found a credit card issued to Lonnie Bond and a Cross pen and pencil set engraved with the initials of Clifford Peranteau. In a letter rack on the floor near Charlie's bed, they found a transit map of San Francisco. Yukon Street, the tiny street on which the Dubs had resided, had been circled in ink. And in a cardboard box beneath the desk, investigators found a dozen videotapes belonging to the Dubs. The labels were inscribed in Harvey's handwriting. Police painstakingly reviewed every tape they found at Charlie's place. It was only by accident when rewinding a movie called *Taboo* that they made an important discovery. At the very beginning of the tape, a macabre real-life scene flashed on the screen. The detectives watched it over and over again to confirm their first impression. What they saw were two bodies, stiff with rigor mortis, in a blue wheelbarrow. Obviously, the killers had taped the burial of two victims and then retaped a movie over the original footage. Police painstakingly checked every other video. On another they saw a split-second glimpse of Kathi Allen.

Investigators were now wrapped up in a macabre game of connect the dots. They had tons of evidence but few bodies. Where were the Dubs family, Peranteau, Jeff Gerald, Charles Gunnar, Donald Lake, Sheryl Okoro, Kathi Allen, Mike Carroll, Brenda O'Connor, Lonnie Bond and Scott Stapely? Normally, police find a body and track down the killer. Leonard and Charlie had turned the tables on them. Police knew they were linked to at least a dozen deaths, but they had yet to find the bodies. They had no evidence to link the bodies they had found to Charlie while the list of missing people with connections to Leonard was growing daily. "Every time this guy met somebody, they wound up gone," remarked a Calaveras County deputy sheriff.

Police got a break a few weeks later when several investigators took a leisurely drive down an old logging road during a noon-hour break. They just wanted to get away from the stink of death. But they hadn't gone very far down the dirt trail when they spotted debris and a mound of fresh dirt on a logged out hillside. Coyotes had unearthed the corner of a sleeping bag and with it another body. It seemed death was everywhere.

The officers returned with San Francisco medical examiner Boyd Stephens, who began to dig carefully through the red soil that was famous throughout the county. Before long he unearthed a blue sleeping bag.

A man's body had been jammed headfirst into the bag. He was dressed in jeans, a shirt and an undershirt. A green plastic garbage bag had been pulled over his head. His hands had been cuffed behind his back, his legs bound with rope, and a gag, consisting of a leather strap and a red rubber ball, had been placed in his mouth. He had been shot in the head with a single .22 caliber bullet. Stephens later identified the man as Leonard's neighbor, Lonnie Bond Senior.

Directly beneath the blue sleeping bag, Stephens found a green sleeping bag containing the body of Scott Stapely. His feet and hands had been bound with duct tape, and he also had been gagged. He had been shot four times, above the right eyebrow, in the mouth, in the right upper shoulder and in the lower right leg. From the position and angle of the wounds, Stephens theorized that he had been on the move when he was shot.

Police were now convinced that many of the people whose names had surfaced at the site were dead. Many had been reported missing within the past year, or their current whereabouts were unknown. The list included Stapely, the three members of the Dubs family, Paul Cosner, Bond, as well as Bond's common-law wife and child. Police told reporters that as many as 25 people could have died at the hands of Leonard Lake and Charles Ng. California already had its Skid Row Slasher, its Zodiac Killer, its Charles Manson, its Juan Corona, its Hillside Strangler and its Freeway Killer. It now could add the Motherlode Murderers to the state's infamous list of mass killers.

Several weeks after the excavation of human remains had begun, police found another pail on a site about three miles away from the cabin that contained Paul Cosner's driver's license and the gun police believe was used to kill him. The identification was in a Philo Motel envelope marked with the name *Cosner*. In the trench near the cabin, they had found the sun visor from the passenger seat of his car. It was punctured with a bullet hole. A corresponding bullet hole existed in the right front headliner. Police recovered two .22 caliber bullets that appeared to have been fired from a Ruger pistol. A police crime scene expert used a chemical on the car to reveal blood spatter marks on the headrest and shoulder area of the right front passenger seat. They also found a bullet hole in the paneling of the passenger side door. From the angle of the shots and the location of the spatter marks, police deduced that Cosner had been shot from behind while sitting in the passenger seat of his car, presumably while Leonard Lake was giving it a test drive. It looked like Charlie had been the backseat trigger man.

By this time Leonard had been removed from life support and was dead. But for a while he lived on in the tales of horror told by his former neighbors. Residents marveled at their near brushes with death. Young women who posed for him attired in camouflage clothes while brandishing machine guns related how weird he seemed. A woman who had made his drapes talked about how he wanted to hire her for other work but how something made her decline the job. A youth who was hired to dig trenches at the cabin arrived at the site with his mother to direct police to more possible gravesites. An old man who once picked up Leonard hitchhiking recalled him muttering about how a woman had driven by earlier without stopping and how it was his lot in life that no self-respecting woman would have anything to do with him. Everyone was outraged that the scripture-reading Charles Gunnar was really Leonard Lake, a cold-blooded murderer who had turned their community into his personal killing field.

Back in San Francisco, Cricket was facing heat from the district attorney's office and from the media for her late-night visit to the Wilseyville cabin. Just what evidence had she removed from the cabin? Were there more videotapes? And where was Leonard's 1985 journal? Cricket dismissed her behavior as an error in judgment. She maintained she had gone to the cabin to retrieve personal photos and sex videos only.

Police now knew she had used the Dubs' credit card in restaurants on at least two occasions. She also had some of Kathi Allen's jewelry. When police searched Cricket's home, they found Kathi's floating heart chain and the size-four wedding ring her mother had given her. They also discovered an assortment of whips and sexual aids. Sheriff Ballard informed the media that he considered her a suspect in the murders. Cricket was urged to return any items taken from the cabin and to cooperate fully. If she did the state was willing to grant her immunity from the fraud-related offenses.

Publicly, Cricket rejected any notion that Leonard Lake was a killer. "The only time he has hunted down and killed people was when he was in the marines," she told reporters. But privately she told San Francisco homicide investigators Ed Erdelatz and Jeff Brosch that Leonard had told her Charlie had killed Don Giuletti, the gay disc jockey, and that he had admitted kidnapping the Dubs and prostitute Sheryl Okoro. She also knew about the bunker, the cell and its purpose, and was able to describe it to investigators.

"What was the cell used for?" Erdelatz asked her.

"Apparently for Leonard to keep someone in."

"Did you ever question Leonard about it?"

"No, I didn't like to think about him doing such things," she replied. "It disturbed me." But she admitted Leonard had told her about Okoro and her black pimp. He said he had made an arrangement to have Okoro for a while, but when they stopped for gasoline on the way to the cabin, he drove off without the pimp. He told her he drugged Okoro so she didn't know where she was.

"He said he had his way with her for several days," Cricket told the investigators. "He said he had sex with her, had his way with her, had handcuffed her, had done what he wanted with her, and even though it might have been—I don't know—painful or severe, she said she didn't mind. I have seen a photograph of her."

Cricket admitted she had used Okoro's name when she participated in a pornographic video and in correspondence with the buyer of the video.

All Leonard had told her about the Dubs, she said, was that he had been hired by someone to kidnap them and had delivered them to others.

"He also said that they had given him a choice of giving him a sum of money or being able to empty the people's apartment," she explained. "Because Leonard liked video equipment, he decided to take that option. Charles Ng helped him."

Cricket also confirmed to investigators that Charlie and Leonard had sexually assaulted an escort from an escort service. Leonard had told her that Charlie had cut the crotch out of the woman's pantyhose and had stabbed the bed with a knife while he raped her. "He apparently was into frightening women—threatening them," she said. "Maybe it helped him sexually, I don't know."

"Did you ever feel that Leonard was going to take your life," asked Brosh.

"No."

"Ever feel threatened?"

"No."

Erdelatz asked Cricket if Charlie was homosexual or bisexual.

"All the time he ever spoke, it was about women. He had dirty pictures of women. He spoke of . . . uh . . . in my words, making love to his pillow while looking at pictures of women."

The police officers asked Cricket if Charlie was involved in sexual activity with Charles Gunnar's children. She didn't think so.

"He may have had photographs," she added. "He seemed to be fascinated by a young girl's blooming body. In some of his photo albums, you will find a particular girl that he followed as she matured, and he was fascinated with how a child turned into a woman. This one girl, he particularly got it on photographs—chronologically."

Cricket gave police possible locations where Leonard may have buried additional evidence: the Greenfield Ranch commune, where he had lived, the 40-acre Indian Creek ranch, where they were living when Charlie was arrested by the FBI, and the house he rented near Garberville. She returned some of the tapes she admitted removing from the cabin, including one showing her and Leonard discussing a burglary they committed together. The tape also showed them discussing Leonard's Miranda Operation. But mere knowledge of a crime wasn't a criminal offense. Police couldn't determine to what extent Cricket had been involved in Miranda.

If Cricket was in touch with Charlie, she wasn't saying. Police knew Charlie had contacted a San Francisco gun shop from Chicago to ask them to ship him an Uzi submachine gun that had been in the shop for repairs. The store had refused to ship the gun to the alias he provided in care of general delivery, advising him they could only ship the gun to a reputable gun dealer, where he could then go to pick up the weapon. He declined. After five days in Chicago, Charlie drove to Detroit with his friend's brother, David Diaz, and crossed the bridge to the Canadian city of Windsor, Ontario. Police tracked him to the small city of Chatham, where he and Diaz parted company. They believed Charlie had hopped a bus to Toronto and had disappeared among its huge Asian community.

The Royal Canadian Mounted Police and Interpol joined the hunt for Charlie, alias Richard Charles Lee and Michael Kimoto. The FBI circulated two photographs of Charlie with the warning that he was believed to be armed: "Extreme caution should be used as subject indicates that he will not be taken alive."

Welcome sign for Calaveras County, which took its name from the river the Spanish called Rio de Las Calaveras, *or "River of Skulls."*

Inspector Ed Erdelatz of the San Francisco police department, the first main investigator on the Charles Ng case.

L–R: Mitch Hrdlicka, District Attorney Investigator for Calaveras County; Carol Waxman, Victim Witness Counselor for Orange County; Inspector Irene Brunn, missing persons unit for the San Francisco police department; John Crawford, District Attorney Investigator for Calaveras County.

L–R: Lieutenant Ron McFall and Undersheriff Randy Garsmuck, both of the Calaveras County sheriff's department; Mitch Hrdlicka, District Attorney Investigator for Calaveras County; Peter Smith, District Attorney for Calaveras County; Carol Waxman, Victim Witness Counselor for Orange County; Inspector Irene Brunn, missing persons unit for the San Francisco police department; John Crawford, District Attorney Investigator for Calaveras County.

16

In the Slammer

Locked in a Calgary police service holding cell, Charlie sat with his head bowed, feeling sorry for himself. He never should have been caught. He never should have given up his gun—even though the policeman had nearly broken his thumb prying the Ruger out of his grasp. Even when they handcuffed his hands behind his back and shoved him into the patrol car, he hadn't quit. He had tried to get at the handcuff key in his jean pocket. But there hadn't been time. They were at the station in a couple of minutes, and the police found the key.

He was a beaten man now and thoroughly humiliated. He had defecated during the struggle with the Bay security guards, and the police had left him to sit in his soiled underwear. Maybe Leonard had been right to kill himself, he thought.

Charlie's long run from justice had sapped him physically, emotionally and financially. The last week had been the worst. He had called his sister collect from Chatham, begging tearfully for help, but she hadn't been very encouraging. Alice had urged him to give himself up. But Charlie had hopped a Greyhound to make the 2,000-mile bus trip to Calgary, hoping she would change her mind when he arrived at her door.

Charlie was down to his last ten dollars when the bus rolled into Calgary, but he was still afraid to approach his sister. He couldn't have known police had been there for most of the previous week. They had staked out the house from a white van parked up the street. It was Charlie's good fortune that they had called off the surveillance team just days before his arrival. But his luck hadn't held.

The security guards who caught him shoplifting at the Bay store had no idea what they had latched on to. If he had managed to get his gunhand free, they wouldn't have lived to tell about it. But he hadn't. And they did.

Now he was finished. He was so ashamed. What was there to live for? A date with the gas chamber in California? Well, screw that. He slipped out of his soiled briefs and fashioned them into a noose.

A constable at the back counter raised the alarm. Jerry Salinger had been doing paperwork when a movement on the security camera monitor caught his eye. He looked up to see a naked man tying a piece of cloth to the bars near the ceiling of the cell. Salinger's cry brought the arresting officers running. When they burst into the holding area, Charlie stepped down quickly and resumed his seat on the bench. He said nothing as they untied his shorts from the bars and left the cell. He kept his head down, eyes averted, mouth shut.

While Charlie sat in stoic silence, police went through the supplies he was carrying when arrested: two pistol clips with nine rounds in each, a wallet containing $10, a handcuff pouch and handcuffs, gloves, a ski mask, a knife and a pouch containing about 50 loose rounds of ammunition. A very lethal arsenal. The cops wondered when he had been planning to use it and on whom.

They pulled him into a police interview room a couple of hours later and asked him a few general questions to confirm that he was who they thought he was. Calgary police detectives Barry Whistlecraft and Peter Jobbins had been tipped off by RCMP in June that Charlie might be headed their way. Whistlecraft, an 18-year veteran who had been called in on his day off, studied the pitiful character slumped in the chair in front of him with his head in his hands. The guy was probably relieved to be captured, he thought. He looked whipped.

"Do you know why you are here?" Whistlecraft began.

"Yes."

"For shooting a guard at the Bay?"

"Yes."

"You have been identified as Charles Ng, who has been in the newspapers. Is that you?"

Charlie didn't reply.

"You are wanted with a Leonard Lake for a series of murders in California, right?" Again there was no reply. Charlie mumbled something the detectives couldn't hear. "Did you know Leonard Lake?" asked Whistlecraft.

"Yes."

"How long have you been in Calgary?"

"A few days."

"Where have you been staying?"

"Nowhere."

"Where is nowhere?"

"The street."

"Where did you stay in San Francisco?"

"I rented a garage from a Chinese couple at 136 Lenox."

Whistlecraft was now fairly certain they had the right guy, but he asked a few questions about Charlie's employer to cinch it for California investigators. He quizzed Charlie about his salary and his boss's name. He didn't ask anything about the killings; he didn't want to screw up the California case. Charlie answered politely until Whistlecraft mistakenly called him Tony, mixing him up with another Hong Kong–born fugitive who had recently been arrested in Calgary and extradited on mass murder charges. Tony Ng had been accused of gunning down 13 people in a Seattle gambling club. He was found by immigration officials hiding out in Calgary during a routine sweep of Chinatown.

"My name's not Tony," Charlie snapped.

"Sorry, Charles," the detective apologized. Then he added, "Some people from California will be coming to talk to you."

Charlie was photographed, taken before a bail magistrate and transferred to the Calgary Remand Centre, the downtown holding facility for prisoners awaiting trial. The paperwork was stamped Saturday, July 6, 1985.

The California cops arrived at noon the following day with about 60 journalists in tow. Whistlecraft picked up San Francisco homicide inspector Ed Erdelatz and Calaveras Deputy Sheriff Norm Varain at the airport and whisked them over to the Remand Centre. Charlie, clad in green prison coveralls, was wearing leg-irons and handcuffs when he was escorted into the small interview room where the three detectives waited. Whistlecraft sat in a chair in a corner. Charlie sat across from Varain and Erdelatz at the table. He sat silent and guarded with eyes downcast. He didn't appear to want to talk to them. Erdelatz had expected as much. He had been running his questions over and over in his mind on the flight. After introducing the officers and reading Charlie his rights, Erdelatz informed Charlie that Leonard had told police all about him. He said police now had the video-tapes and that Cricket was cooperating. The news seemed to get Charlie's attention.

"What did she say?" Charlie appeared to be alert now, but he still wouldn't make eye contact. From the corner of the room Whistlecraft watched, almost in awe, as Erdelatz went to work on him. He didn't raise his voice or pound his fist. He was courteous. But he made an immediate connection with the suspect. He knew how to push all the right buttons. Man, this guy is smooth, Whistlecraft told himself. This guy is really, really good at what he does.

Erdelatz and Varain spent the next two hours laying out the case to Charlie. This is what we've got, they told him. They showed Charlie the transcripts of the videotape and photos of the victims. Then Erdelatz lowered the hammer. "What did you do with the babies? Where are the babies? Did you kill any babies?" Erdelatz stayed on the subject, hammering away, convinced he had struck a raw nerve. Charlie had to respond.

Erdelatz, whose father once coached the Oakland Raiders, had 14 years on homicide, 28 years in total on the force. It wasn't unusual for him to be handling four homicides in a week. Lately, he had been putting in 17-hour days on the Ng task force. When Charlie started talking, he suppressed a smile. He didn't care that Charlie denied killing the babies. Once Charlie started lying, he would eventually trip himself up. Sometimes, in a circumstantial case like this one, contradictions were almost as good as confessions.

Once Charlie started talking, Erdelatz asked him about the killing of Paul Cosner. At first Charlie claimed Leonard Lake bought Paul's car from a fence, but eventually he admitted he had been involved. He claimed he had been waiting on a nearby side street when Leonard took the car for a test drive. Leonard picked him up after killing Paul Cosner, he said. To explain the bullet holes in the car's headrest and door, he concocted a story about Leonard reaching back from the driver's seat to shoot Paul from behind.

"He was dead when I first saw him," Charlie claimed. "I helped Leonard put the body in the trunk."

Charlie said they went to Paul's apartment and grabbed two guns but left without taking anything else when the telephone rang. He told the California cops that Leonard gave the guns to Cricket's father to sell at a flea market. Charlie said he and Leonard drove to Calaveras, dragged Paul's body through the rainy dark night and dropped it into a 4' – 5' deep grave. Leonard was going to go back later to conceal the grave, Charlie said.

When asked about the Dubs' disappearance, Charlie again put all the blame on Leonard. He said his only involvement with the family was when he removed some items from their home. He said Leonard initially told him not to ask what happened to the family but later admitted killing them. Leonard, he said, went to the Dubs' Yukon Street house claiming to want to rent their video camera for a wedding. Then he pulled a gun on Harvey Dubs, handcuffed him and drugged him. When it got dark Leonard dragged Harvey out to his van and forced Debbie to carry the baby, promising to release them after using their credit cards. Charlie said Leonard admitted strangling the two adults and burying them in holes he had dug previously. He said Leonard never explained what happened to the baby. Charlie told the cops that Leonard gave Cricket the Dubs' credit card.

Erdelatz then asked about the shooting of the gay disc jockey and his roommate. Charlie claimed to know nothing about the shootings. He also denied knowing what happened to Charles Gunnar. All Leonard told him the day he arrived back in California, he insisted, was that "Charles Gunnar is no longer with us."

Charlie admitted luring his co-workers Jeff Gerald and Cliff Peranteau into the country to be killed, but he claimed Leonard did the killing. Charlie had little to say about Mike Carroll and his girl friend, Kathi Allen. He admitted he knew Carroll from serving time with him in Leavenworth but claimed not to know what happened to him. He said he saw Kathi at the Wilseyville cabin, but didn't know what happened to her either. He said Leonard told him he "took her for a walk."

Charlie told Erdelatz and Varain that Leonard had shot both Lonnie Bond and Scott Stapely at Bond's cabin, but that he had helped drag the bodies out. "I told him, 'If you want to kill the baby, make sure he don't suffer,'" Charlie told the police officers. He said Leonard put the baby's head between his legs and twisted the body. Police suspected the baby had been bludgeoned in his crib.

Erdelatz showed Charlie photos of Maurice Rock and Sheryl Okoro, but Charlie denied ever seeing them. He told Erdelatz he believed Leonard may have killed them as well as Randy Jacobson by handcuffing them and giving them an overdose of chloroform. The officers talked to Charlie off and on for about five hours, taking only a 45-minute break in midafternoon to review some of Charlie's statements. But when they turned on a tape recorder near the end of the afternoon, Charlie clammed up. They returned in the evening with a concealed tape recorder, but Charlie advised them he was through talking.

Charlie had been contacted by Charles Stewart, head of the Calgary Defense Lawyers Association. Stewart told him that under Canadian law he did not have to talk to police and that he had a right to a Canadian lawyer, who would be provided free under the province's legal aid plan if he couldn't afford one. Stewart didn't take the case himself, but he lined Charlie up with Don MacLeod and Brian Devlin. The pair had arrived at the Remand Centre as he was leaving.

"Hey, you guys," he said, stopping them on the sidewalk. "I just talked to this Charles Ng fella, and he definitely needs a lawyer badly. One of you two guys should see him to tell him I referred you." The lawyers were a natural fit. They had handled the Tony Ng extradition case and had won assurances from the Americans that their client wouldn't face the death penalty.

Whistlecraft was furious at the lawyers for sticking their noses into the case. "In 30 years in the police department I never heard of a lawyer coming down unsolicited, demanding to see somebody," he fumed. Whistlecraft demanded to know why Remand Centre staff had allowed Stewart to see Charlie.

They told him they hadn't wanted to grant him access, but he insisted. "He made such a fuss that we kind of felt that we had to," they claimed.

The California cops were also angry at what they claimed had been the unsolicited legal advice provided to Charlie by Calgary lawyers. California investigators were hoping Charlie would not fight extradition and he could be back in California within days or a few weeks. At worst they hoped he would plead guilty to the Canadian charges stemming from his struggle with security guards and his shooting of security guard Sean Doyle, and be returned to the United States following his conviction.

"If he fights extradition, God knows what legal roadblocks could occur," Erdelatz told reporters after the interview.

Remand Centre staff kept a nightly suicide watch on Charlie, a guard stationed outside his cell updating a log on his status every 15 minutes. Charlie was given only one piece of clothing: a fireproof tear-resistant gown that prisoners called baby-dolls. He received a coarse blanket made of similar material, a mattress and a pillow. He denied being suicidal, but he told a Remand Centre nurse that he was depressed over his confinement. He broke into tears when he talked about the shame he had brought upon his family in Hong Kong.

Charlie appeared in Alberta provincial court the following day and was remanded for psychiatric examination. Although still a suicide risk, he was deemed fit to stand trial. He appeared in court a week later to request a trial by judge and jury on charges of attempted murder, robbery and unlawful use of a firearm. Clad in green prison coveralls and blue tennis shoes, with manacles around his waist, wrist and ankles, he glanced coolly around the downtown Calgary courtroom during his five-minute appearance. His new team of lawyers did not argue for bail on his behalf.

Charlie settled into a routine at the Remand Centre, but medical staff and guards kept him under close observation for a month. It angered Charlie that he had to wear shackles when he went into the prison yard to exercise. The metal cut into his ankle, but he refused treatment for the welts. Eventually, he was given clothing to wear and was no longer required to wear shackles during his hour-long exercise period. He spent his days reading and performing mental gymnastics. He would disassemble and reassemble a rifle in his head or go through the steps of building a house piece by piece. He soon tired of a steady diet of fiction and requested educational material to help him pass the time.

While he professed to have no more suicidal thoughts, guards discovered he had been talking to a convicted child killer in a neighboring cell about killing himself. Guards intercepted a note to Charlie suggesting various ways Charlie could kill himself in prison. Beyond that, Charlie's own father had urged him to kill himself. Nevertheless, it soon became clear that Charlie was no longer a suicide threat. A prison psychologist found he was enjoying his notoriety.

"He is impervious to public censure and goes about satisfying his own needs and goals in a single-minded fashion," the psychologist wrote. He concluded that Charlie craved friendship but only to satisfy his own needs.

The psychologist reported that Charlie perceived the world as a dog-eat-dog struggle where it was acceptable to exploit and manipulate others. He warned that for this reason Charlie should be treated with extreme caution despite his seemingly pleasant demeanor. "He is intelligent, observant and calculating. If the opportunity exists and the probability for success is in his favor, he will try to escape," the psychologist warned.

Back in California, officials began assembling the necessary documentation to apply for Charlie's extradition, telling reporters they most likely would be seeking the death penalty. But Canadian police and justice department officials warned that the stance could have serious implications on the extradition process. Under a 1976 Canada–U.S. Treaty, either country could refuse to extradite a fugitive without assurances that the suspect would not face the death penalty. The clause hadn't been just a Canadian idea. At the time the treaty was signed, Canada had not yet abolished the death penalty, but some American states had. Canada had demanded such an assurance in extraditing Tony Ng on the Seattle slayings earlier and Washington State officials had agreed. Ng's lawyers, MacLeod and Devlin, told reporters they would be seeking the same commitment from California officials.

Charlie, again manacled and accompanied by armed officers, appeared in Calgary provincial court for his preliminary hearing in November. After hearing the evidence, Judge Hubert Oliver remanded Charlie to stand trial the following month. Sean Doyle and George Forster were key witnesses at the trial when it began in Alberta's Court of Queen's Bench before a crowd of local and U.S. reporters and spectators. Doyle, who taught art, English and social studies at Father Lacombe High School, told Mr. Justice Allen Sulatycky that he observed Charlie stealing a two-liter bottle of Pepsi from a basement shelf at the Bay department store in downtown Calgary. He recounted the arrest and struggle in which he was shot in the hand.

"We were squirming around quite a bit," he said. "I was struggling to get hold of the gun, and I thought if we kept the gun on the floor that nothing would happen, and as long as I kept my hand around the trigger then we would be all right. But I was getting severe kicks in the back of the head, and I thought I would not be able to hold on to the gun much longer."

Doyle testified that after Charlie got off the first shot, he had feared someone would get killed and he had redoubled his efforts to get control of the gun. But Charlie began biting his left wrist and forced the gun barrel toward his chest, he said. "I felt my life was in danger, and I thought I would have to try and get that gun away from my chest," he said. "I reached, I shoved my left hand out to try to get the gun away from me. And at that point, the gun went off again. I felt a severe impact and I looked at my hand and I saw a powder burn. I assumed I had been hit. I was suffering quite a bit of pain by that time. I could hear myself moaning from the pain."

Doyle was asked to demonstrate how he was holding the gun when he was hit. He picked it up and was about to demonstrate when he was interrupted by the judge.

"I wouldn't point it around," he said. "Point it down to the floor."

When the prosecutor advised that the gun wasn't loaded, Doyle nervously continued the demonstration, pointing the barrel at the spectators' gallery.

"Don't point it into the crowd, then, please," the judge interjected.

"Certainly not at the defense table," quipped Charlie's lawyer, Paul Devlin. "Defense counsel," corrected MacLeod.

"Don't point it at me either," the judge said.

"This is making me nervous," muttered Doyle.

Later, under cross-examination from Devlin, Doyle was again asked to demonstrate how he held the gun.

"It's definitely not loaded," Devlin said.

"You can point it at Mr. Devlin because he says it's unloaded," the judge added helpfully.

"It's definitely not loaded," repeated Devlin. He continued with his cross-examination, asking Doyle about the struggle. "And all of this struggle took about approximately how long before the second shot went off? From the time you began to struggle with him over the bag to the time when the second shot went off, can you give us any estimate as to what amount of time?"

"It's a really difficult question because going over it in my mind several times, it seems like it was a slow-motion movie," Doyle explained. "I have really no idea of time. I was aware of some things—the gun and the people around and the shots—but the time was," he hesitated, "vague."

"You weren't looking at your watch," the judge added helpfully.

"No."

Forster, the second part-time security guard, testified that he thought Doyle had been shot in the head initially because he saw blood dripping from Doyle's ear after the gun went off.

"Then Sean raised his hand and I saw the bullet wound in his hand," he said. "Sean moaned. He started moaning almost immediately."

Allan DeVries, a former city police officer who was also working at the Bay as a security guard, testified that he pinned Charlie to the floor, trapping his gun hand between his chest and the floor.

"I made no attempts to get the gun," he explained. "I thought it would be safer leaving it where it was. I said we'd just keep him as he is. He isn't going anywhere. We'd wait for city police to get here."

He said police arrived in less than five minutes.

Constable Donald Bishop, a five-year member, said he reached under Charlie and tried to persuade him to release his grip on the gun, but when he refused to voluntarily give up the weapon, he forced it from his grasp.

"I grabbed the hand," he testified. "I indicated to the accused to release the weapon, which he didn't. He tried to draw it out. I then grabbed the thumb of the accused and pried back on it. He then released the weapon. I brought his arm up around the back, put it in another lock and we handcuffed the accused."

Charlie was convicted of armed robbery, aggravated assault and unlawful use of a firearm, but he was acquitted of attempted murder. Judge Sulatycky said he couldn't conclude that Charlie intended to kill anyone, but he sentenced him to four and a half years in prison on the other charges. A severe sentence was required because Charlie had entered the country illegally, had resisted arrest and had used a gun that was "fully loaded, cocked and ready to fire," he observed, adding, "There was not a word said about remorse."

Charlie would have to serve at least 17 months—a full third of his sentence—before he would be eligible for release on parole. California authorities would have to wait more than a year and a half to get their clutches on Charlie, and even then the Canadian federal government would have to agree to surrender him with a death sentence hanging over his head.

In California, Calaveras District Attorney John Martin formally charged Charlie with nine murders, including the slaying of the San Francisco disc jockey. Martin expressed dismay that Charlie would be sent to a Canadian prison rather than back to the United States to face the more serious murder charges.

Doyle and Forster became Canadian celebrities, receiving awards and a commendation from the City of Calgary and an association of private investigators. They even appeared on *Front Page Challenge,* a popular Canadian television show featuring a panel of journalists attempting to guess a news story by asking questions of the newsmakers. The two part-time Bay security guards stumped the panel.

But after the pair had their 15 minutes of fame, they had to cope with the aftermath. Doyle, who had come to Canada from Dublin when he was 17, had the more difficult road. Doctors managed to save the middle finger of his left hand, but he would never regain full use of it despite two operations and months in a cast. When he appeared before the Criminal Injuries Compensation Board, a panel that compensates crime victims, he was advised that he wasn't entitled to much. Had he lost a thumb or index finger, the compensation would have been higher.

"But what about the impediment to my speech?" he asked, his blue eyes twinkling mischievously. The panel looked at him quizzically.

"When someone cuts me off on Deerfoot Trail, how do I indicate to him that I am unhappy with his driving?"

But beneath the Irish banter, Doyle was having a tough time. He had intense hatred for Charlie, and he couldn't let it go. Every night in a recurring nightmare he lined up Charlie in the telescopic sights of a high-powered rifle. But when he squeezed the trigger, he was confronted by Charlie's family. They stood glaring at him as if to say, "You're no better than he is." Doyle finally sought counseling and was found to be clinically depressed. He was advised to take several months off work, both from teaching and working at the Bay. So he stayed home and painted. Eventually, he came to terms with his hatred and forgave Charlie. He wanted to see Charlie punished, but he no longer wanted him dead.

Charlie's conviction came a week before his 25th birthday. He spent Christmas in the Calgary Remand Centre reflecting on where he had been and where he was going. He stood at his narrow window watching the snow blowing over the Rockies and falling on the Christmas shoppers in the streets below. He missed his family. He had read in the newspapers that his sister Alice had disowned him, that she was afraid to admit he was her brother for fear of getting fired from her job at the bank. She didn't even want to come to the prison to see him. He thought back to their childhood together, remembered peering down from the top bunk at his two sisters snuggled in the bed below. He remembered wishing them good-night. A lump formed in his throat and tears rolled down his cheeks. Charlie was feeling very sorry for himself, but he felt not the slightest remorse for his victims.

The Wilseyville General Store and Post Office, where Brunn and Eisenmann were to meet Cricket before visiting the cabin. Evidence found at the cabin led to the international manhunt for Charles Ng.

17

Frog and Slant

EDMONTON ALBERTA / JANUARY 1986

CHARLIE ARRIVED at the Edmonton Max on a frigid blustery day in late January 1986. The sky was overcast, a dirty gray. The view from the window of the prison van as it roared up the Manning Freeway reminded Charlie of Kansas and Oklahoma: flat empty prairie. But it was so white! Here and there headless grain stalks poked through the crusting of snow like stubble on an old man's chin. The place seemed desolate, dead.

The van turned north off the highway onto a narrow country road and after about a quarter mile veered right into the prison parking lot. Charlie did a double take when he noticed electrical cords snaking from under the hoods of the parked vehicles to plug-ins along a fence. What the hell was that all about? The cords, of course, were for the electrical engine heaters needed in subzero weather. Such a necessity was new to Charlie. It reminded him vaguely of the horses tied to hitching posts in cowboy movies.

The van pulled up to a 14-foot entry gate and stopped while prison officials conducted security checks. Charlie looked out the back window through a swirling white plume of vehicle exhaust. God, it looked cold! If he ever broke out of this place, where would he go? He would freeze before he reached the nearest farm.

Charlie glanced at his surroundings as he was marched into the prison admissions area in shackles and the familiar belly chain. There wasn't much to see. Gray. Institutional green. Cinder-block walls. Sliding steel gates clanging open and shut. It was pretty much what the Remand Centre guard had told him to expect.

By now Charlie was used to the routine. He'd been through it at the Pearl Harbor Brig, Leavenworth, the Remand Centre and several county jails in between. The strip search: strangers peering into every orifice, up his nostrils and anus, into his ears and under his tongue. The shower: rubbing the pungent delousing chemical into his hair and waiting five shivering minutes until he was allowed to rinse it out.

The Correctional Service of Canada mission statement was posted on a plaque on the wall near the entrance to the prison and on the first page of the prisoners information handbook. It read, "The CSC contributes to the protection of society by actively encouraging and assisting offenders to become law-abiding citizens while exercising reasonable safe, secure and humane control." The handbook contained a message from the warden and rules regarding security, safety, cleanliness, behavior, dress, movement, telephones and discipline. It also advised prisoners about visits, programs, educational opportunities and prison employment as well as services ranging from religious and recreational activities to crafts, hobbies and haircuts.

Charlie was admitted into the Disassociation and Segregation Unit at the north end of the complex. A gray steel gate separated the 72 prisoners in the hole from the other 170 prisoners. They were usually separated for good reason. Some were violent; some were in danger of violence. Some were both. Charlie was escorted to the lower D range, a long dim hallway with six segregation cells facing a gray cinder-block wall. As the heavy solid-steel door clanged loudly shut behind him, Charlie conducted a casual inventory of his cell. It was about 8' x 12'. On his left, in a corner just inside the door, was a stainless steel combination sink–toilet. On the right-hand wall, a thin striped mattress lay on a steel bed frame bolted to the wall and floor. Along the left wall was a small metal desk with two shelves and an attached stool on a swivel arm. The gray paint on the concrete floor was wearing away in places, exposing the brown base coat. The pocked and peeling gray walls were marked with crude graffiti. A tin mirror about a foot square hung over the sink. A bookcase shelf was anchored to the wall adjacent to the desk. The only illumination, other than the small points of natural light seeping in through the slit windows, shone down from a recessed fluorescent light above the desk. Charlie turned around and looked out through the Plexiglas window in the door. There was nothing to see out there.

Charlie wondered how long this would be home. His cell was the last of six in the dimly lit corridor. He had no idea if the neighboring cells were occupied. He couldn't hear anyone next door. He ambled over to the window and peered out into the prison yard. From his vantage he could see anyone entering the prison from the outside world. But aside from his lawyers, he didn't expect anyone would be coming to see him.

Later Charlie heard other prisoners shuffling up and down the corridor, but he couldn't see anything through the small scuffed window in his door. He heard the occasional clanging of cell doors on the range and the muffled tones of guards and inmates punctuated by an occasional burst of laughter, which seemed out of place in the hole. Charlie sat on his bunk and stared at the wall. He was in the belly of the beast and had no idea how to extricate himself. No windows would be inadvertently left open at the Max.

Over the next two weeks, Charlie was rousted for meals served through a slot in his door, for his weekly shower and for interviews with a counselor and a prison psychology worker. The rest of the time he was left alone to ponder his fate. The highlight of the day, usually at midmorning, was the one hour allotted for exercise in one of two fish tanks on either side of the unit. At least they looked like fish tanks. They were the exercise yards—narrow, fully enclosed cubicles measuring about 20' x 20'. Inmates called them fish tanks or aquariums because the wall separating the yard from the control center was mostly window. Heavy wire mesh enclosed the ceiling, keeping the inmates in but not keeping the elements out. Charlie had cut through thicker stuff when he broke into the Weapons Company armory at K-Bay, but he didn't have any wire cutters this time. It would have been difficult to use them anyhow. Every move he made was monitored by a camera mounted near the ceiling just above the door.

Bundled up against the subzero temperatures in a heavy institutional green parka, mitts and toque, Charlie performed a daily exercise routine: stretching, shadow boxing, kicking and punching a heavy body bag hanging on a chain from a ceiling beam. He had to keep moving to keep warm. When he did his aerobics or jogged in the frigid arctic air, his breath billowed like white fire from the snout of a dragon. The dragon had been his code name in the Marine Corps and his self-ascribed nickname as a kid. Homage to Bruce Lee. He could use his help now.

Charlie was beginning his third week in solitary confinement when he heard the jangle of keys outside his door. He waited but the door didn't open. He heard voices, laughter and then the clang of the cell door next to his slamming shut. During exercise periods over the next few days, Charlie noticed a stocky middle-aged man with a dark complexion and a mop of black hair. He worked out in the opposite exercise court. The man noticed him watching, glanced up with smiling green eyes and acknowledged him with a barely perceptible cocking of his right wrist. Charlie was watching through the Plexiglas square in his door when the prison staff escorted the man back to his cell. Sure enough they took him to the cell immediately next to his. A neighbor.

A few days later the neighbor sent him a note. He heard the rustle of paper as a hand slipped it through the narrow gap under his cell door. One side of the paper was filled with algebra equations. On the other side, in neat handwriting, was a single line: "Got any magazines?" It was Maurice Laberge, who had just been transferred back to the Max after a stint in the Special Handling Unit in Prince Albert, Saskatchewan. For the next several weeks Mo and Charlie corresponded. In prison lingo their notes were called kites because inmates often had to throw them from one cell to another and then reel them back in when their questions had been answered.

Mo obviously knew things. He knew where to get pencils and erasers, who to contact for a tall coffee mug like he had, what books could be found in the library. Mo knew what could be purchased in the prison canteen and when visiting hours began. As a former clerk of the prison grievance committee, he knew a lot about the staff and the inmates, too. He knew the guards' names and what they were like. He knew which requests were likely to be acted upon and which ones were a waste of time. He was working on a university degree.

"Let me check out some of those school courses and books you got," Charlie scrawled in his tall script that tended to ignore the line on the foolscap paper. "Let me see what it is like."

Charlie offered to help Maurice (he always addressed him as Maurice in the early days of their relationship) when Mo was stumped with algebra questions. "Maurice. Send over them algebra text and a pad," he scribbled. "I'll see what I can do."

"Maurice," he would write, "let me check out your razor, will you?"

"Maurice. Where do ya get this type of paper?" he would ask, referring to Mo's lined foolscap pages. "The population canteen or the school?" He would complain about his television reception or fill in Mo about his academic courses. "Just knocked out two lessons in my practical math course myself," he would advise. "Need to chill out a bit."

By April, Charlie was confiding in Mo and seeking his advice on institutional matters. As Mo became a valuable resource for Charlie—a veritable gold mine—Mo was thinking the same about his neighbor. If he played his cards right, Charlie could be his ticket home. Mo began saving the notes they passed back and forth, making sure to carefully date them. When he had collected about a dozen, he would put them in a brown manila envelope, stamp it confidential and mail it to his lawyer, Burke Barker.

Barker, an amiable man in his midfifties with a black beard and a bottomless well of conspiracy theories, was a professor of law at the University of Alberta. He was a maverick, often taking on causes and clients other lawyers wouldn't touch. He was a big supporter of the poor, the hopeless and the downtrodden. He also was a family friend. When Mo, his family and his lawyer had different ideas about the best course to take on a given matter, Barker cleared that up in his usual bombastic style. "Give me carte blanche to do what I see fit or go get yourself another lawyer," he bellowed. Both Mo and his family acquiesced.

Mo wasn't sure what he would do with the notes or just how forthcoming his new neighbor would be, but he knew Charlie was an extremely high-profile criminal who could attract a great deal of attention in media and political circles. It was very likely, he reasoned, that police or prosecutors in California would be interested in what Charlie had to say about his offenses. Mo had seen prison informants testifying at his own first-degree murder trial. He had watched Barker shred their credibility and leave their testimony in tatters. He had learned from their mistakes. But if he had Charlie admitting his guilt in his own handwriting, Mo knew his own credibility wouldn't matter a hell of a lot. So Mo was careful to date Charlie's notes. He also made sure he quickly wrote down anything Charlie told him about the case as soon as possible, including the date, time and place of the admission. What would the state of California pay to have Charlie gift-wrapped for the gas chamber? Mo would see what Barker could get.

If Charlie's admissions didn't secure Mo a get-out-of-jail-free card, perhaps he would write a book about his experiences with Charlie once he was released. If that didn't pan out, he could always use the material for a thesis for one of his degrees. Maybe he would write a book about serial killers he had known. Mo turned on the charm, and soon he and Charlie became pals. What began as a formal relationship between two inmates who addressed each other as Maurice and Charles quickly developed into good-natured bantering dialogue. They made up disparaging nicknames for each other and traded insults and racial slurs daily. Mo called Charlie "Slant," short for "slant eyes," and Charlie responded by calling his French-speaking neighbor "Frog."

"Slant," Mo would write, "your incredibly patient and wise uncle notices that his ungrateful, dog-breath nephew is suffering from a mental disorder brought about by a lack of rice and other gook amenities: cirrhosis of the brain; certainly looks like intellectual AIDS. However, being forever kind, gentle and patient to a fault, your generous uncle will overlook your deficiencies and vagabond memory. How your mangy carcass survived this long is a puzzle."

Charlie would respond in kind. "Froggy, your artistic, talented, youthful and inspiring nephew understands the degenerative and non-adaptability of your frog's brain in prolonged confinement. However, your wise and sensitive nephew is ready to tolerate your senility."

Despite his true motives, Mo tried to be a good friend to Charlie. He offered advice when asked and helped Charlie deal with his confinement. Mo had the experience, having served nearly 10 years in prison by the time he was 34. He had been incarcerated for five straight years—since April 1981—and a lot of that time had been in the hole. While other inmates would pound on Charlie's door, hurling abuse and calling him a baby killer and a skinner (prison jargon for a rapist), Mo offered unconditional friendship, at least on the surface of things. He was supportive. He was amusing. Mo might often tell Charlie how he believed Charlie had serious psychological problems, but he refrained from judging. Mo often actually liked Charlie though he found his clinging behavior very annoying.

In May, Charlie complained to Mo that he was doomed to serve his prison sentence in solitary confinement. "The excuse the keepers here use is that it's for my safety," he lamented to Mo in his rambling scrawl. "But you and I and the guards all know the true reasons. They think I want to get out into population and do some fucker(s) in to get life in Canada and avoid the death penalty in the United States. Or they think I am so good in chop chop [Charlie's term for the martial arts] that if provoked or attacked I might turn around and slay a few."

Charlie asked Mo if he would be better off transferring to Prince Albert, Saskatchewan. Mo agreed that the northern Saskatchewan prison, which was designed for prisoners who needed protection from other prisoners, would be a better place for Charlie. He urged him to apply for a transfer there. But Charlie was full of misgivings and second thoughts. The Max was easier for his lawyer to visit, and he feared that once he got to PA Pen, he could find himself still stuck in the hole.

Mo urged Charlie to go for it anyway. "What I am saying is going to PA is a long process and the opportunity is too good to pass up," he advised Charlie in a lengthy missive. "It's good to explore options. The difference between here and PA is night and day." Mo had spent nine months at PA Pen, and he knew the place pretty well. Charlie followed Mo's advice and put in for the transfer. He was tired of being cooped up in a cell for 23 hours a day. It was wearing on him already. Under "reasons for transfer," he outlined his desire to get into the general inmate population.

"It might be all for nothing," he confided to Mo. "But then, like Rambo said, 'Here at least I know where I stand.'" He added, "It's been nice knowing you, Grasshopper. Hope you can fly soon!"

But Charlie wasn't going anywhere in a hurry. Mo told him it would take at least three months for the request to be processed. In the meantime the pair was granted permission to work out together in the exercise yard. Charlie made the request through channels about three weeks after Mo's arrival from PA Pen. Mo was happy to oblige. Prison officials warned him Charlie might be dangerous. Mo, who had rippling biceps and a crushing grip, just grinned.

"That little shrimp?" he chuckled. "I think I'll be okay."

It wasn't until later that he discovered just how lethal the little shrimp could be. Charlie asked him what to expect in general population. If other prisoners made a move to get him, how would they do it? What would they have for weapons? Would they attack from the front or behind? Where would the attack likely occur? He had Mo act out a few scenarios. It was Charlie's response to the attacks that gave Mo pause for thought. The younger man was quick, and he was deadly. Charlie's moves piqued Mo's interest in martial arts.

"Hey, can you show me how you did that?" he asked.

From that day on, the martial arts became part of their exercise ritual and a major component of the notes they passed to each other's cells. Theirs was a strange pairing. Charlie, at 25 years old, the youthful teacher, and Mo, at age 34, the elder student. He often addressed Charlie as "Master" or "Master Dragon" while Charlie would teasingly call him "Grasshopper" in reference to the old television series *Kung Fu*. In deference to their eight-year age difference, they also frequently referred to one another as "Uncle" and "Nephew."

One day Mo offered to ask his girl friend to find a female pen pal for Charlie. He waited until the guards had come by with breakfast. When he could hear their footsteps fading away and the range door clang shut, he reached under his door and slipped his note through the gap under Charlie's door. Charlie heard the rustle of paper and bent down to scoop it up. While his own handwriting was often an illegible scrawl, he had no difficulty reading Mo's firm even printing. He chuckled as he read the note.

"I am not sure I want to describe you as a pigeon-toed, deviate, dog-breath psychopath from Hong Kong," Mo had penned. "Send me over a description—character and physical attributes (i.e. slant eyes, lizard tongue, orangutan complexion) and I'll incorporate it in my note."

Charlie grabbed a pen and went to his desk to scribble a reply. "Looking for not-too-old/not-too-young, 18 to 35 year old Caucasian or Asian (no nigger). Intelligent (I.Q. More than 80), good looking (I won't fuck anything you won't fuck), marriage-minded, non-prejudiced, sensitive, understanding and yet kinky (pantyhose and lingerie lover) that doesn't give a shit what the media said about the Slant. Also bureaucratic-hating, rice-loving and a passion for the oppressed ricer." He listened at his door for sounds of people in the corridor. Hearing none he reached out and slid the note under Mo's cell door. A lot of their exchanges were like that. Just something to pass the time.

Finally, in May, Charlie began to talk freely to Mo about the charges against him. He told Mo that Leonard Lake's murder of his own brother and his best man while Charlie was in prison would make it difficult for the prosecution to blame Charlie for the other slayings. It created a reasonable doubt. "It shows he was like that before I met him," he told Mo.

He gave Mo the background to his arrest, summarized his capture and told him how he crossed Canada by Greyhound bus with only $400. He talked about the theft of the vise and Leonard's subsequent arrest. And he bragged about his heinous crimes, taking pride in the brutality and ruthlessness of the murders. He told Mo about the videotapes. "That's it, man, the new wave—video crime."

Mo had a difficult time understanding the rationale. "Are you serious?

Why would you videotape it?" He could understand robbing and stealing, and he had been prone to violence himself on occasion, but he didn't understand why it was necessary to kill someone to take their car or their video equipment. "What all did you do to these people?" he wanted to know.

The answer he received made even less sense. Charlie claimed he cut the clitoris off one of his victims. He said he used a chainsaw to sever the testicles off another. He bragged about pouring acid on the eyes and genitals of victims. "The crimes I committed aren't even in the books," he boasted, "and they won't be because the people I killed aren't around to talk about it."

Charlie talked extensively of the pains he and Leonard Lake took to dispose of the bodies, particularly at the beginning before they got lazy and careless. They had destroyed the evidence. No one would ever be able to prove he raped any of his victims because they would find no semen. He said he helped put the bodies on a woodpile, splashed gasoline over them and burned them to cinders.

"It smells like a pig on a spit when they're burning," he told Mo. "If you're hungry, it makes your mouth water. Later you come back and smash the pieces with a spade. When it has cooled, like charcoal, you pick up the pieces of bone that you can see and put them in a pail. Then you spread it in the knee-high grass. It's like spreading pepper on a steak."

In early June, during a morning exercise session, Charlie told Mo about the Dubs murders. They had been talking about Charlie's school years in England. It wasn't a fun time, Charlie told his buddy. "No one cared, no love, no gifts." He said his parents would promise him gifts as incentives for getting good grades, then renege on their promises. Charlie couldn't satiate his hunger for material possessions. That's why the Dubs were killed, he explained. Leonard Lake wanted their video and stereo equipment. Charlie got the VHS movies and documentaries they had taped.

Charlie told Mo he and Leonard sometimes argued over whether they should kill certain people. "But we always reconciled."

"When I made a kill, he would praise me, and it was like positive reinforcement," he explained. "His whole trip was psychological."

Charlie boasted that he and Leonard planned their killings and carried them out like precision military operations. "Lake would tell me what to do and I'd do it," he explained. "Sometimes I knew what he was going to say, so I did it before he told me."

But even from his own distorted view, Charlie thought the Dubs murders, particularly the killing of the baby, were over the top.

"Lake told me it would be a good training experience, like in the SS when they were given a puppy at the beginning of their training and forced to kill it to graduate." Charlie said he killed the mother and her toddler while Leonard took care of the father.

"The baby was a little hard, but the hole [his term for women] was a piece of cake. I don't think they found the spot where we buried them or there would be something in the paper or on the news."

Two days later, again in the exercise yard, Charlie told Mo that he went to a sex club with Leonard's ex-wife one night. She dressed up in black pantyhose for him when he told her they turned him on. "She rubbed her panty-hosed legs all over my back."

Charlie talked about the kind of women who turned him on: sexy small-breasted blondes. "I always wanted a virgin. I was going to keep her in the cell for a long time." But before long his conversation had returned to the murder of the Dubs. It was obvious to Mo that Charlie was bothered by the slaying of the baby. "At first I felt funny about wasting the baby," he said. "Then I figured it was better that way than having no parents."

Charlie reiterated, however, that he had no remorse about killing the baby's mother. It was an unbelievable high. "Killing Deborah Dubs was the first time pulling the trigger made my dick hard," he told Mo. "The begging just before the kill was the best part." He liked the sex with Debbie Dubs the best, and he had kept her panties as souvenirs. He told Mo he thought she enjoyed it. "Daddy dies, Momma cries, baby fries," he chortled. Mo was sickened by the graphic detail yet excited to be getting such detailed information.

Mo couldn't be certain if Charlie was telling him the truth, but he didn't really care. A judge and jury would have to sort that out. When it seemed that half of what Charlie boasted was pure crap, Mo began focusing their conversations rather than just letting Charlie run on. Mo needed more detail about the actual killings. At first Charlie was suspicious. If Mo asked about some detail, he wouldn't respond. But Mo sensed Charlie was really dying to talk about it. Eventually, the information would come pouring out. He would preface his remarks, "My lawyer says I shouldn't talk to anyone, but I guess I have already jumped in with both feet." He told Mo he was responsible for 12 murders: seven men, two women, two children "and one faggot."

"How do they act when you tell them you are going to kill them?" Mo inquired as they worked out on the parallel bars one day.

"One of the bitches offered to be Lake's and my slave forever," Charlie replied.

"Was she on the video?" asked Mo.

"Well, yes. The Allen . . . No, I don't know," he said evasively. "She squealed like a pig."

Charlie told him about the execution-style killings of two of his victims and how he practiced using his martial arts weaponry on one. "I practiced with a throwing star on a frog like you," he told Mo.

"What do you mean, frog?"

"Maybe not a frog, but he had a French name. Peranteau. What do you think? Is that a frog name?"

"What did you kill him with?" prodded Mo. "A star?"

"No. No, I threw the star at him, but I shot him with a .357," explained Charlie, as nonchalant as if he were talking about the weather. "He begged me not to kill him. He offered to be my slave forever, so I let him think I was thinking about it. When I was loading the gun, he was so scared he pissed himself. I put the gun behind his left ear and cocked it slow so he could hear every click. He kept saying, 'Please, please, Charlie.' Lake said, 'Kill the pig.' I said, 'Good-bye, Clifford,' and pulled the trigger."

Charlie admitted he and Leonard had screwed up when they tried to dispose of Peranteau's body. They forgot to remove the handcuffs before they lit their makeshift crematorium, and the police found the evidence at the burn site.

He admitted that he also made a mistake when he kept Peranteau's engraved pen and pencil set, which police later found in his apartment. "One way out would be to say that Leonard gave it to me," he confided. Charlie told Mo he lured Peranteau and Jeff Gerald out to Leonard's cabin with promises of "free pussy and drugs."

"The fuckin' honky called me a chink, so when I killed him I made him say it over and over again."

Charlie's talk about killing rattled Mo. It wasn't so much the details of the slayings or the lack of remorse that shook the hardened convict. He had heard many other lifers callously describe killings. It was Charlie's manner as he described the killings that was chilling. His murky brown eyes brightened. He panted. Drool seeped from the corners of his mouth. He looked like a man on speed, whipping his arms this way and that to emphasize how he slaughtered his victims, pointing his finger like a gun. "Blam!" He savored talking about killing as much as he enjoyed killing.

Charlie was one sick puppy, Mo decided, disguising his feelings behind a disarming smile. He was amassing solid detailed evidence, but he wondered how much more of this guy he could stand. "I can tell you like talking about it," he told Charlie. "Your eyes light up, your mouth salivates, your body vibrates."

"That's my thing, man," Charlie retorted. "No kill, no thrill. That's my passion. Once you get the thrill, you are bored without it."

Charlie claimed he had become addicted to murder. Leonard had to coerce him to make the first kill, but since then Charlie had not needed anyone to push him. "I would kill and Leonard would praise me," he explained. "All my life I wanted this, so I would do anything for him. After I began to like it, it was him trying to kill my passion for the kill. You see, the Marine Corps trained me to be a killing machine, and it's a habit I couldn't break. Not even now. It's here. It's in me. It is me."

Charlie referred to himself as Leonard's disciple. Leonard knew just which buttons to push to set him off. "I was a perfect killing machine, motivated by sex, passion and power," he proudly confided. "No gun, no fun. No kill, no thrill."

But Charlie's regard for Leonard Lake as a father figure had definitely cooled. Charlie felt betrayed by Leonard's suicide and left Leonard as the patsy. As much as he had loved him before, he despised him now. He didn't need him anymore. Leonard couldn't be of any use.

"Lake was a fat, bald, 39-year-old," he spat. "A burned-out Vietnam vet. He liked ugly sluts." Charlie was particularly upset that Leonard had mentioned some of his partner's crimes in his journal, but Charlie was aware the passages couldn't be used against him because Leonard was dead and the writings of a dead man couldn't be tested in court. He told Mo that the sweet part of Leonard's suicide was that he could blame all the killings on him. "I can say it was all Lake and I had no choice."

Charlie lamented that he had placed his life entirely in another man's hands. He would never make that mistake again. He had trusted Leonard, but the man was a bozo. Driving Paul Cosner's car after killing him was plain stupid, he told Mo. "Leonard found a guy who looked like him—this Paul Cosner—and he wanted his car and his I.D. I didn't want to kill that punk, but Lake wanted his fuckin' Honda—a cheap fuckin' Honda." But Charlie said he was in Leonard's debt for putting him up when he was hiding out from the Naval Investigative Service and for bailing him out of jail when he got caught shoplifting waterbed sheets shortly after his release from Leavenworth. The Cosner killing would square them, Leonard had said. So Charlie had sat quietly in the backseat of the car during the test drive, waiting for Leonard to set up the kill. He told Mo they went down a side street and pulled the gun on the guy, but he refused to divulge his bank code or any of his financial information. When it was clear that he couldn't be scared into it, Charlie shot him.

"I shot him in the head," he told Mo during their morning exercise period. "Bang—right behind the ear. Ooo! One bullet and finally I was all paid up with Lake. He made a strange gurgling sound in his throat—a real deep rattle noise."

Charlie often talked about escaping, but Mo hoped he never got the chance. It was obvious Charlie would just pick up where he had left off. "What are you going to do if you escape anyway, Charlie?" Mo asked him one day. "All you like doing is killing people. You need some psychiatric intervention," he suggested.

"This time I will be more careful," Charlie responded. He fancied himself a terrorist in the mode of the international terrorist Carlos the Jackal. Charlie relished the idea of mass murder. Mo thought it was spooky stuff. He drew a chart of various kinds of killers, ranking Charlie just above the "frothing at the mouth mad killers." At the bottom of the chart he noted that Charlie's condition was irreversible and could only be treated with massive doses of electric therapy while seated. Charlie scrawled back that Mo's diagnosis looked more like getting rid of the problem than therapy.

While Charlie went to great pains to project the image of a relaxed, quiet and polite inmate, the more Mo was around him, the more he saw to contradict the façade. They were working out in the yard early one morning when Charlie went berserk. He began punching the cinder-block walls with his fists, striking his knuckles repeatedly against the brick until they bled. He then used his bleeding knuckles to create a polka dot pattern on the walls. Mo watched in disbelief. When he looked down at his own feet, he saw they were spattered with Charlie's blood. He accused Charlie of having a demented fascination with blood and left it at that.

Mo also found it increasingly hard to stomach the notes Charlie passed under his cell door. The crude sketches he had drawn initially to illustrate his karate and other lessons in martial arts became more and more perverse. Most often they depicted oral sex, anal sex, sex with children and even sex with animals. Some depicted torture and assaults on prison staff. One sketch depicted a young woman giving a blow job to a man who held a gun to her head. The woman wore a necklace with the dangling letters that spelled out *cocksucker.* Charlie scrawled a caption: "Blow job at gunpoint; make sure she do it right! Besides, she like it that way." He told Mo he had forced one of his victims to perform oral sex at gunpoint and had pulled the trigger during the assault just to savor the woman's terror. Mo dutifully filed all the sketches away in a brown manila envelope on a shelf in his desk and mailed them to Barker at regular intervals. He feared if he was caught with them during a random cell search, he could get into trouble. He was even more fearful that word would get back to Charlie that he was saving their correspondence.

Eventually, he told Charlie he was thinking about writing a book about Charlie's case when he got out of prison. Charlie wasn't surprised. His lawyer had been approached by several authors and screenwriters. The older convict wanted him to explain why there was so much interest in him. "What makes you so special?" he had asked Charlie at the time. "There are all kinds of serial killers around. We just finished with Clifford Olson. The media wanted to forget about him."

Charlie just laughed. "I'm not your normal serial killer. I didn't go home after and drink warm milk and clean my weapons. I was working." He meant that his killings were all business. He liked the fact that he and Leonard gleaned financial information from the victims and cashed in on their assets. They killed friends and strangers, women and babies. He saw killing as a job, a way of life. They didn't engage in spontaneous acts of violence. He and Leonard planned every killing down to the very last detail. They were true professionals.

So when Mo brought up the idea of writing a book, Charlie was flattered. He was above all else an egomaniac. He liked the idea of having a biographer, someone he could trust to tell the world about the real Charles Ng and not just regurgitate the media hype. But he was mindful of the risk to him. He stressed that he not be portrayed as a child molester.

But Charlie had a darker and more sinister message to follow. He sent Mo a sketch depicting a rat in a courtroom witness box telling a judge about the book. "Yes, my Lord, that is the book inmate Mo was talking about. Yes, that's it," the rat is saying. The book was entitled *The Dragon and the Frog.* The cover showed a frog and a dragon in martial arts combat. It was Charlie's way of warning Mo to step cautiously. Charlie included the rat in many of his incriminating sketches to remind Mo to keep their correspondence to himself as far as Charlie's case was concerned.

Charlie often used sketches to demonstrate his feelings. When he was going through a bout of depression, he sent Mo a drawing of a frog leading a swimming man through turbulent waters. "The nephew thinks his wise, kind and understanding uncle will lead me through the treacherous and stormy sea of betrayals and pains to the wealth, freedom and vengeance of the dry shore," Charlie wrote. "The nephew's mind is going through an extremely confusing and stressful state at this time, but he has faith in his almighty, frog-kicking uncle."

Many of the sketches were simply that—hasty reactions quickly produced, devoid of detail, black ink on paper. But some contained a great more detail and color. Red for blood dripping from corpses, blue for prison blue jeans. Most included a crudely drawn frog or a rat or both. Others included a dog, much like Wubon, Leonard's dog that appeared in the background of one of the pair's videotapes. Mo was always easily identifiable by his bushy eyebrows. Charlie usually depicted himself in glasses. In most of the drawings the characters were labeled, and their comments were scrawled in cartoonlike balloons. Sometimes both men contributed to a sketch, passing it back and forth under the cell doors to add more and more detail.

Charlie rated loyalty above everything else. He had been loyal to Leonard, and he showed it to Mo. But he wanted his loyalty returned. When other inmates abused him or prison staff refused to have anything to do with him, he turned to Mo. He begged Mo to stand by him.

"All I can tell you is that you should recall your first impression of me and stick to it," he wrote. "Faith is most important and I need not tell you that. I know I have no right to ask you to stick by my side; maybe it is better to have no expectation. But I want you to know what . . . I did and did not do."

But it was not an easy relationship. Like a spoiled brat, Charlie demanded constant attention, often interrupting Mo's studies with piddling requests. By August they were really beginning to get on each other's nerves. Things heated up in a spat over Charlie's use of Mo's razor. Charlie would borrow it and not return it promptly. Mo threatened to cut off Charlie's use of the razor and leave him to suffer with the cheap prison-issue razors if he continued to abuse the privilege.

About a week later Charlie went ballistic when Mo refused to help him

224 *No Kill No Thrill*

with his course studies. Mo said he was willing to help Charlie solve the problems, but he wasn't going to do the work for him. Charlie had to try to figure out the problems for himself first. They got into a heated argument during the exercise period. Charlie was wild, swearing at Mo and threatening him. When they got back to their cells, Mo responded with a conciliatory but stern note. "Your ever-forgiving uncle, with a heart as large as the Mediterranean, patient to a fault, youthful and overly gracious, has this to say," Mo began. "Swear, curse, froth at the mouth—I don't care. But under no circumstances are you to ever threaten me again. Because you are an inferior yellow, dog-breath bastard whose mother tried to crush you at birth, I will ignore your first obvious example of hallucinatory transgression. You may get frustrated with your course and I can dig it. I cannot do more than quickly correct it. I just don't have the time. If you have made a good effort, fine. I will help. But not before. Relationships are not bargaining sessions."

Charlie responded with a brief note that he would look forward to serving his uncle with his "mad and sick" cartoons. But within a few days it became obvious to them that the relationship was crumbling. Mo was growing fearful that his friendship with Charlie could hurt his chances at an upcoming parole-board hearing. He was hoping to be transferred out of maximum security, a move requiring the recommendation of prison guards, and he was beginning to hear snide remarks from guards about his cozy relationship with Charlie. Before he could even be considered for a transfer to a medium-security prison, he would have to show that he could function in the prison's general population. But that might not be possible if his ties to a baby killer and skinner created animosity.

"You feel you are carrying a lot of Lake's flack that you don't deserve," he wrote Charlie. "Mo now gets some of Slant's for free and I don't like it—from staff, from prisoners, from the cleaners, from anyone who is told of what is going on. At one point, I didn't know and I didn't care. However, it may be that I now go out to population here and this could become tricky. I do for me what I think is best for me. It is not a putdown on you. What is, is."

Mo had also had more than enough of Charlie's constant talk about the killings. He was sick of it and had asked Charlie to stop talking about it, but Charlie couldn't help himself. Talking about killing excited him. Mo wrote, "Even your conversations give me nightmares. The problem is not between you and I, per se. It's all about who you are and what you have been doing. Enough is enough. In the name of what do I justify regressing on my release plans? Curiosity? This is nuts, Slant. Nuts!!! You must confront your past."

In addition to chattering on and on about the killings, Charlie was often vulgar and uncouth. No wonder he never fit in at any of the private schools, thought Mo. He lacked all social graces. He picked his nose and farted in public and anyone he didn't like he branded as someone who "sucked moose cock."

But Mo had an even better reason for breaking off contact with Charlie. The truth was he didn't have to put up with his crude little neighbor anymore. He had the goods on him. He had more than enough detailed information about the California killings to try to negotiate a deal: hard information he hoped only the real killer could know, information needed to convict Charles Ng of multiple counts of murder. Mo had already dispatched a letter to California authorities offering Charlie's notes and drawings, and it was dangerous to continue the relationship when Charlie could become aware of the betrayal at any moment. Charlie had made it abundantly clear to Mo that the penalty for betrayal was death. While Mo believed Charlie wanted him to tell his story, there was no sense taking any more chances.

When Mo managed to snag a janitorial position, he informed Charlie he didn't want to exercise with him anymore. One of the perks of being the unit cleaner was being able to exercise any time he wanted. He told Charlie he just couldn't handle more talk of killing. "Listen," he said to Charlie. "I don't want to hear about this stuff anymore. I have had enough."

Charlie asked Mo to let him end it. He wanted to tell the prison staff that he didn't want to exercise with Mo anymore. It would allow him to save face. "No hard feelings," he told Mo. "I know the situation."

But Charlie didn't really know the situation. He didn't know about the letter Mo had sent through a friend to San Francisco homicide inspector Ed Erdelatz. The letter, accompanied by one of Charlie's sketches, advised Erdelatz that Charlie had produced a number of sketches detailing the killings.

"What really strikes me as odd is the apparent need that Charles had to talk about his bizarre and grisly exploits," Mo wrote Erdelatz. "By drawing his victims and naming them, he, in some way, was vindicating the horror of what happened and turning it into a form of macabre humor." The letter advised Erdelatz that there were 200 sketches, many of which focused on Kathi Allen, Donald Giuletti and the Dubs. It included the expressions Charlie was fond of saying, "No kill, no thrill"; "papa dies, momma cries, baby fries"; and "no gun, no fun." The letter concluded, "This was not your usual opportunist, but rather a clever and brutally sadistic murderer." Mo included a prison post office box address and a phone number.

If the letter didn't get Erdelatz's attention, the sketch did. Mo had sent Erdelatz one of Charlie's sketches of a figure clad in Ninja attire wreaking vengeance upon the San Francisco homicide department. The sketch showed a figure labeled as Erdelatz being killed by an assassin with a silencer-equipped pistol. All around his fallen body were slain colleagues. The drawing was captioned, "Pay Day for the 187 Task Force's Pigs: Slant moves in swiftly with whispering deaths."

Mo had his hook in the water and he was awaiting the catch of his life. If he snagged Erdelatz, he hoped Barker could negotiate his way out of prison nearly 20 years before the expiration of his sentence. He would have a second chance at life. He was confident Erdelatz would take the bait. How could he ignore it?

Meanwhile, Charlie finally received his transfer to Prince Albert. He and Mo exchanged photographs and promised to keep in touch. In PA Pen Charlie got his wish. He was placed in general population, made friends with several fellow prisoners and helped edit the prison newspaper *Off the Wall.* He had no inkling of the frenzy Mo had stirred up in his wake.

"Pay Day for the 187 Task Force's Pigs," a detail from a Charles Ng sketch that Maurice Laberge sent to San Francisco homicide investigators. It got their attention.

"Statue of Madness," a Charles Ng sketch depicting Leonard Lake.

"Slant's Paradise," a Charles Ng sketch depicting his fantasies: food, women, pornography, murder.

"Remains Claiming Section," a Charles Ng sketch introduced at his trial in which he depicted families claiming the remains of his and Leonard Lake's victims.

"Dinner Time," a Charles Ng sketch in which he recalled eating dinner and watching Leonard Lake torture Kathleen Allen.

"Lake's Baby Dies School," a Charles Ng letter and drawing in which he challenged Mo Laberge not to attach his "square John" ethical standards to Charlie's actions.

The Disassociation and Segregation Unit at the Edmonton Max.

The exercise yard at the Edmonton Max, where Charlie and Mo worked out together and where Charlie began to describe the California murders.

18

On the Case

SAN FRANCISCO CALIFORNIA / AUGUST 1986

M O'S LETTER HIT the San Francisco Homicide Squad on August 11, 1986, like a San Andreas earthquake. Erdelatz immediately called the number Mo had included and was surprised when he reached a prison. He explained to a prison employee who he was, and he verified the basic facts. A correctional officer confirmed that a prisoner named Maurice Laberge was housed in protective custody with Charles Ng. "Yes," the officer said. "They do have access to each other. They have been exercising together for several months."

In fact Mo was almost the only contact Charlie had. The guard offered to contact Mo to get more information for the California police officer. When he called back four days later, he told Erdelatz that Mo claimed to have sent 400 of Charlie's crude sketches to his lawyer, Burke Barker. "Some of the sketches depict you and District Attorney John Martin in various stages of dismemberment," said the guard, relaying information Mo had given him. The officer told Erdelatz that Mo offered to cooperate "if so advised by his attorney."

Erdelatz was unable to reach Barker, but a few weeks later, Mo's lawyer called him back collect. He reached Erdelatz's partner, Inspector Jeff Brosch, instead and told him about the material Mo had procured.

"If this material was ever placed in front of a jury, Ng would fry," Barker told the inspector, hoping to whet the veteran cop's appetite. Barker indicated he would be willing to turn over the material, but only if he got a deal for his client, who was serving 25 years for a robbery he probably didn't commit.

"What do you think we could do for your client?" asked Brosch.

Barker told him to make a deal with Canadian police. "Police in Canada are infinitely corrupt," he told Brosch, warming up for one of his usual rants. "They will do whatever you ask them to do." Barker said his client might need a little cash as well in exchange for the inch-thick file of Ng's drawings. Brosch told him he would need to talk to his superiors. "Call back this afternoon," he said.

When Barker called back, Brosch told him the San Francisco police department was definitely interested, but he needed proof the drawings were legitimate.

"Laberge can attest to that, and I'm sure you have handwriting experts who can verify Ng's handwriting," Baker replied. "He's written captions under most of the sketches." Barker told Brosch the sketches were sexually obscene. He described a few of them over the phone. Brosch could hear the rustle of paper over the telephone line from the desk over 1,600 miles away. "Here's one with a man on his knees facing a man in standing position who is holding a machine gun," said Barker. "It's captioned, 'Please don't shoot. I'll suck.'"

Barker now insisted Brosch not involve Canadian police. He refused to bring the sketches to California and insisted upon receiving advance notice of any plans the San Francisco police might have to come to Canada to retrieve them. Brosch called back a few days later and made arrangements to view the sketches in Barker's office on the University of Alberta campus two weeks later. Erdelatz ignored Barker's request about leaving Canadian officials out of the loop. About a week before the meeting, Erdelatz called the Edmonton police service to request help in obtaining the sketches. He briefed them on the case and explained the predicament. He told them Charlie was wanted for 12 murders and was believed responsible for another 13. Now this lawyer had sketches, which experts had verified had been drawn by Ng, and wanted money for them.

"We're not prepared to pay a nickel for the drawings," Erdelatz snarled. "If this Barker is a lawyer, he has a duty to turn the documents over to police." He urged Edmonton city police to seize the sketches or he would take them himself without a search warrant. Edmonton police weren't confident that they could obtain a search warrant since the crimes involved were committed outside of Canada. They told Erdelatz they would have to check with Ottawa.

Brosch flew into the Edmonton International Airport the day before his scheduled meeting with Barker and met with police and justice officials in a federal justice department building downtown. Nine people attended the 3:00 P.M. meeting, including Shelagh Creagh, a prosecutor who would be handling Charlie's extradition hearing. RCMP Sergeant Ray Munro was there, too, following the orders of his boss, Chief Superintendent Gordie Grieg. Creagh said she would look into obtaining a search warrant under the Extradition Act. Ray, she said, would be the primary investigator because the Extradition Act came under federal authority. After a half hour of discussion, they decided to await the results of the meeting with Barker. Perhaps he would hand over the sketches, and they wouldn't need a warrant.

A city police homicide detective named Tom Peebles drove Brosch to a hotel near the university campus the next morning. Since Barker had insisted that Canadian police not be contacted, Brosch took a cab to his 9:30 A.M. meeting at the Law Centre. He arrived early but found Barker waiting in his office. After exchanging pleasantries, Brosch got down to business.

"Do you mind if I look at the sketches?" he asked. Barker produced five large manila envelopes and invited Brosch's inspection. Before he had viewed even half of the first envelope, Brosch knew the sketches were well worth the trip. He told Barker the sketches were important evidence in the murder case, and he wanted to take the material with him.

"No way!" retorted Barker. "You get nothing until I get help for my client."

"Just what do you expect us to do?" asked Brosch.

Barker told him to inform Canada's attorney general how important the material was to his case and ask him to release Mo. Barker said he believed the endorsement of the San Francisco police department would win Mo's early parole on a sentence that wouldn't expire until 2007. Mo was eligible for parole as early as December 1989, but given the judge's remarks at his sentencing, it was very unlikely Mo could be paroled before 1999 unless he cut a deal. Barker said Mo had to get out of prison soon or he would be killed because he had blown the whistle on corrupt guards. His life was in danger.

Brosch offered to write a supportive letter to Mo's parole board.

"That's not good enough," snorted Barker.

"That's about the best we can do," Brosch replied. "I'll talk to the DA, but I doubt we can do much more than that. Now what's this about cash?"

Barker told him Laberge's family had spent $10,000 on his legal expenses and it would be nice to recover it, but his client's freedom was more important than money. Brosch asked to photocopy the sketches and Barker told him to pick out six. When Brosch picked out 56, Barker reluctantly agreed to let him photocopy the bundle. But when they finished photocopying the last of the sketches, Brosch told Barker he wanted the originals.

"In California it's against the law to withhold evidence," he told Barker.

Barker exploded. His face grew red and he began yelling at the cop. "Don't you dare threaten me," he shouted. "If you try anything funny with the local cops, the sketches will disappear and you will never see them again." Then shaking a finger at Brosch, he warned him to stay away from Mo.

Unperturbed, the policeman sat flipping through the sketches while he waited for Barker to cool down. As he went through the stack, he noticed Mo's notes.

"Is this Laberge's writing?" he asked.

Barker confirmed it was. Mo had written down Charlie's admissions as he made them, he explained. "He took complete and detailed notes," he continued. "He's a very intelligent man. It gets him into trouble sometimes because he is smarter than the guards."

The meeting lasted almost until noon. Finally, Brosch got to his feet and advised Barker that he would get back to him about his request after he had talked to the district attorney in California. He took a cab back to the hotel and met Peebles. He was pretty happy with the morning's work. He had walked out of Barker's office with 56 photocopies of Ng sketches. It was a start.

Back at the federal department of justice that afternoon, the officers met again with Creagh, Ray Munro and a few other city police officials. They were later joined by Bruce MacFarlane, a senior justice department official. Creagh and MacFarlane explained that they would not be able to obtain a search warrant under the Extradition Act because there hadn't even been a formal extradition request from the American government. Perhaps there might be a way of pursuing a search warrant under a breach of Canadian law. They decided to examine the possibilities and meet again the following morning.

At 8:30 A.M. they reconvened at the Bowker Building, near the provincial Legislature, with senior officials from the provincial attorney general's department. Both the deputy minister and the assistant deputy minister joined the group of police officers and prosecutors to discuss a plan to pursue charges against Barker that would enable them to seize the original sketches. The only option, they decided, would be to charge him with obstruction of justice, but success seemed remote. It would be difficult to win the argument in court that Barker was obligated to turn over documents to police in another country. Even if they could convince a judge to sign a search warrant to empower them to seize the sketches from his office, how did they know he hadn't moved them? The meeting broke up without a definite plan. Everyone was worried that Barker might destroy the documents if he was slapped with charges. Police decided, however, to keep the option open by gathering evidence on Barker's bid to use the sketches to obtain cash and freedom for his client.

To that end, when Brosch returned to Barker's office for a second meeting at 2:00 P.M. that day, he was wearing a listening device concealed under his clothing. Peebles and two other officers delivered Brosch to the same hotel where he had picked up a taxi the previous day. With the California cop on his way to the rendezvous with Barker, the Edmonton detectives set up in a parking lot just northwest of the lawyer's fourth-floor office and activated the listening and recording equipment.

Barker seemed to suspect Brosch might be wearing a wire. He sat on the opposite side of the room and kept his voice low—almost in a whisper.

"Well?" asked Barker.

"I talked to my DA, and he's interested in this stuff," Brosch began. "He's concerned that we're not getting the originals. He says there's nothing he can do with copies."

"He'll get the originals when he agrees to help my client," Barker promised. He added that Mo would have to be available to testify in order to have the sketches introduced in court. "The state of California is not all that different than out here. It's got to be introduced through a witness." The problem, Barker continued, was that it was going to be difficult to have a serving Canadian prisoner travel to the United States to testify. There really wasn't a precedent for that. How could a convicted felon be moved across the U.S. border? And it would be unlikely that he could swear the testimony in Canada because Ng's defense team would want to cross-examine him on his evidence.

"That looks like it's going to be a monumental task, the way I see it," Brosch agreed. "We'll have to look into it." He asked Barker if he could bring local police into the case. Barker dismissed his concerns with a wave of his hand.

"There's nothing they could do for you anyway," he snorted. "You would just be wasting everybody's time."

Brosch said the Calaveras district attorney, as well as the families of the victims, were anxious to learn any information that might lead to bodies still unrecovered. Police had yet to locate the bodies of the Dubs family, Ng's co-workers and the female victims. According to Mo's notes, the bodies of the Dubs had been buried, and it might be still possible to recover them.

"Well, there may be more sketches, but I can say in all honesty that I don't know if there's any more," said Barker. He refused to hand over the originals until his client was paroled. "If he can be paroled without a fuss, if that parole can be set up in such a way, then he can go to California while on parole."

"I'm kind of caught in the middle," protested Brosch. "My guys tell me I need the original stuff. We're not going to deal in the dark." He told Barker that in a high-profile case like Ng's, every aspect of the prosecution would be under intense public scrutiny. There could be no secret deals. Maybe the public reaction would be favorable to paroling Mo to testify against Charlie. Perhaps Mo could be portrayed as a hero for coming forward with evidence critical to securing a conviction.

"Laberge doesn't want to be a hero," snapped Barker.

Brosch asked Barker again about payment. How much did Mo want? "You mentioned a $10,000 legal fee? Is that it?"

"I pulled that out of the air," admitted Barker.

"Is that the bottom line, or are we talking about a higher figure?"

"I don't even want to talk about that," Barker responded. He didn't think involving cash in the deal was a good idea. Cash wouldn't help Mo much. It could just taint the whole deal. Barker suggested that with the support of U.S. officials, perhaps Mo could be transferred to a medium-security prison like Bowden Institution, north of Calgary. He would be safer there.

"He's a super intelligent guy, but he just gets into more damn trouble," Barker explained. "But he'd be better off in Bowden because most of the inmates there are lifers." He told Brosch that arranging Mo's transfer would be a good opening point for the negotiations. If they could get Mo transferred, they could have copies of all his documents and interview him. They agreed to talk again.

Brosch headed back to San Francisco at noon the following day. Back at the office officers clustered around a drawing that depicted Charlie wearing a sign stating, "No Death Penalty." He was walking with the aid of a cane toward the American border. The cartoon was captioned, "After 30

Years Extradition." Charlie was gleefully proclaiming, "Hee, I did it!" Mo is shown offering congratulations: "Well done, Slant." The sketch alarmed Canadian police and prison officials when they saw it later. It demonstrated that Charlie was contemplating killing a guard or police officer to receive a life sentence for murder in Canada. When a copy of the sketch was turned over to Charlie's keepers in Saskatchewan, they immediately placed him back in solitary confinement. It took him some time, but Charlie was eventually able to figure out what had prompted the move.

The wiretap on Barker hadn't been very successful. There were huge gaps in the tape during which the electronic device had failed to pick up Barker's voice. He also didn't appear to have made any admissions that could form the basis of a criminal charge. Police decided to wait for the extradition process to begin before going after the original sketches. Brosch kept a line open to Barker in the hope that Mo would help them recover the bodies of Harvey, Debbie and Sean Dubs. But he didn't pursue any plans to spring Mo from captivity. They decided to let him sit for a while.

Ray Munro flew to California to assess the status of the case against Charlie. Canadian justice officials wanted him to be able to provide direct evidence to the court on the basic facts of the case. When he arrived to review the files and interview the lead investigators, Ray was shocked to discover that police in San Francisco and Calaveras were locked in a jurisdictional battle. The investigation lacked a central focus, and evidence was scattered between the two locations. Communication between the two police forces was lacking, and at times they seemed to be running at cross purposes.

It also appeared to Ray that both investigation teams had put together a great case against a dead man. They had plenty of evidence to convict Leonard Lake but little direct evidence to connect Charlie to the murders. They didn't seem to realize they had to prepare the case on paper and submit it to the Canadian courts in order to extradite Charlie.

California police officials were both bemused and confused by the appearance of a Mountie and wondered quite openly what the hell Ray was doing there. But Ray and San Francisco Assistant District Attorney Paul Cummins hit it off immediately. When Ray visited Cummins' office, he was

surprised and impressed to see a photograph of Cummins taken with President John F. Kennedy. The photo had been taken in 1963, just shortly
before Kennedy was assassinated. Cummins, just 17 at the time, had been
invited to the west wing of the White House to meet the president after
being named San Francisco's top student athlete of the year. While in San
Francisco, Ray also met with Erdelatz and Brosch. He went on to San
Andreas to meet County Sheriff Claud Ballard and Calaveras District Attorney John Martin. Ray was joined on the trip by Shelagh Creagh and Bruce
MacFarlane, who were anxious to see for themselves the case they would
have to fight. Charlie was a ward of the Canadian courts, and it would be
up to them to make sure the Americans had a solid case against him to justify the extradition. When Ray returned from the 10-day fact-finding trip,
he produced a written report of his findings for the two prosecutors, outlining a lengthy list of perceived deficiencies in the case. They had hoped to
find enough solid evidence to eliminate the need to use a jailhouse informant, but it now looked doubtful they could get by without Mo Laberge and
Charlie's sketches. Not much else existed to connect Charlie to the victims.

For more than a year the extradition case lay dormant while American
officials sorted through the evidence. Charlie struck up a new friendship
with a prisoner in solitary confinement at Prince Albert Penitentiary and
began exercising with him. He was obsessed with escaping and tried to
enlist help from everyone he met. Meanwhile, Mo pursued his studies at the
Max, taking courses in assertiveness, communications, behavioral sciences,
substance abuse and domestic violence. And Ray was preoccupied with the
Hinton train wreck that killed 22 people in the Rocky Mountain foothills
west of Edmonton. He also had set in motion plans to interview key American witnesses in the case. Canadian government officials would have to
send a diplomatic note to the American government seeking permission to
do the interviews. The FBI would have to track down the witnesses and
make the arrangements. It would take time.

Finally, in November 1987, California state officials filed the application for extradition and the process began. Ray flew to Saskatoon to apply
for a warrant of apprehension that would authorize him to remove Charlie

from prison for his first appearance at the extradition hearing. With the paperwork in hand, he drove north to Prince Albert to collect his prisoner.

It was a cold November day. The season's first snow crunched under the tires of the rental car as Ray and two Saskatoon RCMP officers drove up to the large cement buttress that enclosed the prison. Ray signed in and walked through to the prison administration area, where he waited with the warden for guards to bring Charlie from his cell. Charlie arrived in handcuffs and drab green prison garb. Ray introduced himself and explained what he was doing. An RCMP aircraft would fly them to Edmonton for the court appearance the following week. Charlie would have a chance to meet with his lawyers.

Charlie listened politely and when he spoke he addressed Ray as sir. In the warrant Charlie was accused of 25 offenses relating to the kidnapping and murder of 13 victims. He also was accused of being an accessory in the murder of car dealer Paul Cosner, of trying to kill San Francisco resident Richard Carrazza and of stealing from the Dubs' home.

Ray shackled Charlie's feet and escorted him into the prison yard, where an unmarked police car was waiting. They drove out of the gate toward the Prince Albert airport, about a 15-minute drive from the prison. Ray rode in the backseat with Charlie. He had left his .38-caliber revolver back in Edmonton. He thought it would be safer that way. He didn't want to give Charlie an opportunity to grab a weapon and make his escape. There was enough firepower in the vehicle already. Both the police officer and the prison guard in the front seat were carrying weapons.

Aboard the RCMP Twin Otter aircraft, Ray slid into a seat across the aisle from Charlie, about five seats behind the pilots. He was less worried about his proximity to Charlie during the 90-minute flight to Edmonton than he was about the snarling police dog sitting in the seat directly behind Charlie. Charlie, restrained in handcuffs and leg-irons, said little during the flight and appeared oblivious to his surroundings. He had been instructed by his lawyer, Don MacLeod, not to engage in conversation with the police officers.

Ray was surprised at how unassuming Charlie appeared. He was extremely quiet and polite. Almost timid. Although he was 26, he looked much younger. When he was wearing his glasses instead of his contacts, he looked almost bookish and nerdy. No one passing him on the street would suspect he was a horrific killer. This, thought Ray, made him all the more dangerous.

It was still daylight when they arrived at Edmonton Institution and Charlie was booked into his cell. He met with MacLeod the following day and appeared in court at Edmonton's inverted pyramid–style courthouse on November 20, 1987. Charlie was expecting to be greeted by a swarm of media when he arrived at the courthouse, but Ray took him into the building through an underground entrance. A number of reporters were on hand for his court appearance, but there wasn't much to write about. The hearing was postponed. When the day finally arrived, Charlie sat in the wooden prisoner's box in shackles. For the most part he kept his head down and his mouth shut, staring unblinkingly at the judge. The appearance was a mere formality. The court heard motions to close the proceedings to the media and set the date for the five-week hearing the following spring. It would begin May 24, 1988.

Bruce MacFarlane told reporters that the issue of whether Canada would allow the extradition in the face of California's stated intention of seeking the death penalty would not be decided at the hearing. He said it would be decided by the federal justice minister once the hearing concluded. The hearing would only determine whether the United States had sufficient evidence to prove Charles Ng had committed the offenses. Lawyers representing the United States would have to establish their case in court, and Charlie's lawyers would have an opportunity to test their evidence in cross-examination. But no one, least of all Charlie, was ready to proceed to that stage yet.

Police ferried Charlie back and forth between Edmonton Institution and the courthouse in an unmarked car, using a different route every time. There was concern that some of Charlie's military buddies might attempt a commando-style rescue operation. One route took Charlie past a trailer park that had been devastated by a tornado. Charlie was fascinated by the devastation wreaked by the twister that had struck the city in July. The tornado had skirted Edmonton's eastern outskirts and ripped through the Evergreen Mobile Home Park, killing 27 people and injuring 300 others along its 25-mile path. It also had caused more than $300 million in damage. Charlie asked Ray so many questions about the twister that the police officer decided to swing through the trailer park so Charlie could see for himself the swath the storm had cut. Much of the wreckage had been cleared away, but the bulldozed lots served as grim reminders of the people who had lived and died there just a few months earlier.

Ray returned to California after Christmas to check on progress in the case and to see what had to be done in Canada to assist in the extradition. The prosecution would present most of its case through affidavits from American witnesses. Ray was anxious to see what Charlie's military buddy Hudson would have to tell him. Charlie had been calling John Hudson and Michael Diaz frequently throughout 1984 and 1985 to brag about his escapades, but the two ex-marines were thin on details. However, Hudson, a slim dirty blond with a southern drawl could help the prosecution lay out its conspiracy theory. If police could prove that Charlie and Leonard had conspired to kill their victims, then the absence of witnesses to Charlie's involvement in the actual killings could be overcome. Hudson recalled numerous conversations in which Charlie talked about the Brotherhood and Operation Miranda. He agreed to testify at the extradition hearing.

In March 1988 Ray tracked down and interviewed witnesses involved in Charlie's arrest. A week later he headed up Highway 2 to Edmonton to determine just how much cooperation the Mounties could expect from Maurice Laberge. It was a warm clear spring day at the end of March, a nice afternoon for the drive to the prison. The snow in the fields was melting rapidly. Soon the farmers would be in the fields.

The RCMP sergeant had called the prison's head of security, Jack Arrowsmith, to arrange the meeting. Since Ray had put a few of Arrowsmith's clients into the prison, he planned to slip in through the prison's shipping and receiving door, where he wouldn't be spotted. Word that the head of RCMP homicide was visiting the joint would spread rapidly through the prison. Ray, dressed in a white shirt and brown slacks, tie and corduroy jacket, stopped in at the front gate shortly after 1:30 P.M. He checked his .38, picked up a visitor's pass and waited for Arrowsmith to show him in the back way. He didn't have to wait long.

Arrowsmith escorted him to a bare interview room near the Disassociation and Segregation Unit and instructed a guard to bring Mo from his cell. Ray glanced around the room while he waited. A table, a couple of chairs, painted cinder-block walls. He had been thinking about what to say to Mo. He hadn't called ahead to advise Mo he was coming. He expected the prisoner to be wary—possibly even angry—over his sudden appearance so long after he had sent his juicy evidence to the Americans.

Ray decided there was really only one way to play it. He would simply ask for Mo's cooperation. He would ask him if he was willing to turn over the sketches and help in the investigation. Ray would advise him that if he refused, RCMP would subpoena both the sketches and his testimony. Negotiations were not an option. Either Mo helped voluntarily or he just helped.

Like most cops Ray didn't like having to deal with inmates. They were always after something. And surprise, surprise—they usually couldn't be trusted. From what he knew about Mo, he expected nothing different. Mo was a career criminal who had grown up in an era when cons negotiated deals with cops. When Mo was committing crimes, cops didn't always have money to buy information, and they couldn't always promise protection for witnesses in danger. So cons and police did a lot of bartering over charges and information. Smart cons like Mo would break into a sporting goods shop, steal a large number of guns, bury them and then trade them in exchange for breaks when they were arrested for other offenses. They would say they knew where someone had hidden a stash of stolen guns and play it for what it was worth. They knew politicians were pushing to rid the streets of illegally obtained weapons, and police were always under pressure to recover them. It wasn't until police began recovering the same guns again and again that they realized the game being played. Mo came from that school. Well, Ray wasn't playing.

Ray knew Burke Barker, too. He was familiar with Barker's general mistrust of police, corrections officials, judges and the justice system. He

244 No Kill No Thrill

kind of admired the maverick lawyer. If he was having a coffee in the court-house cafeteria, Barker would join him and growl and rant and philoso-phize. But Ray was prepared to go straight back to his office to start draw-ing up subpoenas to serve on both Barker and his client if Mo started play-ing footsie with him.

But Mo was not the least bit riled when he walked in the door in his prison greens. When Ray introduced himself without offering to shake Mo's hand, the prisoner unleashed a disarming smile.

"How are you?" he asked. "You must be here about Ng?"

When Ray explained the situation, Mo said he would cooperate. He allowed Ray to take down an official statement to that effect. He didn't ask for anything in return, and Ray offered nothing. But both men knew Mo was approaching his first real crack at parole, and cooperating with the authorities on a complex, high-profile international case could help him. Ray was on his way back to Edmonton in a matter of minutes, pleasantly surprised at how well the interview had gone. He hadn't wanted to talk about the case with Mo. He was worried about contaminating the witness. He wanted the evidence Mo gave to come from Charlie alone and no other sources. With a record like Mo's, it was a cinch the defense would attack his credibility and motivation. But if his evidence was clear, unadulterated and corroborated by detailed notes and sketches in Charlie's own handwriting, Mo would provide an incredible bonanza for the prosecution.

19

The Hit List

PREPARATIONS for Charlie's extradition hearing were well underway in the spring of 1988 when Canadian government lawyers handling the case in Edmonton got an urgent missive from police in Saskatchewan. Charlie, it seemed, was planning to have them killed.

About a month before the hearing was to begin in Edmonton, police in Saskatoon arrested a small-time hood and sometime police informant who had been involved in a hit and run. The 41-year-old drifter faced a lengthy prison term for repeated drunk-driving infractions and for driving with a suspended license. He wanted to deal. He said he had valuable information to trade about a serial killer. He told his police handler that he had been in prison with a man who wanted someone to do a whack of killing for him. The informant, who had a record longer than his legs, never mind his scrawny, scarred and tattooed arms, claimed that documents still in his wrecked Pontiac Ventura at the police impound lot would back up his claims. He directed police to bring back a cheap vinyl suitcase stashed in the trunk. In the suitcase police found a handwritten list of witnesses and prosecutors in the case against Charles Ng, complete with addresses and phone numbers. There were asterisks beside some of the names.

"These are the people he wanted killed right away," the informant explained. Charlie had told him that killing Canadian justice department lawyers Shelagh Creagh and Bruce MacFarlane would likely delay the extradition proceedings by several years. "He wanted me to follow them home from the courthouse," the informant explained. "He said it was not a busy courthouse, and they would never think they were being followed. He wanted them both killed."

Charlie wanted to enlist his prison pal to murder about 20 people in order to break the links in the chain of evidence against him. The accused killer had numbered the targets on the list so they could discuss them without tipping off guards who might be overhearing them or intercepting their mail. "I am listing everyone so you can refer to them by number in the future or vice versa," Charlie had scrawled across the top of the list headed "Extradition Affidavit Index." He added, "Most of them are insignificant paper pushers."

The Saskatoon cop and his partner knew they had stumbled on to something significant, but with their limited knowledge of the California murders it was all very confusing. They talked to their informant for three and a half hours at the Saskatoon provincial courthouse, scarcely believing what he was saying. Their informant, whom they nicknamed Sam, claimed Ng was believed responsible for 27 murders in California. He said Ng planned to kill again while in prison. The cops got on the phone to Prince Albert Penitentiary to warn them about Charlie's stated intention to kill a prison guard in order to avoid the death penalty in California. Prison officials, courtesy of Mo and other inmates, were already well aware of Charlie's intentions. The cops tracked down extradition lawyer Shelagh Creagh in Edmonton, who put them on to Ray Munro.

The RCMP sergeant had recently been transferred to Three Hills, Alberta, a small farming community just an hour's drive north of Calgary, where he had been assigned to operate as the RCMP's uniformed detachment commander. On the surface, it seemed a bizarre move by the federal policing agency at the time, but within the RCMP, advancement beyond the rank of sergeant usually required a candidate to command a detachment.

Most of these detachments were in small towns because the RCMP had a contract with the Alberta government to supply policing in municipalities that didn't have a police force. They also patrolled provincial highways. Ray's transfer, however, had come at an inopportune time. His involvement in the Ng case was expanding as the extradition hearing loomed. But the transfer was the next logical step for the veteran cop, who was now 39 and had been in plainclothes most of his career. He had been in homicide for 14 years and actually would have welcomed the change if he hadn't had so damn much on his plate.

Ray had been assigned the Three Hills duty along with an additional six-week assignment as the lead investigator at the Calgary Winter Olympics. His Olympics duties had kept him occupied until mid-March. When the Saskatoon cops called for him in late April, Ray suggested they get a taped statement from the informant that he would use as a basis for his own interview. He stressed the importance of the evidence and the drawings. If nothing else it was important corroboration of Mo's evidence against Charlie.

After being briefed by Ray, the Saskatoon cops sat down with their informant with the tape recorder rolling. Sam had a criminal record dating back to 1964 when he stole a car in London, Ontario. He had his first drunk driving charge in Hamilton two years later. From there he had racked up offenses from coast to coast. Rape. Armed robbery. Attempted murder. Uttering threats. A dozen charges of driving while impaired and leaving accident scenes. He had proved to be a valuable snitch for the Saskatoon cops, who first encountered him being beaten outside a city bar. One of his ears was partially severed in that brawl, but he declined to lay a complaint against his attackers. When police picked him up for driving with a suspended license shortly after, he offered to be their snitch if they didn't charge him. And he kept his end of the bargain. In the course of a few months, he tipped them off about a series of farm machinery thefts, a burglary gang, a number of welfare frauds and three separate gangs involved in armed robberies, drug dealing and major thefts. And he worked cheap, seldom asking for money and occasionally paying it back at a later date. But this time he had informed the Saskatoon cops that he wanted money for his information and that he wanted to avoid going back to a federal prison, where his reputation as a snitch could come back to haunt him.

Sam had met Charlie in the segregation unit at the Prince Albert Penitentiary in September 1987 while he was serving an eight-year sentence for armed robbery. Ignoring the other prisoners who were out for their hour of exercise in the warm spring sunshine, Charlie had struck up a general conversation with Sam about penitentiary life. The second time out Charlie had told Sam a bit about his stint in the Marine Corps and about how he valued loyalty above all things. In a prison filled with young men, Charlie was drawn to Sam, nearly 13 years his elder, in the same way he had been drawn to Leonard and Mo. He needed a surrogate father in his life. He needed his advice, friendship and loyalty. Sam was impressed by the young man's intelligence. The two bonded almost immediately.

Within five days Charlie began talking about his need to find a trustworthy cohort to assist him. He said he was looking for someone willing to go to the United States and kill witnesses and prosecutors from California to Tennessee. At first Sam thought Charlie was joking, but detecting an earnestness in Charlie's voice, he listened politely. Feigning interest he asked for the kinds of details an assassin would need to know if he was seriously contemplating the assignment. Sam bragged about his own checkered past, exaggerating his exploits and trying to sound as if he was capable of murder, but he had no interest in getting involved in heavy crime. Charlie was taken in. He thought he had found his man. He excitedly told Sam that when they returned to their cells after exercise period, he would provide him with a schematic drawing of the home of one of the men he wanted killed in California.

Back in segregation, Charlie sketched a rough drawing of the home and the street, and the trees and buildings that could be used for cover. He put the drawing in his towel, reached through the bars and tossed the bundle toward Sam's cell, two doors down the range. Sam reeled it in, read it and filed it away. Like Mo he recognized its value as a potential bargaining chip should he have another encounter with police or prison officials.

Even if Sam had been a pathological killer rather than a petty crook, he would have been hard-pressed to find the motivation to do Charlie's bidding. Charlie admitted he didn't have any money to pay for the killings. All he could offer was his undying loyalty. If Sam helped him escape, Charlie vowed to pull off a few bank jobs that would handsomely reward Sam's loyalty. All Sam had to do was drive the getaway car. Charlie had a dream of stealing a motorhome and traveling from town to town, raping and robbing and hiding out in the woods. Beautiful sexy women would be no problem. They could just grab them off the streets.

Once he believed Sam would do his bidding, Charlie spelled out in detail the people he wanted killed and his reasons. He had been giving his hit list a lot of thought. He told Sam he had been spotted coming out of a house where a murder had been committed. He needed those witnesses, two women, killed. A friend in Kansas also needed to die. He told Sam that John Hudson, a former Leavenworth prison mate, was blabbing to the cops about information Charlie had given him about the bunker and his sex slaves. Hudson worked at a fast-food restaurant, and the best way to get him would be to shotgun him in the parking lot, he told Sam.

Charlie figured he would need the help of ex-marines to spring him from prison. He showed Sam plans for a commando-style raid on the guards transporting him to and from his extradition hearing in Edmonton.

"He laid out the groundwork for how they traveled from the Edmonton Max to the downtown facility where they hold court," Sam explained. "He suggested the car be stopped and the driver shot and the unarmed officer in the back [Ray Munro] be shot, too."

The schematic drawing Charlie gave to Sam detailed the layout of the home of Dennis Moving co-worker Perry McFarland. Charlie told Sam he had planned to go to the man's place and rape his wife and kill her in front of him before killing him. He said he had always had this fantasy but had never had a chance to act it out. He also wanted to steal their two vehicles: a Toyota pickup and a Dodge Omni. Charlie expected McFarland would be called to testify about the day he had showed McFarland some blood on his shoe and asked McFarland to guess whose blood it was. When McFarland guessed it was Charlie's blood, Charlie had laughed and said it was a "nappie-head's blood [the blood of an Afro-American]." Charlie hated blacks.

He told Sam he also wanted his boss, Dennis Goza, killed because he had told a private investigator working for Charlie's lawyer that Charlie wasn't at work on the days his co-workers were murdered. Charlie wanted three other company employees killed as well. He told Sam to kill them all at once when they took their morning coffee break. He said they always went to the same place.

"He gave me a detailed description of these people's movements," Sam told police. "Some of it he wrote down. He said if I needed weapons, the place to get them was the police officers' homes in Calaveras County because it was a very isolated area. He suggested I just go up there, kill them and take their weapons out of their homes.

"He was very adamant. He wanted them dead. He seemed to be very vindictive." Since reading a *Penthouse* magazine article about his case, Charlie also had deadly plans for his partner's ex-wife, Cricket. The article revealed that Cricket had provided information to the police. Charlie complained that because of Cricket he would never get a fair trial. He wanted her dead.

"Apparently, she had given other interviews to other scandal sheets over the past year, and she stopped because her lawyer told her that she could implicate herself in the murders," Sam told police. Charlie told Sam about the videotapes and suggested that one showed Leonard, Cricket and him having sex with dead bodies.

Sam admitted he had no idea why Charlie chose him as his confidante. He had read newspaper stories of the murders and was well aware of Charlie's notoriety. "I don't know for what reason he chose to talk to me, but he did, for whatever reasons." But he said Charlie was suspicious almost to the point of being paranoid. That worried Sam. Charlie always talked about killing a prison guard, but Sam figured he would settle for killing a fellow inmate, especially if he thought the inmate was ratting him out. He might get only five years in prison for killing an inmate, but he could always kill another later.

Most of the names on Charlie's hit list came through the private detective hired, at California state expense, to assist the defense, Sam said. "The man seemed to give him a lot of information about people's movements, where they lived, their phone numbers. A lot of these things he got from his investigator, he gave to me to help in the quest to eradicate these people from his life." In addition to hiring a private investigator on his behalf, the state also shelled out $2,000 for a computer to help Charlie keep tabs on his court documents, he said.

Knowing that Sam was soon to be released on mandatory supervision (the Canadian equivalent of time off for good behavior), Charlie devised a plan to continue communicating after Sam left prison. Charlie instructed Sam to have some envelopes printed with his lawyer's name and return address because guards weren't supposed to read the privileged correspondence between inmates and their lawyers. Charlie instructed Sam in the preparation of invisible ink that wouldn't appear unless the page was heated. He also taught Sam jargon from the game Dungeons and Dragons so no one could understand their messages.

Sam had told Charlie he had an ex-marine buddy who might be willing to help with Charlie's escape. His friend, whom they code-named Ollie, after Oliver North, would be invited on a fishing trip—code for the killing of John Hudson in Kansas—and bowling—code for the murders of the California witnesses. If he wrote, "I went to the movies," it meant he had done a reconnaissance of the target. If he said, "I saw Harry last night," it meant the person had police protection. If he wrote that he would have a cup of coffee on April 16, it meant Charlie would be scooped out of prison by helicopter in broad daylight, and if it was a cup of hot chocolate, it meant they would break Charlie out at night. If he said Eddie was coming with him, it meant he would be using plastic explosives to blow his way into the prison. Charlie also devised terms for booby traps, safe houses and stabbings.

Charlie would send letters to Sam in care of Rodger Henry, General Delivery in Saskatoon. He asked Sam to send him information on karate killing blows because, for security reasons, it wasn't available in the prison library. Charlie gave Sam a crash course in everything from the use of burglary tools to the acquisition of silencers and the construction of pipe bombs. He told Sam where to find books on guerrilla warfare and survivalism and how to steal identification documents.

Sam told the city cops that Charlie scared the crap out of him. "I think he would take my life in a minute if he thought I was jerking him around." He said that as he was leaving the prison, Charlie had handed him a note to thank him for his friendship and to remind him of his duty to him. He scrawled, "Hard to put into words. I want to let you know I am proud to be your friend/family and trust that I won't be waiting in vain. Take good care and I'll see you when the day comes. For the meantime, happy hunting." The note included a sketch of two men in a jeep with a machine gun mounted on it heading to San Francisco. The caption read, "Here comes the rat patrol." He also gave Sam a photo of himself with a big smile on his face, sitting cross-legged on the floor in a Nike T-shirt, jeans and sneakers. Sam gave Charlie a sweatshirt.

When Ray interviewed Sam about a week after he had spoken to Saskatoon police, he was curious to know just what Charlie planned to do when he escaped from prison. Sam said he wasn't planning to disappear. "He wants to become a terrorist. His goal was once he got out of jail, he would be free to go on a crime spree. He intended to amass $100,000 to $200,000 and then go into Europe. He wants to become more dangerous and renowned than Carlos, the well-known European terrorist."

Ray quickly ascertained that Charlie had talked in generalities to Sam about his crimes with the exception of the killing of San Francisco disk jockey Donald Giuletti. Charlie was worried that Giuletti's roommate, Richard Carrazza, could identify him. He was apparently still unaware that Carrazza had failed to pick him out of a police lineup in Calgary. Ray asked Sam if Charlie had any unique expressions.

"Well," replied Sam, "I heard him say, 'Daddy dies, momma cries, baby fries,' but his favorite thing was, 'No kill, no thrill.' When he talked about past crimes, he would say these phrases and giggle." Sam was committed to testifying against Charlie if required, but Ray wondered how useful he would be. His reputation as a snitch who would sell anyone out for money or favors did not make him a very credible witness. Still, police thought Sam could be useful. Through him they could keep tabs on Charlie and possibly obtain more evidence to use against him at the extradition hearing.

Police engaged Charlie in correspondence using the codes that Sam provided. Charlie wrote that he had heard that Sam had been arrested following an accident. "Believe my heart sank when I learned of it, but now am glad you seem to be okay. I hope you have a chance to complete your correspondence courses and have had a good chat with Ollie about the fishing trip. For now, keep the faith, stay sober and keep me posted." In his cryptic letter, Charlie was inquiring whether Sam had obtained fake identification for him and if Sam's mercenary friend was willing to help him break out of prison.

Sam's response a few days later kept Charlie's hopes alive that plans were underway to assist him from the outside. "Heard from Ollie. He's been making plans to get down there for a day or so to visit. Is most excited about his fishing trip. He's a real movie buff so is going to stop in Edmonton and PA on his way down here by car. Got one of my correspondence courses going. Am still working on acquiring another." Police were advising Charlie that Sam's friend was planning to do a reconnaissance of the Edmonton and PA prisons and that Sam had lined up a set of fake identification and was working on a second set.

If Charlie's spirits were lifted by the letter, he didn't indicate it in his reply. He was depressed. Spring was coming, the snow was melting and he was stuck in prison with lousy food and "more noisy punks."

"These days I get more restless and distracted, like a kid waiting for his promised present, which I trust you understand," he wrote. In code he informed Sam that he hadn't found new addresses for some of the targets on his hit list, but he was still hopeful Sam would carry out the murder missions. He was also curious when the jail break might come together. "I assume Ollie wasn't too lucky on his SE Asia fishing trip. Hope he plans to try his luck fly-fishing this trip. Did he say (roughly) when he will cast his lines? Did he have any problems getting his equipment together? If he plans to drop by for a surprise visit, let him know I will be at this address for a while. But do ascertain the day in advance because a screw-up would be extremely embarrassing—not to mention costly."

Charlie followed up with a note the next day to advise Sam he was about to be shipped to Edmonton for court appearances leading to his extradition, but he didn't expect to be away from Prince Albert for long. Sam responded with another upbeat letter advising Charlie that his military friend had engaged a helicopter pilot to assist in the jail break.

Charlie replied in mid-May. He didn't know when he would be shipped back to Prince Albert. "Send my greeting to Ollie and I hope you fare well on your correspondence courses. Tell him I really miss fishing. And I count on you to win some bowling bouts for me."

"One last thing," he scrawled across the bottom of the page, "in case I won't be fishing soon, would it be possible to spare $200 in a money order so I can buy that typewriter I desperately need?" He wrote again two weeks later. In a long, rambling and self-pitying letter, he brought Sam up to speed on his extradition case. "My actual hearing will commence on October 17, 1988 and will last six weeks or more," he explained. "Security measures to and from the airport/court and inside the courtroom is provided by the RCMP emergency response team with MP5s and 9 mm automatics. Belly chain and leg-irons all the way. Therefore I am not looking forward to the arduous event."

He wished Sam the best and advised him not to "sweat it" if their communication broke down. He asked him to acknowledge his letter with a postcard. "In this no-win situation I am contained in, when almost everyone is either cashing in, ratting about and/or sinking me, one thing that keeps me going is a man like you who still holds values like loyalty, courage and friendship high."

He got his return postcard from Sam via the police.

Charlie's mention of everyone cashing in was a direct reference to Mo. He now suspected Mo was going to testify against him at his extradition hearing. And he figured it was likely Mo who had turned over the sketches to prison authorities that ended his stint in general population. Soon after his return to the Max, Charlie put in a request for Mo to cut his hair. Mo refused, saying he would only cut Charlie's hair if Charlie was in restraints. A few days later, when Mo was about to enter the exercise yard, he noticed Charlie there. He stood in the doorway a moment wondering if he dared enter the exercise area. Ray had instructed him not to have any further contact with Charlie, but how could he not go out without Charlie becoming suspicious? He stepped slowly into the yard, leaving the door behind him open a crack in case he had to make a hasty retreat. He welcomed Charlie back to the Max, and they made small talk for a few minutes. Charlie told him about Sam and asked if Mo knew him. When Mo said he didn't, Charlie told him about the escape plans he and Sam had concocted. He also told Mo about his hit list. Before long Charlie broached the subject of the sketches. He asked Mo directly if he had turned them over to prison officials. Mo denied it. He could tell Charlie was extremely upset, and he was worried that the conversation would turn violent. The next 75 minutes were among the longest of Mo's life. He felt like he was locked in a tank with a piranha. It was a relief when the guards summoned them back to their cells. But the next day the guards let the two out for exercises at the same time again.

Mo wasn't sure what to make of the situation. Was Charlie pissed at him or not? Charlie had given the sketches to him, and now the prison officials had them. It wasn't too difficult to put it together. Was Charlie waiting for a chance to strike a killing blow? As time went on, Mo began to doubt that Charlie intended him harm. Maybe his initial impression about Charlie wanting his story told was correct. Maybe in Mo's case Charlie's desire for notoriety was greater than his need for vengeance. They went out together in the yard, picking up where they had left off nine months earlier. Charlie started talking about the Dubs. Mo was all ears. He knew through his lawyer that the San Francisco police were anxious to recover their bodies. Mo asked Charlie where he and Leonard had dumped them. Charlie stooped over and drew a map in the dirt. He said the burial site was about three miles from Lake's cabin and up a steep hill. Leonard had picked the spot one day when he was out walking his dog. Charlie said they spent two days digging the hole, which was on federal land. It was tough digging, pick and shovel work like he was used to in the marines. "We went down about this deep," he said to Mo, gesturing to his chin with his right hand. He said they dug the grave several days before they went into San Francisco to grab the Dubs. He said Leonard had drugged the couple, and they had still been groggy when he'd asked Charlie to kill them. Charlie said he used the cord of a soldering iron. "It was easy," he told Mo. "After I killed them we loaded the bodies into the Volkswagen camper and drove up the hill. We dropped the baby and the bodies into the hole and filled it with dirt. We went back a couple of days later and spread some more dirt around so there wouldn't be any indentation when it rained."

Mo pressed Charlie for more detail about the location of the grave. Charlie told him it was difficult to get the vehicle up the steep trail so they had to drag the bodies through the pines to reach the site. It was wet and slippery going.

"How did you feel when this was happening?" asked Mo.

"I was on a mission. I wanted to do it and get it over with."

When Mo contacted Ray to let him know what he had learned, Ray was furious. "I thought I told you to stay away from that guy!" He talked to the prison's security officer and made sure the pair didn't exercise together again. Ray relayed the information to Calaveras County, where the sheriff's deputies launched another search for the Dubs. Charlie's map, which Mo duplicated back in his cell, was too vague to be of any real help. They came up empty.

Things weren't going very well for Mo either. After testifying at the preliminary hearing of the murder case against fellow prisoner Daniel Gingras, Mo was advised that he was going to be transferred to the maximum-security Kent Institution, the sister prison to Edmonton Max, located near Mission, British Columbia. Mo had been working hard to win a transfer to the medium-security Bowden Institution, north of Calgary, where he felt he would be able to function in population without fear of being killed by another prisoner. Inmates who testified against their fellow inmates tended to have short life spans in maximum-security jails. Survival was difficult among killers already serving life terms who wouldn't pass up a chance to earn money and power by erasing a rat.

There was more. After Mo had testified at Gingras' preliminary, Mo's sister received a call from the accused killer claiming that he knew where to find her and that it might not be in her best interests if her brother testified against him at his trial. Now, Corrections Canada officials wanted to send Mo into general population.

Panic-stricken, Mo got on the phone from the Calgary Remand Centre to Ray Munro, urging him to do something to block the transfer. "If they send me there, I won't survive past dinnertime," he predicted.

Ray, who had spent the summer preparing a four-volume court brief for the extradition hearing, made a number of calls and finally managed to delay the transfer. Prison officials agreed to send Mo to the Regional Psychiatric Centre in Saskatoon for anger management therapy until after he testified at the extradition hearing and Gingras' trial. It was only a short-term solution. Police would have to find a safe institution to house their informant after that. Ray called in Sergeant Ray Ambler, a longtime RCMP acquaintance who coordinated the force's witness protection program. Ambler enrolled Mo in the program, pledging to work with prison officials to ensure his safety while he was incarcerated. The deal also called for further protection should Mo still be in danger after his release from prison. He was their baby now.

"After 30 Years . . . Extradition," a sketch by Charles Ng depicting his goal to remain, by whatever means, including murder, in Canadian prisons until California had abandoned the death penalty.

20

Tug of War

IN MID-OCTOBER 1988 Sharon Sellitto pulled her suitcase out of the closet at her home in San Francisco's Glen Park and began packing for a trip to Canada. The autumn trek to Edmonton was not going to be a vacation. The outspoken 41-year-old former dancer and circus performer was heading to the Alberta capital to glare into the dark empty eyes of the man accused of murdering her brother, Paul Cosner. She had waited a long time for the opportunity.

When a reporter from the *Edmonton Journal* called her, she took time from packing to explain why she wanted to attend the extradition hearing. "I want to see Charles Ng in person," she explained. "I want to come and hate him close up." Sellitto had carried on a one-person campaign since her brother had disappeared in November 1984. Paul had been her only brother, and for much of her life, especially after her parents divorced and her stepfather died, he was the closest thing she had to a father. She was initially furious at the incompetence of police, at their seeming reluctance to even search for her missing brother. Now she was outraged at the legal maneuvers undertaken by Charles Ng and his lawyers to drag out the extradition process and nearly as furious with Canadian authorities for allowing it to happen. She had read that Canada had refused to extradite World War II Nazis to face post-war justice at the Nuremberg trials, and she was anxious to ensure her brother's accused killer didn't avoid his date with the California gas chamber.

"I want to see, in person, the process that's put us through hell—the Canadian extradition process," she said. "We were thrilled when Ng was caught up there," she told the reporter, "but we've been put on hold for three and a half years by your judicial process."

A groundswell of public opinion was sweeping across Canada, urging the government to send Charles Ng back to face his accusers. Led by the Ottawa-based Victims of Violence movement, Canadians were circulating petitions and writing letters to politicians demanding the fugitive be sent back immediately without waiting for assurances that he wouldn't face the death penalty. It was the movement, headed by Gary and Sharon Rosenfeldt, that had invited Sellitto and the families of other murder victims to Canada to attend the extradition hearing. The former Edmonton couple had met Sellitto when they had driven to San Francisco to protest Canada's extradition policies in front of the Canadian consulate a few weeks before the hearing. The Rosenfeldts knew the pain the families were suffering. Their own child, along with 10 others, had been murdered by Canada's most reprehensible serial killer, Clifford Olson, just six years earlier. They had watched their son's killer play the system, even receiving cash to reveal where he had hidden his victims' bodies. Gary Rosenfeldt, a stocky middle-aged man with curly brown locks, had founded the organization in Edmonton to help victims in Alberta, and it quickly grew into a national organization with chapters in communities from coast to coast.

Now Gary Rosenfeldt was upset over the Charles Ng case. He wanted to show Canadians the faces of the suffering families and force them to deal with the death-penalty issue on an emotional rather than philosophical level. He had made personal contact with several of the families as part of a bid to show them that Canadians cared about their plight. He and his wife had been speaking at a conference on victims of crime at the University of Michigan in Ann Arbor in May when he discovered Brenda O'Connor's family lived in Coldwater, just an hour away. Gary and Sharon were excited about making contact but apprehensive about how they would be received. They knew the trauma that turns families into victims often shatters their trust in people, causing them to sometimes react with hostility to anyone breaching their privacy. Richard O'Connor, Brenda's father, took the call with a fair amount of surprise, bewilderment and skepticism, but he invited the Rosenfeldts to the family's home and greeted them warmly. The meeting was highly emotional with Brenda's tearful siblings clustered around, but through a frank discussion of the issues in the case, the two families forged a bond that transcended governments and borders.

The Rosenfeldts had traveled to California to meet Sharon Sellitto in June. When they learned she had been refused an interview with the Canadian consul, who even refused her phone calls, they called the media and demonstrated with a crowd of supporters outside the consulate office until they were invited in for a meeting. They were making a difference and winning the admiration of Americans, especially the victims, with their vocal stance. When the date of the extradition hearing was announced, Victims of Violence contacted the families and invited them to Edmonton, offering to defray some of the cost if they needed financial assistance.

"We're hoping that throughout the five-week hearing that we can bring in a steady stream of victims' families," Rosenfeldt told reporters in Canada. Charles Ng's extradition hearing was a hot issue in the United States, and Rosenfeldt was determined to make it a hot issue in Canada. He already had the attention of the White House. The office of U.S. Vice-President George Bush had contacted the organization for its views on the case.

Sellitto, too, had been writing letters to politicians on both sides of the border, from San Francisco City Hall to the White House and Parliament Hill. By the time she arrived in Edmonton the day before the hearing was scheduled to commence, she had worked herself into a rage. She stepped in front of the cameras and microphones and warned Canadians that their country was going to become a haven for killers if they didn't start sending them back to face justice. Start with Charlie, she demanded.

"I think it's fine for your country to have no death penalty, if that's

262 No Kill No Thrill

what you want," she continued. "But why are you making it applicable across the border? It's none of your concern what we do with our criminals."

In stark contrast to Sellitto's belligerence, her 64-year-old mother, Virginia Nessley, choked back sobs as she told reporters that she was anxious to talk to Canada's justice minister Ray Hnatyshyn about the case. "I'd like to know if he has any children," the still-grieving Ohio woman said through her tears. "Does he have one child he could spare—because I didn't." She described the death of her son as a personal holocaust and doubted, at the speed the case was going, that she would live long enough to see his killer brought to trial.

Security at the Court of Queen's Bench was tight. Spectators, having walked through a gauntlet of reporters and photographers outside the concrete building, had to pass through a metal detector and a throng of heavily armed police to reach the entrance of Courtroom 417. Guards asked Sellitto, who had her long blonde hair tied in a bun, to remove her hairpins and let her hair fall to her shoulders. Once inside, she sat with her mother in the front row, impressed by the solemnity of the proceeding. Red-coated Mounties in Stetsons and knee-high brown riding boots were stationed around the courtroom. On a table at the front of the room, the evidence lay in heaps. Ray's handiwork was there—four black binders, each four inches thick. There were hundreds of pages of affidavits, evidence from the pathologists and crime-scene investigators, the police identification specialists, the handwriting experts—the culmination of years of work by police in many cities. The U.S. case was outlined in a single foot-thick document adorned with a red ribbon and a gold seal. Ray sat nervously at the prosecution table. This was his baby. If the case failed it would be his neck on the block.

The crowd waited quietly in anticipation of Charlie's arrival, tipped off by the sudden attentiveness of the security detail. They could hear him coming from a long way off, the faint jingle of his chains growing louder as he approached through a hidden corridor inside the bowels of the court building. When he finally emerged he was shackled at the wrist, waist and ankles, and clad in prison clothing—dark green slacks and a green zippered jacket over a navy blue T-shirt. He was 27 now and looked like he had put on 10 pounds.

Nessley's heart pounded as he shuffled to the prisoner's box. Her clenched hands trembled, but she kept her eyes locked upon him as if she were trying to burn a hole right through him. Her daughter mouthed "bastard" as he went by. How unspectacular he is, she mused. How ordinary. He's not very big and tough at all without a gun or a knife in his hands. She stared at him in the prisoner's box, where he sat with his head bowed. She was pleased that he appeared uncomfortable. His leg twitched nervously, and his Adam's apple quivered uncontrollably.

The courtroom was called to order when Justice Marguerite Trussler took her seat on a raised dais at the front of the courtroom. A stern-faced woman in a black judge's robe with a red sash, she was a relatively new appointment to the bench. The hearing got off to a slow start as both sides spent a good deal of time arguing over the admissibility of evidence. But when federal prosecutor Bruce MacFarlane referred to the case as "The People of the United States against Charles Ng," it was a tiny victory for Sellitto. It was no longer just her fighting alone for justice. It was no longer the City of San Francisco. Or the State of California. It was now the United States of America. It sounded so important.

MacFarlane began by describing the brotherhood Charlie and Leonard Lake had formed—an evil partnership created for the purpose of kidnapping and enslaving women to fulfill their brutal sexual fantasies. Operation Miranda. He told the judge that he would present a mountain of evidence—100 affidavits, testimony from 15 witnesses and a videotape—over the coming weeks.

Sellitto walked out of the first three-hour session feeling better than she had in months. "I am not so filled with rage now," she told a waiting throng of reporters. The evil that had terrified her all this time had been pulled out of the darkness and thrust into the light of day, where it had been stripped of its menacing power. "We don't have to sit at home going crazy over it in private anymore, making ourselves sick."

On the second day, Charlie again sat quietly in the prisoner's box, flanked by two heavily armed RCMP Emergency Response Team members. The previous day he had nearly slipped out of his handcuffs when an ERT member let his attention stray. Ray was rotating the officers on Charlie's detail every two days to prevent them from becoming too complacent. Ray had no doubt that Charlie would make a break for it if he thought he had a good chance of getting away. MacFarlane started the day by describing how Leonard and Charlie opened post office boxes under the names of their victims to siphon off money still coming to them. The pair didn't just kill their victims, he explained. They stole their lives and stripped them of everything of value. MacFarlane was setting the tone for what would follow, and the proceedings settled into a routine. Day after day, week after week, MacFarlane continued to outline the case set out in more than 200 pages of affidavits. He called witness after witness. Sellitto and her mother and stepfather eventually returned to their homes, but their seats in the courtroom were soon filled with members of other victims' families.

Richard and Sharron O'Connor arrived in early November to add their voices to the growing lobby. They warned Canadian minister of justice Ray Hnatyshyn that he would take a lot of heat from Canadian voters if he failed to send Ng back. They urged the justice minister, who was already the target of a massive letter-writing campaign, to take steps to speed up the extradition process. Ng's lawyers had revealed that they intended to appeal an unfavorable decision all the way to the Supreme Court of Canada, a move that would delay Charlie's murder trial for years.

Dwight and Lola Stapely flew from Los Angeles to see the man accused of murdering their son, Scott. Lola, a heavyset woman with a penchant for flowery dresses, fixed her eyes on Charlie and glared at him for two straight days. The Stapelys weren't prepared for the shockingly cold climate in Canada's northernmost large city and headed back to southern California early after the hearing went into one of several closed sessions to hear the testimony of protected witnesses.

Raymond Joseph Leveque Munro took the witness stand on Halloween as one of the last six Crown witnesses. The previous Friday the roly-poly Mountie had been in the courtroom as the M Ladies videotape was played. He had seen the tape at least 10 times, so he focused his attention on the accused. As Charlie sat in the prisoner's box watching the tape on a small television screen, he appeared to be actually salivating during the scenes in which Kathi Allen and Brenda O'Connor had been forced to disrobe. Drool leaked from the corners of his mouth. Munro was repulsed. Ray knew what Charlie had done, knew what he was capable of doing, but he was still filled with revulsion watching Charlie's reaction to the videotape. Even in front of a courtroom, he was very obviously enjoying himself.

Ray was called upon to give background on two witnesses who were still scheduled to present evidence, Mo and John Hudson, who were testifying anonymously as John Doe 1 and John Doe 2. The prosecution elected at the last moment not to call Sam, the Prince Albert Penitentiary inmate whose testimony Ray felt would corroborate Mo's evidence about Charlie's sketching ability. Later a police handwriting expert would testify that Charlie drew the captions on the sketches, but no evidence would ever be tendered to prove that Charlie drew the sketches himself. Ray described his involvement in securing Charlie's sketches and outlined his dealings with Mo. He explained that he had met with San Francisco police inspector Jeff Brosch when he arrived in Edmonton and had been involved in a number of meetings with high-level justice department officials to determine how best to obtain the evidence. Police had seized the originals of the sketches only a week before the hearing was slated to begin. Ray described his meetings with Charlie and Mo and also verified that one of the voices on the videotape was Charlie's.

Ray Ambler, the RCMP officer in charge of the RCMP witness protection program, followed Munro to the stand to explain why Mo required protection as a result of his testimony against multiple murderer Daniel Gingras. Ambler was grilled extensively about the protection deal by Charlie's lawyer, Don MacLeod, a 35-year-old workaholic from Calgary.

MacLeod, a graduate of the University of British Columbia, had a reputation as a bit of a bulldog. He was a dirt biker and a hockey player and co-chaired the Canadian Bar Association's southern Alberta criminal justice section. After four years in corporate law, he had jumped into criminal and civil law and had handled everything from thefts to murders. Over the last eight years he had taken on a number of unpopular high-profile cases, including the case of a man claiming to have been assaulted by police and a man fired from the University of Calgary over a PCB spill.

MacLeod wasn't sure if his appointment to Charlie's defense team was a blessing or a curse, but he suspected it was the latter. He hadn't worked so hard on a case since he had represented Seattle fugitive Wai Chiu (Tony) Ng in the fall of 1984, and he remembered vowing at that time never to touch another case like it. Then Charlie's case fell in his lap, and he couldn't pass it up. He was the most qualified Alberta lawyer for the job, and in terms of legal issues, he found the case irresistible. He was having to break new ground. Since the Canadian Charter of Rights and Freedoms had come into effect in 1982, no one had raised the issue of whether the death penalty constituted cruel and unusual treatment. And the actual criminal case was staggering—12 murder charges, 26 charges over all. It was likely going to be the longest extradition hearing in Canadian history. The caseload was crushing, and it would increase as he rushed to meet deadlines in the time-limited appeals.

MacLeod's defense of Charles Ng was high-profile and was sparking heated debate over the death penalty in Canada. MacLeod was even getting a hostile reception from people on the street. He had received death threats. In addition to being attacked for representing Charlie, he was also being blamed for delaying the process. But he gave no quarter. The criticism only drove him to work harder. He took the case because he staunchly opposed the death penalty. He made no bones about it. "I hold the view that as a society we should hold ourselves to a higher standard of conduct than the conduct we ascribe to people we label as criminals," he explained. "I think there has to be another way."

Now, with a chance to prevent at least one man from being subjected to what he termed "ritual murder," MacLeod went after the deal RCMP had made to secure Mo's testimony. Just what was the prisoner's motivation? Did police offer to help get Mo out of prison in exchange for his assistance in the Ng and Gingras cases? Ambler, a lanky articulate Mountie, denied it.

"It was emphatically told to him, 'No, we have no control over

Canada Corrections and National Parole and what they do with you,'"
he testified.

"The question is this, though," MacLeod pursued the officer. "You
would advise the National Parole Board that he had been of assistance?"

"Oh, yes, yes," agreed Ambler. He explained that if necessary, in the
event of Mo's release from prison, the RCMP would relocate him and his
family, give him money for living expenses, provide him with job retraining
or help to obtain further education. They also would help Mo find a job.
They had made the commitment to him in writing.

"It wouldn't be up to him," Ambler explained. "It's solely on our judgment to determine whether there is a threat. If there is a threat, we will take
the necessary action. If there is no threat and there is no need to assist, we
won't."

Ambler explained that RCMP believed someone might try to kill Mo,
and for that reason he had been transferred out of Edmonton Max to the
Corrections Canada Regional Psychiatric Centre in Saskatoon. The contract
on Mo's life had been confirmed by prison guards. It was taken seriously.

MacLeod continued. "The threat doesn't end today or tomorrow or
next week with respect to rats who give evidence?"

"No," replied Ambler.

"And in fact, the existence of a threat continues upon parole release of
rats should people be aware of their identity and location?"

"That is correct."

MacLeod's repeated reference to Mo as a rat prompted an objection
from MacFarlane. "This is a court of law," he complained. "It's not a back
alley."

"My hands are clean, My Lady," retorted MacLeod.

"You might be able to find a better choice of words, Mr. MacLeod,"
the judge admonished him.

MacLeod was engaged in a two-stage battle to save Charlie. The political battle over whether Canada was obligated to seek assurances against the
use of the death penalty would be fought on another day. But first he would
try to convince Justice Trussler that there was insufficient evidence to justify

Charlie's extradition to the United States. And the best shot he had to shred the prosecution's case against his client was to destroy its star witness, Mo Laberge.

Mo spent nearly four days on the witness stand in the closed courtroom testifying in detail about his many conversations with Charlie. He explained that Charlie and Leonard had a brazen scheme going to bleed the victims of their financial assets before they were killed.

"They would attempt to wring out the maximum benefit from these victims," he told Justice Trussler in response to questioning from MacFarlane. "And some of the things they did seemed kind of crazy. They would find out if people were on unemployment or had paychecks coming, and these people would be interrogated and questioned to find out every last detail about their financial situation. Then the person was kept alive long enough to get these things through a series of post office boxes and phone calls and letters." Charlie told him the proceeds of the crimes were usually split three ways—between Leonard, Charlie and Leonard's family. The profits were fairly meager because many of their victims had little.

"I asked him why they were killing these kind of people," Mo said. "He [Charlie] said, 'You don't miss nobodies.'"

Referring to the notes he started recording in April 1986, Mo said Charlie wasn't altogether happy with the rapport Leonard had with Cricket. "He felt that Lake trusted Cricket far too much, and Charles saw her as being a very weak individual who abused sex, drugs and alcohol, and therefore was very vulnerable." He said Charlie despised people who used drugs and alcohol.

MacFarlane wondered why Charlie opened himself up to Mo. "Did Mr. Ng at any stage in these early discussions indicate to you why he was prepared to be so candid with you?"

"Well, that was one of the amazing things," Mo responded. "When I asked him about it, he said his lawyer told him not to talk to anybody. He would say that and out it would come. I was the first person that he had the opportunity to be with since his arrest for shoplifting in Calgary who wasn't either a lawyer, prosecutor, a police officer or a prison guard. I was the first friendly face that he had probably spoken to since the shoplifting. And he needed to get it out. He needed to talk to someone about it. And he did."

Mo said that when he asked Charlie how many people he had killed and how they broke down in terms of age and sex, Charlie initially told him he had killed nine victims—four women and five men. Sometime later Charlie told him he had killed 12 people in total: "three women, two babies, six men and a faggot." He said Charlie talked at length about shooting gay disk jockey Donald Giuletti because that was the first kill he claimed to have done on his own. Mo said Charlie told him he shot Giuletti three times in the head, but he had been seen by the man's roommate.

"Did Mr. Ng mention the roommate's name to you?"

"Yes, he did," Mo replied. "I don't have it written down, but it seems to me it is a name like razzle dazzle." (The name was actually Richard Carrazza.) Charlie also told Mo that once, when Leonard was sexually assaulting a captive, Charlie cooked himself a meal and ate it while watching.

But one of the most important details that Mo recalled from his conversations with Charlie was the distinct and jarring sound of the handcuffs and leg-irons on the videotapes of Kathi Allen and Brenda O'Connor. "You can hear the handcuffs clicking in the video," Charlie had told him. Mo testified that Charlie also told him the two women captives had their hands cuffed behind their backs. Those details added credibility to Mo's testimony. With no opportunity to have seen the video himself, he could not have known these facts unless Charlie had told him.

Midway through the second day, MacLeod got his chance to cross-examine Mo. He focused on Mo's lengthy criminal record. Mo admitted he had stolen a car, a recreation vehicle, tires, even equipment from a hospital while visiting his badly burned cousin. He also admitted he had been charged with assaulting his former girl friend in 1976, pushing her in the presence of a police officer. He was asked about several other assault convictions. MacLeod warned Mo to answer truthfully. "I should warn you," he said testily, "I'm going to check every word you're saying."

Mo just shrugged. "That's fine."

MacLeod brought up an old allegation that Mo had once sexually assaulted a child. It was an offense for which he was never charged and one he had never admitted. Mo maintained that if the attack occurred, it was committed by an accomplice and not by him. MacLeod attempted to pursue the matter and very quickly drew objections from MacFarlane. MacLeod switched tactics and suggested Mo had an extensive career as an informant. Again Mo denied the allegation. MacLeod asked him about the prison-yard murder of Tennessee racketeer Tim Collins. Mo pointed out that the jury found him not guilty. As the testimony wrapped up for the day, Justice Trussler had another subtle admonishment for MacLeod.

"May I have your assurance you are not going to try to retry Mr. Laberge on the Collins matter?" she asked.

"You may have that assurance, My Lady," he replied.

Before and after court, Mo was walked unmanacled to a nearby hotel room where he was allowed to shower and change into and out of the clothes his parents brought him to wear while he testified. He wore prison garb to and from RCMP cells in the Edmonton suburb of St. Albert in the evenings, but he put on slacks, a shirt and dress shoes for court. In the evenings police took him to trendy Jasper Avenue restaurants for dinner. He was not perceived as a security threat. He had too much to lose. The day-room the police kept at the hotel was a welcome respite from a prison cell, and his handlers consented to allow his family to visit him there before they took him back to the jail. Police encouraged the contact. It made Mo feel human again. It seemed to him a small perk for risking his life to testify against Charlie and that other mad-dog killer, Gingras.

RCMP had the other informant, known only as Sam, stashed away in their cells in another Edmonton suburb, the community of Sherwood Park. They went to great lengths to keep Mo and Sam apart for fear of having their evidence tainted. Neither man knew the other, and police wanted to keep it that way. Their common link was Charlie, and they saw the same man from different perspectives. Charlie had candidly given Mo details of his killings. He had talked so freely that Mo was convinced he really wanted Mo to tell his story, perhaps so that his prowess as a killer would be more widely known. With Sam, Charlie had talked incessantly about escaping and about having the people killed who betrayed him or could testify against him. Surprisingly, Mo was not on Charlie's hit list.

MacLeod used his second day of cross-examination to press Mo for details about his activities in the Disassociation and Segregation Unit and to ascertain just how much access Mo had to Charlie's court materials and outside media reports about the case. He seemed to be building a case to show that Mo had manufactured his so-called evidence from news reports embellished with his imagination. Mo claimed to have no access to Charlie's files and very little access to newspapers. He told MacLeod he wrote down only the most dramatic admissions and the dramatic quotes—the words that stuck in his mind after they finished their exercise sessions in the prison yard. He said at the beginning he wrote down general things about Charlie's background he thought were interesting and might be helpful if he wrote a book or thesis—things about Charlie's upbringing and military career.

"This was just kind of general stuff," he told MacLeod. "I had no idea he was going to get into this kind of gory detail."

MacLeod asked him about sending his notes and the sketches to his lawyer. It was something he didn't do with the notes he kept of his conversations with Gingras. Mo responded that he had a total of four pages of notes from his conversations with Gingras, and those were notes he had recorded in French.

"He just did not ramble on like Charles Ng did," Mo explained.

At times the dialogue between the lawyer and the witness became heated. At other times court officials could barely refrain from laughing at Mo's witty retorts. MacLeod pressed Mo to admit he had lied at his Lethbridge trial, claiming innocence, in a bid to avoid going to jail. He suggested Mo might be lying now to get out of jail.

"You don't like being in jail much, do you?" he asked Mo.

"I'm getting older. It's not quite as much fun as it used to be."

MacLeod produced a sketch Charlie had drawn that depicted Mo involved in the prison-yard killing of the Tennessee racketeer. The lawyer asked Mo if it was an accurate depiction of any discussion Mo and Charlie had of Tim Collins' murder. Mo said the drawing was based on newspaper coverage of the case and not anything he had told Charlie.

"So what you're basically saying is though this cartoon is in bad taste and perhaps exhibits a bizarre sense of humor, it doesn't depict something that actually happened?"

"That's correct," Mo conceded.

MacLeod asked to have the sketch tendered as an exhibit. "It has to do with the issue of whether or not cartoons allegedly provided to this witness by Mr. Ng depict real events or not," he told the judge. "We have this witness testifying that it does not depict a real event."

"Well, he may have said that," Justice Trussler agreed, "but I think he also said that it depicted Mr. Ng's perception of what happened. This was a cartoon that was drawn before Mr. Laberge ever spoke to Mr. Ng."

Switching tactics, MacLeod asked Mo if he was occasionally addressed by inmates and guards in the hole as a senior corrections officer. Mo denied it. He asked Mo if he had a toaster and porno movies in his cell and had pizza delivered there. Mo denied that, too, but he admitted he had a computer, television and VCR, which he had purchased himself, in his cell. Noting that Mo had testified that Charlie liked to "make love" to his pillow while looking at pornographic photos, MacLeod asked Mo if he engaged in deviant sexual practices while in prison.

"The integrity of my pillow was safe at all times," he assured the lawyer.

MacLeod wound up his cross-examination by asking Mo what he expected to gain by testifying against Charlie at his trial in the United States. "Have you made arrangements whereby you might obtain financial or other rewards should you be called upon to give evidence?"

"No."

"Are you telling me here today, under oath, Mr. Laberge, that should you be called upon, you will neither seek nor accept any reward, advantage or consideration of any kind?"

"That's correct."

"Do you hope, Mr. Laberge, one day to write a book about your noble adventures with Mr. Ng?"

"I don't know," Mo conceded. "It's getting kind of complicated."

"You told us earlier on that your primary objective when all this began was that you were thinking of writing a book?"

"Life was simpler then," Mo replied.

"So you have changed your mind now, and you're offering yourself to us as a completely rehabilitated, publicly motivated, good citizen. Is that it?"

"Did I say that?" inquired Mo, his bushy black eyebrows raised in mock surprise.

Exasperated, the lawyer wound it up. "I suppose the best place to end this examination is where it began, Mr. Laberge," he concluded. "And that is you have been a liar in the courts in this province. Correct?"

"That's correct, sir," Mo agreed.

When Mo was excused he was escorted out of court by a beaming Munro. The veteran Mountie was pleased with Mo's performance on the stand. He never appeared rattled. His evidence was clear and succinct. He handled the questions about his credibility with aplomb. It was about the best evidence Ray had ever heard from a witness, never mind a jailhouse witness.

There was no question Mo was good. But he'd had a life's worth of experience testifying in court and watching witnesses give their evidence. It was where he had picked up the idea of making detailed and dated notes. But he was quick on his feet, and his intelligence had shone through.

In the back of the courtroom, others also nodded in approval. San Francisco Assistant District Attorney Paul Cummins was impressed. The burly and balding 42-year veteran didn't like to use prison witnesses, and he almost never did. His view was that when you throw mud, you dirty your hands. Often it was purchased testimony. The risk of tainting the case was too great. But this Mo character was another story. This guy was good. And he backed up his testimony with notes and drawings.

Charlie's defense team was also taken aback. MacLeod had been confident he could smash Mo's fragile credibility, but the wily con had kept dancing out of reach. Shortly after Mo's testimony, MacLeod contacted the Rosenfeldts to ask them to inquire whether the families of the victims would support a deal. He said Charlie might waive extradition and plead guilty in exchange for an assurance that he wouldn't face the death penalty. The Rosenfeldts gathered with family members and asked them what they thought. There was little discussion. The families sent back a resounding no. They would put their faith in the process despite MacLeod's warning that the case could drag on another three or four years.

MacLeod had hoped to have the victims' families on side when he approached the California prosecutors, but he made the pitch to them regardless. He found Cummins and Munro having a coffee together after court adjourned. The courthouse basement cafeteria was nearly deserted at 3:30 P.M. on a Friday afternoon. MacLeod glanced around to make sure no reporters were in earshot before speaking. He suggested there was room for negotiation and that it might be worthwhile to explore the possibility of coming to some agreement regarding Charlie's return and plea. What Charlie wanted was some guarantee that the district attorney would not seek the death penalty. Cummins liked the idea but said he had to talk to the Calaveras County District Attorney John Martin as well as his own boss in San Francisco. But a deal waiving opposition to extradition and involving, say, 12 guilty pleas to murder in exchange for 12 life sentences with no eligibility for parole (what prosecutors called LWOPs) would avoid what was now expected to be a lengthy extradition process and a costly trial.

Cummins knew that if Charlie was extradited and his trial was held in San Francisco, he would be unlikely to win a death sentence anyway. He hadn't tried a death penalty case in four years. The last one he had tried, a case involving two men who kidnapped a child for a ransom and then beat him to death, ended with the jury recommending life without parole. Polls of San Francisco's liberal residents traditionally showed that they opposed the death penalty by a factor of more than two to one. San Francisco residents traditionally supported legalizing marijuana and prostitution. Even Charlie Ng had a chance to get a hung jury in his town. But Cummins made no commitments. He had to check with his superiors.

Munro took it all in with a bemused grin. It seemed a reasonable offer, but he realized, of course, he was looking at it from an entirely different perspective. American district attorneys are political creatures. They are elected to office. And Charlie was a poster boy for the death penalty. It would be a tough sell.

Back in California, there was a flurry of action in the offices of the district attorney and attorney general. Calls came from the families of the victims. Sellitto, by now a confirmed skeptic, thought the plea bargain was a trick and that once back in the United States Charlie would change his plea.

California's terse answer came back to Canadian officials the middle of the following week. Thanks, but no thanks. And the meter began running on what would ultimately become the longest and most expensive trial in California history.

The extradition hearing continued, but MacLeod wasn't optimistic about the outcome. He had pinned his hopes on establishing that it would be very dangerous for justice to accept Mo's word, but the drawings and notes backed up so much of what he had to say. They had a ring of authenticity that the court could not disregard. MacLeod argued that the identification of Charlie's voice on the videotapes was insufficient to tie him to the murders of Mike Carroll, Kathi Allen, Lonnie Bond, Lonnie Bond Junior, Brenda O'Connor and Scott Stapely. He called only four witnesses. Justice Trussler reserved her decision.

Mo had enjoyed his brief taste of freedom. It had been great to walk the streets again, to enjoy food in a restaurant, to stop at a convenience store to buy a newspaper—all little perks one does not enjoy in prison. He had even purchased a lottery ticket at the mall near the hotel that police were using. Lottery tickets were a novelty for him. They were just being introduced when he was arrested in the Lethbridge holdup, and he had never had a chance to try his luck. He was in the back of a police car on his way to Calgary to testify at the Gingras trial when he remembered to check his ticket with the numbers in the local paper. The first number was a four. He looked at his ticket. He had a four. Great. The next number was an eight. He had that, too. He had the next number, a 17, as well. With heart pounding he looked at the remaining numbers. He had one of the remaining three. He couldn't believe it. A winning ticket!

"Hey guys!" he exclaimed to the cops in the front seat. "I got four out of six! I wonder what would have happened if I had got six out of six?"

The two cops in the front seat didn't even look back. "You would have been shot trying to escape," deadpanned the driver.

Trussler wasted little time in reaching her decision. She came down with her ruling November 29, 1988, just a few weeks after the conclusion of the case. In a courtroom packed with spectators and journalists, she ordered Charles Ng returned to the United States to face trial on the majority of the 25 charges against him.

She said she was satisfied, based largely on Mo's evidence (he was identified as John Doe I in the transcript of the ruling), that Charlie was part of a conspiracy to kidnap, rape and kill. She ruled there was insufficient evidence to extradite Charlie on the charge of being an accessory after the murder of Paul Cosner, although there was evidence of other offenses against him. She also ruled there was insufficient evidence to support the kidnapping charges against Charlie in the cases of Allen, O'Connor and Lonnie Bond Junior.

Charlie, who had entered the courtroom shackled at the wrists and ankles with his thumbs hooked on the pockets of his jeans, sat emotionless as the judge read her 17-page decision. She glanced up at him as she read the conclusion: "I am issuing a warrant for the committal of Charles Chi-tat Ng to the nearest convenient prison with respect to 19 offenses where he is to remain until surrendered to the United States of America." The accused raised an eyebrow in mock incredulity.

The judge advised Charlie he had 15 days to appeal. In the meantime she was forwarding the hearing transcript and her decision to the federal minister of justice, who would ultimately decide if Charlie was to be returned to California. It was unclear who would make the decision since Canadians had just gone to the polls in a federal election and the new government cabinet had not yet been appointed.

California Governor George Deukmejian was pleased with the ruling but stressed that his satisfaction was tempered by the knowledge that it could still be months, if not years, before Ng was back in California state jurisdiction.

"There are few crimes in modern times as heinous as the atrocities attributed to Ng," he told a news conference in California. "In the interests of justice, I am today asking Canadian authorities to make as swift a determination as possible in this particular case so his guilt or innocence can be adjudicated in California."

Spurred by the California governor and Canadian citizens, Canadian authorities were chugging along as fast as they could. But encumbered by an extradition process desperately in need of streamlining, there was little hope of a quick resolution as long as Charles Ng fought every step of the way. And fight he would.

Murder victim Paul Cosner with sister Sharon Sellitto. Throughout the long years during which Charles Ng fought extradition from Canada, she relentlessly fought for justice for her brother.

Charles Ng's cell in the Disassociation and Segregation Unit at the Edmonton Max.

21

The Adopt-a-Con Solution

EDMONTON ALBERTA / DECEMBER 1988

A FTER MADAME JUSTICE TRUSSLER'S RULING, calls for Charlie's immediate deportation to the United States grew louder. Many Canadians were incensed by his lawyer's claims that various appeals of the ruling could drag on for years. Their rage intensified when Victims of Violence president Gary Rosenfeldt, who jumped into the fray with zeal, discovered that Don MacLeod's legal bills for Charlie's defense were being picked up by taxpayers. Forty-two thousand Canadians signed a petition demanding Ng's immediate deportation. It was forwarded to the federal parliament through Ontario Tory backbencher Bill Domm, who urged his government colleagues to draft a new law that would automatically ship accused American killers back for trial.

MacLeod filed Charlie's appeal December 7, 1988, arguing that his client's rights had been breached when Justice Trussler refused to hear evidence regarding the death penalty. MacLeod had wanted to call a witness to California's last gas chamber execution to demonstrate the cruelty of execution. Meanwhile, federal prosecutor Bruce MacFarlane assured reporters that the court was making a special effort to hear the case quickly. However, he said, it would likely be the spring of 1989 before the appeal was heard.

Not everyone felt Charlie was manipulating the Canadian extradition process. The *Edmonton Journal* delivered a reasoned editorial warning that no matter how repulsive Ng's alleged crimes might be, they did not justify removing his right to a fair hearing. "Ng, if he is guilty as charged, has destroyed enough," the Pulitzer Prize–winning paper cautioned. "We cannot allow him to force us, out of our revulsion for his crimes, to destroy a fundamental principle of justice as well."

Charlie was ill when the February 1, 1989, hearing date rolled around. His lawyer was granted a one-day adjournment. After brief arguments the following day, Court of Queen's Bench Judge Paul Chrumka upheld Trussler's ruling. But within moments of the ruling, Charlie instructed MacLeod to file another appeal at the next court level.

While the extradition case was creeping its way through the courts, Ray Munro was finding little time to run his Three Hills detachment. He was getting no respite from the Ng case. The RCMP's Columbo got a call early in the year to attend a meeting of U.S. investigators to help plan for Charlie's eventual trial.

Ray headed down to San Andreas for the meeting. He felt a little uncomfortable walking into a room full of Americans from several different police agencies, but he was confident in his knowledge of the Ng case. He brought along the four-volume brief on the case he had prepared for the extradition hearing. Although some American investigators seemed puzzled by the involvement of a Canadian Mountie in their case, San Francisco Assistant District Attorney Paul Cummins and Calaveras District Attorney John Martin made it clear they wanted Ray on the team. His participation was one of the few things they had agreed upon. They recognized that through his involvement in the extradition hearing, Ray was in the best position to identify weaknesses in the prosecution's case. He could also shepherd the Canadian witnesses, particularly Mo, who wouldn't likely testify without Ray at his side. The investigators agreed to form a special task force to assemble and correlate all the information collected to date. It was time to begin the painstaking process of gleaning each fact required to win a conviction on each charge.

A formal request to put Ray on the team was made to the Commissioner of the RCMP in Ottawa. "My official request to you is for the assignment of Sgt. Ray Munro to assist as a consultant and liaison person in this trial preparation," San Francisco District Attorney Arlo Smith wrote Norm Inkster on March 20, 1989. "I believe he has already logged more hours in this case than anyone down here." He advised that Ray's expenses would be paid by a special state investigation grant that had been given to Calaveras County. The task force would operate at least three months, Smith wrote. "My sincere hope is that you will look favorably upon this request to help ensure Mr. Ng receives the quantity and quality of justice he deserves." Of course, Paul Cummins was behind the letter. He was extremely impressed by Ray's extradition brief.

Inkster approved the request. It was in Canada's best interests to help the Americans successfully prosecute Charlie and, at least inside legal circles, the action might help offset the animosity against the Canucks for the delay in sending Charlie back to face trial.

Sorting out the logistics was a little tougher. Ray was, after all, supposed to be running a detachment. He couldn't just leave. Finally, a plan was hatched to send Ray down to Sacramento for three out of every five weeks. California authorities rented Ray a car to drive the 1,540 miles between Alberta and California—a trip he became accustomed to making in about 30 hours. Usually, upon his return to Canada, he was required to drive two hours north to K–Division headquarters in Edmonton to report to his boss. Then it was back down to Three Hills to clear off the paperwork stacked on his desk.

Fortunately, Three Hills was a quiet community, and the RCMP corporal who was Ray's second in command was a competent administrator. The residents never did question why the RCMP detachment commander, the equivalent of a town police chief, was so frequently absent or why he drove a rental car with California license plates. But that was just the beginning of the strange goings-on at the detachment office.

Meanwhile, Ray also had to keep tabs on his star witness. Mo had a parole hearing scheduled for late March, and he was quite anxious. His initial application for day parole in February had been rejected, but board members agreed to hear a new application the following month.

RCMP and prison and parole officials devised a plan to send Mo to a minimum-security halfway house on the west coast. With a $500 price on his head—a lot of money inside the prison, where currency was banned—Mo's life was still in grave danger. Police knew they couldn't keep Mo indefinitely at the Corrections Canada Regional Psychiatric Centre in Saskatoon. It was a treatment center, not a holding facility for threatened convicts. Mo had received an angry reception from RPC inmates after returning from the extradition hearing the previous fall, but they eventually accepted him back in their midst, despite the fact that he was now a known rat.

Ray Ambler and Ray Munro made the five-hour trek from Edmonton to Saskatoon to attend Mo's hearing and to bring him back to testify at further proceedings against Gingras. They were prepared to support his move to a halfway house or his transfer to a safer prison. They were not prepared for the decision that was handed down.

The board rejected the halfway house plan. They felt Mo still hadn't demonstrated he was able to function in prison society, much less society outside the prison fences. Mo's history of manipulating the system appeared to have backfired this time. The board members did not want to be responsible for him for the 18 years he would be on parole before his sentence officially expired.

Mo was devastated. His two police handlers were merely confused. They had been given the impression the halfway house plan had been agreed upon by all parties and the board would rubber-stamp it. Now they had to figure out what to do with Mo to keep him from being killed before his scheduled testimony.

The drive back to Edmonton was a quiet one. No one said much for the first 100 miles. Mo slumped in the backseat, staring vacantly out the window, wondering how he had gotten into such a fix. His life was worthless now. If they returned him to Edmonton Max or Kent or Prince Albert, his many enemies were bound to kill him for ratting out Gingras or Ng or

both. He had been hoping his newfound police allies would have the necessary clout to spring him, but now he realized he was just a pawn. While
Mo felt sorry for himself, his two handlers in the front seat kept running
the plan over and over in their minds, trying to figure out how it had gone
off the rails.

By the time the three men stopped for dinner in Lloydminster, an oil
town straddling the Alberta–Saskatchewan border, they were ready to hash
it out. Toying with a medium-rare steak at a roadside gas station restaurant,
Mo blamed the predicament on himself. He was convinced there was a conspiracy against him as a result of his stinging assessment of prison officials
in the essay he wrote on the Gingras case. They were just getting even with
him.

The cops didn't really buy the conspiracy theory, but they sure felt
snookered. No one had signaled any problem with the release plan before
the hearing. The cops suspected Mo's caseworker was simply overruled or
that there had been a bureaucratic mix-up. But what could they do with Mo
now? There was no precedent to follow. They had an informant in limbo.
He had no home institution. No plan. Nothing.

Mo turned up the heat. He threatened to back out of his agreement to
testify against Charlie and Gingras if the safety issue wasn't addressed. Why
should he stick his neck out without protection? Back in Edmonton, Mo's
handlers called an emergency meeting with the prosecutors in both cases to
review the options.

Both prosecutors still wanted Mo's testimony. They were willing to
look for a way to soothe Mo's fears. Ray Munro eventually came up with a
new plan. He called it the Adopt-a-Con Solution. He offered to take Mo
into his personal custody at the Three Hills RCMP detachment for 90 days,
long enough to get Mo over the hump and give police and prosecutors more
time to work out a permanent solution with prison and parole officials.

Federal prosecutor Bruce MacFarlane was skeptical. "Are you sure you
want to do this?" he asked Ray.

Ray wasn't thrilled about the prospect of taking Mo home with him,
but he didn't think they had any other options. If the RCMP wanted to

maintain the integrity of its fledgling witness protection program and the safety of its witness, it seemed the only way. Ambler was on side. Mo was ecstatic, but Ray was preoccupied with finding a way to put the proposal to his supervisors. It seemed a situation in which it would be better to ask for forgiveness than for permission.

Much to the dismay of RCMP management, once more Ray Munro was setting an unorthodox precedent. His boss, still trying to adjust to the fact that he had a detachment commander living part-time in California, could only shake his head.

Ray wasn't worried about Mo escaping. Mo was too smart to risk all when he knew he was so close to earning his way out of prison. He had a perfect opportunity to prove he was capable of being on the outside. Besides, Mo was beginning to trust Ray—no mean feat for a guy who had never trusted anyone his entire life. He was beginning to realize that if Ray gave his word, he delivered.

Although Ray probably wouldn't have admitted it to anyone, he was growing fond of the convict. The pair had spent considerable time together during the extradition hearing, and Ray liked Mo's style. They both had what Ray liked to call the jazz: a shared love of excitement. Ray sometimes wondered, reflecting on his own impoverished upbringing, how close he had come to taking Mo's path.

During the Gingras trial in Edmonton, Ray arranged for Mo to meet with *Edmonton Journal* cop reporters to discuss his revelations about the prison's handling of Gingras. The two veteran reporters didn't quite know what to make of the con. But they didn't trust him. They told him they couldn't accept what he was offering without corroboration and advised Mo to take his concerns to Scott Newark, a local prosecutor who had been looking into the Gingras fiasco on his own time. Mo eventually had an audience with John Weir, a prominent Edmonton lawyer who had been appointed to conduct a one-man independent inquiry into Gingras' case.

Later, when Mo had finished testifying at the Gingras trial, he hopped in Ray's car with all of his worldly possessions—his computers and school books—and they drove to Three Hills. Mo used one cell reserved for juvenile offenders as his bedroom and another as his office. Breakfast and lunch were served to him in his cell, but Ray or one of the six officers at the detachment would take him out for dinner to a local restaurant. Mo kept track of his daily escorted absences into the community, which Ray would check and sign off.

Mo was still an exercise fiend who prided himself on maintaining a high level of physical fitness. Under the watchful eye of a Mountie escort, he would run two to five miles a day at the local outdoor track to keep the fat off his body. He was just under six feet with a muscular build and hands the size of shovels. He didn't touch cigarettes. In fact he had a mild allergy to cigarette smoke and could barely cope with the ever-present wreath that hung around his chain-smoking handler. He spent his time in cells pursuing his academic studies. He was working on a bachelor of administration degree and had just won the province's Louise McKinney award for academic excellence. He hoped to attend university upon his release and work on a master's degree in business administration.

Mo hadn't been in Three Hills long when the detachment got a visitor from California. Paul Cummins came up in April 1989 to seek Ray's help in charging Charlie with the murder of Paul Cosner. He also wanted to interview Mo to find out what Charlie may have said to him about the slaying. Police believed Cosner had been killed in San Francisco, which put the case in Cummins' jurisdiction.

Cummins, who had helped in the 1970s prosecutions of some notorious California race murders known as the Zebra killings, was floored by Three Hills, population 5,000. The countryside seemed so empty compared to California. But that was hardly surprising. Three Hills was a very peace-loving community, home to the Prairie Bible College and a few houses and stores. Cummins called it "the home of 29 churches and one bar." It was a far cry from his town, a city of 500,000 scattered over 37 square miles of steep hills and plunging coastal valleys. San Francisco averaged 120 homicides a year. Three Hills averaged about 60 arrests in total.

Cummins met up with Ray at the RCMP detachment and explained what he needed. Later in the day the pair slid over to the nearby community of Trochu, which was hosting a rodeo in its hockey arena. The fireplug of an assistant district attorney was so mesmerized by the ground-pounding fury of the bucking broncs and bulls that he almost didn't catch the voice behind him.

"Hi Paul!"

He turned to find Mo grinning broadly at him from the stands. He was taking in the show with an off-duty RCMP officer. Mo, Cummins discovered, was a cowboy himself, a real rootin' tootin', horse-riding, bull-dogging stockman. Mo explained to the American visitor that he had once run a few head of cattle himself, and he was hankering to set up another ranch once he made parole. In the meantime he was content to take correspondence courses, testify against bad guys and, when he was really bored, mow Ray's lawn.

Cummins spent about four hours interviewing Mo at the Three Hills detachment to determine the extent of Mo's knowledge about the Cosner killing and any other murders that may have occurred within San Francisco city limits. The following day Cummins went on to Edmonton to meet the prosecutors who had dealt with Mo in the past. Ray chauffeured Cummins around Alberta in the detachment's unmarked vehicle and made the introductions. The two really hit it off on the four-day visit. "The only thing we didn't do was cut our veins and join blood," Cummins later joked. Ray took his guest on a weekend jaunt to Banff and Lake Louise, knocking him out with the area's spectacular mountain scenery and then scaring the hell out of him with a wild ride through a blinding spring blizzard on their return. Amused, Cummins began to wonder if Ray shouldn't be locked up and Mo shouldn't be running the detachment.

In a bid to advance Mo's case for parole, Ray arranged for him to go on unescorted passes to work at a nearby Bible camp on the Red Deer River. Mo did manual labor, helping out wherever he could. Three days a week, RCMP officers would drop Mo off at the camp in the morning and pick him up in the evening to bring him back to his cell.

About a week after Cummins' visit, the Alberta Court of Appeal again upheld Charlie's extradition. The following day Ray flew down to California to swear to the court that he had served the extradition warrant on Charlie. It was time to begin warming up the wheels of justice in the United States. When Ray returned, Mo's 90 days in his custody were just about up. Ray took Mo in to see his parole officer in Edmonton to try to find a place in the prison system for him.

On the way over to K–Division headquarters, Mo wanted to stop at the drugstore at nearby Kingsway Garden Mall to pick up a few toiletry items. Ray did some banking and went to wait for Mo outside the drugstore. As he arrived he saw Mo coming out of the store with security guards hustling after him. Mo had slipped a bottle of aftershave and a few other items—about $20 worth of goods—into his pocket and had been caught. As he was being led away, Mo looked back at Ray to see if he was coming to his rescue.

Ray sighed. What was the man thinking? He didn't have any reason to steal. The Mounties were reimbursing him for his living expenses while he was in the witness protection program. But Mo had to push the envelope. He was obviously not ready for parole.

At first Mo was very arrogant and cocky with the store security staff, but when city police arrived and he realized he was going to be arrested, he became suddenly quiet. Ray was steaming inside. He asked city police to deposit Mo at the St. Albert RCMP detachment when they were finished booking him on theft charges. Then he left. He would let the system deal with Mo.

Ray didn't see Mo again for a month. When he learned that Mo had been sent to the medium-security prison at Bowden, north of Calgary, Ray asked Ambler and another Mountie to pay him a visit. "Go ask him why he's an asshole," he suggested. When it came time for the good cop–bad cop routine, Ambler was always the bad cop. He made a point of demonstrating that he wasn't Mo's pal and he wasn't Mo's mother. Ambler had never really trusted Mo. The way he saw it was that sometimes you have to deal with the devil, and there was no doubt in his mind Mo was the devil.

Mo was surprised when the two uniformed Mounties strode in to see him in Bowden. They rubbed it in pretty good. They wanted him to realize just how quickly his dream could evaporate. All it took was one false step, one bonehead move, and he could be behind a fence until 2007. Ambler was careful about what he said to Mo, cautious about not going over the line. He always suspected Mo might just turn around and write a book about him and Munro. He was always calling them a pair of paralegal psychopaths. But it seemed to Ambler that every time he saw Mo, he was in the midst of a crisis. Now he was desperate to get back into the RCMP's good graces. But Ambler wasn't interested, and Ray, still seething over being burned, was ignoring him. Mo would have to come up with some new twist to get their attention.

It didn't take him long. Soon Regina city police were calling Ray to ask him about Mo's reliability in relation to a high-profile prairie murder case. Mo apparently had contacted them with information about former Saskatchewan provincial cabinet minister Colin Thatcher, who had been convicted of killing his estranged wife, JoAnn Wilson, in January 1983. Thatcher was seeking a review of his life sentence based on new evidence uncovered by a private investigator. Mo claimed to have information about a weapon used in an attack on Wilson, but if the Regina cops wanted it, they had to go through his handler: Ray.

Mo told the cops that Thatcher had fenced stolen goods for him prior to them both being sent to Edmonton Institution. He claimed he assisted Thatcher, the son of the province's former premier, in acquiring a firearm and a secondary car, which he believed was used in one of the assaults on Wilson. Mo said he gave Thatcher a handgun that he stole in a burglary in the southern Alberta city of Medicine Hat. He was willing to swear to it.

Ray was skeptical. It was indeed quite a coincidence that Mo would have information in yet another high-profile case. "He's grasping at straws to get back into my good books," Ray theorized. He considered the information valueless since Thatcher, whose case had spawned several books, was already serving his life sentence, and his appeal had been denied. But the Regina cops were still very, very interested. Mo had told them that Thatcher had used two handguns—a black one and a silver one—in the attacks. It was a fact the police had not released publicly. The cops wanted a statement.

But Ray had enough on his plate without taking on another of Mo's make-work projects. He returned to California for task force duty in July, August, September and December. He stayed in a motel and later a furnished apartment in Rancho Cordova, a community of about 60,000 just east of Sacramento on the road to Lake Tahoe. The team, headed by Special Agent Martin Ryan and consisting of investigators from Calaveras County and San Francisco, worked out of a state bureau of investigation field office.

The work was tedious. There were volumes and volumes of paper. Investigators sifted through the files to try to match the pieces of evidence with the crimes. The evidence for each murder was broken down into three categories: physical evidence, eye witnesses and admissions. They were expanding Ray's conspiracy theory and boosting his four-volume brief to an incredible 52 volumes. Ray attacked the work with a vengeance, often working until late in the evening or even midnight. He had no distractions. There wasn't anything to do back at the Days Inn but watch television. Ray had spent 14 years as a homicide cop. He joked that the report they were producing on the Ng task force was a thesis for his master's degree in homicide. It was a challenge to take such a massive amount of evidence and break it down into useful elements. It was a lot like writing a book—a litany of death. But the process was painstakingly slow. They had no sophisticated computer programs. The best they could do was assemble the evidence by hand and punch it into a basic word-processing program. The job that had been expected to take three months was now expected to drag out more than twice that long.

In January 1990 Ray and another task force member flew to Nashville and Oklahoma to interview two of Charlie's former Leavenworth prison mates.

Ray got a few strange looks when he showed up at the Nashville city police homicide department to ask for their help in setting up the interview. None of the homicide detectives had ever met a real Canadian Mountie before, and they had to ask him several times to explain why he had been seconded by the state of California to assist in a serial murder case. There were plenty of jokes about Stetsons and horses, but the amiable Canuck soon had them chuckling with him rather than at him. He had brought along a sizeable collection of uniform shoulder flashes and pins to hand out as well as a mounted photograph depicting three RCMP sergeants in their various uniforms over the force's history. The Americans loved the stuff.

The first former prisoner Ray interviewed was a former military helicopter pilot Charlie had tried to recruit into his brotherhood. The man, now in the dry-cleaning business, had been located by the FBI. He told Ray he saw Charlie almost daily while he was in Leavenworth and had listened to his wild fantasies. He always thought they were just that. He had never given any credence to them. During a four-hour interview, he told Ray about letters and photographs Charlie had received from a buddy in California. It seemed the guy was building some sort of dungeon or bunker. He sent along photos of the bunker in various stages of construction. The information was useful, but Ray doubted the man would be required to testify at the trial.

Ray flew into Oklahoma City the next day to meet with John Hudson, the fellow prisoner Charlie had visited after leaving Leavenworth. Ray had interviewed him previously, before the extradition hearing, but he used the opportunity to introduce him to Larry Copland, the Calaveras County deputy sheriff on the task force. Hudson told the investigators that Charlie had called him often during the killing spree, always prefacing his calls with the greeting, "Brother, it's me." While Ray and Copland were in Nashville and Oklahoma, other task force members were in New York and Chicago interviewing other prospective witnesses. When they returned to Sacramento, they compared notes. The case was coming together.

Ray was doing such a great job running his Three Hills detachment from Sacramento that his bosses promoted him to staff sergeant and gave him command of a larger detachment. The Cardston detachment in southern Alberta just north of the Montana border would require more attention. It was 1990, a summer of native unrest in Canada. It began with a violent struggle over gambling in which two men were killed at a Mohawk reserve near Cornwall, Ontario, and spread to a 78-day standoff between

Canadian soldiers and Mohawks at Oka, Quebec, just outside Montreal. Tensions with Cardston-area natives were climbing over the construction of a dam across the Oldman River, which ran through the area. Ray had his hands full, barely avoiding a gun battle with a militant native group called the Lonefighters. When he was summoned back to Sacramento for a meeting of the task force in November 1990, he was happy to have a break from the tension. But his good humor rapidly dissipated.

All the Ng task members were on hand when the California attorney general was presented with their finished product. The media were summoned to a press conference to follow, including the major networks. But the real news was going on behind closed doors. California's assistant attorney general made it clear at the meeting that the state was not prepared to waive the death penalty for Charlie. Regardless of what the Supreme Court of Canada decided, the United States of America would do whatever was necessary to bring Charlie back to face murder charges. They were prepared to come and get him, to seize him and take him back forcibly.

Ray was stunned. He looked around the room to see if it was all just a joke. No one was laughing. His American colleagues stared back with somber expressions. The threat was clear. Ray got on the phone to federal prosecutor Bruce MacFarlane, who had recently been appointed assistant deputy attorney general of Canada. MacFarlane flew down immediately to meet with California state officials. California's assistant attorney general reiterated for MacFarlane what he initially had told Ray. He thanked Canada for its efforts, but put Canada on notice that Charlie was returning to face the death penalty regardless of what the court decided. When MacFarlane suggested Canada might be forced to deport Charlie to Hong Kong if the U.S. refused to waive the death penalty, he was told Charlie would never make it there. The U.S. official stated that the United States would consider a midair interception to prevent Charlie from reaching Hong Kong. MacFarlane raised his hands and pleaded for reason. "Just hold on there," he said. "I don't even want to discuss that. I'm not even going to go there."

The threat had the desired effect in Ottawa. Ray was summoned to a January 1991 meeting to brief senior justice department officials. The big

292

question was what do they do with Charlie if the court ruled that Canada should require assurances that the death penalty not be imposed. How serious was the American's threat? It wasn't without precedent. California agents had gone into Mexico previously to bring to justice drug dealers who killed a Drug Enforcement Agency officer. Americans had gone into Panama to arrest dictator Manuel Noriega when he annulled the presidential elections after an opposition victory. And they had invaded Iraq when Sadam Hussein ignored a January 15 deadline to get out of Kuwait. The war chiefs had dubbed the operation Desert Storm. What were they planning next, Ray wondered. Arctic Storm?

22

Back in the USA

OTTAWA ONTARIO / FEBRUARY 1991

A DETERMINED GAGGLE OF PARKA-CLAD PROTESTERS stamped their feet in the snow outside Canada's Supreme Court, trying to keep warm as they waited for the media to arrive. It was February 21, 1991, more than five and a half years after Charles Ng had been arrested in Calgary and the battle to extradite him was still raging. Charlie had fought extradition every step of the way and had turned Canada's multi-leveled extradition process into a laughing stock. Now, on this bitterly cold day in Ottawa, the nation's capital, the Supreme Court was going to wade into the fray. Families of several of the victims made the trek from California and Ohio to remind Canadians that it wasn't just a philosophical battle over whether or not one favored the death penalty—the victims in this tragedy were real. The shivering grim-faced Americans marched in circles in the snow, wearing placards bearing photographs of their murdered kin.

Dwight and Lola Stapely, whose son Scott had been murdered, made the trip up from Los Angeles. And outspoken Sharon Sellitto, accompanied by her mother from Ohio, came up from San Francisco prepared to duke it out with the bleeding heart Canucks who seemed intent on denying her murdered brother justice. San Francisco Assistant District Attorney Paul

294   No Kill No Thrill

Cummins, who had spent most of the last two decades prosecuting killers and arsonists, had come to watch the arguments and report back to his political masters. And, of course, Gary and Sharon Rosenfeldt were there with the Victims of Violence organization, using the reporters and television cameras to pressure the court and federal politicians to deport Charlie immediately. They had now collected 100,000 signatures on petitions in support of their position.

Amnesty International was there, too, taking the unpopular opposite point of view. Amnesty lawyer David Matas had been given 10 minutes to present his argument to Canada's high court. Spotting the Amnesty lawyers in the jam-packed courtroom, Sellitto thought, Oh, good, they've come to support our cause. But when she realized they were fighting to save Charlie from the death penalty, she became incensed. The Gulf War was raging and the best use they could make of their resources was to try to save a psychopathic monster who murdered women, children and babies? She could barely restrain herself from attacking them physically. "If we haven't been through enough already," Sellitto lamented, "now we have to deal with these hypocritical bastards."

Sellitto was quickly becoming the most prominent spokesperson for the victims' families, although she didn't claim to speak for them, and they didn't always agree with what she said. But she was a media magnet. Blonde and fit, she was photogenic and articulate. And she spoke her mind. God, how she spoke her mind. In the vernacular of journalists, she gave good quote. While some of the families recognized that Charlie's defense attorneys, Don MacLeod and Michael Burt, were just doing their jobs, Sellitto openly despised them and had no qualms about making sure they knew it. As the Supreme Court hearing was about to be called to order, she climbed an ornate staircase up to a balcony and looked down upon the men seated at the defense table. Sellitto had seen MacLeod arguing for Charlie's rights at the extradition hearing in Edmonton. "What about my brother's rights?" she had muttered. She blamed MacLeod for the delays in getting her brother's killer back to face his accusers. She had even less respect for Burt, the 39-year-old New York-trained San Francisco public defender. Sellitto had seen him pandering to the compassionate instincts of jury members. It made her nauseous. She once saw him show jurors a baby photo of a three-time killer who was on trial for injecting another man with rat poison. The photo depicted the killer at the age of three, decked out in a sailor suit in his mother's arms. "The bastard," Sellitto hissed when Cummins pointed him out at the defense table. Some Canadians apparently shared her view of the lawyers. One stranger had told her that he hoped she got Charlie back to the U.S. soon. "And take his lawyers with him," he added.

Still plagued by telephoned death threats for taking the case, MacLeod had been invited by court security officials to enter through a side door. An armed court security officer was glued to his side. The 38-year-old bachelor should have been exhausted from the crushing workload, but today he was pumped with adrenaline. It was his big day, the biggest case of his life, and he was ready. He had already made an oral argument to the federal justice minister Doug Lewis and had backed it up with 70 pages of documents. He had filed 2,100 pages of documents with the high court for this day. He knew his argument better than he knew his best friends, many of whom he hadn't seen for some time, what with the 100-hour weeks he was working. The public may have seen him as standing in the way of justice, delaying at every turn, but for MacLeod, the case had been a series of gut-twisting, heart-pounding sprints, racing to meet one document filing deadline after another. He was practically living in his downtown Calgary office.

MacLeod was set to argue that the death penalty constituted cruel and unusual punishment under Canada's Charter of Rights and Freedoms. Since the Supreme Court would be hearing arguments on two similar cases at once, MacLeod would be joined by counsel for Joseph Kindler, another American fugitive arrested in Canada. Kindler had been convicted of two murders in Pennsylvania in 1985, but after a jury recommended the death penalty, he escaped from jail and fled to Canada.

MacLeod had spent a great deal of time studying exactly how the state kills and had a sheaf of affidavits attesting to the cruelty of death by poisonous gas. "The pain, which is similar to that experienced during a heart attack, is felt immediately in the arms, shoulders, back and chest and intensifies as less and less oxygen reaches the body's tissues," he explained in his brief. "The condemned experience pain, great agony and extreme anxiety. The execution takes twelve minutes. During much of that time the con- demned persons remain conscious. They gasp and convulse repeatedly. They may drool, urinate, defecate, vomit and experience muscle contractions. Witnesses describe gas chamber executions as horrible, painful, cruel, degrading, unconscionable and horrifying. "MacLeod wrote that one person who had viewed California's last gas chamber execution—the 1967 execution of 37-year-old cop killer Aaron Mitchell—called it the most horrifying and dehumanizing experience of his life.

When court was called to order and the seven justices, including two women, filed in to take their places on the bench, MacLeod hammered them with argument after argument that submitting Charlie to execution by the State of California was a violation of his rights under the Canadian Constitution.

"Clearly, over the last 50 years, there has been a progressive and increasingly rapid evolution away from the death penalty," MacLeod argued, noting that 13 American states and the District of Columbia had abolished the death penalty. "That evolution has led almost all Western democracies to abandon it. Canada, both domestically and internationally, has taken a stance in opposition to it. Life imprisonment is a valid alternative. The death penalty is indeed cruel and unusual, grossly disproportionate, not in keeping with the dignity and worth of the human person and thus a penalty that always offends section seven of the Charter."

The defense lawyers would try to force the Canadian government, through the Supreme Court, to invoke Article 6 of the Canada–USA Extradition Treaty, which enabled either country to refuse extradition if the death penalty was sought. At the time the treaty was ratified in Canada on March 22, 1976, Canada still had the death penalty on its books and some American states had already abolished it. However, no one had been executed in Canada since 1962, and the move to ban executions entirely was gaining ground at the time. In a free vote in the House of Commons later in 1976, the death penalty in Canada was abolished. The issue was revisited in 1987, after Charlie's arrest, and again Members of Parliament were asked to vote according to their conscience rather than along party lines. They voted 148–127 against reintroducing the death penalty. Now the court was being asked to reexamine the extradition treaty in light of the new Charter.

In an extremely rare move, Canada's federal cabinet had decided in June 1990 to refer Charlie's case directly to the Supreme Court, thus shaving a couple of years off the extradition process by avoiding a federal court trial and appeal. The ministers asked the court to answer a complex question: Would surrendering Charlie to face the death penalty be a violation of his rights under the Canadian Charter of Rights and Freedoms? Cabinet also wanted the court to determine if the justice minister had made any legal errors in deciding to surrender Charlie without first seeking assurances that the death penalty would not be imposed.

Justice Minister Doug Lewis had already decided that Charlie could be extradited. He said Canada had a discretionary power to ask for assurances against the use of the death penalty in special cases, but Charlie's case did not warrant it. "I have concluded that it would be unwise and indeed quite wrong for me to seek to limit the full application of California law to Ng," he had advised MacLeod. Lewis was also unswayed by the cruelty argument. "The method used in California has been in place for a number of years and has found acceptance in the courts in the United States." He said he also had to consider the consequences of seeking assurances against the death penalty in such a high-profile case. "If it were generally accepted that, by fleeing to Canada, a person accused of capital murder could escape exposure to the death penalty, I think it is foreseeable that Canada would become a safe haven for such criminals," he continued. "In my view, such a prospect is simply unacceptable." MacLeod responded by launching a civil suit against the justice minister for violating his client's rights.

California Governor George Deukmejian had raised the haven issue several years earlier in a letter to Prime Minister Brian Mulroney. "While I am strongly committed to the death penalty as an appropriate punishment in certain cases, I also understand that your country does not impose the death penalty and is reluctant to return fugitives to the countries that do," he wrote. "If, however, such reticence results in the denial of Mr. Ng's extra-dition, it could have the unfortunate consequence of making Canada a haven for death penalty fugitives."

Don MacLeod attacked the safe-haven argument in the Supreme Court, recognizing that it might be a pivotal point. He told Chief Justice Antonio Lamer and the six other black-robed judges that no statistical evi-dence supported the claim. Charlie came to Canada to seek help from his sister—not to dodge execution, he said. "Until we see some evidence that in fact capital fugitives are flocking to Canada in order to avoid the death penalty, it can't be raised as a reason not to seek an assurance."

The Calgary lawyer was brilliant in his first Supreme Court appear-ance—reasonable, logical and forceful. He would concede later, without a hint of modesty, that it was the best day he ever had in a courtroom. But when the court adjourned at 4:30 P.M., it left the parties with no hint of how it might rule on the matter. It was anybody's guess.

Sellitto might not have been impressed with MacLeod's argument, but she was impressed by the formality of the proceedings. It made her feel that the murder of her brother was at least being taken seriously. She kept up a running commentary during the hearing, calling Charlie and Kindler "mur-dering pigs," oblivious to the fact that Kindler's parents were seated direct-ly behind her. Many of the lawyers' arguments were references to precedents set in other cases. Pretty boring stuff. But suddenly Sellitto's ears perked up. What were the lawyers saying? They were talking about sketches. What sketches?

Federal prosecutor Bruce MacFarlane had produced a fat manila enve-lope containing incriminating sketches that Charlie had drawn in prison. He passed a sheaf of papers to each of the lawyers. The families looked blankly at one another. It was the first they had heard of any such evidence. Although the sketches had been introduced by Mo Laberge and the informant known as Sam three years earlier during the extradition hearing, it had been done in secret. Suddenly, the existence of the drawings was out in full view.

While the families of the victims tried to get a fix on exactly what this new evidence was and how important it might be for the prosecution,

Charlie was blissfully unaware of the latest developments. He was stuck in solitary confinement in the Prince Albert Penitentiary, unaware of how dangerously close he was to being whisked back to the United States. California police and U.S. federal marshals were waiting in Edmonton, ready to pounce on him and spirit him back to the States should the judges rule immediately on his case. If they ruled Charlie could be extradited, they planned to fly immediately to Prince Albert in a small RCMP Twin Otter aircraft, scoop up Charlie and fly on to Lethbridge, Alberta, where a larger jet would be waiting to take him to California. It didn't happen. The court didn't come down with a ruling for another seven months.

In the interim a number of Canadian politicians blasted the country's convoluted extradition process. The former speaker of the governing Progressive Conservatives demanded an amendment to the Canadian Constitution to prevent illegal immigrants from qualifying for protection under the Charter of Rights and Freedoms. Even Alberta Premier Don Getty, a former quarterback in the Canadian Football League, waded in with a few bone-crushing hits. He had Don MacLeod in his sights. "A large part of our problem is the lawyers that milk the system, keeping people like Charles Ng in Canada," he remarked in the provincial legislature. MacLeod fired back the following day with a statement chastising the premier and calling his remark "unjustified and unpardonably ill-informed." He said Getty's remarks demonstrated an ignorance of the facts and a basic misunderstanding of the constitution.

Another Alberta politician, Stockwell Day, expressed anger over the fact that taxpayers were not only footing the bill for Charlie's legal expenses, but also for his Athabasca University courses. Day, who would later make a run at becoming Prime Minister of Canada, called the situation "odious." Charlie was taking a psychopathology correspondence course through the university. He also was enrolled in a psychology course through British Columbia's Simon Fraser University, but this course he was paying for himself. It involved counseling women.

Charlie's sentence for wounding Calgary security guard Sean Doyle expired during the summer, but a judge ordered that he continue to be held in custody under an extradition warrant. No one wanted an accused killer wandering Canadian streets.

The new justice minister, Kim Campbell, who would go on to briefly become Canada's first female prime minister, tabled legislation in the autumn of 1991 to speed up the extradition process. The time involved in processing Charlie's case was a prime example of a system that was too cumbersome, she said. The changes were made with input from both lawyers in the case, MacLeod and MacFarlane. The new legislation cut the number of possible extradition appeals from seven to four, effectively trimming two years off the process.

Meanwhile, Charlie, now almost 31 after entering his sixth year in Canadian prisons, was still trying desperately to get out of solitary confinement. He was being housed in a super maximum-security unit with 40 other prisoners at a cost of nearly $62,000 a year, and he hated it. He applied to Canadian Corrections authorities for a transfer to the Regional Psychiatric Centre in Saskatoon, Saskatchewan, a few hours south of Prince Albert, but the request was rejected. Charlie settled for anger management courses at the prison.

Charlie should have been settling in for the long haul. His lawyers in California were saying that even if he were extradited immediately, he probably wouldn't go to trial for another five years. Burt was upset that his defense team wouldn't receive the funding or the authority to begin working on the case until Charlie was extradited while the state had been going hard at it since establishing the Ng task force in 1989. "They've had an army to prepare it, and we won't be allowed to prepare until Ng is in the country," he lamented. Ng's other U.S. attorney, San Francisco lawyer Garrick Lew, conceded the cost of the trial would dwarf anything the State had ever seen and could climb higher than $15 million.

"We're looking at an enormously difficult trial," Lew told journalist Rick Mofina, a Calgary crime writer who had dogged the case for years. Mofina wasn't just following the case through the courts. He had been keeping tabs on Charlie in prison, writing to him since December 1990, pressing him for an interview. Finally, succumbing to Mofina's persistence,

Charlie wrote back. "I am feeling more and more a part of the human community and a stranger to myself," he confided to Mofina. "Although I am standing alone, I am still able to carry on. For how long, I don't know."

Most of Charlie's letters to people he thought might help him with his complaints against Corrections Canada dripped with self-pity. But in his September 12, 1991, letter to Mofina, Charlie responded to the journalist's query about his view of the death penalty with a passage from an essay by French writer Albert Camus. In "Reflections of the Guillotine," Camus argued that capital punishment was the most horrific of deaths because it was the most premeditated. "For there to be equivalence, the death penalty would have to punish a criminal who had warned his victim of the date at which he would inflict a horrible death on him and who, from that moment onward, had confined him at his mercy for months," Camus wrote. "Such a horrible monster is not encountered in private life."

The death penalty question was causing extreme anguish behind the ornate doors of Canada's Supreme Court. After much soul-searching, the Court sent out an advisory that it would announce its decision on September 23, 1991. The victims' families huddled by their phones for word to come down from Ottawa. "We just hope and pray the decision is in favor of sending Ng back without conditions," said a worried Rosenfeldt. "If it's not, I don't know what we will do."

As the families and their supporters began their vigil, the RCMP stepped into high gear with its own program. Word had come down from the top that not a moment was to be wasted should the court endorse Charlie's extradition. The plan to whisk the accused killer out of the country had been modified to ensure there was an RCMP jet at the Prince Albert airport capable of making a quick exit from Canada. Ray Munro headed down to California to help arrange the reception while RCMP Sergeant Ray Ambler handled the Canadian end. He arrived at the prison the night before to take prison staff and the U.S. Marshals on a dry run through the process. The necessary paperwork had been prepared in advance. It would be a precision operation with precautions in place to guard against any moves by Charlie or outsiders to abort it.

MacLeod had served notice that he would appeal an unfavorable Supreme Court ruling to the United Nations court at the Hague and asked the court to advise Canada not to immediately extradite the fugitive. The court had complied with the request, but no international law compelled Canada to agree. MacLeod could only hope that Canadian officials would be sufficiently concerned about the international ramifications of ignoring the United Nations' request to delay sending Charlie back to the U.S.

His fears were not groundless. The Supreme Court decided by the narrowest of margins that Charlie could be extradited without assurances that he would not face the death penalty. In speaking for the 4–3 majority, Justice Gerard La Forest called his crimes "almost unspeakable" and stressed that the extradition was necessary to prevent Canada from becoming a haven for fugitives.

"The possible significance of the temptation of an accused to escape to Canada should not be overlooked," he wrote. "Counsel has led evidence before us to show that, since 1976, approximately 300,000 homicides have occurred in the United States. As this court has recognized previously, the two countries have a long and relatively open border and similar cultures, which makes the possibility of an escape over the border much more likely." He noted that both Charlie and the other fugitive, Kindler, committed crimes in Canada. "This would seem to be precisely the kinds of individuals the minister would wish to keep out."

La Forest would later call the decision his most difficult in 12 years and more than 1,500 cases on the Supreme Court. "Ng really tore me apart," he said upon his retirement in 1997. "I have never had any doubt about the correctness of my view since, but I had a very difficult time with that."

However, Mr. Justice Peter Cory, in putting forward the dissenting opinion, couldn't understand why the Charter's protection against cruel and unusual punishment didn't apply to Charlie. "In my view, since the death penalty is a cruel punishment, that argument is an indefensible abdication of moral responsibility," he wrote. "Historically, such a position has always been condemned. The ceremonial washing of his hands by Pontius Pilate did not relieve him of responsibility for the death sentence imposed by others."

Justice Cory said Canada had an obligation not to extradite a person to face cruel and unusual punishment. He rejected the safe-haven argument, saying that it had not resulted in an exodus of fugitives to Europe, which refused to extradite fugitives to countries without assurances that the death penalty wouldn't be invoked.

The court didn't rule on whether the death penalty itself violated the Charter but hinted it likely did. Six of the judges expressed opposition to capital punishment in the ruling, signaling to the country that should Parliament ever consider restoring the death penalty, it would probably be rejected by the country's highest court.

The decision came down at 8:00 A.M. Saskatchewan time. At 8:20 a call came through to Prince Albert Penitentiary from the federal justice minister's office advising that the extradition had been approved. The justice official who took the call at the prison flashed a thumbs up to the warden and Ambler, who were waiting by phones in nearby offices to pass on the word to the guards and waiting aircraft. The team jumped into action.

Guards and U.S. marshals were dispatched to Charlie's cell. Charlie, bewildered, initially balked at the transfer and refused to go without speaking with his lawyer. The guards assured him that he didn't have a choice. He was leaving, and he was leaving now. With a video camera rolling, they marched him to the rear of the prison, where a van and a half dozen police escort vehicles were waiting. The caravan of eight vehicles, 18 police and correctional officers and a police dog and his handler arrived at the airport at 8:43 A.M. Only the *Edmonton Journal* was on hand at the RCMP hangar to see a morose-looking Charlie half dragged aboard the twin turbo-prop aircraft. By 8:50 A.M., they were in the air. Several of the guards and police officers who stayed behind applauded as the wheels left the ground. It was a popular sentiment. One Canadian newspaper would run Charlie's Folsom Prison mugshot the next day on its front page under a screaming headline: "Good Riddance." Charlie's six-year, $2-million hiatus in Canada was over.

Ambler, armed with an electric stun gun, sat directly behind Charlie on the plane. He stayed close to the plane's intercom system in order to advise the two RCMP pilots of any problems in the passenger compartment.

He had been advised that justice officials would call him on his cell phone if it was necessary to turn back. Charlie, dressed in dark blue prison coveralls, sat in leg-irons, with his hands in cuffs and linked to a chain around his waist. He sat quietly, still peeved at not being able to talk with his lawyer. He was surrounded by several U.S. marshals, Task Force Commander Martin Ryan and Calaveras County Sheriff Bill Nuttall. All were unarmed. Restrictions against bringing firearms into Canada or taking them from Canada to the U.S. convinced the multi-jurisdictional police team to opt for a strong physical presence, restraints and the stun gun to prevent Charlie from trying to escape. In any event they didn't want a gun battle on the plane.

The Beechcraft King Air crossed into the United States about 80 minutes later. If Canadian authorities had wanted to reach Ambler on his cell phone to order him to bring Charlie back to Canada, they wouldn't have had much luck. He discovered it wasn't working. The plane touched down in Boise, Idaho, just before noon, and the police officers disembarked from the aircraft to clear customs. Ambler and a marshal stayed on board with Charlie. Ambler didn't want Charlie setting foot in Idaho and triggering another state-to-state extradition process. He provided Charlie with a plastic container to use as a urinal before they took off for McClellan Air Force Base near Sacramento.

About two and a half hours later, Ambler heard the pilot on the intercom: "Hey, Ray, take a look out the window," he called from the cockpit. "You ain't ever going to see anything like this in your life again." Peering out his window, Ambler saw what looked like at least 100 police cars parked on the tarmac below, all with their roof lights flashing. Media vans were visible along both sides of the road leading into the base. The moment the RCMP aircraft touched down and came to a halt, it was surrounded by police vehicles. As the aircraft door was opened, Ambler could hear the distinctive *ta-chung, ta-chung* sounds as the waiting police officers racked the slides on their shotguns. The plainclothes Mountie decided to let a uniformed marshal lead the procession off the plane.

Charlie kept his head down and his eyes on the ground as he was escorted from the aircraft and to a waiting van by an entourage of California state corrections officers in crisp new uniforms. He was off to the infamous Folsom Prison with a helicopter escort. He wasn't going to like his new home one little bit.

Task Force Commander Ryan told waiting reporters he was glad the trip from Canada had been uneventful. "It's been a long six years," he said. "Now we're ready to proceed with Phase II."

Back in Canada, MacLeod filed an appeal to the United Nations Human Rights Committee, but he couldn't stop Charlie's swift extradition. He was furious that RCMP had surrendered Charlie to the U.S. before he even had a chance to tell him about the decision and what it meant. He had been given assurances that he would be able to talk to his client. "What difference would another 20 minutes have made?" he fumed. "What was the hurry? It was just plain stupid!"

Canada's justice minister Kim Campbell told reporters that, although she had carefully considered the request from the United Nations committee to delay extradition until it had heard MacLeod's appeal, in the end, she rejected it. "I had to make a judgment call, and I determined my greater obligation was to serve the cause of justice by surrendering Charles Ng," she said.

When the United Nations came down with its decision three years later, it ruled 14–4 that Canada ignored its obligations under the International Covenant on Civil and Political Rights when it extradited Charles Ng. The United Nations urged Canadian officials to press the United States not to seek the death penalty against Charlie, and it appealed to them not to make the same mistake again.

Ray Munro was in Calaveras County for Charlie's first appearance at the courthouse in San Andreas. He had been asked to be on hand to answer the court's questions about Charlie's incarceration in Canada, should they arise. A surreal scene greeted him as he rolled up to the Justice Center, a flat-roofed two-story modern structure with an historical mural painted over the pair of double main entry doors. Police snipers were stationed on the rooftop, and snarling police dogs ringed the building. Inside, spectators were checked through a metal detector and frisked for weapons before they were allowed to enter the courtroom. Reporters and cameras were everywhere.

Charlie was escorted into the building from a prison van parked at the back door. Several relatives of Charlie's victims were also on hand. Sharon Sellitto, now a familiar face at his proceedings, was part of Charlie's welcoming committee. She had driven up from San Francisco for the 2:30 P.M. hearing. Now she waited in a packed and noisy courtroom for his grand entrance. A rattling of chains signaled his appearance. A hush fell over the room as a rear door opened and a pair of massive guards the size of refrigerators strode in. A perceptible gasp arose from scores of throats as Charlie, looking all the more diminutive between the two giants, shuffled into view. As the guards chained Charlie to his chair, Michael Burt rose and placed a reassuring hand on his client's back. Charlie was frightened, but he struggled to keep his face impassive and his fear masked.

Clad once more in a prison jumpsuit, and manacled hand and foot, Charlie spoke quietly to Judge Douglas Mewhinney with no hint of emotion in his voice. He kept his eyes fixed toward the front of the court during the 15-minute appearance, not once looking into the packed spectator's gallery as he was arraigned on 11 murder charges. A guard with a short-barreled shotgun stood at his side, and front-row spectators were warned by Calaveras County deputy sheriffs not to make any sudden movements in the courtroom.

Dian Allen drove three hours from the San Jose area, south of San Francisco, for the brief view of the man she believed had killed her sister, Kathi. "I wanted to see him face to face," she told reporters outside the court. "I wanted to see what kind of person would do this."

Meanwhile, Charlie was extremely unhappy to find himself again in solitary confinement. But, now an experienced jailhouse lawyer, he began launching a blizzard of complaints about his treatment and the violation of his rights. He complained about his food, about his lawyers and even about getting carsick in the prison van while being transported the 30 miles between Folsom and San Andreas. He complained about being locked in a small cage, like Hannibal Lecter in the movie *Silence of the Lambs,* during breaks in court proceedings. But his biggest beef was the refusal of the court to allow him to be represented by San Francisco Deputy Public Defenders Michael Burt and Garrick Lew. Judge Mewhinney assigned two new lawyers to defend Charlie because he was concerned that Burt, who was representing two other accused killers facing the death penalty, was much too busy to take on such a massive case. Burt had his hands full representing mass murderer Richard Ramirez, the killer known as the Night Stalker. Forty-one-year-old Lew, a University of California graduate, had told the court he wouldn't take on Charlie's defense without his partner, Burt. Mewhinney dumped Charlie's case on two local defense attorneys, James Webster and Thomas Marovich. Both were capable enough. Both had experience in capital cases, and Marovich was a former county district attorney. But Charlie didn't want them, and his objection would drag the case on for years. When he was ordered to stand trial in November 1992, his defense team was optimistically predicting the case could begin within two years. But then legal hurdles initiated by Charlie resulted in eight trips to California's Supreme Court for resolution. He played a game of musical chairs with his lawyers and judges, too, turning the case into a national embarrassment. He went through 10 judges and four defense teams, chewing up the calendar with three dozen pretrial motions and pushing his trial date further and further into the future.

One psychology professor who chronicled the case in a book about serial murderers estimated that Charlie, who was barely 25 when he committed the crimes, could be 50 before he is executed. The families of the victims were beyond discouraged. Sharon Sellitto complained that it was hard to get swift justice when all the lawyers were billing by the hour. She said she was tempted to leap over the rail that separates the courtroom spectators from the lawyers, but she didn't know who to strangle first.

"We have no hope at all," she lamented. "It is like trying to hurry a glacier. It is shameful." She told journalist Rick Mofina that the case evoked images of Dante's *Divine Comedy.* "You know the inscription over the gate to Hell, where it says 'Abandon all hope, ye who enter here?' Well, that about sums it up for me."

Charles Ng, in restraints, looks morosely out the window during his extradition flight to the United States. Ray Ambler of the Royal Canadian Mounted Police sits behind him.

Charlie is escorted from the aircraft at McClellan Air Force Base near Sacramento. One of America's most notorious mass murderers was finally back home to face his accusers.

Charlie is escorted into the van waiting to carry him to Folsom Prison.

23

On the Outside

I F MO WAS AT ALL REPENTANT over his drugstore shoplifting escapade, he didn't let on the next time Ray stopped by to see him at Bowden Institution. The big cowboy just turned on a huge grin and shrugged. "Hell, we're all expected to screw up. It's part of the process," he said.

His plans for parole were proceeding. By the fall of 1991, even as Charlie was en route to California, Mo was making a pitch for full parole. He had spent the past year on a day-parole program, working in the community in the daytime and returning to his prison cell every night. The program was set up by the RCMP, who paid him $1,800 a month to cover his expenses for food, lodging and transportation. Mo kept a basement suite apartment in Three Hills for daytime use when he wasn't doing volunteer work at a church camp. The RCMP was still honoring the promise they had made to protect him from any fallout as a result of his testifying in the Gingras murders. That obligation remained as long as the threat to his safety did. Although Mo couldn't change his name or appearance while on parole, he was encouraged to keep a low profile in a central Alberta farm community, where he was unlikely to encounter anyone from his past. This time he behaved himself. No screw-ups.

When Mo applied for full parole, the board members listened atten-
tively. Mo was not a typical inmate. Super intelligent. A member of the
Mensa Society. A university degree. Strong family support. A record of
cooperation with police and prison authorities. It looked like he finally had
his head on straight. The parole board agreed that he was ready to resume
his place in society. As he walked out of prison he believed in his heart he
had earned his way out. There was little doubt his extensive involvement in
the Ng and Gingras cases and his studious behavior in prison had shaved 16
years off his 25-year prison term. It was a remarkable feat given the judge's
condemnation of him at his trial.

Mo believed he really had changed. He was done with prisons. He had
spent too much of his life in a cell. But he knew he deserved it. He had been
a one-man crime wave. In a space of 14 years, between 1968 and 1982, he
had racked up 45 criminal charges. He couldn't get those lost years back, but
he was only 39. He knew he had the smarts, and he was willing to work
hard. He could salvage what was left of his life. He had time.

Fresh out of jail, Mo met a deeply religious young woman and wooed
her off her feet. He still had the charm, the friendly crinkles around his eyes,
the giant hands with their reassuring grip. With graying hair and a tattoo of
Thumper Rabbit on one arm, he hardly seemed menacing. Before long his
new love was pregnant with his child. But it didn't last. His boy was still a
toddler when the relationship fell apart.

Mo was working as a foreman at a southern Alberta ranch. He enjoyed
the stress-free environment and didn't mind getting his hands dirty in an
outdoor manual labor job. It paid a decent wage and it kept him out of
trouble. It felt great to be astride a horse again. On his days off he pulled
his horse trailer down to Calgary to take his young son horseback riding on
the hills overlooking the city. He loved being out with kids, horses, dogs
and elderly people, and that's how he spent his time whenever he had the
chance.

Ray, who was still commanding the RCMP detachment in Cardston,
Alberta, would drop by frequently to see how he was doing. The Mountie
was still running back and forth between Alberta and California to testify

at various court hearings related to Charlie's case. Although he had been present, he had not been called to testify during Charlie's first appearance in Calaveras County. When he flew back a month later for a hearing into Charlie's super maximum-security designation, he testified that Canadian officials had housed Charlie in special facilities because he was perceived to be dangerous and an escape risk. The testimony pretty well killed Charlie's chances of being housed at the Calaveras County jail. Being locked up 23 hours a day was making Charlie stir crazy. He became extremely obsessed with food. He was always hungry, and the fare never measured up to his expectations. He became preoccupied with trivial things like needing his hair and fingernails trimmed. And at night he was very often lonely and depressed.

But he never gave up the notion of escaping and was always hoping he would get a chance. Guards found he had stashed a razor blade in the light socket in his cell. After one visit from his lawyer, Charlie removed a sharp metal clasp from a manila envelope, but then left it in the booth when he realized he would be searched before returning to his cell. Outwardly, however, he maintained his model behavior. Always polite. Always obedient.

Meanwhile, Mo's release from prison simplified life for Ray and the American authorities. It would have been extremely difficult, if not impossible, to transport a serving Canadian prisoner to the United States to testify in a court proceeding. With his extensive criminal record, it would still be tough to get Mo across the border, but the Canadian government could apply for a special permit, and Ray, of course, would be responsible for him while he was in the United States. There was nothing, however, to compel Mo to go. His decision would be strictly voluntary. And even Mo wasn't sure whether he wanted to testify in the case or not. For one thing, American justice officials wanted him to take a polygraph test, and he was balking. He didn't trust the lie detector, and he didn't trust cops. He feared that once he was on U.S. soil, American officials would grab him and incarcerate him as a material witness to ensure he would be available for trial. He contemplated washing his hands of the entire affair, and he went so far as to send a letter to American authorities demanding special treatment. He didn't want to get involved without assurances they would provide for his safety under the American witness protection program operated by the U.S. marshal's office.

Ray was never sure if Mo was prepared to testify, either. One day he seemed to be leaning one way and the next day, the other. Perhaps the prosecutors could enter the sketches and his evidence from the extradition hearing without calling Mo to the stand. It came as somewhat of a surprise to Ray when Mo called in February 1992 to say he was willing to meet with U.S. officials about testifying.

The meeting with Calaveras District Attorney John Martin and Deputy Attorney General Sharlene Honnaka in Rancho Cordova didn't go well. Mo came across as hostile, obstinate and arrogant. He demanded to be allowed to testify under an alias for his protection. He was worried that by testifying at such a high-profile case, he would be exposing himself and jeopardizing his safety. If he had to relocate after testifying at Charlie's trial, he wanted the U.S. government to pick up the tab. But Martin and Honnaka refused to bargain. They wouldn't offer Mo anything for his testimony—not even protection—and refused to consider having Mo testify anonymously. This case had to be transparent. They didn't like the idea of calling a jailhouse informant, and they were very worried Mo would taint their case. If it became known during the trial that Mo received anything for his testimony, it could severely damage not only Mo's credibility but the credibility of the entire case. Martin and Honnaka wanted to use the sketches and Charlie's admissions to Mo about the killings, but not if the case was jeopardized by Mo. The two sides were at an impasse.

As they were heading to the airport to return to Alberta, Ray and Mo were chatting about life on the outside. Ray wanted to know how Mo was coping. Whether he was able to stay away from crime. Whether he missed the excitement and adventure of his old life.

"How are you handling the jazz?" Ray wanted to know.

At that moment they were passing an 18-wheeler on the freeway. Mo's eyes were riveted on the truck. In huge letters across the side of the trailer was the name *Brinks*. Mo didn't say anything for a few moments. He just stared. "Jeez, would you look at that?" he finally mumbled. "If I had known they hauled tractor-trailer loads of money around here, I would have moved down here a long time ago."

A few months later Ray received a call from Mo, who had just landed a job on a cattle ranch near Rocky Mountain House, just west of the foothills.

"Hey, Columbo, I just had to phone you," he told Ray. "I am still dreaming about that 18-wheeler. If I made a score like that I'd have a condo in the Caymans and a Mercedes in the garage." Mo still hadn't decided if would he testify against Charlie. Now that he was out of prison, what was the point?

A year passed before Mo made his next move. He called Ray and told him he was willing to take the polygraph test. Ray figured he must be getting bored not being the center of attention anymore. They flew down to Sacramento almost immediately for the test. It was a whirlwind trip. They arrived one day, took the test the next and flew back the following day.

The test produced mixed results, but it was more than enough to satisfy the California prosecutors. Mo was asked questions about evidence he had given at the extradition hearing. "Did Charles Ng tell you that he killed Kathi Allen?" he was asked. Mo answered yes, and the machine registered that his statement was true. "Did Charles Ng tell you he killed Brenda O'Connor?" Again Mo answered yes, and the device confirmed the answer. But when Mo was asked if he had told the truth at the extradition hearing and he answered yes, the machine registered that he was being deceptive. The same reading came up when he was asked if he had made notes of Charlie's comments immediately after their conversations. Mo admitted that sometimes he hadn't made the notes until the following day. The polygraph technician advised Ray that Mo had passed the test. He was back in the limelight again, California's star witness against Charlie—provided there ever was a trial.

The case was bogging down horribly. Charlie was still adamant that, although penniless, he had a right to be represented by the lawyers of his choice, Michael Burt and Garrick Lew. He had no faith in his court-appointed lawyers, Marovich and Webster. He launched a $1-million mal-practice suit against the pair. He refused to speak to them. The frustrated attorneys asked to be removed from the case, but their request was denied. Charlie applied to the court repeatedly to be allowed to try the case him-self. Before long there was such a procession of lawyers and judges involved that it was beginning to look like a serial lawyer case instead of a serial mur-der case.

It was all very perplexing for renowned California lawyer Ephraim Margolin, a veteran constitutional lawyer who worked out of an office over-looking San Francisco's Union Square. Margolin had been involved in the case peripherally since Charlie took flight from South City Lumber in South San Francisco. When Charlie was finally extradited, Margolin had acted on behalf of Lew to argue that the San Francisco attorney should be allowed to defend him. He went so far as to guarantee to Judge Mewhin-ney that if Michael Burt was also assigned to the case, they would be ready for a preliminary hearing within eight months. Mewhinney was dubious about the guarantee and opted instead to appoint Marovich and Webster. "They are willing to do it in six months, so I am appointing them," Mewhinney told Margolin. Margolin responded wryly, "Thank-you, your honor," which, as Margolin later put it, is what you say to a judge when you are being screwed.

"We drove back to San Francisco celebrating," he recalled. "Nobody wanted Charlie's case, but Garrick made the effort out of loyalty to his client." Margolin said the Sonoma lawyers denied they ever promised to be ready for the preliminary in six months. Later Margolin was invited by Mewhinney to appeal the decision to the California Supreme Court, which he did on behalf of Charlie. He lost the argument by a 4–3 decision. Had the margin been reversed, Margolin would later lament, it would have saved California taxpayers and the families of Charlie's victims years of anguish and expense. Charlie continued his fight to have Lew and Burt represent him for seven years. He drafted a flurry of motions and applications, and argued for a change of venue, claiming he could not get a fair trial in Calav-eras County. He petitioned the court to move his case to San Francisco, where juries were so solidly against the death penalty that no one had been sentenced to die in several decades.

The trial was eventually moved out of Calaveras County, but not to any defense-friendly locale. Charlie was to be tried in Orange County, a judicial district at the opposite end of the spectrum from liberal San Francisco. The crime-weary residents living in and around Los Angeles had no qualms about the death penalty. They had sent a stream of killers to San Quentin's death row, where more than 500 were waiting to die, and they were waiting for a governor with the balls to resume the executions.

Governor George Deukmejian was their man. In 1992 California executed its first death row inmate in 25 years, the 195th man to be executed by lethal gas in the state. The following year, a second California man was executed, but by then the state allowed condemned inmates to choose between lethal gas and lethal injection.

Orange County residents may have been supportive of capital punishment, but the county didn't want the case. It couldn't afford it. Some bad stock investments had forced the county into bankruptcy, and there was barely money for necessary services, let alone what was expected to be the longest and most costly trial in California history. Finally, in March 1995, Orange County officials agreed to take on the trial provided the state and Calaveras County covered the costs. A trial date was set for September 6, 1996, but lawyers on both sides doubted it would begin before the fall of 1997.

Charlie's defense had landed in the lap of William Gorman Kelley, an experienced 48-year-old Orange County deputy public defender who had handled a number of high-profile murder cases. He had just finished a trial that had been going on for about two years when he was approached to take Charlie's case. Kelley thought it over for a week. He knew it would be a huge sacrifice for his career and his family, but it would also be the most challenging case he was ever likely to see. Kelley agreed to take over the 10-year-old case, although he admitted he had second thoughts when he saw the tractor trailer back up to the office door and unload a staggering six tons of files. There were 750 binders, each three inches thick, as well as 3,000 pieces of physical evidence to weed through. "My mouth was hanging open as they were bringing it in," Kelley later told reporters. "I was sitting there thinking to myself, What have I done?" There would be no early trial. The case was a monster.

A tall lean man with short dark hair and a sharp beak, Kelley was no stranger to controversy. He had often taken repulsive cases other lawyers shunned. In the mid-1980s, he had defended a pedophile accused of sexually assaulting blind paraplegic girls, aged 8 and 9, whom he had spirited away from a children's home where he had worked. The case of the Highland Home Kidnapper had triggered a major scandal and intense media coverage. No one in the public defender's office would touch it. Kelley requested the file.

Kelley had enrolled in college with the dream of being a painter, a sculptor and a filmmaker, and he earned a degree in fine arts. But when he was working on his master's, he got involved in an avant-garde project examining the validity of courtroom photographs. The idea of going into law got planted. He had been hoping to get a university teaching job with his master's degree, but there wasn't a lot of demand for art teachers. His girl friend, a law student, suggested he give law school a try. He was midway through his second year and still doing freelance commercial artwork on the side when he got hooked by trial work. He discovered that he could make the courtroom his canvas. He loved the action in the courtroom, and he realized he could use his creativity just as well there.

Fate made Kelley a defense lawyer. He had started out on the other side, clerking in the San Diego district attorney's office. When he followed his girl friend up to Oregon, he first tried to get a job with the DA's office there, offering to work 20 hours a week for free. But they didn't like Californians there. So he trotted over to the public defender's office, where they were thrilled to accept all the free help they could get. He later landed a job but eventually moved back to California, where the money was better.

It wasn't long before Kelley became involved in several controversial cases. He endured public loathing by winning an acquittal, after two trials, for a driver involved in a vehicular homicide. The crash on the Pacific Coast

Highway had killed a teenage girl and seriously injured seven others. The case spawned the formation of a Mothers Against Drunk Driving chapter in Orange County and sparked new drunk driving legislation. In 1987 Kelley took on another unpopular case stemming from the death of three police officers who were killed while chasing a stolen car. The deaths occurred when two police helicopters involved in the 50-mile chase collided. The driver was convicted of three counts of second degree murder, but Kelley had the charge reduced to involuntary manslaughter and the sentence reduced from three life terms to nine years.

His two most recent high-profile cases had been notorious homicides. He had defended Gregory Sturm in a 1990 case in which the fired auto parts store employee tied up three store employees and then executed each with a bullet in the head. The man's guilt was admitted, but Kelley fought through two trials in a bid to save the man from the death penalty. The case is still under appeal. In another 1990 case Kelley represented a woman accused of stabbing her sleeping husband to death. He proved she was attacked by her abusive husband in the kitchen and actually stabbed him while defending herself as the fight raged through other rooms in the home. She was acquitted.

When Charlie's case arrived at his door, Kelley had a lot of catching up to do. He would rise at 5:00 A.M. and head into the office to read the extensive files on the case, usually not getting home until midnight. Once in a while he took a Sunday off. The case was going to be a long haul. There would be many 100-hour weeks. But the biggest difficulty he faced was an uncooperative client. Charlie didn't want him, didn't like him and, at times, refused to even talk to him.

"Mr. Ng is not speaking to or cooperating with me on any matter," Kelley complained in a motion to the court. "I believe this is a result of psychological problems he is having." Kelley argued that his client was mentally incompetent and unable to properly instruct his counsel. Charlie argued that his lawyer was professionally incompetent and should be dismissed. A psychiatrist who treated Charlie told the court that while Charlie understood the charges against him, he was suffering from an obsessive compulsive disorder and depression. At one point Charlie had Kelley removed from the case, only to hire him back again.

Upheavals in the case weren't confined to the defense. Calaveras District Attorney John Martin was appointed to the bench, leaving his associate Peter Smith to prosecute the case. And after his boss lost a hard-fought election for district attorney in San Francisco, Assistant District Attorney Paul Cummins was removed from the case by the victor. Cummins had been trying to lay three more murder charges against Charlie, but he never could convince Martin they could win convictions. The charismatic Irish Catholic was disappointed to go, believing he was a victim of politics, but he had a lot of respect for Deputy Attorney General Sharlene Honnaka, who was named his successor. Following a game of musical chairs with the judges, which saw two judges challenged by the defense and one challenged by the prosecution, a hard-nosed taskmaster and ex-marine named John Ryan was assigned the case. Kelley admired Ryan, who had been the judge on the bench when he defended the Highland Homes Kidnapper a decade earlier. Ryan seemed determined to end the litany of delays and get on with the trial as soon as possible.

But Charlie wasn't going quietly into the night. He was still pressing to get Lew and Burt on the case. Ryan, like his predecessors, was very quickly becoming exasperated. "Everything we do in this case seems to go in circles," he lamented at one point. "We have to break the circle and move forward."

Back in Alberta, Ray still worked occasionally for the State of California *versus* Charles Ng. He went to Vancouver to interview a man who had been visiting and corresponding with Charlie in the Prince Albert Penitentiary. Ray discovered the man, who was also Chinese, belonged to a prison fellowship group. He said only once had Charlie broached the subject of his offenses and that he had advised him it was not a good idea to discuss them.

Ray later returned to Vancouver, joined by Calaveras cops John Crawford and Larry Copland, to interview a man who had served in the marines with Charlie back in 1982. The former Marine Corps corporal told RCMP that Charlie claimed he had killed a woman at the Rainbow Car Rental agency on the marine base at Kaneohe Bay, Hawaii. A woman named Jackie Ryder had been killed there that year, and the murder had never been solved.

"The first I heard about the murder was from Charlie himself," the ex-marine told a Mountie. "He was telling me, in his own words, 'I wasted some bitch.' He was pretty excited about it. He said he had entered the car rental, just whipped open the door, stuck his gun in and popped her in the chest or face somewhere, I assumed, with his .45 that he had purchased earlier."

The ex-marine said Charlie never really explained why he did it. He said on another occasion he had to talk Charlie out of wanting to kill a military policeman who had whacked him over the head with a night stick. "Charlie was a little unstable," he explained. "He took offense really easily." The ex-marine said Charlie once claimed to have attempted to slash a hitchhiker's throat in a rental car, but the guy got away. He also said Charlie claimed to have killed people in Hong Kong by firing random shots into a crowd from his apartment window.

"He had a real hate on for women. He didn't like women at all one bit. But yet he acted quite unstably if you called him gay or faggot, which I did many times." He told the cops that once, when the two were on their way to shoot their weapons on a gun range, Charlie told him that he loved him. When he laughingly called Charlie a faggot, Charlie pointed his loaded weapon at him.

He told the Mounties he last saw Charlie shortly after he was rearrested in California and on his way to the brig in Pearl Harbor to face court martial for the armory burglary. When he heard Charlie was on the run for a string of murders in California, he assumed he was coming north to Canada to seek sanctuary with him.

Charlie's buddy was asked why he came forward to police. "I've been thinking about it for a long time," he explained. "I suppose maybe the family would like to know how their daughter died or who did it. It might take a load off their mind. And I figure Charlie's going to fry anyhow for these other murders down in California. Hopefully, they will keep him locked up for a while, and he won't be a threat to me." He added that if Charlie went after him, Charlie should know he would "definitely come out shooting."

Charlie had been asked about the Ryder killing when he was arrested in Calgary, but he had refused to say anything about it. But he had told a lawyer back at his court martial in Hawaii that he had killed two people in Hawaii. Investigators followed up on the ex-marine's information to see if they could link the Ryder killing and any other homicide to Charlie, but they didn't have much luck. The information was too sketchy. Too much time had passed.

Kelley was traveling across Canada as well. Starting in Nova Scotia and then heading to Ottawa, he continued west through Winnipeg to Calgary, Edmonton and Vancouver, searching out and interviewing potential witnesses. Many of them were people who had dealings with Charlie and Mo: police officers, guards and convicts, even Mo's family. In June 1996 Kelley decided it was time to meet Mo himself. He asked Ray if Mo would fly down to Sacramento for an interview with the defense team. Ray left it up to Mo to decide, but he thought it would be a good idea for the two men to size each other up. It would give Mo a taste of what he could expect at the trial, and it would give the prosecution an opportunity to see how well Mo stood up to Kelley's attack.

It was warm, in the mid-90s, when Mo and Ray arrived in Sacramento, a nice change from Alberta, where the snow had been falling just two weeks earlier. They met Kelley and his investigator, Richard Sakobuchi, on July 2 at a downtown office building. Mo had brought along a copy of his notes of his conversations with Charlie and the sketches Charlie had drawn for him. They sat in a pile on a table in front of Mo along with a copy of his testimony eight years earlier at the extradition hearing in Edmonton.

Kelley asked him if he had any other sketches and notes aside from the ones he had turned over to his lawyer. Mo responded that if he did, they would be in Ray's possession. Ray told Kelley he had a sealed box belonging to Mo, but he hadn't opened it to see if there were other drawings. Neither

Ray nor Mo had any objections to turning over anything they found in the box. Kelley asked Mo if he had ever used a pseudonym or alias. Mo said he had occasionally used the name Pat Reimer, and he also had used the name of his brother Rene when his own driver's license was suspended. Kelley wanted to know if every conversation between Mo and Ray had been recorded.

"Just what do you mean by conversations?" asked Ray. "We've been having conversations over the past 10 years. Every official conversation has been recorded."

"What do you mean by official versus unofficial?" asked Kelley.

Ray said he didn't consider general conversations about the status of Charlie's case to be official. "There's probably been no official involvement with Mo since 1990."

"Okay, I notice you call him Mo," Kelley asked suddenly. "Is he, Mr. Laberge, a friend of yours?"

"Oh, definitely," Ray agreed, nodding.

"Oh," Kelley said, slightly taken aback. "How long have you been friends?"

"Well, I'm gonna say we evolved to become friends," explained Ray. "I've known him for 10 years now." He didn't volunteer that Mo affectionately called him Columbo and had mowed his lawn when he had been living in Three Hills, but he made no attempt to hide the relationship that had grown between them.

"How long have you considered him your friend?"

"I'm gonna say it just developed. You know, when I say friend, I mean friend, a business associate."

Kelley shifted direction. He began questioning Mo about his involvement in the RCMP witness protection program. Mo became a little testy, balking at answering questions that didn't pertain to Charlie's offenses. He maintained that his involvement in the program had nothing to do with any perceived threat from Charlie. Kelley questioned Mo about whether he ever viewed any of Charlie's legal material or if he had ever read Leonard Lake's diary. Mo denied ever doing so. Kelley asked him about a jail guard who claimed Mo had read the diary and described parts of it to him.

"Okay," Kelley went on. "If he testified that in fact you actually did describe it to him, he'd be lying then?"

Mo chuckled. "Yeah, okay, he just got whacked for perjury so he could lie about that, too," he said.

"He got what?" asked the astonished lawyer.

"He got whacked for perjury."

"How do you know?"

"He got caught tampering with odometers," retorted Mo. "It was in the papers recently."

"So he's no longer a jailer, apparently?" Kelley asked.

"No, no, no, no," chuckled Mo. "I think he might even be in jail."

Kelley asked Mo if he would draw him a sketch of the exercise area where Charlie and Mo had worked out daily. Mo declined, suggesting that Kelley ask the institution for a photograph of the exercise area.

"So you are unwilling to draw it for me?"

"Not interested," responded Mo. He was enjoying himself now. "Get Charlie to draw it for you."

Kelley asked Mo if he ever drew a sketch for Charlie. Mo recalled drawing the chart that compared Charlie to Canadian serial killer Clifford Olson and other killers. He told Kelley that Charlie got upset about that one.

"I told him the only cure for him was massive shock therapy," Mo explained.

Mo was asked several times about whether he had committed any offenses since his release. He said all he had were a few traffic tickets and maintained he had not been questioned as a suspect in any crimes. Kelley asked him about his plans to write a book about Charlie. Mo explained that it would have been a book about serial killers and likely would have included information about Daniel Gingras as well. He said he would not have written it until after his release.

"What were you intending to do with the book?" asked Kelley. "Sell it?"

"I would have sold it for sure," responded Mo.

"Just to make money?"

"Absolutely!"

"You were going to base an entire book upon that three- or four-month relationship?" Kelley wondered.

"The information I had in that three-month period was fairly dramatic and fairly extensive," countered Mo.

Kelley switched back to the witness protection program.

"Have you ever said you wouldn't have testified or didn't want to participate in any further criminal proceedings until certain arrangements were made for you?"

"No."

"Okay, hang on a second," sputtered Kelley. "Um, oh boy! Um, when did your time under the witness protection program begin?"

"I can't figure out if it ever really began!" Mo responded.

"Well, did you ever actually live under the auspices of the witness protection program?"

"Uh, actually, I don't know," answered Mo.

As the interview went on, the pair became more and more testy. Mo was getting angry at the questions and Kelley more and more frustrated with Mo's responses. He asked Mo if he would object to being fingerprinted. Mo advised him to get a copy of his prints from the RCMP.

"Since you are in this country, it would be real easy for us to get them," Kelley countered.

"The answer is no." Mo had his back up now. "No pictures. No fingerprints."

"Do you have something to hide?" badgered Kelley.

"I'm not charged with anything here," snapped Mo. "I have got nothing to hide!" Finally, Ray agreed to provide a set of Mo's fingerprints if they were requested through the proper authorities.

Once he had Mo worked into a bit of a lather, Kelley asked him about the allegations that he had once sexually assaulted a young boy. Mo again denied it, as he had at the extradition hearing and at Gingras' trial. Kelley asked Mo if he had ever discussed the offense with nurses, psychologists or

324 No Kill No Thrill

psychiatrists when he was being held at the Corrections Canada Regional Psychiatric Centre in Saskatoon. Mo agreed he had.

"You never admitted it?" continued Kelley.

"No, what I did, in fact, was submit the transcript of the testimony, and I accepted responsibility for what was on the transcript."

Kelley asked Mo if he would voluntarily allow him to seek his medical records from the Regional Psychiatric Centre. Mo refused permission.

"You can hassle me all you want," he told the lawyer. "I'm not gonna do it."

"Well, if I did have such reports like that, would you be willing to look at them and tell me if they are true or not?"

Mo said he wouldn't look at the reports.

"So if a psychologist says in his report that you said you sexually assaulted this boy by putting your fingers into his rectum, you say he is a liar?"

"Best talk about it with him," Mo replied.

"Do you deny telling him?"

"I don't want to deal with it," Mo answered.

"Would you like to see the report?"

"Nope."

"You're gonna have to deal with this some day."

"Perhaps."

"Your credibility is going to be an issue in this case," continued Kelley. "You understand that?"

"Absolutely."

"And part of your credibility is being open about your life?"

"Oh, I don't know. I have no interest in bolstering my credibility. I could care less."

"You could care less if you are believed or not?"

"That's right."

"You don't give a shit what the jury thinks?"

"I don't give a shit what the jury thinks."

"Do you want to testify?"

"No."

"Are you planning on coming down here to testify?"

"I haven't made up my mind yet. My personal opinion is you should just tell him to plead guilty."

"Why did you come here today?"

"For your benefit. The prosecution asked me to come." Mo had actually thought he had information that could be useful to Charlie's defense. He thought Kelley was making a mistake by taking a confrontational approach when he could help Charlie's cause by probing the relationship between the two inmates. Mo was willing to help convict Charlie but didn't want him executed.

"So if they ask you to come testify at the trial, you're gonna do the same thing?" continued Kelley. "You're just gonna come on down?"

"I may do that."

"Why would you do that if you really don't want to testify?"

"It may be my duty."

Kelley went back to Mo's prison records, trying to convince him to give permission to see them. He wanted to try to make him defend Mo's credibility. Mo wouldn't bite.

"When the boy testified that you sexually assaulted him, was he lying?"

"I don't even want to respond to that garbage," Mo snarled. Kelley prodded Mo again to give him permission to take his fingerprints. Finally, he pulled out a court order and insisted Mo obey it. It was dated March 5, 1996, the date Mo was to have been interviewed. Mo had cancelled because of the death of an aunt. During a break and a meeting with prosecutors Honnaka and Smith, Ray offered again to provide Kelley with a copy of Mo's prints. Kelley grudgingly agreed that would suffice.

It was getting late in the afternoon when Kelley pulled his trump card. He handed Mo a report from a psychiatric nurse and asked him to read it. When Mo saw the confidential medical file, he went ballistic. Ray tried to calm him, suggesting to Kelley they take a break. He asked if Mo could keep the copy of the report that had been handed to him. Kelley refused.

"Where did you get that from?" snapped Mo.

"Hand me that report, Mr. Laberge," responded Kelley. "It doesn't belong to you."

"It is mine," retorted Mo.

"Mr. Laberge!" Kelley raised his voice. The two men faced each other, their faces red with anger. Kelley turned to Ray to ask him to control his friend, but Mo was wild.

"I'll punch him!" he seethed, raising a menacing fist.

"Let me talk to him," Ray intervened, trying to be the peacekeeper.

"Those are my documents!" Mo repeated.

"Mr. Laberge, you are going to give it to me," ordered Kelley.

"No, I'm not!"

Ray appealed to his friend. "Mo," he cautioned.

"I'm not giving it to him," he told Ray.

"Mo," Ray tried again.

"Where did he get it from? Where did he get it from?!"

"Return the document!" Kelley ordered.

"I'm not returning it," Mo retorted. He was almost spitting angry. "It's mine. You have no business having it. That's stolen goods, sir, that do not belong to you."

Kelley appealed to Ray. "Mr. Munro, will you direct him to give me that?"

"Yeah, yeah," Ray replied.

"I won't do it!"

Ray tried again. He asked the others to leave him alone in the room with Mo. Kelley wouldn't leave without the document. Mo again raised a clenched fist to the lawyer.

"No, don't hit me," Kelley warned.

They had to call in Deputy Attorney General Honnaka to break up the melee. A squat solidly built Hawaiian-born woman, Honnaka eyed the combatants as Kelley explained the situation.

"He's refusing to turn it over," he complained, "and the RCMP, the Royal Canadian Mounted Policeman, Mr. Munro, is sitting here doing nothing."

"It's not yours," interjected Mo.

"Hi!" beamed Honnaka, flashing a bright smile to diffuse the anger in the room. But Kelley and Mo continued to chirp at each other. Honnaka tried to separate the bickering parties. She suggested the defense lawyers leave the room so they could talk to Mo. But Kelley didn't want the prosecution seeing his ace card, which was now crammed in Mo's back pocket. After a few questions to determine the origin of the document, Honnaka ordered Mo to return it. He flung it down and stormed out of the room.

"Oh, Mo, don't run out," Ray muttered at his disappearing back.

By the time Ray caught up to Mo on the sidewalk outside the office, Mo had already calmed down. He was even able to joke about the angry exchange, but Ray's eyes had been opened. He had always known Mo had a violent temper. He had seen Mo's lengthy prison record and the violent offenses listed on it. The bar fight where he had blinded a man with a beer glass. The fight at the wedding when he had beaten up the best man. The burst of road rage when he had pulled out a rifle and fired at two men who had beaten him up. But it was one thing to read about it and another to see the man so enraged, so barely able to contain his anger.

Peter Smith was amazed at Mo's behavior. One minute childish and totally irrational and the next calm and collected and philosophical. "It was the most amazing transformation in a personality I had ever experienced in my life," he recalled later.

Ray was glad he had suggested Mo bring his wife along on the trip. He would find comfort there. Jade, who had flown into San Francisco on a separate flight and driven with them to Sacramento, was intelligent, level-headed and very independent. Mo had been lucky to find her.

They had met in the autumn of 1993 when Mo was working as foreman in charge of 4,000 head of cattle at a feedlot north of Calgary. Jade, a local veterinarian, had come out to do a postmortem on a dead cow. She was cutting delicately around the internal organs of the bloated carcass when she accidentally punctured the stomach. The ruptured organ sprayed both her and Mo with the foul juice of the rotting beast. They laughed about it then, joking with one another as they cleaned up in the office and had a coffee together. Mo was drawn by her infectious laugh and her huge hazel brown eyes. He had asked her out on a date, but the 27-year-old brunette looked at his gray hair and politely declined.

"How old are you anyway?" she had asked.

"Forty-one."

"Well, I think you are a little too old for me," she replied.

"Well, what does age have to do with it?"

His persistence eventually wore her down and they began dating. About four months into the relationship, he asked her to accompany him to a family wedding in Moose Jaw. In their motel room together, she began asking him questions about his past, about the past jobs he had held. She finally gleaned from him the fact that his work had something to do with finances.

"Were you a banker?" she asked.

"No."

"A financial planner?"

"Nope."

She couldn't narrow it down. Finally, giving it up, she teased, "You robbed banks?"

"Yup," he said, his eyes twinkling.

"You're not serious?"

"Well, it wasn't banks," he explained. "But I was a robber." He explained that he spent time in jail for that phase of his life and that he had worked on his education while in prison. Jade didn't really know what to think, but she stuck it out with him in Moose Jaw for the weekend. At the wedding she met Mo's huge family and marveled at the way he interacted with them. He was close to most of his brothers and sisters, particularly his eldest brother, Roger, and very devoted to his mother. He spoke openly of his past when she asked him specific questions, but he never really told her more than he thought she needed to know. She was satisfied with that.

Jade and Mo were married on a cool, damp and cloudy day in June 1995. It was a casual ceremony, Mo in blue jeans adorned with a big shiny belt buckle, white shirt, bolo tie and a black flat-brimmed cowboy hat.

They roasted beef over a pit, had a dance in a machine shed, splashed around in a rented hot tub. Jade didn't know anything about Mo's involvement in the prosecutions of Daniel Gingras and Charles Ng until well after she met Ray. He had dropped in to see Mo, who introduced him. "Honey, this is Ray. He's a Mountie." Although Ray had been invited to the couple's wedding, he hadn't attended. He was laid up with a broken collar bone after wrecking a car on a southern Alberta highway. He struck a hapless horse that had wandered out onto the road. It was a convenient excuse, however. Ray never intended to go. He wanted to keep his relationship with Mo strictly professional. But it would be tough.

Mo never talked about Gingras. Jade sensed there was some deep-rooted hatred between the two men, perhaps even fear. But Mo often spoke about "the little Chinaman." He was still wrestling with the decision of whether to testify at Charlie's trial. He felt a sense of duty, not so much to his sense of justice, but to Charlie. He truly believed Charlie wanted his story told. It was no surprise to him that his name hadn't been on Charlie's hit list. He had felt genuine affection for the little man—although he despised what he had done—and Mo never once felt as if he was betraying their friendship by testifying. Their relationship was full of contradictions. Mo didn't believe in capital punishment, yet he knew his testimony could help send Charlie to the gas chamber. He didn't understand how Charlie could enjoy the act of killing.

"If I ever had to shoot a man, I would shoot him in the legs," he once told Ray during one of their trips to California. "I just couldn't take away a life."

Newly married and living in the country, Mo had a good life, and he knew it. But Ray could sense a change gradually coming over him, and he didn't like it. Although Mo denied he had succumbed to the lure of the jazz, the man's behavior was setting off alarm bells in Ray's head. Living the life of a cowboy with a new bride who worshiped him didn't seem to be enough for Mo. The couple had bought an acreage with a spectacular view of the mountains, and Mo had remodeled the farmhouse into a dream home. But Mo still wasn't content. He wanted more. He quit his job at the feedlot and went into business with his brother Lucien and another man, buying and selling vehicles around the province. He wanted to make a lot of money fast and then retire.

Every time Ray saw Mo, he became more uneasy. Mo seemed to know a lot about things he shouldn't know. He would often drop broad hints that he knew details of certain crimes. Ray knew that if Mo was hanging around with other ex-cons, he was violating his parole. Mo maintained he just happened to hear about this or that, but his demeanor suggested otherwise. He was also drinking hard again, so much so that Ray took to making sure Mo had a ride home after their meetings. Mo's propensity for hard drinking and fast driving was dangerous. He had been lucky so far. He had only been nabbed for speeding. Ray warned Mo to stay away from his criminal pals. He also alerted RCMP colleague Ray Ambler, who was in charge of criminal investigation for the area. He asked Ambler to keep a close eye on Mo. He feared Mo was up to no good.

On the outside, Mo tried to turn his life around while working on a ranch.
After years of imprisonment, he especially savored the great outdoors.

Maurice Laberge exchanges vows with
Jade at their wedding in 1995.

Ray Ambler of the Royal Canadian Mounted Police.

24

The Jazz

IT WAS A SUNNY TUESDAY in mid-July 1997 when Silver Dollar Casino owner Frank Sisson wheeled his white Dodge Dynasty into the parking lot of his Calgary bank. The sky was a brilliant blue. To the west, sunshine danced off the snowcapped Rockies. Sisson, a 57-year-old leather-faced former rodeo cowboy, had just finished doing his annual tour of duty working security at the Calgary Stampede, which had wrapped up two days earlier. He was looking forward to an easy day at his casino, restaurant and bowling alley in southeast Calgary. It was about 10:30 A.M. when he pulled the big car to a stop and reached across the seat for the black bank deposit bag that contained about $8,000 in cash, a good chunk of the previous night's video lottery terminal receipts. As he opened the door and swung his feet onto the pavement, he was startled to see a white truck roaring across the parking lot toward him. When it skidded to a halt just a few feet from his door, a man with a large black handgun and a black balaclava jumped out to confront him. The gun was pointed at Sisson's face.

"Give me the money," the gunman shouted. "Give me the bag!"

"What?" Sisson still couldn't believe this was for real. It was broad daylight, for Christ's sake.

"Give me the money!" the gunman yelled again.

"Fuck you!" Sisson shouted, swinging a wild right at the man's head.

The enraged gunman jumped back and fired several shots point-blank at Sisson's bowed legs. Sisson went down like a tree from a chain-saw. The gunman scooped up the bag of money, leaped back in the truck with his partner and roared out of the parking lot. The truck smashed into two parked cars as the pair made their escape. Sisson, in shock and bleeding badly from his bullet-riddled legs, rolled over to catch a fleeting glimpse of the truck's license plate number before it disappeared from view. Ignoring the waves of pain washing through his body, he kept repeating the plate number until he had it memorized. It wouldn't do much good. The robbers switched to another vehicle four blocks away.

Drawn by the sound of the gunfire, several bystanders rushed to Sisson's aid. He handed one his cell phone and asked him to call his wife. "Don't get her all in a panic," he advised. He hollered to others to call 911. A woman answered that they already had put in the call. Sisson remained conscious until police and the ambulance arrived, cursing loudly as the attendants destroyed his new cowboy boots to get at the wound in his left foot. They were halfway to the hospital before it dawned on them to check his other foot. He had been shot in his right leg as well. By the time he arrived at the hospital, he was down several pints of blood. Doctors didn't know if they would be able to save his left leg. The bullet had entered just below the knee and exited out his heel, ripping muscle and pulverizing bone on the way through. "Shit," exclaimed Sisson when he realized it was the same leg he nearly lost once before. "That's the same damn leg that got ripped up by a Brahma bull."

The July 22 robbery was front-page news in Calgary. The crusty casino owner was practically a celebrity in the town. He was a vocal spokesman for Alberta's burgeoning gaming industry, a proponent of video lottery terminals in bars and lounges. He wasn't a guy to be pushed around. Police placed a guard on his room and registered him under an alias in case his assailants wanted to come back to finish the job. Calgarians flooded the hospital with 350 get well cards and letters while the media cranked up the heat on Calgary city police to nail the robbers. They got their first break when a witness came forward to identify the second getaway vehicle. He had encountered the robbers as they were making the switch and had yelled at them to move out of his way, but he clammed up quick when he saw they had guns. Now police had a solid lead. The robbers were driving a Chevy Suburban. Police got another break when an off-duty police officer arrested a man who appeared to be getting ready to set fire to a vehicle north of Calgary. The man was Mo Laberge. The vehicle was a Chevy Suburban.

Mo's wife, Jade, received a call from Mo to pick him up at the RCMP detachment in Airdrie, north of Calgary. When she arrived she was stunned at his appearance. He had been severely beaten resisting arrest. The off-duty policeman had to knock him unconscious to detain him. Mo had a bloody bandage around his head. "Don't worry," he soothed her. "There's an explanation." Mo had to come up with a humdinger for police. He claimed that his brother Lucien and another man had taken his vehicle without his permission and had used it for a getaway vehicle. When he found out about it, he was livid and demanded they fix the problem. His vehicle was fairly well known in the area, and he didn't think it would be long before police came knocking at his door. Mo told police that his brother's accomplice, a salesman at a Calgary car dealership, had stolen a Chevy Suburban from the lot and had brought it out into the country, where he planned to torch it to throw police off Mo's trail. Mo said he talked the salesman out of the plan and was walking away from the vehicle with the gas can when he was arrested.

Police were understandably skeptical. There were several unsolved robberies in the Red Deer and Edmonton areas that could have been the work of an experienced armed robber like Mo. A supermarket and a casino had been hit in Red Deer. There had been a home invasion in Sherwood Park, an Edmonton suburb. The RCMP made it clear to Calgary city police and police in other jurisdictions that if they found evidence that Mo was involved in crimes, they should pursue charges against him. Sisson's shooting in Calgary had a much higher priority than the conviction of Charles Ng in California. Ray Munro advised California authorities that Mo was on thin ice and could very well fall through.

But Mo was very convincing. He said he knew where the gun and the money from the robbery were stashed. He told police the salesman had a black Jeep for sale on the car lot and the gun and money were stashed inside. Police obtained a search warrant and went in at night to recover the gun and the money. Mo had been correct. They found a .38 caliber revolver and a bag of money. But it wasn't the .357 that had shot Sisson, and they couldn't prove the money was from the heist. However, it was obvious to police that Mo was in tight with the robbers. One or both had told him about the money. Police set up surveillance on the Jeep and watched from cover as the salesman tore the vehicle apart the next day looking for his stash. To cover things up police sent around a couple of detectives who claimed to be investigating a series of car burglaries in the area by a fictitious young offender. They asked the salesman if anything was missing out of his Jeep. They told him the kid they apprehended said he took some money from the vehicle. The salesman didn't bite. But the cops didn't care. They had now covered the disappearance of the money and the salesman would not suspect Mo or his brother or them for that matter of taking the money.

Mo told police the disappearance of the cash had caused a rift between his brother and the salesman. Lucien was complaining he was being squeezed out of his cut. Mo was confident his brother would give a statement fingering the salesman for the shooting, and he offered to try to get the salesman to confess to the shooting on tape. Fearing charges of entrapment, city police declined the offer, but Mo was insistent. He told them he was inviting the salesman to a restaurant where he would try to get him to say something incriminating. "You can come if you want," he said. "Sit nearby. Listen in."

Afterward, he met the officers outside the restaurant. "I got him to talk about it," he said excitedly. "Did you get it?"

"No," they replied. "We couldn't hear a word you guys were saying."

Eventually, the RCMP offered to help Calgary city police with electronic surveillance. They didn't have any difficulty putting a wire on Mo. If the salesman incriminated Mo in the offense, it wouldn't be a shock to them. As usual Mo had a plan. He figured he would casually remark that he had been over to the Silver Dollar Casino for lunch and had seen Sisson "gimping around." The bait proved to be sufficient. The salesman couldn't resist remarking that he should have killed Sisson instead of just shooting him in the legs. But the conversation was fairly cryptic with both men using street slang. The meaning of the remark would be open to interpretation in court. Police kept trying.

So Mo introduced the salesman to an RCMP agent, hoping that a professional could pry the information about the Sisson robbery out of him. It had been easy enough to set up. Mo and the salesman were sitting in a restaurant having lunch when Mo's cell phone rang. He spoke to the caller, hung up and told the salesman a good friend of his was in town and he was going to pop by for a coffee. He hinted the man had done time. The plan was to lure the salesman into bragging about his own resume. But police never got much for their effort. The salesman was no dummy.

Seven months after the robbery, Mo asked Ray if he would meet him and his brother Lucien for lunch at the Crossroads Motor Hotel in Calgary. Lucien had agreed that later that day he would go to the RCMP General Investigation Service's office to make a statement about the robbery. Ray met the pair at the restaurant at 12:15 P.M. They took a booth by the window overlooking the parking lot and made small talk for a while, talking about Mo's new hairstyle and glasses. After a few minutes Mo asked Ray what his brother could expect when he went in to give his statement. Ray said there were two investigators waiting at the GIS office, an RCMP officer and a city cop, and they wanted to hear what Lucien had to say. They might want to ask him some questions.

"Are they going to arrest him?" asked Mo.

Ray told the brothers that police hadn't told him they were planning to arrest Lucien, but a lot would depend on what he had to say.

"Charges will probably be laid in due course," Ray explained. He said if Lucien went to meet the cops, he should expect to testify at the trial. And if he gave his word that he would honor a subpoena, Ray would recommend he should be released until the trial. Lucien was worried the trial might have an effect on an ongoing battle he was having with his estranged wife over access to and custody of his child. Ray told him that police would be discreet.

"Are you comfortable with this?" asked Ray.

"Yeah," he replied. "I just want to get it over with."

"I think you are doing the right thing," replied Ray. He assured Lucien that when there were mitigating factors in a case, the courts took them into consideration.

They ate and Ray picked up the lunch tab. As they walked through the lobby toward the street, Lucien remarked, "This has gone a lot farther than what I signed on to do." The threesome drove together to the Stockman's Building, where the GIS offices were located, Ray and Mo in front, Lucien in the rear. "Will they ask about Red Deer?" asked Mo, referring to a casino robbery in the central Alberta city.

"They probably will," replied Ray. He turned to look back at Mo's brother. "Just be honest and forthright regarding your involvement in all offenses. They'll be interested in everything you can offer regarding the planning and circumstances surrounding the offenses and the use of firearms."

"Lucien had nothing to do with any guns!" snapped Mo. Mo led the way to the second floor where the offices were located. Ray stayed for the introductions and then slipped away. He returned two hours later and drove the pair back to the Crossroads. Lucien said the interview had gone okay.

Police eventually tracked down the gun used to shoot Sisson, tracing it back to the salesman. They then arrested Lucien, who had admitted he was the salesman's wheel man for the Sisson robbery. Lucien maintained he was not a willing participant to anyone being shot. He fingered the salesman as the shooter. When police picked up the salesman a week later, after they were sure he was sweating with the knowledge that his accomplice had been arrested, he hired a lawyer and offered to plead guilty to possession of a firearm. The case began to wind its way through the courts.

It looked like Mo was in the clear. Or was he? If he testified against his brother and the salesman, what would they tell police about Mo's involvement in the Sisson robbery and other crimes they had pulled off together? Police were now investigating armed robberies in Medicine Hat and Saskatoon that seemed to have Mo's fingerprints all over them. It was really starting to look bad for Mo.

During the winter Mo made repeated trips to see the Calgary detectives investigating the case, answering their questions and providing information to fill in the gaps in the stories. He was under pressure in the Ng case as well. Charlie's lawyers were pressing an Alberta court to investigate whether Mo had perjured himself at Charlie's extradition hearing. They wanted Madam Justice Marguerite Trussler to order four witnesses to testify about Mo's admissions that he had sexually assaulted a boy during one of his crimes. Charlie's trial was only six months away and the defense wanted to prevent Mo's damning testimony from ever reaching the ears of a California jury. If he was convicted of perjury, the prosecution would have to drop him off the witness list or risk tainting their case. The RCMP hired Red Deer lawyer Gordon Yake to act for Mo; Don MacLeod represented Charlie. Police felt obligated to help Mo protect his family. If the defense was successful in getting access to Mo's medical files, it could expose Mo's family to risk because the documents identified them and indicated where they lived. Yake argued that allowing the application would be an invasion of Mo's privacy and would be contrary to national interests, including sovereignty. MacLeod argued that Mo had waived his privacy rights and that international courtesy and the search for the truth were paramount. After several days of secret hearings in Edmonton between March 11 and May 19, 1998, Justice Trussler denied the application. Two of the witnesses the defense wanted to call worked in prison psychiatric facilities, and the judge was worried inmates would refuse to participate in treatment programs if their medical records weren't kept strictly confidential.

Mo wasn't around when the hearing wrapped up. He had headed to Saskatoon on business. While he headed east, his wife was going the opposite direction. Jade planned to go camping with her brother near Rocky Mountain House after the May long weekend, Canada's Victoria Day. Before she left, Mo told her how much he loved her.

Mo returned from Saskatchewan on the afternoon of May 19. When he checked his telephone answering machine, messages were waiting for him from Ray and Yake. He had won the case. Charlie's application had been denied. Mo was in a cheerful mood when he climbed back into his big black Suburban and headed to the nearby town of Crossfield to grab some dinner at a restaurant. He had a bowl of soup and a Caesar salad and chatted with the waitress and the cook, whom he knew well. He always dined there when Jade was out of town. As he wished his friends a good night and left them shortly after 11:00 P.M., he appeared to be in good spirits.

Fifteen minutes later the 46-year-old cowboy robber with a passion for fast cars was dead. A farmer reported the accident on a secondary road north of Calgary. It was near seeding time, and he had been working late in his fields, preparing the soil for his crop. He told police he was pulling a cultivator and harrows down the road with his four-wheel drive tractor when he noticed the headlights of a vehicle approaching from behind. When he saw the lights dip briefly from view before reappearing over a small hill a mile back, he figured he had ample time to swing the huge unit off the road before it reached him. He was wrong.

Police estimated the Suburban was traveling about 100 miles an hour when it hit the two sets of harrows and the blades of the cultivator. The Suburban flew off the road on impact and burst immediately into flames. Police at the scene checked the charred license plate. When they discovered who they were dealing with, they called the RCMP's General Investigations office in Calgary. Ray, who was now working out of Edmonton as an RCMP Customs and Excise officer, was also immediately alerted. He raced to the scene, two hours away. By the time he arrived, police had illuminated the entire crash scene with emergency flood lights. Mo's truck, smashed and burned, sat smoldering in a field about 100 yards off the road. It was a clear crisp May night. There had been no rain, but a heavy dew was settling on the wild grass growing along the road. The crash had occurred just six miles from Mo's house. His charred body, hanging out the passenger door, was barely recognizable as human. The first officers at the scene had found Mo's briefcase and his Rolex watch. Police also found about $23,000 in 20, 50 and 100 dollar bills drifting around the crash site on an evening breeze out of the Rockies. Ray and RCMP Corporal Dahl Chambers, who had dealt with Mo in the past, counted the money together. They thought it had been ejected on impact from a cash box Mo had hidden in the engine compartment of his truck. His wife later confirmed that he kept large amounts of cash hidden there.

Chambers had called his supervisor in Calgary to ask that a homicide investigator be sent to the scene, someone with no affiliation to Mo. He wanted the investigation thorough and by the book. Then he called a meeting to brief all the accident investigators at the scene. He advised them that Mo had been a suspect in the Sisson robbery, that he was in the RCMP witness protection program, that he was to testify in a serial killing case in California and that some people wanted him dead. If this was a simple motor vehicle accident, as it appeared, he wanted to be able to prove it.

Had someone killed Mo? Had he killed himself accidentally or deliberately? Was it really Mo in that truck? All police knew was there were no skid marks at the crash site. Either the brakes didn't work or they hadn't been applied.

Later that morning Ray called Jade on her cell phone to break the news and to make sure she would be okay. If there was a hit on Mo, if someone had tried to kill him, they might try for her, too. When she learned who was calling, Jade assumed the worst. She sank to her knees and listened to his voice.

"There's been an accident with the Suburban," he explained. "There's a body which hasn't been identified yet, but I'm pretty sure it's Mo. I found his watch. I know it is his watch. I have seen it on him. Are you still there?"

"Yes," she managed to gasp.

"I need to know the name of his dentist."

Jade gave him the information.

"Are you all right?" asked Ray.

"Yes," she said. Ray asked her to come down to the crash site. "Have your brother drive you," he suggested.

"What is it, Jade?" her brother asked after she hung up. "What's wrong?"

"He's dead," she said, slumping to the ground. She would go to the crash scene, but first she wanted to go for a walk in the woods and sit by a stream and be by herself for a while. Remembering Mo.

Police found several more pieces to the puzzle over the next few days, but they still weren't sure what it all meant. Mo had checked his life insurance policy just four days before the crash. He had also recently been to his dentist's office. And the day he had been in Saskatoon, a hotel had been robbed of $46,000. His take, if he and a partner did the job, would have been about $23,000.

Mo's funeral was held in a Catholic church in Airdrie, north of Calgary. Ray was there and spoke a few words at the ceremony. He told the crowd, which included Mo and Jade's family and Mo's parole officer, that he considered Mo a friend. He said they tried to keep their relationship professional, but over a decade of trials and tribulations, it had grown personal.

"Mo had a very cavalier and carefree spirit which made it very easy to like him as a friend," Ray explained. "We enjoyed many fun-filled memorable times together as well as many tough and trying times throughout difficult periods in both of our lives."

Mo's eldest brother, Roger, gave the eulogy. It was simple, but heartfelt, a snapshot of what everyone who knew Mo was feeling. "Mo, you pushed the limit in everything you did," he said, "and you thrived on being on the edge. From your early childhood to the very end, your nature was to challenge everything. . . . No matter how exhilarating or dangerous the situation, you always told me to go for it because only the good die young and what a shame not to have lived life to the limit. Mo, you lived life to the limit."

Jade echoed those sentiments in her husband's obituary. "He will be remembered by his family and friends for his exuberance, entrepreneurial spirit and his unwavering view of life as a journey," she wrote. "Every man dies, but not every man really lives. Mo really lived." She remembered what Mo had told her once about life. "You've never lived until you've almost died—and for those who fight for it, life has a flavor the protected will never know." In memory of her husband, a tree was planted in Calgary's Fish Creek Park, the same park where Charlie had hidden out 13 years earlier.

About a month after the funeral, Ray received a call from Lucien. He wanted to meet with Ray right away and asked him if he would come to Saskatoon. Ray suggested that if he wanted to meet, he should come to Edmonton. They finally settled on a Smitty's Pancake House in Red Deer, an hour and a half south of Edmonton.

Lucien was waiting in the parking lot when Ray drove up at noon. They walked in together and took a table near the front counter.

"How are you doing, Lucien?" Ray inquired as they both ordered coffees and were handed menus by the waitress.

"Not well," he replied morosely. "Not well at all. The past six weeks have been really bad, ever since the newspaper stories about me and the robbery. My poor mother is taking it hard."

Ray assured him he hadn't talked to the press.

"I'm in real trouble," moaned Lucien. "And the only person who can help me is dead!" He told Ray that Mo had assured him nothing would happen to him regarding the Calgary charges.

"What ever gave you that idea?" Ray was incredulous.

"Mo said all I had to do was give a voluntary statement and it would all be taken care of." Lucien also denied he had been the one who had sexually assaulted the teenager Mo was accused of assaulting. He said he hadn't even been in town when the offense occurred. "It's the same as Calgary," Lucien continued. "I had nothing to do with it."

"You didn't participate in the Sisson robbery?" Ray was stunned.

"No."

"Who did?"

"It was Mo and that car salesman," Lucien said. "All I did was meet them, and Mo gave me the Suburban to drive."

"If you had nothing to do with it, why did you confess to it?"

"I just did it to keep Mo from going back to jail," Lucien explained.

"Mo came crying to me for help and begged me to accept the blame for the robbery. He said nothing would happen to me. That you would take care of it."

"What do you mean?"

"I had no reason to disbelieve him. But then Mo died and I didn't hear from you and I started to get worried."

"There was never any deal like that," Ray explained.

"What do I do?"

Lucien was nervous and confused.

"Mo must have told you about what happened?" Ray insisted.

"He did not. All I found out later was that my phone was tapped." Lucien seemed totally unaware of how Mo had been caught attempting to dispose of the Suburban and how he had spilled his guts about the robbery. Ray repeated that from day one investigators had been working on the premise that Lucien and the car salesman were responsible and that Mo was assisting them.

Lucien was stunned. "He used me," he sputtered. "He set me up for a fall!"

He appealed to Ray again. "What should I do now?"

Ray told Lucien he couldn't offer him any legal advice, but he would be wise to seek legal help.

"There's more, and I don't think you are going to like it," Lucien said. He went on to tell Ray that Mo was involved in a recent hotel robbery in Alberta and during the course of the holdup, the hotel clerk had ripped off Mo's mask. That's what inspired Mo's new look. He wanted to look more like Lucien.

"Was Mo armed?" asked Ray.

"Yes."

"Did he fire a shot?"

"He popped one off so the clerk would leave him alone so he could get away."

"I always suspected Mo did that job," Ray told Lucien. "There's no doubt he would have found himself back in jail, probably by the end of summer, if not for this particular robbery then for his involvement in the Sisson offenses."

"How is all this going to affect you?" Lucien asked Ray.

"Don't worry about me," responded Ray. "I am a big boy and I have been around the block a few times."

Lucien told Ray that one time he was at the bank with Mo when a Brink's truck rolled up and a guard went in and came out with four bags of money. Mo asked Lucien if he would help him knock the guard off.

"I told him no way," Lucien replied, gesturing with his hands.

"Was Mo into armored cars?" Ray inquired.

Lucien didn't answer. Finally, he said, "He was using you guys as alibis. He figured he could knock off an armored car on his way to court." Ray started thinking about the times Mo had come into Edmonton unannounced to see him. He arrived one evening after an armored car holdup had occurred in Calgary.

"Was Mo involved in that robbery?"

Lucien said he didn't know, but he was at Mo's place, helping him plaster his house, when Mo took off.

"I was mad," Lucien admitted. "You cannot do the plaster work I was doing alone. I had to redo it two or three times." Lucien said the salesman dropped Mo back at his house later in the day.

The two men made small talk while they dug into the soup and clubhouse sandwiches. When the plates and bowls were cleared away, Lucien asked Ray if he could recommend a lawyer. Ray jotted down the name of a Calgary firm of criminal lawyers and picked up the tab for lunch. He told Lucien he would check on the armed robbery.

"It won't be too useful now, but at least you can write it off your books," Lucien remarked. "There's a lot of other stuff I could tell you about Mo."

Lucien's revelations caused a nightmare for the prosecution in the Sisson case. In the end they stayed the charges against Lucien. It looked doubtful they could ever get a conviction once the defense lawyers trotted out Mo's past.

Ray breathed a sigh of relief. Maybe it was for the best that Mo would not be testifying at Ng's trial. There were far too many skeletons in the man's closet.

As the trial approached, Ray's caseload increased. He spent a great deal of time trying to locate witnesses for Charlie's lawyer, Bill Kelley, and he went on a few missions for the prosecution as well. He located Charlie's former landlord in Vancouver and transported him to California to testify at a pretrial hearing in August 1998. In September he went to Calgary to locate and advise seven Canadian witnesses the prosecution intended to call. Among them was former Bay security guard Sean Doyle, the father of the boy who had found Charlie's lean-to in the south Calgary park, the arresting officers and prison officials who had witnessed Charlie writing on prison documents. Several had retired. One police officer had taken a job as the chief of a tribal police force.

Jury selection began on September 14, 1998. Finally. The candidates were selected from a pool of 3,000 in an effort to find sufficient jurors who had not been contaminated by the massive press coverage of the murders. The courthouse's eleventh floor resembled an airport departure gate as members were dismissed and new prospects were ushered in. Judge John Ryan thinned the crowds quickly when he asked how many could spend the next nine months to a year in court.

Mo wouldn't be there, although some people, including Frank Sisson, still expected him to turn up. Such was Mo's life that no one was really sure where fact ended and fiction began.

Mo and "Sam" weren't the only two Canadian convicts to contact police about Charlie. Ray had to stifle a laugh when he learned that Canada's most notorious serial killer, Clifford Olson, was trying to get into the act. Olson, renowned for his efforts to draw attention to himself, had contacted California prosecutors through Canadian External Affairs to say that he had important information about Charlie. It didn't take a lot of detective work to determine that while both killers had served time in the Prince Albert Penitentiary, they had never been there or in any other federal institution at the same time. Ray advised the prosecutors that Olson would be of little value to them as a witness even if he were telling the truth. "In my opinion the only reason Olson is coming forward is to generate publicity for himself," he explained.

Meanwhile, Charlie was also seeking attention through a flurry of complaints about his treatment and his first media interviews since his arrest. He complained about his food, the strength of his prison-issue eyeglasses, his being prevented from practicing origami—the Japanese art of folding paper into tiny animals. He was locked up 23 hours a day in Folsom's 500-inmate isolation unit, and he craved social contact. He hated the way he was depicted in the media. He hated being called a monster and a master manipulator. He even hated being blamed for all the trial delays.

Charlie should have adapted well to prison life. He had always been a loner and had always felt uncomfortable in social settings. He had gross feelings of inadequacy, was unhappy with his physical appearance and often felt ill at ease mentally. It quickly became apparent to the stream of psychiatrists visiting him at Folsom that he embraced the repetitive orderly life of prison, where even the simplest decisions were made for him. He had been institutionalized most of his adult life—at private schools, in the marines and in prison. Even at the age of 37, it was a difficult chore for him to decide what clothes he should wear every day. Despite all his complaints, he seemed to function well in the prison environment. He spent four hours a day studying law, boning up for his case, and buried himself in military books, magazines and biographies of his idol, Bruce Lee. He even learned how to build and refinish furniture. But he was starving for companionship. He missed the uncle–nephew relationship he had enjoyed with Mo more than he cared to admit.

Although he reacted to news of Mo's death with typical restraint, deep inside he was saddened by his friend's passing. Mo—like Leonard and like his lawyer friend Michael Burt—had been a father figure for him. Now two were dead, and the courts refused to reunite him with the third. They were substitutes for the father Charlie never had, for the father who had bound him and beat him as a child, for the father who was never there, for the father who sent him away when he was growing up and trying to become a man. Now, with Leonard and Mo gone, Charlie was clinging to Burt desperately. Having Burt represent him had become an obsession. Only Burt could save him. He showered the San Francisco lawyer with cards and origami, professing his devotion to the man. "The more I think of you, the more I miss you," he wrote on one of his spectacularly folded paper animal creations. "The more I think of you, the more I need you. You are the best there is! Peace in every crease; love in every fold. I will never let go of you in my heart."

In his media interviews Charlie attempted to paint himself as an ordinary guy. "I'm just like everybody," he told the *Orange County Register* in October 1998. "I have feelings. I need to eat, sleep. I need to have friends." He struggled to disassociate himself from the ex-marine whose motto in life was now so widely reported: "No kill, no thrill; no gun, no fun." Anxious to shed the monster label, he now contended that was just locker-room talk. He never meant it literally. Heaven forbid.

He saw himself as quiet, socially unsophisticated, retired, perceptive and sensitive. He was hurt that people didn't see him as a good person. He blamed the media for that. No wonder the families of the victims hated him. The media was putting all the blame on him. He really wasn't so bad, but he admitted to the *Sacramento Bee* he would have difficulty proving it. "With the stigma attached to me, I have my work cut out for me."

It was a stigma Bill Kelley was working hard to overcome as he prepared to defend Charlie on charges of killing seven men, three women and two babies over the space of nine months. Prior to the trial the brash 50-year-old lawyer released a videotape that Leonard Lake had made while Charlie was still in Leavenworth prison. He allowed a TV station to air portions of the Miranda tape, in which Leonard revealed his twisted plan to capture young women and enslave them as sex objects for his personal gratification. There was Lake, reclining in his big easy chair, telling the world that he planned to use women like books, to enjoy them for an hour or two and then put them away until he wished to use them again. "What I want is an off-the-shelf sex partner," he coolly explained. With Kelley's bold release of the tape prior to the trial, the 18-year veteran defense attorney was laying the groundwork for his contention that Charlie had been Leonard's stooge. He maintained that Charlie had been compelled to participate in Leonard's Miranda fantasy as a result of his cultural background, his upbringing and his resulting psychological problems. Kelley's sole focus was to help Charlie escape the death penalty. He believed he could do it. He felt confident he could get a hung jury and negotiate a plea bargain that would spare Charlie's life. It was not impossible.

Mo poses in front of the Chevy Suburban that may have been the vehicle in which he died.

The charred hulk of the Suburban in which Mo died. Approximately $23,000 drifted in the breeze around the scene.

25

Voice from the Grave

THE TRIAL OPENED at the Orange County Courthouse on October 26, 1998, exactly 13 years, 3 months and 20 days after Charlie's arrest in Calgary. As she walked into the courtroom, Sharon Sellitto had a sinking feeling in the pit of her stomach. After so many years and so many delays, she couldn't convince herself the trial was beginning. So much time had passed since her brother disappeared that she had doubted his killer would ever be brought to justice. The night Paul Cosner vanished, Ronald Reagan was president of the United States and the Berlin Wall still stood, protecting communism from the ravages of the free world.

The Stapelys, making the half-hour trek to court from their Garden Grove home, also shared in that sense of trepidation. They had exhausted their $65,000 life savings traveling to Canada and into northern California to attend most of Charlie's previous 70 hearings. Both now in their 70s, they had feared they might not live to see this day. "We never thought it would take this long," lamented Lola. "When it gets down to the wire, you realize how tired you are and how hurt. And you wonder, how much more can I take?" Several witnesses had already died, including Debbie Dubs' father, Jim Nourse, and Calaveras Sheriff Claud Ballard. The case had already cost California taxpayers $10 million, and it was feared the number could double before a verdict was reached.

As they walked through the heavy oak doors of the court on that first day, the families had no idea what lay in store for them. Had they known, they may have had second thoughts about being there. The tears began to flow even as the court clerk read off the names of their murdered relatives. The names were posted on a large board at the front of the courtroom. Sellitto was so wound up she could scarcely breathe.

Deputy Attorney General Sharlene Honnaka made brief introductory comments to set up the scene at the Wilseyville "killing field and mass graveyard," telling the jury the case was about 12 people, most of whom had vanished without a trace. Then she switched on a videotape, the "M Ladies" tape, which put Charlie at the scene of the abductions of Kathi Allen and Brenda O'Connor. The families, courtroom spectators and jurors watched in shock as the women were given their choices: be sex slaves for Leonard and Charlie or die. With horror etched in their faces, they saw Charlie, stripped to the waist, hack off Brenda's blouse and bra with a knife.

"You can cry and stuff like the rest of them, but it won't do you no good," he is heard, chuckling on the tape. "We are pretty coldhearted."

The jury of 14 women and four men, including six alternates, watched in astonishment as Leonard Lake told Kathi Allen, "If you go along with us, cooperate with us, we'll be as nice as we can to you within the limits of keeping you prisoner. If you don't go along with us, we'll probably take you into the bed, tie you down, rape you, shoot you and bury you." For several agonizing seconds, the courtroom was silent, all eyes locked on the image of the terrified woman on the screen in front of them. Then they heard Leonard's cold voice blurt from somewhere off-camera, "Sorry, lady. Time's up. Make your choice."

Honnaka showed another brief segment. It was Kathi, clad only in pantyhose, giving a back massage to Charlie as he lay naked on a bed.

"You'll be hearing other evidence about the defendant and about his long-term plan," Honnaka continued. "You'll hear his co-workers say that they frequently heard him say, 'No kill, no thrill; no gun, no fun.'"

Charlie, dressed in a blue shirt, white slacks and sneakers, kept his eyes locked on the video screen in front of him without once ever looking at the jury. Now 38 he was no longer the lithe and agile young man who could barely be restrained by security guards when he was arrested in Calgary. He was a plump awkward-looking man with thick black-framed glasses and a crew cut. His shirttails hung down over his pants covering the remote-controlled stun belt around his midriff, which made him look even more obese. One false move and he would be hit with 50,000 volts. With the exception of the courtroom security officials, no one was giving him much attention. All eyes were riveted on the video monitors.

Family members watched in stunned silence. Some had been aware of the videotapes; some had even read the transcripts that had been released the day before the trial, but seeing it as it happened was absolutely horrifying. "I just didn't expect being hit between the eyes so early," Sellitto told reporters during the morning break. "I was just so surprised to see all that tape within the first 20 minutes of the first day after waiting so many years to find out what happened. It was shocking. It was stunning."

"I can't imagine what the rest of it will be like," worried her mother, Virginia Nessley. She said she was grateful that the families of the two women depicted on the tape were not in the courtroom to have to watch the horror movie. But back in Coldwater, Michigan, Brenda O'Connor's shocked parents watched the scene on their television set. It would be their last glimpse of their daughter—a gut-wrenching image of her terror. Like most other victims, her body had never been recovered. All that was left of Brenda was small pieces of teeth and bone.

When court resumed, Kelley countered with a video of his own. He played the 18-minute Miranda tape for the jury, letting jurors see the man Charlie claimed was responsible for all the murder and mayhem: Leonard Lake. Kelley told the jury that Leonard probably did have help, but he claimed it was mainly from his ex-wife, Cricket. He did his best to counter that powerful scene of Charlie hacking and slashing at Brenda's clothing. He reminded the jury that the prosecution's case was built entirely on circumstantial evidence. "There's not going to be anybody that says, 'I saw

Charlie kill somebody,'" he explained. "I'm not saying Charles Ng is an angel. He is obviously not. But he is charged with murder, with ending people's lives—not cutting off people's clothes."

Kelley told jurors that the prosecution was going to use the testimony of Maurice Laberge, who had died recently in a car accident, as its "big link" in the case because the Canadian convict claimed Charlie confessed to the crimes while they were incarcerated together in Canada. But he counseled jurors to discount what the man would say. "To call him a career criminal is an understatement." He said Mo was a pathological liar who couldn't be trusted, a child molester who was prone to violence. To hear Kelley tell it, Mo was far worse than his client. He was depicted as a piece of scum who contrived a story to buy his way out of prison. Kelley was very convincing. As the case progressed, jurors would come to see Mo through Kelley's eyes, but nothing the skilled defense attorney could say could keep them from wondering how Mo got such detailed information about the killings.

Over the next weeks the prosecution laid out the case against Charlie in minute detail. They called family members to testify that their kin had not been seen or heard from since their ill-fated involvement with Charlie and Leonard. Police had found five relatively intact bodies in Wilseyville but had only small fragments of 10 of the 12 people that Charlie was charged with killing. It was necessary to show that the lives of these people had ended.

Grandmother Sharron O'Connor arrived from Michigan to take her turn in the witness stand. She glared at Charlie, reviewing the videotaped scene of her daughter over and over again in her mind. Charlie would see only her rage, not her sorrow. "I didn't want him to see me cry because I hate him, and I didn't want to give that to him," she later told reporters. "I won't give that to him." O'Connor, whose daughter, Brenda, son-in-law Lonnie Bond Senior and grandson Lonnie Bond Junior had lived next door to Leonard, refused to get upset when testimony in court suggested her daughter's common-law husband had set up a methamphetamine or speed lab in the A-frame cabin outside Wilseyville. "I knew all about this, and I decided it didn't matter," she explained.

It was more difficult for the Stapelys to hear that their son, Scott, was also involved in the illegal drug lab. When that evidence came out during the trial, the couple fled the courtroom. Lola felt as if her heart was about to explode. As she hobbled from the courtroom, she was convinced she was having a heart attack. Her doctor later confirmed she had suffered an anxiety attack at the shock of hearing the allegation against her son. It was just too upsetting to hear that Scott, who had founded the San Diego chapter of the crime-fighting Guardian Angels, might have been involved in anything illegal. "This is all just a horrible shock," Lola explained to reporters. "It goes so much against the grain of everything he had done." She refused to let the revelation tarnish her memories of her son. The couple had practically constructed a shrine to Scott in the foyer of their home with mounted photographs of him from cradle to grave. They conceded he may well have known about the drug operation, but they would never believe he played any active role in it. The thought was just too painful.

RCMP Staff Sergeant Raymond Joseph Leveque Munro wasn't called to the stand until mid-November. The prosecution enlisted the 30-year veteran Mountie to introduce several of Charlie's sketches as court exhibits as well as portions of Mo's testimony at Charlie's extradition hearing a decade earlier. Not only would Ray read Mo's testimony into the court record, but he would have to defend it from Kelley's efforts to discredit it and Mo. It took 12 minutes to read Mo's extensive criminal history into the court record. Ray explained that Mo had been placed in a witness protection program and over the course of 14 months had been paid about $36,000 in Canadian currency for living expenses.

He described, reading Mo's words from the extradition hearing, how Mo had met Charlie and exercised with him daily, and how, as time went on, he had begun making detailed notes of their conversations when Charlie volunteered information about his offenses. He explained that Mo had received about 150 morbid sketches from Charlie, which Mo had also kept and mailed to his lawyer. He said Charlie was particularly worried about the videotape Leonard had made of Kathi and Brenda, the tape in which he used a small knife to cut off Brenda's T-shirt.

Ray read an excerpt from Mo's testimony in which he described a crude sketch Charlie had drawn, depicting himself eating rice and watching while Leonard assaulted Kathi with a whip. In the sketch Charlie is telling Leonard, "Rice is ready! Dinner time!" Another excerpt of Mo's earlier testimony described a grisly sketch in which people are retrieving small bags containing the remains of their dead children from pathologist Boyd Stephens. The bags are labeled with names Dubs, Allen and Bond. Through Ray the prosecution entered a third sketch showing Charlie and Leonard burning bodies on a fire and a fourth depicting Charlie sitting on a cot in a San Quentin prison cell years later. On the cell wall behind Charlie, the slogan "No kill, no thrill" was scrawled. The adjoining wall was covered with captioned drawings of 12 murder victims.

Kelley's animosity for Ray seeped through from time to time in his cross-examination of the Mountie, forcing Judge Ryan to intervene to remind the pair to stick to questions and answers. Kelley thought Ray had allowed himself to get too close to Mo. Privately, he called Ray "slime."

The defense lawyer would make much of the inconsistencies in Mo's testimony at previous court hearings regarding his alleged sexual assault on a boy. The incident was coming back to haunt Mo even in death. It was apparent that Mo had denied it repeatedly in court, but he had admitted it at least four times to prison and parole officials.

Kelley wanted to know about a November 17, 1997, taped interview in which Ray had questioned Mo about the contradictions. When Ray had asked Mo if there was ever an intention by him to mislead prison or parole authorities by admitting the sexual assault he claimed not to have committed, Mo had explained that he accepted responsibility for the crime in order to earn his release from prison. He felt that if he didn't admit the crime and show remorse, he would never be paroled. So he told Ray he played along with the parole officials even though he wasn't the one who committed the crime. He had always maintained that an accomplice had committed the sexual assault.

Judge Ryan, a 63-year-old former Orange County deputy district attorney, seemed to enjoy Ray's courtroom demeanor, particularly when the

Mountie addressed him as "My Lord." Ray explained in court that in the Canadian judicial system, which borrows heavily from the British, prosecutors and defense attorneys also refer to each other in court as "My Friend."

"I think we should adopt some of the Canadian language," Ryan chuckled as Ray left the stand.

Ray's testimony on behalf of Mo Laberge was pivotal because it enabled the state to enter Charlie's sketches into evidence. Even without Mo the drawings connected Charlie to the killings in a manner that could not be easily refuted. Mo's collection of Charlie's grisly art spoke volumes.

Kelley argued strenuously that the sketches provided by Mo were just cartoons and not admissions of guilt by his client. "The testimonial gloss that Maurice Laberge placed on the meanings of those drawings is no more credible than that of any other career robber–burglar–pedophile–perjurer," he argued. But a handwriting expert who followed Ray to the stand testified that while it couldn't be proved conclusively that Charlie drew the pictures, he did write the damning captions and comments on the crude illustrations.

The prosecution had other evidence aside from the sketches and Mo's posthumous testimony. It called a stream of 60 witnesses over four weeks to describe the links between Charlie and the murders. Police witnesses testified about what they found at the Wilseyville cabin as well as what articles belonging to the victims were found at Charlie's apartment and in his possession when he was arrested in Calgary. Co-workers testified about Charlie's fixation with killing, his continual recitation of the slogan "No kill, no thrill" and his animosity toward the two co-workers he was accused of killing. His boss produced records demonstrating that Charlie was not working at his moving company job on the days the murders occurred and that he had in fact called from Wilseyville to ask for time off in some cases.

Kelley, closely following his strategy of resurrecting Leonard Lake, opened his defense with an intensive examination of the warped ex-marine's life. One of his witnesses was a screenwriter who had adapted John Fowles' novel *The Collector* for a movie. The story of the lovesick butterfly collector had spawned the Miranda Project in Leonard's mind. Kelley called former neighbors, former wives, family and friends to paint a bleak portrait of the man Charlie claimed was responsible for all the killings. He called a woman who described how she had been raped by Leonard after he had persuaded her to pose for photographs. At times spectators and family began to wonder just who it was who was on trial.

Kelley also worked hard to put the spotlight of blame on Cricket, who had been granted immunity from 18 murders in exchange for her cooperation with police. He noted that Charles Gunnar, the best man at Leonard and Cricket's wedding, was shot with two different weapons, one of which was a gun police had found in a hollowed-out book at Cricket's house. Kelley pointed out to the jury that Charlie was in Leavenworth at the time of that murder. So who likely fired the other gun? In a spate of dramatic courtroom theatrics, he scooped up Cricket's MAC-10 automatic pistol and began waving it around in front of the jurors. "Why does a 41-year-old teacher's aide have a gun like this?" he wondered aloud.

Courtroom spectators buzzed in anticipation when he called Cricket to the witness stand. They gaped as the mysterious dark-haired woman, dressed in black, entered the room. Kelley showed her a copy of her immunity agreement and read it into the court record. Then, with a hint of the creative flourish he had retained from his university days, he turned to the jury and said, "No more questions, your Honor." Spectators gasped. At the prosecution table, Honnaka and Smith huddled in a hasty whispered discussion. Smith had prepared a cross-examination, but was taken completely by surprise when Kelley opted not to ask a single question. There was nothing to cross-examine. Was there anything they could get from this witness that would help their case? No, they decided. Smith advised Judge Ryan that the prosecution had no questions for Cricket. With that, Leonard's ex-wife was dismissed. She walked swiftly from the room while the crowd sat in stunned silence. Judge Ryan caught Kelley's eye and allowed a hint of a smile.

The defense team had claimed that after Cricket had been granted immunity for the 18 murders, she admitted having discussions with Leonard about cutting up Gunnar's body with a chainsaw. When Leonard told her that he wanted to get rid of Gunnar, she had replied, "Oh yeah, don't be ridiculous. How are you going to do it? You can't even pick the man up. Are you going to cut him up?" Charlie's lawyers claimed that Cricket had at times introduced her ex-husband to people such as Charles Gunnar and that she had endorsed Gunnar's social security checks. And in one porno tape Leonard and Cricket made together, they are seen discussing Leonard's sex slave plan.

"Leonard and Cricket even made a homemade video of themselves where they actually got a photo album out, containing photos of young women, and they are talking about some of these women disappearing," Kelley told the jury.

Through December the defense called more than 60 witnesses of its own, before breaking for Christmas, and then it called 20 more in January. The defense had decided not to call Charlie to testify. Kelley and his team of Lewis Clapp and James Merwin had considered it but had changed their minds when Judge Ryan ruled that the prosecution would be allowed to cross-examine him about all the murders, the videotapes and the incriminating statements he made to Mo in prison. They feared it would be too damaging to their client to put him on the stand and subject him to withering cross-examination. After barely mentioning their client's name for weeks while pointing the finger at Leonard and Cricket, it seemed most unwise to put the focus back on Charlie just before the jurors went off to decide his fate. They closed their case, and both sides prepared their closing summations.

Honnaka and Calaveras County District Attorney Peter Smith made extensive use of the videotapes and sketches to demonstrate to the jurors why they must find Charlie guilty of the murders. In a dramatic summation that had jurors and spectators clinging to every word, Honnaka explained that if Leonard and Charlie conspired to kill the victims, it didn't matter which one pulled the trigger. They were equally guilty. They pulled numerous segments from the tapes to show the two had forged an evil bond. Honnaka produced the sketch at San Quentin depicting Charlie in his cell with trophy photos of all his victims with the exception of Scott

Stapely. Placing the sketch on an overhead projector, Honnaka told the jury, "Ladies and gentlemen, this is an admission by the defendant that he killed all these people."

Smith, a wiry hatchet-faced man with chestnut hair, green eyes and gold wire-rim glasses, finished the prosecution's summation the following day. Smith came from a long line of lawyers. His father, Jerome, had been an appellate court justice in San Francisco. His sister was a lawyer and his cousin was a lawyer. "We're all Irish Catholics," he said by way of explanation. "That's why we're all lawyers." Smith apologized as he prepared yet another video sequence for the jury. "I know this is disturbing to watch, and I know it is disturbing to listen to. But if you can put that aside when you deliberate and watch this videotape and you listen to the words that are spoken, you will gain a wealth of information. It captures the raw emotions of what was going on. It captures the true essence of what they were doing." The soft-spoken district attorney directed the jurors to just watch and listen and not to look at the transcript they had in their hands. Many of the jurors had as hard a time watching the tape now as they had earlier in the trial. Smith played the clip of Brenda O'Connor begging to be reunited with her baby, the most emotional scene on the tape. The anguish in her voice reverberated through the packed courtroom.

"Not only can you hear her words, but you can actually feel them," Smith noted after the segment was played. "You can feel the terror. You can feel the desperation in her words." He played other clips in which Charlie and Leonard could be heard snickering, clips, Smith told the jury, demonstrating how truly coldhearted they were. He showed the clip where Leonard told Charlie to put Kathi through the shower, a clip that he said showed how the men treated her "like a piece of meat." He said the video gave the jury a front-row seat to the crimes. He played a segment in which the men advise Kathi that they had killed her boyfriend, Mike Carroll. He pointed out how they talked about him in the past tense. He concluded his two-hour summation with the most dramatic video segment: Charlie hacking the clothing off of a terrified Brenda O'Connor.

The defense was expected to begin closing arguments the following day, but in a most bizarre twist in a case full of twists and turns, Charlie moved once again to dismiss his lawyers. He wanted to testify, and Kelley had overruled him. He wanted a chance to refute the damning evidence of his dead friend, Mo, and he was determined to do it against the most strenuous advice of his lawyers. Judge Ryan refused to dismiss Kelley, but he allowed Charlie the right to speak to his own defense against the wishes of his counsel. The defense team scrambled to prepare a framework for his testimony.

Wearing the same pink shirt he had worn through most of the trial, but with the stun belt removed, Charlie hunched forward in the witness box and maintained that the sketches, which he called cartoons, were satire meant only to pass the time in solitary confinement. They were not intended as an admission of anything. He said he and Mo shared in their creation. "He would draw part of the cartoon and slide it over to me, and I would embellish it and send it back." He claimed Mo coaxed him to draw cartoons related to the charges. He said he called the sketch of the San Quentin scene "Doomsday Fantasy" because it was meant to reflect the "hang him" attitude of people and the probable futility of his claims of innocence. He claimed Mo had drawn the photographs of the victims on the cell wall in the sketch and asked him to put captions on them.

"Every time I send him a cartoon like this he would laugh and prompt me to do more," Charlie testified. He claimed he had lent Leonard's diary to Mo, not realizing Mo was a jailhouse snitch. It was from Leonard's diary and other court records that Mo was able to create the false confessions.

A harried Clapp, at times stumbling through disjointed questions, asked Charlie if he ever told Mo he had burned the bodies so he didn't have to worry about a corpse ever turning up that police could link to him.

"No, never."

"Did you ever tell Maurice Laberge that a complete family you killed was the Dubs family and that Sean Dubs was only 16 months old?"

"No."

"Do you have any idea where Maurice Laberge would have got that information?"

"From the media, from articles about my case and police reports," replied Charlie. "I heard him talking about my case with other inmates and correctional officers."

"Did you ever tell Maurice Laberge that 'Deborah Dubs was good to my dick. She could control her hole muscles'?"

"Oh no, never," Charlie said. "I never talked about my—" He stopped himself before he blurted out the word "victims" and finished "in terms of these victims, what I knew about or what I didn't know about it."

Charlie had a tougher time explaining his presence at the Dubs' house after their disappearance. He had been positively identified by neighbor Barb Speaker. "Leonard came to me one day and basically told me to help him out with a job. He drove me to this place, gave me a key and told me to go into the apartment, where there should be a sea bag and also a flight bag right next to the doorway. To come down and put it in the trunk of the car."

"Do you know what happened to the Dubs family?"

"At that time, no."

"Did you tell Maurice Laberge that 'killing Sean Dubs wasn't easy, but it was just business, just part of the operation'?"

"No."

Charlie may have thought he was gaining points by denying that he had killed the Dubs, but his admission that he went to their home the following day was a critical point for the prosecution. It made his denial very difficult to believe.

Out in the courtroom foyer during a recess, Lola Stapely summed up his testimony with one word. "Lies," she said.

The prosecution was somewhat surprised by the defense strategy of introducing Mo's statements in the form of questions to Charlie. Just the extensiveness and detail of the allegations had to affect the jury as Charlie attempted to deny the incriminating statements one by one.

Back in the courtroom, Clapp made an attempt at damage control. "Would it be accurate to say that just about anything Leonard Lake told you to do, you would do?"

"No," replied Charlie. "There's a line that I wouldn't cross. Either hurting or killing somebody, something serious like that, I wouldn't do it."

But Charlie had trouble explaining why he cut Brenda's T-shirt and bra off and why he made crude comments on video. "I thought it was something that would get Leonard erotically turned on," he said, adding that he made the comments "in the heat of the moment" to ensure the women complied with Leonard's directions.

Charlie said he fled to Canada not because he was fleeing a murder rap but because he knew the car they were using was stolen. He claimed he fled because he feared he would be deported if it was discovered he was in the United States illegally. But he admitted to helping Leonard bury Lonnie Bond Senior and Scott Stapely. He said Leonard asked him to help him bind the bodies, place gags in their mouths and stuff them in sleeping bags to make it appear that the murders had been biker-style executions. Charlie claimed he didn't know Leonard planned to kill the women he had kidnapped. He was just helping Leonard gain their cooperation and compliance, he testified. For two days Clapp continued the strategy of putting forward statement after statement Laberge had attributed to Charlie, and Charlie denied every one. It was as though he thought he had a giant eraser and could simply erase the prosecution's case by denying it.

But any advances Charlie may have made for his cause were quickly reversed when Honnaka began her crisp cross-examination. Charlie didn't have an explanation for how Mo knew that the sounds of handcuffs could be heard clinking on the videotape. He finally had to concede that the knowledge may have inadvertently come from him. How could Mo know that the two women in the video had their hands cuffed behind their backs? Charlie couldn't explain. How could Mo say Kathi was forced to wear pantyhose with a ripped crotch if he hadn't heard that from Charlie? Or how he could say Brenda was "a skinny speed freak" if Charlie hadn't told him? How would he know if she was long and lean or short and fat? Charlie couldn't explain.

"Didn't get it from you though, right?" Honnaka asked.

"No, not that I know of."

She asked Charlie what he was doing during the six hours that Leonard spent in San Francisco waiting to kidnap Kathi. If he knew what Leonard was up to, why didn't he leave?

"He told me to stay in the house, to wait for him," Charlie finally replied.

When testimony resumed the following Monday, Honnaka kept hammering at Charlie. She asked if he had ever told Mo about a sexual technique he had used, which Charlie called the "asshole death grip." It involved anal intercourse with a woman while she was being strangled with a pair of pantyhose.

"No, I never did," he replied.

Honnaka then produced a sketch depicting Charlie sexually assaulting a woman in that manner. She asked Charlie to read his own handwriting on the sketch. He dutifully read, "I'm gonna give you Master Ng's asshole death grip, bitch!"

She asked him if he ever told Mo he killed babies. When he denied it, she produced sketches he had drawn of "Slant's Day Care," "Lake's Baby Dies School" and a third sketch depicting Charlie cooking a baby in a wok—all sketches related to the killing of babies. Honnaka slapped the wok sketch on the overhead and asked him if he had written the words on the sketch. Charlie said he had.

"Can you tell us what the words say in that little bubble coming out from the figure labeled Slant?" she asked.

"It say, 'Ahi-ya! Daddy dies, momma cries, baby fries,'" Charlie read.

"What is this picture saying: that the baby is about to be cooked—is that right?"

"No, this is a ridiculous satire," Charlie replied, glaring defiantly at the prosecutor.

Honnaka went next to the day-care sketch and asked Charlie to describe what was in the sketch. Charlie explained that the drawing showed a baby microwaved and placed on a plate. He said he made the drawing as a result of being taunted as a baby killer by other prisoners on the range. The third sketch depicted Leonard drowning a baby in a rain barrel while another figure is shown grabbing a baby by the hair and giving it a judo chop to the neck. A third figure is smashing a pillowcase, apparently containing an infant, into a wall. Across the top of the sketch Charlie had scrawled, "Uncle Mo. Don't try to attach your square John ethical standards to your nephew's works of art. Whatever makes you laugh adds another day to your old age."

Charlie dismissed the sketch as another attempt at black humor. He said Mo loved his artwork—the sicker the better. "He will just jump up and down and bang on the wall and get off on it. He enjoy it and praise me about it. I didn't know at the time he was saving all this stuff to set me up. It was my way of ridiculing the charges." The jury was visibly having a hard time with Charlie's explanation. It was difficult for them to find any humor in drawings that depicted killing babies.

Honnaka asked Charlie what he had meant when he told O'Connor on the videotape she could "cry and stuff like the rest of them," but it wouldn't do her any good. "What do you mean by 'the rest of them'?" she inquired.

"There's no 'rest of them,'" Charlie said lamely.

Honnaka would later say that cross-examining Charlie was the most fun she ever had in a courtroom. She gave him little opportunity to make denials and focused on every contradiction. Every word out of Charlie's mouth was taking him another step closer to death row. Much of Mo Laberge's extensive evidence and a number of additional sketches would not have been introduced had Charlie not taken the stand.

Kelley could only sit and try to take it. He winced as the case he worked so many hours to build was ripped apart bit by bit. "Imagine taking four years to build a house and the day before you move in somebody puts a match to it and burns it down," he would later explain.

Honnaka used her unexpected second summation to ridicule Charlie's claim that he had never had sex with his women captives. "Is that believable, ladies and gentlemen, given what you're hearing and what you're seeing on the videotape? Did you see the smile on his face when he cut that bra off?" Who was it, she asked, who had enticed Charlie's co-workers to

Wilseyville? And what happened to them once they got there? "We know what happened to people who went up to Wilseyville. They died." Whether Charlie pulled the trigger or not, he was just as guilty of murder.

Kelley made a valiant attempt to repair the damage, but there wasn't much he could do. He attempted to recall Cricket to the stand, but the prosecution objected and the motion was denied. Cricket wasn't even in Orange County any longer. She had gone back to her new life, and new husband, in San Francisco.

Sensing the jury's anger after seeing, time and time again, his client threatening the two women in the videos, Kelley used his closing argument to remind them to keep their emotions in check. "Everybody else can say, 'Let's take him out back and shoot him,' but you don't get to. You've got to leave that emotion at the door." He pointed out that Charlie hadn't been charged with sexual assault or kidnapping and that was all the tapes showed. "I'd be the first one to stand up and say, 'Guilty as charged,' if those were the charges." But no matter how many times the prosecution played the tapes, they never showed Charlie killing anyone, he continued. He produced a life-size photograph of the man he claimed was the real killer: Leonard Lake. He produced a billboard with targets painted to represent the victims, but the ploy backfired. Many jurors found the prop offensive, and the judge ordered him to dismantle it.

"How can we avoid Leonard Lake?" Kelley asked. "Is there any doubt that if there is a kingpin in this whole thing, he's the man?"

Following Kelley in a one–two defense punch, Clapp asked the jury why the prosecution never called Cricket. Then he answered his rhetorical question: "Cricket was not called to testify because of the harm she could have done to their case." He noted that the immunity extended to Cricket in 1993 meant she could not be charged in connection with the 12 murders that Charlie was accused of committing or an additional six murders attributed to Leonard. Clapp noted that a calendar Cricket turned over to police was missing the three crucial months when most of the murders occurred, so investigators couldn't be certain of her whereabouts on any of the dates of the killings.

When the defense wrapped up its summation on February 7, 1999, Mo, now deceased eight months, took center stage. Clapp tried once again to discredit the jailhouse informant whose voice from the grave had such a crippling effect on Charlie's claims of innocence. He took the jury through Mo's evidence, point by point, to establish inconsistencies. Mo got the hair color of this victim wrong, Clapp said. Mo claimed Lonnie Bond Senior had been tortured with a chainsaw, but the man's body showed no signs of mutilation. He reminded jurors that Mo was paid money by the police, that he earned early parole, that he was placed in a witness protection program. But he couldn't overcome the damage done by the incriminating sketches, in Charlie's handwriting, the videotape and Charlie's kamikaze testimony. The trial drew to a close three and a half months after it began. Charlie's fate was now in the hands of the 12 women and men.

The jury deliberated for nine days before reaching a verdict, which came down on February 24, 1999. The day before they had come out to ask specific questions relating to the murder of Paul Cosner. Cosner's sister was struck by a horrible sense of foreboding. Sharon Sellitto didn't sleep at all that night, tossing and turning, worrying about the outcome. It had been too long and too hard for the trial to go off track now. She couldn't fathom why the jury was hung up on Paul. But hung up it was. Other than Lake's diary, which was not admitted in the trial because it was considered hearsay evidence, there was precious little to put Charlie at the scene of Paul Cosner's murder. Mo's evidence wasn't very helpful on that count. He had testified at Charlie's extradition that the car salesman had made a rattling sound when he was shot. But he also quoted Charlie as saying they had driven nails through his hands, which didn't seem likely if the slaying had occurred as police experts suspected. The trajectory of the bullets, determined from the holes found in Cosner's Honda, and the blood spatter marks, strongly suggested that he had been shot from behind while sitting in the passenger seat of his car. But since Charlie wasn't a very proficient driver, it had to have been him in the backseat. Surely, the jury could see that, Sellitto thought.

But when the families filed into the courtroom on Wednesday, February 24, 1999, the foreman's announcement sent an icy sliver into their hearts. The jury was unable to reach a verdict on one count. "Oh, no," moaned Sellitto. "Not Paul!" She had been assured by Sharlene Honnaka the day before that it was unlikely the jury would get hung up on a single charge, but now it had happened. Now she waited anxiously as Judge Ryan polled the jurors to determine if there was any possibility of reaching a verdict. Two jurors said there was no chance. Ryan declared a mistrial on the one count, but no one knew which count it was. The court clerk read out the verdicts. On the charge of murdering Sean Dubs. Guilty. On the charge of murdering Debbie Dubs. Guilty. On the charge of murdering Harvey Dubs. Guilty. And on and on it went. The families cheered and wept simultaneously. But when the last name was called, the celebration stopped. It suddenly became clear to everyone that Paul Cosner's name was not on the list. "Oh, my God, no!" cried Sellitto, rushing from the court with tears streaming from her eyes. She couldn't believe it.

Losing Paul had been a nightmare so horrible she couldn't imagine anything worse. But now this. It was like the jury had spit on her. It wasn't reasonable. It wasn't sensible. It was like Paul didn't matter to them. To wait 14 years for justice and then for justice to be denied was almost more than she could stand. When she got over her devastation, she grew livid. How could they have done this? How stupid were they? It was Paul's car that broke the case, for God's sake!

A week after the verdict, Sellitto headed back to Ohio. She went home and stayed indoors for the most part, unable to summon up the courage to step out of the door. When she did go she dressed in hats and big sunglasses to hide her appearance. She didn't want to talk. She couldn't talk. When an old lady came up to her on the street and put her hand on her wrist and told her it was okay, she burst into tears. But as time passed she got angrier and angrier. She broke things. She went into her garden and ripped it apart, hurling morning glories and moon flowers and pansies around the yard. It made her feel better.

The prosecution was happy with the outcome. They knew they had six solid cases, but couldn't predict what the jury would do with the other six.

In the end, Mo reaching out from the grave to point the accusing finger at Charlie had cinched it. Charlie hadn't been able to sit still for it. He needed to respond. "I think Mo Laberge and the drawings had a lot to do with Charles Ng getting on the stand," Peter Smith would say later. "The defense really threw the door wide open when they had Ng on the stand and started talking about the comments he made to Mo Laberge. They were sunk when Charlie opened his mouth."

The penalty phase was set to begin in March. Sellitto, still angry and bitter, decided to go. Maybe it would be good therapy. Maybe she could find out what went so horribly wrong with her brother's case. She packed the car and drove 2,800 miles with her stereo blaring. Maybe she would get a kick out of hearing what a wonderful guy Charlie was. How he got led down the garden path. She could meet his origami buddies and his Oklahoma lover. She was too consumed by her brother's case to stop now. It had become her life. It was costing her relationships, marriages. It was her obsession.

A long line of Charlie's advocates marched to the stand to plead for the ex-marine's life: army buddies, prison buddies, his Oklahoma one-night stand. Sellitto tried not to laugh out loud, restraining herself so that she wouldn't be ejected. Boston psychiatrist Stuart Grassian said Charlie suffered severe personality problems stemming from his strict upbringing in Hong Kong. He said Charlie, however, lacked the inner rage that motivates cult leaders like Charles Manson and Jim Jones. He was much more likely to swig back poisoned Kool-Aid if someone he respected urged him to do so. "He has a pretty substantial dependent personality disorder," Grassian explained, adding that he was surprised Charlie was so docile and compliant and hadn't acted out in prison or court. He also was compassionate. While housed in prison in Canada, he used his prison wages to sponsor two Korean orphans for adoption. Sellitto was nearly gagging by this time.

Charlie's aunt talked about her nephew as a regular kid, nice but a bit shy. She showed the jury greeting cards he made for her while in prison. She showed them photos of him in short pants posing with his cousins and sisters. "I feel it's a real pity that just because he knew some bad people he became what he is," she sniffed. A fellow prisoner testified by video that

Charlie had saved him. Convicted murderer and rapist Lance Blanchard praised Charlie for changing his life by introducing him to Taoism. "I will not harm another human being," he said to muffled guffaws in the courtroom. "I have learned to, no matter what, give respect to everybody."

Practically the entire jury was weeping by the time Charlie's father, Kenneth, got off the stand. In a repeat of his testimony at Charlie's court martial, the elder Ng took the blame for the sins of his son. In halted English the retired 69-year-old Hong Kong camera salesman explained that he may have raised Charlie too strictly, binding his hands and beating him with a cane and the handle of a feather duster when he misbehaved. He said his wife and Charlie's sister, Betty, had often tried to stop him from punishing the boy in that fashion. "Yes, of course I regret," he said when he was asked if he wished he could raise his son over again. Then in obvious understatement, he said, "But maybe it's too late." Charlie sat stonefaced during his father's emotional testimony while four jurors wiped their eyes with tissue. "I come to visit him," his tearful father went on. "That is all I can do because there is no way I can help him now." He wiped his eyes with a handkerchief as he left the stand.

Charlie's mother was the final witness. While jurors again blinked back tears, Oi Ping Ng, testifying through a Cantonese interpreter, pleaded for her son's life. She said she also carried a burden of guilt for not intervening to spare her son from the beatings that defense lawyers were insisting were the trigger that sent him on a murdering rampage more than a decade later. "Of course, I love him very much," she said. "Ever since he was in jail, I never had a good day. I think about him all the time." Charlie stared straight ahead. His lawyer later told reporters he was crying for the first time.

The prosecution countered by switching on the VCR to remind jurors there was another side to this loving, caring, sentimental young man. Smith replayed the scene of Brenda crying out, "That's my baby!" and Charlie replying that her baby was "sleeping like a rock." Jurors wept as they watched the scene for perhaps the dozenth time. Smith referred to Charlie as "a rather despicable person" who had earned the death penalty with his heinous crimes. The young district attorney displayed his own photo gallery of the 12 victims: "young people on the verge of blossoming life." He pointed out that Charlie had made victims of his own parents. He noted that Charlie's parents had given him a privileged life, giving him love and sending him to the best schools. They weren't to blame for the monster he became.

Charlie's lawyers maintained that life in prison was harsh enough punishment. "You may decline to do another senseless killing," Clapp told the jurors. "It is for each of you to determine what the appropriate sentence is without vengeance in your heart. You are not anyone's personal executioner. The families of the victims here are not owed death."

The jury deliberated for two days before returning to their homes for the weekend. During the break one of the female jurors received a bizarre telephone call. A soft-spoken man with an Asian accent, identifying himself as Charles, asked her if she was on the Ng jury.

"Is this Charles Ng?" the astonished woman asked.

"Oh, I am sorry," he replied. "I just wanted to tell you that you are very nice."

"How did you get my number?" she demanded.

"I had a friend help me."

"You can't call me," the juror exclaimed before hanging up the phone.

The woman called the bailiff, who checked the Orange County holding cells where Charles was being jailed during the trial. Officials confirmed that Charles had been on the telephone at the time the juror received the call.

After extensive questioning at a secret hearing held on the Monday morning, the juror convinced Judge Ryan she could remain fair and objective and would not mention the incident to fellow jurors. Judge Ryan was determined that he would not let Charlie trigger his own mistrial by tampering with a juror.

"A defendant cannot be allowed to get jurors kicked off the case during the deliberation process," he ruled. "He can't force a mistrial through his conduct."

The point quickly became moot. The jury came in with its verdict and its recommendation that Charlie receive the death penalty. One by one the individual jurors were polled for their vote, and one by one they called for death. It was now left to Judge Ryan to either accept or reject the recommendation. But it was looking grim for Charlie. Even Kelley was resigned to defeat.

Calaveras County District Attorney Peter Smith.

At Charles Ng's sentencing, Sharlene Honnaka, Deputy Attorney General for the State of California, talks to Calaveras County District Attorney Peter Smith.

Charles Ng's defense attorney, Bill Kelley.

The Orange County Courthouse, where Charles Ng was tried.

Files of evidence against Charles Ng. The case had dragged on for years and had cost millions of dollars.

Murder victim Scott Stapely's pickup truck held in the impound at the Calaveras County Courthouse.

"Daddy Dies, Momma Cries, Baby Fries," a grisly Charles Ng sketch introduced into evidence after Charlie took the stand in his own defense. The prosecution grilled him unmercifully about the meaning of this and other drawings.

"San Quentin, Years Later," Charlie's cartoon pictures of his victims decorating his wall, another drawing introduced during cross-examination.

26

Day of Reckoning

SANTA ANA CALIFORNIA / JUNE 1999

OUTSIDE ORANGE COUNTY'S COURTHOUSE in sun-bleached Santa Ana, an elderly gentleman hawking the *Los Angeles Times* watched curiously as a small crowd gathered in front of the coffee wagon on the sidewalk. He had seen them often enough to recognize who they were, even though he didn't know their names. Few people really did. For the previous eight months, the jurors in the California Superior Court had been addressed only by numbers or referred to by nicknames they had been given by spectators. Today they got their names back.

They didn't have to be in court for the June 30, 1999, sentencing hearing. They had already fulfilled their duty, a service some had dubbed "the jury duty from hell." But they had invested so much emotion in the $13-million case that they were anxious to see firsthand how it turned out.

The group that gathered on the sidewalk against a backdrop of palm trees and flowers had become extremely close-knit over the many months. They had come to know each other like family, shopping together, relaxing at backyard barbecues and calling one another frequently for comfort during rough times. The strain of working on such a lengthy case and continually viewing horrific videotape evidence had taken a crushing toll on them all. Some members were having recurring nightmares of the videotaped scenes involving the two captive women.

"Every time I saw them I would get a chill," said 34-year-old Bonnie Reinhardt, a young, big-boned, dark-haired juror from nearby Anaheim. "I can still see that video in my head. I haven't slept normally in months. But I think being here for the sentencing will help."

Alternate juror Patti McSwain, a U.S. postal service letter carrier, wasn't so sure she would be able to get over it so quickly. "I feel like I have been through a war," the tall redhead lamented as she waited for the sentencing hearing to begin. "I feel like a victim now along with the families. I can't believe the effect it has had on me and the other jurors. We had no idea." Like many of the jurors, she had accepted the county's offer of therapy, and it had been her therapist who had suggested she attend the sentencing hearing.

A camera crew from ABC's *20/20* waited patiently for the jurors to assemble and then filmed their entrance into the building. Up on the eleventh floor, family members, jurors and members of the media mingled outside Judge Ryan's court, waiting for the doors to swing open. Sharron O'Connor, mother of murder victim Brenda O'Connor, went from juror to juror, exchanging hugs and pinning their collars with tiny glass angel brooches she had brought for them from Michigan. Several family members rushed over to hug 32-year-old Mauricio Velarde, the amiable 13-year veteran U.S. Marine Corps sergeant the jurors had chosen as their foreman. Velarde, now in the reserves, worked for the Santa Ana police and school district patrolling school campuses. Just off duty he was still dressed in his Marine Corps uniform.

Velarde's presence on the jury had been a surprise to everyone, including himself. During jury selection the defense had lost count of the number of challenges remaining and discovered they had none left when they tried to block a middle-aged female court clerk from serving on the jury. Judge Ryan allowed both the defense and the prosecution one more challenge. The defense used its challenge to reject the court worker. The next juror called was Velarde.

It was a most embarrassing mistake by the defense, which had hired a jury consultant to help in its selection of jurors. It now had a serving Marine Corps reservist judging the fate of a disgraced ex-marine. The revelation sent a ripple of laughter through the klatch of victims' families who sat through the session. Virginia Nessley predicted Velarde would be named foreman and won a bet from her daughter, Sharon Sellitto, when the jurors announced their choice the following day.

"Is the jury consultant going to be here today?" Nessley had inquired loud enough for Charlie's lawyer, Bill Kelley, to hear.

"No, she went to remedial math class today," replied a smirking Sellitto.

Kelley turned around to glare at the pair. "That's mean," he said. "That's not funny at all."

"Oh, yes it is," replied Sellitto. That exchange had set the tone for the relationship between the two over the next eight months as they came to despise the very sight of each other. Kelley would spitefully remark later that for all the sobbing Sellitto did in court, he never saw a real tear. He believed that the Ohio woman had made her brother's death her *raison d'etre* and was using the tragedy to put herself into the spotlight. The friction had intensified throughout the trial, and it was anticipated that the final salvos in the battle would be fired today.

But Sellitto had her sights set on the jurors. She couldn't forgive them for failing to convict Charlie of her brother's murder. She wanted to grab them and give their heads a shake.

When the doors finally opened, the jurors took their seats in the spectators' gallery while photographers filed into the jury box for the camera angle they had been denied throughout the trial. Judge Ryan was open to cameras and tape recorders in his courtroom, providing the tape was not broadcast and no photos were taken of the jury members or him.

The now familiar clinking of Charlie's chains signaled his entrance into court. A door near the front of the courtroom opened, and he shuffled in with his escort of county sheriffs, shoulders hunched, head bowed, lips pressed tightly together. He was wearing a light blue shirt, open at the neck. Shutters clicked and motor drives whirred. A British documentary film crew had set up alongside the other television cameras at the front of the court to the judge's right. This could be the last time anyone would see Charlie for a long time.

Judge Ryan walked gingerly to his place on the bench. Two weeks earlier he had undergone full knee replacement surgery, and he was still a little tender.

As usual Charlie and his defense team had prepared a raft of motions for him to consider before he got down to the business of the day. They complained that the judge hadn't responded in a timely fashion to motions to dismiss the verdict and to order a new trial based on Charlie's absence from the secret jury tampering hearing. Lawyer Lewis Clapp also advised the court that Charlie sought an adjournment because he had only managed a couple of hours of sleep the previous night. Apparently, he had been up all night researching case law that showed that an accused must be given at least eight hours of sleep before being dragged into court. Clapp blamed his client's sleepless night on overzealous prison officials who strip searched him, fingerprinted him and ordered him to pack up for his impending transfer to San Quentin.

"It is, at least in the jail's mind, a foregone conclusion that what is going to happen here today is already a done deal," Clapp complained. Judge Ryan noted that many of Charlie's motions had been written earlier in the day.

"It was obviously written by someone who has full control of their faculties," he noted. "He is alert now and he knows what is going on. And your motion, if there was a motion, is denied."

James Merwin, the motions lawyer on the defense team, spoke to the other issues. Judge Ryan asked him how he was supposed to respond to the motion within the allotted time period if he had been in bed full of morphine. "Mr. Merwin, I was in no shape to even read those papers at that time." Merwin also argued that Charlie had the right to be at the tampering hearing. He called it a key hearing. Honnaka responded that it was ludicrous for Charlie to be seeking relief based on the fact he had made improper contact with a juror. Midway through her argument, Clapp interjected to advise the court that his client appeared to have dozed off.

"Mr. Ng," the judge called from the bench. "Are you able to listen to what is going on?"

"No, I am unable to concentrate," Charlie replied.

"Why?"

"I am real tired." He told Judge Ryan he had stayed up all night, packing and finishing up the motions he had filed, on his own behalf, today. The judge indicated that Charlie seemed alert enough to proceed.

"He is not falling asleep, Mr. Clapp," he said icily. "That is perfectly clear to the court."

When Honnaka concluded her argument, the judge advised the defense team that he had reviewed his earlier decisions and didn't see that he had made any errors in law. It was time to get on with the business of the day.

Clapp argued that there was no evidence to prove Charlie was the actual killer, so he didn't deserve the death penalty. He requested the court to reduce the sentence to life without parole. It seemed a fairly halfhearted plea for mercy. Kelley would contend later that the defense team had made a succinct argument on paper. Calaveras District Attorney Peter Smith argued that the videotapes, the sketches and testimony of witnesses clearly indicated Charlie intended the victims to die, so whether he pulled the trigger was irrelevant.

Judge Ryan went through all the evidence, including Charlie's assault on Bay security guard Sean Doyle. He noted the schemes were most certainly devised by Leonard Lake, but Charlie was a willing accomplice. He examined Charlie's actual role in the killings. For that he relied on Mo Laberge's evidence. "Even if some of the statements attributed to him by Mr. Laberge were false or exaggerated, his participation could hardly be labeled relatively minor," Ryan noted. "Mr. Laberge had too many details. And, of course, the jury heard Mr. Ng offer excuses which were far too many excuses for everything."

Judge Ryan considered the evidence of three psychiatrists suggesting that Charlie had a dependent personality. But he wondered aloud how a person with such a severe mental deficiency could teach Taoism to a violent murderer, edit a prison newspaper, complete college courses, break into a military armory, escape from a Hawaiian island, hide out in California and later flee to Canada. "And that was ignoring the fact that Mr. Ng has taken on almost every trial judge he has ever appeared before." He looked at the mitigating factors as well: that Charlie was mistreated by his father, that he had been kind to his aunt and that he had remained compliant and passive in prison despite being placed in isolation and at times being abused. When you add it all up, as the jury had, the aggravating factors outweighed the mitigating factors, he said.

Smith asked if the victims' families could have an opportunity to speak. Judge Ryan agreed, despite Kelley's complaint that it would be redundant since the judge had already said he would not consider it.

"I don't think it's appropriate," interjected Kelley. "It doesn't have anything to do with anything. You are not going to listen to them to decide whether or not Mr. Ng gets life or death."

"I believe the statute had other reasons in mind for allowing the victims to make statements," Judge Ryan replied. He explained that the law permitted victims to speak not just for the purposes of sentencing but to help them deal with the psychological pain of their loss.

"I am not sure the courts are designed for the purposes of allowing people to vent their frustration and anger directly to a defendant when a defendant has to simply sit there and listen to it," Kelley argued. He told Judge Ryan that if he was going to permit the families to speak, Charlie wanted permission to leave the court. His request was denied. But before the victims got a chance to speak, the courtroom was cleared for Charlie to make one more application to have his lawyers dismissed. Judge Ryan held a 75-minute in-camera hearing to listen to Charlie before denying the motion and recalling the sentencing hearing. When the public hearing resumed, Ryan said he had been advised by the Orange County jail that if Charlie had been up all night, it had been because he was working on his court documents, not because of anything his captors had done. He also noted that during the just-concluded hearing, Charlie had made an articulate and well-reasoned pitch to rid himself of his lawyer. "He was certainly alert, aware and able to participate effectively in that hearing," the judge advised.

During the recess, 40-year-old William Peranteau, whose baby brother, Clifford, had been murdered, stood in the foyer surrounded by reporters. He was holding a photograph of Cliff taken at a company picnic in Pennsylvania 21 years earlier. William was crying as he talked to reporters. "My tears are not only for my brother but also because I have seen so many others hurt. They lost somebody for no reason at all." He held up the photo of his brother. "This is all we have," he sobbed. "Paper."

His remarks were in stark contrast to those of David Bond, who attended the hearing from Freemont, Indiana. "My brother and his wife and baby were murdered, and I want to see this fucking dog get the death penalty," he seethed. "He killed my family, and I want him dead."

In court Peranteau was the first family member called to speak. He talked about his mother's suffering, about the last Mother's Day card she received from her son—a card asking his mother's advice about marriage and expressing optimism he would land a new job that would allow him to leave the moving company where he worked with Charlie. William said his mother would not want Charlie to ever be released from prison and the best way to ensure that would be to put him to death. He called Charlie a coward. And then he sat down. Around him tears flowed freely and throats ached.

Dian Allen, who resembled her murdered sister, Kathi, kept her comments brief. She told the court she didn't have any fancy speech. "I just wanted to come up here and tell you that my sister was loved and is missed very, very, very much. I lost my mother due to this, and I was left to deal with it myself, and it has been very, very hard." She asked that Charlie be put to death. "We can't give him an opportunity to ever hurt anyone again."

Jeff Nourse, a cousin of Deborah Dubs, spoke on behalf of his family. "Nothing can bring back the Dubs family to us," he nervously told the court. "It was so sad because they were just beginning to start their lives together, and they had so many plans for it, and they were dear people. They would have been an asset to us all." He said his family supported the jury's death penalty recommendation.

When it was his turn to speak, most of David Bond's anger had given away to sadness. He talked about the ordeal his family had been through since his brother, Lonnie Wayne Bond, and his nephew, Lonnie Wayne

Bond Junior, had been murdered. He said the last 14 years had been hell, and it was time for it to come to an end. "The victims and the victims' families need to have this over."

Sharron O'Connor spoke of her love for her daughter, Brenda, and how they liked to bake cookies and make candies together at Christmas. "She was a beautiful person—not a speed freak like Charles Ng would like you to believe," she said. "May God forgive me, but I want Charles Ng dead." She read letters from her daughters. Her 42-year-old daughter, Sherry, demanded vengeance. "I want him to feel afraid and petrified that he is going to die." Her 41-year-old daughter, Debbie, wrote about the pain Charlie had inflicted upon her personally but rejoiced in the fact that her newest granddaughter, Brenda Lee, would carry on her sister's name. Then she expressed disappointment that the families didn't get a choice in the means that would be used to send Charlie to hell. Kelley, who had objected to attacks on his client in the earlier addresses, bit his tongue.

D.J. Stapely, 49, who worked in a state hospital for the criminally insane in Ataskedero, talked about his relationship with his much younger brother, Scott. Then he read a statement on behalf of his father. The letter from Dwight Stapely talked about how he was trying to cope with his son's violent death. "I scream thinking of the terror Scott must have felt waiting for the final killing shots—one in his mouth and one in his head. I have cried and cried." His wife, Lola, also spoke of her unending grief. "There are times, many times, Dwight and I cling to and hold each other. We sometimes cry for hours and hours." She said Charlie had sentenced the families of his victims to a living death with no possibility of parole.

Charlie sat expressionless with head bowed through the stream of heart-wrenching statements. After the families had spoken and wiped away their tears, a solemn Judge Ryan announced his decision. He looked down from the bench upon Charlie and denied both the motion to change the jury's verdict and the application for a new trial.

"It is the order of this court that you shall be punished by death," he ruled. "Said penalty to be inflicted within the walls of the California State Prison at San Quentin in the manner prescribed by law at a time to be fixed by this court in a warrant of execution." Charlie sat stonefaced at the end of the defense table under the watchful eye of eight armed deputies. He didn't flinch.

District Attorney Peter Smith announced that he was withdrawing the Paul Cosner murder charge. Over Kelley's objections Smith invited Sellitto to speak. She had prepared a powerful statement, an indictment of evil, and she was determined to give it, regardless of whether the jury convicted Charlie of murdering her brother or not. The evidence, had they seen it all, was irrefutable.

"We have patiently and not so patiently been waiting for the time when the system would be forced to hear what the far-reaching effects and pain and loss the crime of murder causes, and these murders in particular, and this murder in particular—"

Kelley was on his feet objecting. "Well, I am sorry, I am going to have to object," he began. "This is inappropriate, your honor. Mr. Ng hasn't been convicted of—"

"I am just getting to that part," interjected Sellitto.

"Just a minute, Ms. Sellitto. You don't have the floor right now." Turning to Judge Ryan, he continued. "He hasn't been convicted of Mr. Cosner's murder. In fact seven jurors acquitted him. This is starting to sound like victim impact testimony. And right now there is no proof beyond a reasonable doubt that Mr. Ng is guilty."

"We all understand that, Mr. Kelley," Judge Ryan replied.

"Then what is the point of this?"

"She wants to be heard," the judge explained gently. "We are going to let her be heard." Kelley sat down.

Sellitto thanked the judge and continued. She explained that just when it seemed that her family would have vindication, the jury deadlocked on her brother's murder, despite the fact that Leonard Lake was driving her brother's car when he was arrested, despite the fact that Charlie admitted to helping bury the body, despite the fact that in his diary Lake had documented Charlie's involvement.

"We were stunned," she told the court. "It was breathtaking, dumbfounding, heartbreaking beyond belief. We couldn't even comprehend it. And now it is over, and we will have to live with the verdict, for that is the law."

She lamented that her brother didn't get to appeal. She said his only mistake was placing an advertisement in the *San Francisco Chronicle* to sell a car: "A few lines in the newspaper became an invitation to two monsters named Lake and Ng, who thrilled themselves with dreams of profit, new identities and murder. They learned that the ability to kill was the purest form of power. And the exercise of this power was the greatest thrill of all."

In a strong and powerful voice that had a spellbinding effect on the spectators in the packed courtroom, she described how the two men had tricked her brother and killed him. Their act began what she termed "a long-night's journey into unknowing" because it left her family bereft of clues to Paul's disappearance. She lamented that Lake and Ng's vicious act thrust her family into a judicial system geared almost exclusively to the accused, "where cleverness, deception and intimidation and massaging the rules seem more important than the truth."

Sellitto was just getting warmed up. She credited Paul Cosner with stopping the killing. It was the arrest of Lake in Paul's car and the clues inside the Honda—his blood, bullet holes, weapons and the utilities bill—that led to the investigation into the murders. She talked about how she and her mother spent nearly all their savings traveling to Charlie's hearings in Canada and the United States because they wanted him held accountable.

"If we were allowed to give a victim impact statement, I would say simply this: Charles Ng has shown nothing but contempt for life, for law, for anything and everything good. He has killed many people and for no other reason than his own amusement. And all the way he has not shown any remorse nor the capacity for it." She paused for effect. "For this reason, if not for my brother's murder, he must be put to death."

Sellitto, with fire now dancing in her green eyes, glared over at the defense table, where Charlie sat with his head bowed and his back toward her. "To see him right now and to know he is finally going to pay for these crimes is to forget him," she said, winding up. "He used to tell people he could be invisible. Well, now he is going to be. He'll be gone and we'll be free."

Charles Ng confers with Lewis Clapp, one of his defense attorneys, at his sentencing.

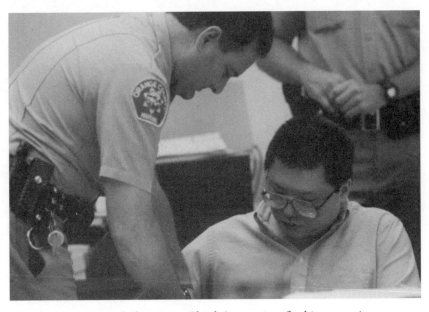

Orange County marshals remove Charlie's restraints for his sentencing.

His day of reckoning at hand, Charles sat quietly and glumly as the death sentence was pronounced.

L–R: Sharron O'Connor, Dian Allen and Sandy Bond at Charles Ng's sentencing, the city of Santa Ana, California, in the background.

Epilogue

A BLANKET OF FOG hung over the San Mateo Bridge as Sharon Sellitto headed east from San Francisco early on October 23, 1999. By the time she reached the 580, headed toward Stockton, another day of brilliant California sunshine was dawning. She fumbled for her sunglasses and turned down the visor to fend off the blinding rays as her Toyota thumped noisily over the uneven pavement. Sellitto had been looking forward to this trip with a mixture of anticipation and dread. But when she heard that the Calaveras County district attorney's office had planned a memorial service for the victims of the Wilseyville murders, she knew she had to go.

There had been many things she felt she had to do since the trial had ended and Charles Ng had been sent off to San Quentin's death row. Much of it hadn't been pleasant, but some of it had been perversely satisfying. After Sellitto had stormed out of court over the verdict, a juror had approached her to explain why they hadn't been able to agree that Charlie had killed her brother. At the touch of the hand on her shoulder, Sellitto had whirled around and blasted the juror. "Don't even talk to me," she had hissed. "There's nothing you can say. Don't touch me. Don't breathe in my face. I don't ever want to be spoken to by you."

She hated them. Hated them all. How could they have screwed up so badly? She had been devastated. But when she recovered from the initial shock, she had kicked herself for refusing to listen to the juror. She did want to know what happened. But even more she wanted to show them they had been wrong and that Charlie had helped kill Paul. She wanted to prove it to them. Oh, how she wanted that chance.

She had been cruising down the Pacific Coast Highway thinking about what an idiot she had been when her cell phone rang. It was another juror.

"A bunch of us are getting together for dinner at a restaurant, and we wondered if you would like to join us," she had inquired. This time Sellitto accepted gratefully. She had spun a U-turn on the highway and raced back home to gather up the proof she intended to fling in their faces. She had grabbed the passage in Leonard's diary in which he described picking up Charlie to help him kill Paul. She dug out Charlie's admission that he had helped bury Paul's body. She also had dug out the transcript of Charlie stumbling to explain how Leonard shot Paul from behind while the two were sitting in the front seat of Paul's car. She had collated the material, highlighted the pertinent passages, stapled it together and raced to a restaurant in Tustin, not far from the courthouse.

She arrived to find several jurors seated around two tables in a corner of the noisy family restaurant. Eventually, they all showed up, except for one alternate, but they were all nervous about the meeting. The juror who had first approached Sellitto admitted she was still afraid the angry woman would deck her. But when Sellitto approached the table, they greeted her warmly, and she tried to be nice in return. She had decided while driving to the restaurant to keep her mouth shut and listen to what they had to say because she really did want to know what logic they had used to reach their verdict.

The emotional meeting lasted five hours, continuing on the sidewalk even after the restaurant had closed. In the end Sellitto wasn't able to contain her anger. It gushed out in a verbal torrent. She showed them the proof that Charlie killed her brother. She told them how mortally they had wounded her. She made them cry. And she wept herself.

Everything came out. They hadn't seen the diary and they hadn't seen

Charlie's Calgary statement because the evidence had not been admitted into court. The diary hadn't been admitted because it was hearsay evidence and the man who wrote it was dead. Charlie's lawyers had argued to admit some of it with the references to Charlie deleted, but Judge Ryan had ruled that would be misleading. Since Charlie's Calgary comments had been prefaced by his statement that his lawyer had advised him not to talk, the prosecution didn't think they could get it into the court record. And Charlie's lawyers had succeeded in convincing at least one juror that Mo had no credibility, and she refused to believe anything Mo had claimed Charlie told him about Paul's murder. Other jurors wondered if it had been Leonard's ex-wife in the back of Paul's Honda. There were many reasons why the jury brought in the verdict it did, but in the end none of them made sense to Sellitto. She thought they still had enough evidence to convict.

The jurors met with the other families in the Orange County courthouse after the sentencing. It was something both jurors and families felt they needed to do to put the case behind them. They had felt stifled after spending months in the same room without being allowed to speak to one another. Now they could tell each other how they felt and release all the emotions that had been bottled up inside. So they sat around the table at the courthouse and hashed things out. Before they parted, the families applauded the jury members for doing the best they could. Sellitto and her mother refrained from joining in.

The justice system didn't normally permit such blood-letting after the fact. And seldom did it hold a funeral for the victims and build a monument with taxpayers' money. But this was a highly unusual case. The costliest. The longest running. Among the most grisly. Everyone needed help to put it behind—not just the jurors or the families of the victims but the investigators and prosecutors as well.

The service had been the idea of San Francisco Medical Examiner Boyd Stephens, who had spent months attempting to identify the remains that had been excavated from the Wilseyville property. As a man who dealt so closely with death and its impact on the living, Stephens was acutely aware that the families needed a chance to pay their last respects to their slain kin. Funerals had not been held for most of Charlie and Leonard's victims because, with only a few exceptions, their bodies had not been recovered. At Stephen's suggestion the Calaveras County district attorney's office purchased a stone crypt made out of locally hewn marble for $9,000 to inter about 60 pounds of human remains—mostly small pieces of charred bone—that had not been identified. They acquired a plot at the People's Cemetery in San Andreas and arranged a small memorial service for family, friends and investigators at the local funeral chapel.

Sellitto wasn't convinced it would bring her closure, but it had to help. Her parents had purchased a plot with a headstone for Paul in Ohio, but he was not there. His body was never found. At least in San Andreas, she could gather with the other families around the crypt. She didn't know if she could pray. She still blamed God for allowing it to happen. Later she would head up Blue Mountain Road past Wilseyville to say a final farewell.

As she drove across the flat orchard country around Stockton, closing in on the Sierra foothills in the horizon, her thoughts turned to the people who had been touched by the tragedy. This could be the last time they all got together, although most wanted to attend Charlie's execution, when and if it ever occurred. Sellitto had already called San Quentin to make a reservation. But prosecutors warned that with all the appeals it might be a 14-year wait. Sellitto wondered how many parents of the victims would be around to see it. Her own mother was 76.

The families, scattered across the United States and from extremely diverse backgrounds, had turned the one thing they had in common into a helpful crutch. They all had each other's phone numbers and email addresses and tried to help each other through the tough times. They had helped each other pull through an experience so torturous and appalling that it was beyond even the imagination of most people. But they were living it. They were surviving.

The San Andreas Memorial Chapel was located on the main road in San Andreas, a white stucco building with ornate windows and a red gable roof. When Sellitto arrived, a small crowd was already gathered near the chapel entrance getting reacquainted. Hugs and handshakes all around.

She recognized most of them, either from personal dealings or seeing them testify at Charlie's trial. San Francisco police officer Irene Brunn had been promoted to inspector four years earlier. She had just turned 60, had nine grandchildren and needed a cane to get around. Her talkative sidekick Tom Eisenmann, now 56, had a few more gray hairs but was aging well. Calaveras County district attorney's office investigator Mitch Hrdlicka, who almost caused a mistrial when a juror began chatting with him about his array of flashy ties, was there in a slightly more subdued silk creation and his trademark Birkenstock sandals. He was accompanied by two women Sellitto later learned were his daughter and girl friend. Sellitto spotted several investigators from the county sheriff's department and the woman who had been Orange County victim–witness counselor during the trial.

Sellitto also recognized John Kallas, the man who had spotted Charlie stealing the vise from South City Lumber. The spry 75-year-old had driven down with Gary Hopper, a South San Francisco police officer who had been on the scene when Leonard had gone into convulsions at the police station. And the distinguished-looking gentleman with the camera was Dr. Boyd Stephens. The medical examiner now believed there may have been remains of as many as 25 people, including three babies, recovered from Wilseyville.

Many of the family members were not as accustomed to the San Andreas heat as the locals and had gone inside to seek refuge from the blazing sun. Sellitto slipped in past Barbara Speaker, the Dubs' neighbor who had spotted Charlie leaving the family's home after their disappearance, and took a seat in the front row nearest the podium. Across the aisle Lauren Bradbury, a work colleague of Harvey Dubs, was gently stroking the petals of a single white lily in her lap.

Dian Allen, who had rented a black Mustang to drive up from Monterey, sat beside Bradbury. The two had become fast friends, and Dian, a 30-year-old single mom, craved her friendship. In her struggle to deal with the murder of her older sister, Kathi, she had nearly self-destructed. She got angry at God. She got angry at life. She tried to drink herself to death. She attempted suicide. She tried everything to kill the pain. "One day I decided, for some reason, God is keeping me here. I can hold on to this pain and this anger or I can live life." In the end she chose life. She was adamant about her choice now. "I am a fighter," she explained. "Nobody is going to take me down."

Sitting near the rear of the chapel, Debbie Dubs' close friend, Karen Tuck, sat quietly with her husband. Not a day went by when she didn't think about her friend. Deb's aunt and cousins had driven up from San Francisco. The Stapelys, their health now ailing, had made the trip up from Los Angeles in their van. Dwight and Lola had given Scott's beloved sailboat to the Boy Scouts. It broke their hearts to sail it. It reminded them too much of their loss. Brenda O'Connor's mother, Sharron, and a sister, Debbie, came in from Michigan, courtesy of a national television talk show that had carried many programs about the case and its aftermath.

Hrdlicka had sent out 70 invitations, mostly to family members and selected investigators. It was to be a quiet affair. No advance publicity. No television cameras. Ray Munro had wanted to attend, but the adventurous Mountie was off to Kosovo to command a 200-member multination police detachment in the war-torn European state. He still couldn't shake the jazz.

Ray, who had received commendations from Canada and the United States for his role in the case, was having a hard time believing Mo Laberge was dead. He wasn't alone. Calgary casino owner Frank Sisson still believed Mo was out there somewhere. "I wouldn't be surprised if he walked up to me one day and tapped me on the shoulder," Sisson said. "And a lot of the police think the same way. There's too much coincidence. It wouldn't surprise me a damn bit." There was no question Mo was smart enough to pull it off. But Mo's widow, Jade, was left striving to get over the loss of her husband. Whatever he may have been in the past, whatever he was made out to be in the courtroom, that wasn't the man she had known for five years. She wouldn't make excuses for him. He had hated it when people did that. He had always said he did what he did because that's what he wanted to do. He had been hooked on the jazz. "He just found ordinary life too dull for him," she said after his death. "He saw things differently than anyone I ever met. I cherish my memories of him. It was the best time of my life.

It would have been great if the jury had seen Mo as he was and not as a paper monster."

Back in Calgary, former Hudson's Bay security guards Sean Doyle and George Forster finally received the $25,000 reward offered by the City of San Francisco for Charlie's capture. Doyle had lobbied against sending Charlie to his death, but the argument didn't find much favor with the victims' families. "I don't want him to get away with it. I just don't want to be dragged down to that level," Doyle explained. "Maybe we should start looking at why these people are doing what they are doing and take steps to change it. Maybe we should be focusing more attention on how we raise our kids and maybe we wouldn't be producing things like Charlie Ng."

Sellitto didn't see Deputy Attorney General Sharlene Honnaka in the chapel. Honnaka, traveling in Europe, had sent flowers and her regrets through Calaveras District Attorney Peter Smith. Bill Kelley, who had lost his father and sister during the trial, headed off on holiday to Scotland after the sentencing. He had not been invited to the service. Nor had his defense team. But it was a good turn out. About 50 people filled the dark-stained wooden pews.

The soft strains of organ music signaled to the late arrivals that the service was about to begin, and a local female soloist, Marlene Bach, opened with a mournful song. Tears began flowing before she reached the end of the first stanza. At a podium at the front of the chapel, Smith welcomed the guests over the muffled rumble of a Harley-Davidson at a bike shop next door. Pastor Carl Johnson, who had been the local minister when the murders were discovered, came out of retirement to conduct the service. Hrdlicka, barely containing his tears, talked about the fantastic people he had met through the course of the investigation and trial. Members of the audience were invited to speak. Most offered thanks to the investigators and court officials who had worked for so many years to secure justice for their kin and for the other family members who had helped them through it. A few chuckled aloud when Sellitto rose from the front pew and turned to face the assembly. "You knew I couldn't keep my mouth shut," she said, smiling. The anger was gone now. Her face was serene. She rested her cheek on the palm of her right hand and began remembering Paul.

She talked about the old two-story house they lived in as children, about how as a nine-year-old she had lived in fear of horrible creatures she believed were lurking in the cellar, ready to pounce on her and drag her into the coal furnace. She would leap into bed with the light on so no monster hiding underneath could grab her ankles. She didn't want to tell her mother she was afraid of the dark. She had confided instead in her brother. And every night he would come in after she was in bed and turn out the light for her.

"I just always thought he would be there to do that," she sobbed.

After the service the group moved to the cemetery, guarded by a civil war cannon, on a sunny hillside overlooking San Andreas. They crowded around the marble headstone to read the inscription, which had been written by Hrdlicka's friend: "In Wilseyville we found you, our lost ones. Though taken in darkness, you will forever live in light. Rest in Peace." Smaller letters proclaimed, "Victims of the 1984–85 Wilseyville Mass Murder." Family members went up one by one to say their last good-byes. Some scattered rose petals, others left photographs, flowers or newspaper clippings. After most had left, Lauren Bradbury laid her white lily on the stone and read a letter she had written to Harvey Dubs in the wee hours of that morning. Between laughter and tears, she reminisced about the good times they had shared before he vanished. She told him how hard his friends had searched and how much they missed him and his family. Then, choking back sobs, she revealed a terrible guilt that had haunted her for 15 years. She had taken the phone call from his killers and had been immediately suspicious when they identified themselves as relatives and claimed Harvey had been called away to a family emergency. But she hadn't immediately called police. "I was young and I was afraid of myself overreacting," she sobbed. When police later suspected the family had been kidnapped, she had replayed the call over and over in her head, trying to remember something that might help. But there was nothing. No clues.

"If I could have given the cops something to go on, maybe they would have located the callers sooner and saved you—maybe they would have saved others," she cried. "So many people. So much horror."

Up the road in Wilseyville, 74-year-old Wes "Pop" Kirk, a tall bearded man in a straw cowboy hat and suspenders, was selling items out of the back of a truck in the shade of a couple of oak trees. He remembered Leonard Lake selling everything from household items to light fixtures—the property of his victims—from the same spot, the corner of Rail Road Flat Road and Blizzard Mine Road, 15 years earlier. Pop was joined by a 38-year-old George Blase, a casual laborer who had lived in Wilseyville all his life. Perched atop a plastic milk carton case in filthy jeans, in a grimy yellow shirt and an even filthier baseball cap, Blase smiled a crooked-toothed grin and chimed in. He remembered the Chinaman all right, remembered seeing him jogging the five miles from the cabin to the general store. He said he always wondered about those two. "Once when I was visiting my girl friend, who was a neighbor of theirs, I heard screams coming from their place. I asked my girl friend, 'What the hell are they doing over there?' She said, 'Oh, they're just partying.'" Pausing, Blase looked up from the cigarette he was rolling in his lap and added sadly, "Then people started to disappear."

The man who purchased Leonard's cabin, Reg Heijne, didn't attend the Wilseyville memorial service. While many locals continued to shun his property, he was comfortable there. Sometimes after sunset, he would sit on his step and listen to the sweet strains of gospel music drifting through the trees from the Bible camp up the road. Whatever others thought about the horrifying past of his property, he couldn't imagine a more peaceful place. Perhaps places, like people, could eventually cleanse themselves of their past.

San Quentin Prison, where Charles Ng awaits execution on death row.

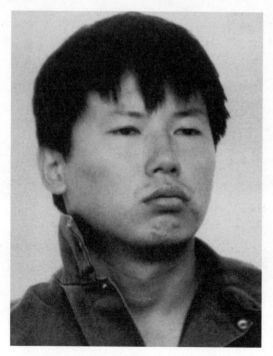

Charles Ng's Folsom Prison mug shot.

Cairn erected by the State of California in Calaveras County in memory of the victims.

L–R: George Blase and "Pop" Kirk sell goods at the roadside location in Wilseyville used 15 years earlier by Leonard Lake to dispose of his victims' property.

About the Authors

GREG OWENS is currently city editor at *Pacific Daily News* in Guam. Prior to this, he spent 16 years as a writer and assistant photo editor for the *Edmonton Journal*. Much of that time was spent as a crime writer, and he has covered virtually every natural disaster in Alberta. His critically acclaimed book, *The Third Suspect*, co-authored with David Staples, is a national best-seller about nine murders at Giant Mine, Yellowknife, in 1992. Owens shared a National Newspaper Award for his in-depth reporting on the subject.

DARCY HENTON won a National Newspaper Award and the Canadian Association of Journalists top investigative journalism award for a story he co-wrote on the torture–murder of a prisoner by members of the Canadian Airborne Regiment in Somalia. His book *Boys Don't Cry*, co-authored with David McCann, documented Canada's largest child sexual abuse scandal. Henton has worked at the *Toronto Star*, *Edmonton Journal* and *Calgary Herald* during his 21-year career in daily newspapers.